Rick Steves'

PRAGUE

& THE CZECH REPUBLIC

Rick Steves & Jan (Honza) Vihan

CONTENTS

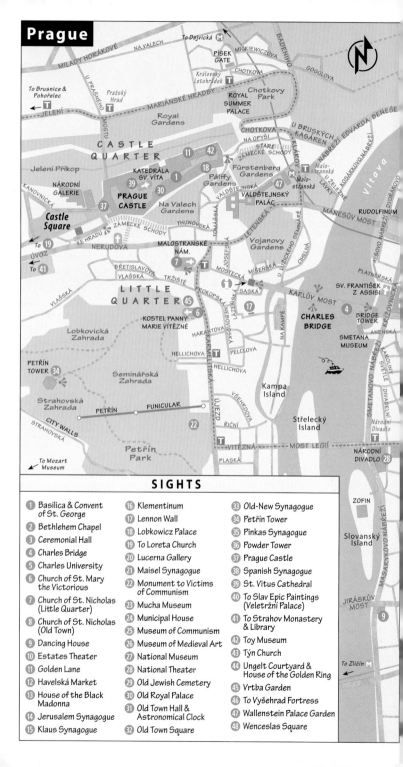

Prague

SIGHTS

1. Basilica & Convent of St. George
2. Bethlehem Chapel
3. Ceremonial Hall
4. Charles Bridge
5. Charles University
6. Church of St. Mary the Victorious
7. Church of St. Nicholas (Little Quarter)
8. Church of St. Nicholas (Old Town)
9. Dancing House
10. Estates Theater
11. Golden Lane
12. Havelská Market
13. House of the Black Madonna
14. Jerusalem Synagogue
15. Klaus Synagogue
16. Klementinum
17. Lennon Wall
18. Lobkowicz Palace
19. To Loreta Church
20. Lucerna Gallery
21. Maisel Synagogue
22. Monument to Victims of Communism
23. Mucha Museum
24. Municipal House
25. Museum of Communism
26. Museum of Medieval Art
27. National Museum
28. National Theater
29. Old Jewish Cemetery
30. Old Royal Palace
31. Old Town Hall & Astronomical Clock
32. Old Town Square
33. Old-New Synagogue
34. Petřín Tower
35. Pinkas Synagogue
36. Powder Tower
37. Prague Castle
38. Spanish Synagogue
39. St. Vitus Cathedral
40. To Slav Epic Paintings (Veletržní Palace)
41. To Strahov Monastery & Library
42. Toy Museum
43. Týn Church
44. Ungelt Courtyard & House of the Golden Ring
45. Vrtba Garden
46. To Vyšehrad Fortress
47. Wallenstein Palace Garden
48. Wenceslas Square

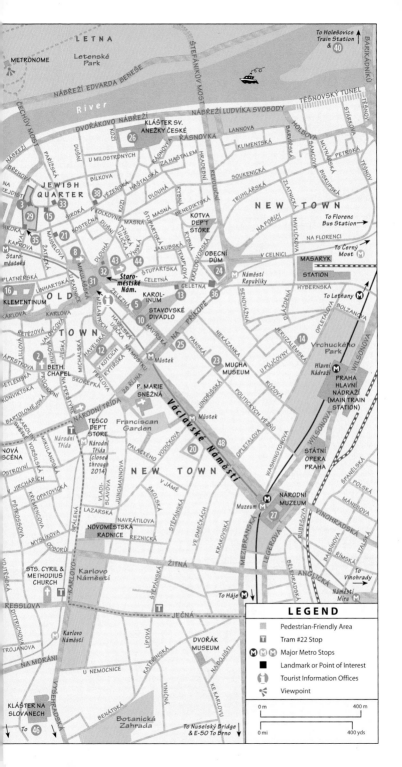

Na zdraví! (Cheers!)

Gothic spires of Týn Church

Domes and towers of Prague's skyline

Mucha stained-glass window, St. Vitus Cathedral, Prague

Charles Bridge with Prague Castle (upper right)

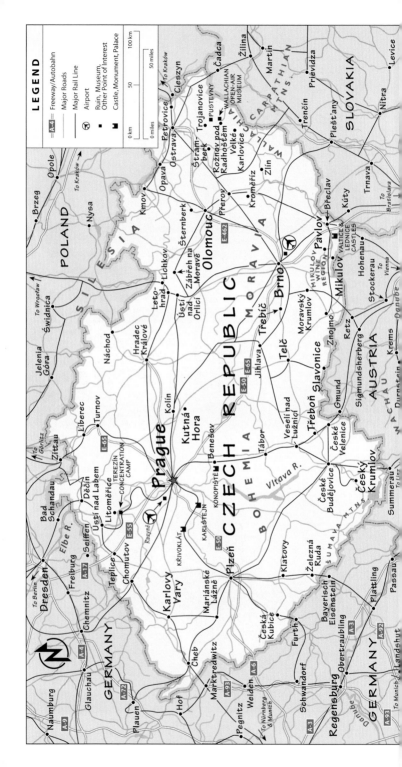

Rick Steves'

PRAGUE

& THE CZECH REPUBLIC

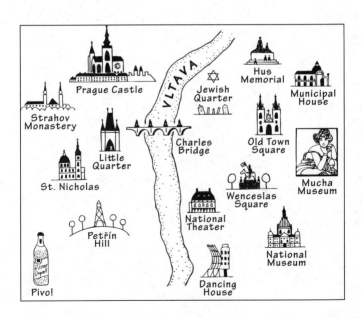

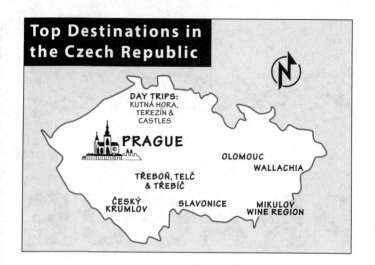

Top Destinations in the Czech Republic

DAY TRIPS:
KUTNÁ HORA,
TEREZÍN &
CASTLES

PRAGUE

OLOMOUC

WALLACHIA

TŘEBOŇ, TELČ
& TŘEBÍČ

ČESKÝ
KRUMLOV

SLAVONICE

MIKULOV
WINE REGION

INTRODUCTION

Wedged between Germany and Austria, the Czech Republic is one of the most comfortable and easy-to-explore countries of Eastern Europe. After the fall of communism, the Czech capital, Prague, quickly became one of Europe's most popular destinations. Come see what all the fuss is about...but don't overlook the rest of the country. Even in a quick visit, you can enjoy a fine introduction to the entire Czech Republic.

This book focuses on Prague, but also includes my favorite small-town and back-to-nature destinations in the countryside. If you want to experience the best two weeks that the Czech Republic has to offer, this book has all the information you'll need.

Experiencing Czech culture, people, and natural wonders economically and hassle-free has been my goal throughout three decades of traveling, tour guiding, and writing. This book is selective, including only the top destinations and sights. For example, the Czech Republic has dozens of charming medieval towns, but I take you to only the most pleasant: Třeboň and Slavonice.

The best is, of course, only my opinion. But after spending half my adult life researching Europe, I've developed a sixth sense for what travelers enjoy.

About This Book

Rick Steves' Prague & the Czech Republic is a personal tour guide in your pocket. Better yet, it's actually two tour guides in your pocket: The co-author and researcher of this guidebook is Honza Vihan, a Prague native who leads Prague and Eastern Europe tours for my company, Rick Steves' Europe Through the Back Door. Together, Honza and I keep this book up-to-date and accurate. For simplicity we've shed our respective egos to become "I" in this book—though

INTRODUCTION

Map Legend

⅃ Viewpoint	✈ Airport	)▭(Tunnel
♠ Entrance	ⓣ Taxi Stand	▱ Pedestrian Zone
❶ Tourist Info	◨ Tram Stop	------ Railway
WC Restroom	Ⓜ Metro Stop	.... Ferry/Boat Route
♜ Castle	Ⓑ Bus Stop	⊢—⊢ Tram
⬚ Church	℗ Parking	Stairs
▪ Statue/Point of Interest	)(Mtn. Pass	- - - - - Walk/Tour Route
◎ Fountain	⬚ Park	- - - - - Trail

Use this legend to help you navigate the maps in this book.

at times, you'll know from the intimacy of some of the comments that Honza is sharing his own uniquely Czech perspective.

The first half of this book focuses on Prague, following this format:

Orientation to Prague includes specifics on public transportation, helpful hints, local tour options, easy-to-read maps, and tourist information. The "Planning Your Time" section suggests a schedule for how to best use your limited time.

The **Old Town, New Town, Little Quarter,** and **Castle Quarter** chapters describe Prague's most important districts and their sights. The **Beyond the Core** chapter visits Alfons Mucha's must-see *Slav Epic* masterpiece and takes you on a self-guided walk through peaceful, view-filled Vyšehrad Park.

Sleeping in Prague describes my favorite hotels, from good-value deals to cushy splurges.

Eating in Prague serves up a range of options, from inexpensive eateries to fancy restaurants.

Shopping in Prague gives you tips for shopping painlessly and enjoyably, without letting it overwhelm your vacation or ruin your budget.

Entertainment in Prague is your guide to fun, including a wide array of concerts and nightclubs—as well as other Czech entertainment options, from the unique Black Light Theater to hockey and soccer games.

Prague Connections lays the groundwork for your smooth arrival and departure, outlining your options for traveling to destinations by train, bus, plane, or with a private driver.

Day Trips from Prague outlines easy visits to nearby sights at Kutná Hora, Terezín, Konopiště Castle, Karlštejn Castle, and Křivoklát Castle.

The second half of the book, **Beyond Prague,** is devoted to the rest of the Czech Republic, describing farther-flung destinations

Key to This Book

Updates
This book is updated regularly, but things change. For the latest, visit www.ricksteves.com/update.

Abbreviations and Times
I use the following symbols and abbreviations in this book:

Sights are rated:

▲▲▲	**Don't miss**
▲▲	**Try hard to see**
▲	**Worthwhile if you can make it**
No rating	**Worth knowing about**

Tourist information offices are abbreviated as **TI,** and bathrooms are **WC**s. To categorize accommodations, I use a **Sleep Code** (described on page 20).

Like Europe, this book uses the **24-hour clock.** It's the same through 12:00 noon, then keeps going: 13:00, 14:00, and so on. For anything over 12, subtract 12 and add p.m. (14:00 is 2:00 p.m.).

When giving **opening times,** I include both peak season and off-season hours if they differ. So, if a museum is listed as "May-Oct daily 9:00-16:00," it should be open from 9:00 a.m. until 4:00 p.m. from the first day of May until the last day of October (but expect exceptions).

For **transit** or **tour departures,** I first list the frequency, then the duration. So, a train connection listed as "2/hour, 1.5 hours" departs twice each hour, and the journey lasts an hour and a half.

elsewhere in the country. Each one is covered as a mini-vacation of its own.

At the end of the book, you'll find these chapters:

The **Czech History** chapter explains the complicated, tumultuous, and ultimately uplifting background of this country.

The **appendix** is a traveler's tool kit, with telephone tips, useful phone numbers and websites, transportation basics, recommended books and films, a festival list, a climate chart, a handy packing checklist, and Czech survival phrases.

Browse through this book, choose your favorite destinations, and link them up. Then have a great trip! Traveling like a temporary local, you'll get the absolute most out of every mile, minute, and dollar. As you visit places I know and love, I'm happy that you'll be meeting some of my favorite Czech people.

Planning

This section will help you get started planning your trip—with advice on trip costs, when to go, and what you should know before you take off.

Travel Smart

Your trip to the Czech Republic is like a complex play—it's easier to follow and to really appreciate on a second viewing. While no one does the same trip twice to gain that advantage, reading this book in its entirety before your trip accomplishes much the same thing.

Design an itinerary that enables you to visit sights at the best possible times. Note holidays, festivals, colorful market days, and days when sights are closed.

If you have only a few days for Prague, remember that the impressive sights of the Jewish Quarter are closed every Saturday, and other museums (particularly in the Old Town) are closed on Monday. Monday can also be a problem day outside of Prague, as many Czech museums are closed.

To get between destinations smoothly, read this book's appendix for tips on taking trains and buses, or renting a car and driving. A smart trip is a puzzle—a fun, doable, and worthwhile challenge.

When you're plotting your itinerary, strive for a mix of intense and relaxed stretches. To maximize rootedness, minimize one-night stands. It's worth taking a long drive after dinner to get settled in a town for two nights. Every trip and every traveler needs at least a few slack days (for picnics, laundry, people-watching, and so on). Pace yourself. Assume you will return.

Reread this book as you travel, and visit local tourist information offices (abbreviated as TI in this book). Upon arrival in a new town, lay the groundwork for a smooth departure; get the schedule for the train or bus that you'll take when you depart. Drivers can study the best route to their next destination.

Get online at Internet cafés or at your hotel, and carry a mobile phone (or use a phone card) to make travel plans: You can find tourist information, learn the latest on sights (special events, tour schedules, etc.), book tickets and tours, make reservations, reconfirm hotels, research transportation connections, and keep in touch with your loved ones.

Enjoy the friendliness of the Czech people. Connect with the culture. Set up your own quest to find the ultimate characteristically Czech pub. (Anything with an English menu doesn't count.) Once inside, ask the locals to recommend the best beer, and make it your goal to get the most interesting story you possibly can out of them.

The Czech Republic at a Glance

▲▲▲**Prague** The Czech capital and one of Europe's most romantic cities, boasting a remarkably well-preserved Old Town with top-notch architecture from every era; a sprawling hilltop castle; a thriving New Town packed with slinky Art Nouveau facades; a historic and well-presented Jewish Quarter; fascinating and inspiring tales from its rocky late-20th-century history; countless lively pubs serving some of the world's best beer; and enough museums, churches, gardens, and other attractions to entertain any visitor.

▲▲**Day Trips from Prague** A wide range of easy side-trips, including Kutná Hora, a workaday Czech town with an offbeat bone church, fine cathedral, and silver mining museum; Terezín, a sobering memorial to the victims of the Nazis; Konopiště Castle, the opulent but lived-in former residence of the Archduke Franz Ferdinand; dramatically situated Karlštejn Castle; and the genuinely Gothic hunting palace of Křivoklát Castle.

▲▲**Český Krumlov** Charming, picturesque, and popular mid-size town huddled under a colorful castle and hugging a river bend in the Bohemian hills, made to order for canoeing, hiking, and people-watching.

▲**Třeboň, Telč, and Třebíč** Three different southern Bohemian towns, each with a claim to fame: Třeboň, surrounded by artificial lakes; Telč, with a spectacular main square; and Třebíč, with echoes of Jewish history.

Slavonice Tiny town hugging the Austrian border, ideal for hiking into a pastoral countryside dotted with evocative, never-used WWII fortifications.

▲▲**Olomouc** Moravian cultural capital and thriving university city, with a grand square (crowned by Europe's biggest plague column), churches, museums, stinky cheese, vibrant everyday life, and an opportunity to side-trip to the country's top Rococo château in nearby Kroměříž.

▲**Wallachia** Time-passed, mountainous corner of Moravia, with a fine open-air folk museum at Rožnov pod Radhoštěm and a mountaintop retreat at Pustevny.

Mikulov Wine Region The Czech Republic's top wine-growing area, with the home-base village of Pavlov (wine cellars and fun water activities), the historical town of Mikulov (synagogue museum), and the impressive castles-and-gardens complex of Lednice and Valtice.

Slow down and be open to unexpected experiences. Ask questions—most locals are eager to point you in their idea of the right direction. Keep a notepad in your pocket for confirming prices, noting directions, and organizing your thoughts. Wear your money belt, learn the currency, and figure out how to estimate prices in dollars. Those who expect to travel smart, do.

Trip Costs

There are two price tiers in the Czech Republic: Prague, and everywhere else. Outside of Prague, you'll be amazed at the low prices for accommodations, food, transportation, and sightseeing. In Prague, you'll find prices closer to the Western European range. Prague hotels are particularly expensive, often surpassing Western prices. But even in Prague, things that natives pay for—such as transportation and food (in local-style, rather than tourist-oriented, restaurants)—are very affordable. Despite the expense of Prague, if you avoid overpriced restaurants on the main tourist drag, and if you use my listings to stay at only the best-value hotels, a trip to the Czech Republic can still be substantially less expensive than a trip to Western European destinations.

Five components make up your trip costs: airfare, surface transportation, room and board, sightseeing and entertainment, and shopping and miscellany.

Airfare: A basic round-trip flight from the US to Prague can cost, on average, about $1,000-1,800, depending on where you fly from and when (cheaper in winter). If Prague is part of a longer trip, consider saving time and money in Europe by flying into one city and out of another (for example, into Prague and out of Vienna).

Surface Transportation: Point-to-point train and bus tickets within the Czech Republic are inexpensive—a second-class train ticket from Prague to the farthest reaches of the country won't run you more than about $40. Renting a car is convenient for exploring the Czech countryside, but doing so is much more expensive than public transportation (figure about $650 per week, including gas and insurance). Leasing can save you money on insurance and taxes for trips of three weeks or more. Car rental and leases are cheapest when arranged from the US. Those with more money than time can consider hiring a car with a private driver (a full-day, round-trip excursion from Prague to Český Krumlov runs about $220; see page 197). Train passes normally must be purchased outside Europe but aren't necessarily your best option—you may save money by simply buying tickets as you go. Don't hesitate to consider flying, as budget airlines can be cheaper than taking the train (check www.skyscanner.com for intra-European flights). For more on public transportation and car rental, see "Transportation" in the appendix.

Room and Board: You can manage comfortably in Prague in 2014 on $130 a day per person for room and board. This allows $10 for lunch, $20 for dinner, and $100 for lodging (based on two people splitting the cost of a $200 double room that includes breakfast). Outside Prague, hotel rates plummet to $70 or less for a decent double, and food prices also drop—making $50 a day per person a reasonable budget in the Czech countryside. Even in Prague, students and tightwads can eat and sleep for $40 a day ($25 for a bed, $15 for meals and snacks).

Sightseeing and Entertainment: Sightseeing is inexpensive here. Most sights generally cost about $5-10. A few biggies cost more (such as Prague Castle—$13) or much more (the Jewish Quarter—$24), but that's rare. Most sights offer senior and student discounts; always ask. Figure $25-30 for concerts, Black Light Theater performances, and other splurge experiences. You can hire a private guide for as little as $130 for four hours. An overall average of $30 a day works for most people. Don't skimp here. After all, this category is the driving force behind your trip—you came to sightsee, enjoy, and experience the Czech Republic.

Shopping and Miscellany: Figure $1-2 per stamped postcard, coffee, beer, or ice-cream cone. Shopping can vary in cost from nearly nothing to a small fortune. Good budget travelers find that this category has little to do with assembling a trip full of lifelong and wonderful memories.

Sightseeing Priorities

Depending on the length of your trip, and taking geographic proximity into account, the following are my recommended priorities:

3 days:	Prague
4-5 days, add:	Your choice of nearby day trips (Kutná Hora, Terezín Memorial, and the three castles: Konopiště, Karlštejn, or Křivoklát)
5 days, add:	Český Krumlov (and skip day trips)
7 days, add:	Olomouc
8-9 days, add:	Třeboň, Telč, and Třebíč
More:	Your choice among Šumava, Wallachia, Slavonice, or the Mikulov wine region with Lednice-Valtice

This list assumes you're primarily interested in the Czech Republic. But note that Prague also splices neatly into a wider-ranging trip that can include such nearby destinations as Vienna (4-6 hours by train), Budapest (7-8.5 hours), Kraków (7.5-8.25 hours), Munich (6.25 hours), and Berlin (4.5-5 hours).

INTRODUCTION

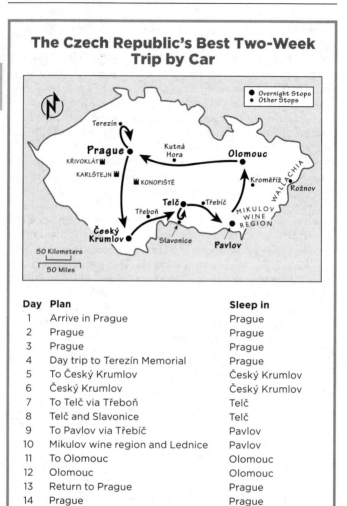

The Czech Republic's Best Two-Week Trip by Car

Day	Plan	Sleep in
1	Arrive in Prague	Prague
2	Prague	Prague
3	Prague	Prague
4	Day trip to Terezín Memorial	Prague
5	To Český Krumlov	Český Krumlov
6	Český Krumlov	Český Krumlov
7	To Telč via Třeboň	Telč
8	Telč and Slavonice	Telč
9	To Pavlov via Třebíč	Pavlov
10	Mikulov wine region and Lednice	Pavlov
11	To Olomouc	Olomouc
12	Olomouc	Olomouc
13	Return to Prague	Prague
14	Prague	Prague

When to Go

In Prague and the Czech Republic, the "tourist season" runs roughly from Easter through October. July and August have their advantages, with the best weather, longer days (daylight until after 21:00), fewer tourists in Prague than in the peak months of May, June, and September, and busy festivals held in small towns around the country. In spring and fall (May, June, Sept, and early Oct), the weather is milder, and the colors and scents are more powerful.

Winter travelers find the concert season in full swing, with re-markably fewer tourists—but outside of Prague, many sights are ei-

The Czech Republic's Best 12-Day Trip by Bus and Train

Day	Plan	Sleep in
1	Arrive in Prague	Prague
2	Prague	Prague
3	Prague	Prague
4	Day trip to Terezin Memorial	Prague
5	To Český Krumlov	Český Krumlov
6	Český Krumlov	Český Krumlov
7	To Telč via Třeboň	Telč
8	Telč and Slavonice	Telč
9	To Olomouc via Třebíč	Olomouc
10	Olomouc	Olomouc
11	Return to Prague	Prague
12	Prague	Prague

With more time in the Czech Republic, consider a pair of other destinations that are a little more difficult, but still possible, to reach by public transportation: Hikers enjoy Wallachia, which fits easily into the above schedule after Olomouc (make your home base in Trojanovice). Wine lovers head for the Mikulov wine region, easiest to visit between Telč and Olomouc (make your home base in Pavlov).

Beyond the Czech borders, you could visit Budapest, Hungary, and Kraków, Poland—each an easy, direct night-train trip away from Prague (or an even quicker connection from Olomouc). For more on these destinations beyond the Czech Republic, see the current editions of *Rick Steves' Budapest* and *Rick Steves' Eastern Europe.*

ther closed or open on a limited schedule. In December, you'll find Christmas markets on main squares around the country, fragrant with the scent of hot wine with cloves. After a quiet Christmas season, Prague explodes with fun on New Year's Eve, teeming with thousands of Germans and other Europeans. In January and early February, when few tourists come, chances are you will wake up to a Prague silenced by the wistful glimmer of snow, which quickly melts in the Old Town but stays on the ground at Prague Castle and on top of Petřín Hill. Seeing the Charles Bridge blanketed by fresh snow makes the hours spent out in the cold worthwhile. Frequent pub stops, with lots of plum brandy and hot wine, are essential at this time of year—and they bring you closer to local life. Winter can linger, but Prague usually turns green with spring around mid-April. Use the climate chart in the appendix as your Prague weather guide.

Know Before You Go

Your trip is more likely to go smoothly if you plan ahead. Check this list of things to arrange while you're still at home.

You need a **passport**—but no visa or shots—to travel in the Czech Republic. You may be denied entry into certain European countries if your passport is due to expire within three to six months of your ticketed date of return. Get it renewed if you'll be cutting it close. It can take up to six weeks to get or renew a passport (for more on passports, see www.travel.state.gov). Pack a photocopy of your passport in your luggage in case the original is lost or stolen.

The Czech Republic has joined the open-borders Schengen Agreement, eliminating checks at **border crossings** when traveling to and from neighboring countries. You'll simply zip through the border without stopping. But when you change countries, you still change phone cards, currency, and postage stamps.

Book rooms well in advance if you'll be traveling during peak season (May-June and Sept) or on any major holidays or festivals (see page 354).

Call your **debit- and credit-card companies** to let them know the countries you'll be visiting, to ask about fees, request your PIN code (it will be mailed to you), and more. See page 13 for details.

Do your homework if you want to buy **travel insurance.** Compare the cost of the insurance to the likelihood of your using it and your potential loss if something goes wrong. Also, check whether your existing insurance (health, homeowners, or renters) covers you and your possessions overseas. For more tips, see www.ricksteves.com/insurance.

If you're planning on **renting a car** in the Czech Republic, bring your driver's license and an International Driving Permit (see page 343). Confirm pickup hours; many car-rental offices close Saturday afternoon and all day Sunday.

If you're bringing a **mobile device,** download any apps you might want to use on the road, such as translators, maps, and transit schedules. Check out **Rick Steves Audio Europe,** featuring audio tours of major European sights, hours of travel interviews on Prague and the Czech Republic, and more (via the Rick Steves Audio Europe smartphone app, www.ricksteves.com/audioeurope, Google Play, or iTunes; for details, see page 49).

Check the **Rick Steves guidebook updates** page for any recent changes to this book (www.ricksteves.com/update).

Because airline **carry-on restrictions** are always changing, visit the Transportation Security Administration's website (www.tsa.gov) for an up-to-date list of what you can bring on the plane with you...and what you have to check.

Practicalities

Emergency and Medical Help: In Prague, dial 112 for medical or other emergencies and 158 for police. To summon an ambulance, call 155. If you get sick, do as the Czechs do and go to a pharmacist for advice. Or ask at your hotel for help—they'll know the nearest medical and emergency services. (See "Medical Help" on page 40 for pharmacy and hospital locations in Prague.)

Theft or Loss: To replace a passport, you'll need to go in person to an embassy (see page 339). If your credit and debit cards disappear, cancel and replace them (see "Damage Control for Lost Cards" on page 15). File a police report, either on the spot or within a day or two; you'll need it to submit an insurance claim for lost or stolen railpasses or travel gear, and it can help with replacing your passport or credit and debit cards. For more information, see www.ricksteves.com/help. Precautionary measures can minimize the effects of loss—back up your digital photos and other files frequently.

Time Zones: The Czech Republic, like most of continental Europe, is generally six/nine hours ahead of the East/West Coasts of the US. The exceptions are the beginning and end of Daylight Saving Time: Europe "springs forward" the last Sunday in March (two weeks after most of North America) and "falls back" the last Sunday in October (one week before North America). For a handy online time converter, try www.timeanddate.com/worldclock.

Business Hours: Most stores are open Monday through Friday from roughly 10:00 to 18:00 (17:00 outside Prague), Saturday morning until lunchtime, and closed Sunday. Tourist shops in the Old Town and small grocery stores around Prague are open daily until at least 20:00.

Sundays have the same pros and cons as they do for travelers in the US—sights are generally open but may have limited hours, shops and banks are closed, city traffic is light, and public-transportation options are fewer.

Watt's Up? Europe's electrical system is 220 volts, instead of North America's 110 volts. Most newer electronics (such as laptops, battery chargers, and hair dryers) convert automatically, so you won't need a converter plug, but you will need an adapter plug with two round prongs, sold inexpensively at travel stores in the US. Avoid bringing older appliances that don't automatically convert voltage; instead, buy a cheap replacement in Europe.

Discounts: Discounts are not listed in this book. However, many sights offer discounts for youths (up to age 18), students (with proper identification cards, www.isic.org), families, seniors (loosely defined as retirees or those willing to call themselves a senior), and groups of 10 or more. While some discounts are technically available only for Czechs or citizens of the European Union (EU), they are sometimes are granted to travelers too—always ask.

Online Translation Tip: You can use Google's Chrome browser (available free at www.google.com/chrome) to instantly translate websites. With one click, the page appears in (very rough) English translation. You can also paste the URL of the site into the translation window at www.google.com/translate.

Money

This section offers advice on how to pay for purchases on your trip (including getting cash from ATMs and paying with plastic), dealing with lost or stolen cards, VAT (sales tax) refunds, and tipping.

What to Bring

Bring both a debit card and a credit card. You'll use the debit card at cash machines (ATMs) to withdraw local cash for most purchases, and the credit card to pay for larger items. (Due to problems with fraud, try to avoid using your credit card to pay for goods or services in Prague.) Some travelers also carry a third card, in case one gets demagnetized or eaten by a temperamental machine.

For an emergency stash, bring several hundred dollars in hard cash in $20 bills. If you need to exchange the bills, go to a bank; avoid using currency exchange booths because of their lousy rates and/or outrageous fees.

Cash

Cash is just as desirable in the Czech Republic as it is at home. Small businesses (hotels, restaurants, and shops) prefer that you pay your bills with cash. Some vendors will charge you extra for using a credit card, and some won't take credit cards at all. Cash is the best—and sometimes only—way to pay for bus fare, taxis, and local guides. Paying in cash also protects you from potential credit-card fraud.

Throughout Europe, ATMs are the standard way for travelers to get cash. But stay away from "independent" ATMs such as Travelex, Euronet, Cardpoint, and Cashzone, which charge huge commissions and have terrible exchange rates.

To withdraw money from an ATM (called a *Bankomat* in the Czech Republic), you'll need a debit card—ideally with a Visa or MasterCard logo for maximum usability, plus a PIN code. Know your PIN code in numbers; there are only numbers—no letters— on European keypads. Although you can use a credit card for an ATM transaction, it only makes sense in an emergency, because it's considered a cash advance (borrowed at a high interest rate) rather

Exchange Rate

Though the Czech Republic joined the EU in 2004, it continues to use its traditional currency, the Czech crown (*koruna,* abbreviated Kč).

20 Czech crowns (Kč) = about $1

To roughly convert prices in crowns to dollars, drop the last digit and divide in half. So that tasty lunch for 160 Kč is about $8, the souvenir Czech puppet for 450 Kč costs roughly $23, and the taxi ride for 2,300 Kč from the airport is...uh-oh.

Many hotels, restaurants, and shops do accept euro bills (but not coins or large bills). You may even see hotel rooms or souvenirs priced in euros (€). In this case, remember that €1 = 27 Kč = about $1.30. If you're using euros, expect bad rates and your change in *korunas.* If you're just passing through, your euros will probably get you by—and they can actually be helpful in an emergency. But if you're staying awhile, get the local currency.

Check www.oanda.com for the latest exchange rates.

than a withdrawal. Try to withdraw large sums of money to reduce the number of per-transaction bank fees you'll pay.

For increased security, shield the keypad when entering your PIN code, and don't use an ATM if anything on the front of the machine looks loose or damaged (a sign that someone may have attached a "skimming" device to capture account information). Some travelers make a point of monitoring their accounts while traveling to detect any unauthorized transactions.

Pickpockets target tourists. To safeguard your cash, wear a money belt—a pouch with a strap that you buckle around your waist like a belt and wear under your clothes. Keep your cash, credit cards, and passport secure in your money belt, and carry only a day's spending money in your front pocket.

Credit and Debit Cards

For purchases, Visa and MasterCard are more commonly accepted than American Express. Just like at home, credit or debit cards are accepted by big hotels and shops. Although larger restaurants take credit cards, it makes more sense to pay in cash—particularly in Prague, where it's unwise to entrust your credit card to potentially unscrupulous waiters.

When I travel, I typically use my debit card to withdraw cash to pay for most purchases. I use my credit card only in a few specific situations: to book hotel reservations by phone, to cover major expenses (such as car rentals, plane tickets, and long hotel stays), and to pay for things near the end of my trip (to avoid another visit to the ATM). While you could use a debit card to make most large purchases, using a credit card offers a greater degree of fraud protection (because debit cards draw funds directly from your account).

Ask Your Credit- or Debit-Card Company: Before your trip, contact the company that issued your debit or credit cards.

• Confirm that your card will work overseas, and alert them that you'll be using it in Europe; otherwise, they may deny transactions if they perceive unusual spending patterns.

• Ask for the specifics on transaction **fees.** When you use your credit or debit card—either for purchases or ATM withdrawals—you'll typically be charged additional "international transaction" fees of up to 3 percent (1 percent is normal) plus $5 per transaction. If your card's fees seem high, consider getting a different card just for your trip: Capital One (www.capitalone.com) and most credit unions have low-to-no international fees.

• If you plan to withdraw cash from ATMs, confirm your daily **withdrawal limit** and if necessary, ask your bank to adjust it. Some travelers prefer a high limit that allows them to take out more cash at each ATM stop (saving on bank fees), while others prefer to set a lower limit in case their card is stolen. Note that foreign banks also set maximum withdrawal amounts for their ATMs.

• Get your bank's emergency **phone number** in the US (but not its 800 number, which isn't accessible from overseas) to call collect if you have a problem.

• Ask for your credit card's **PIN** in case you need to make an emergency cash withdrawal or encounter Europe's "chip-and-PIN" system; the bank won't tell you your PIN over the phone, so allow time for it to be mailed to you.

Chip and PIN: While much of Europe is shifting to a chip-and-PIN security system for credit and debit cards, the Czech Republic still uses the old magnetic-swipe technology. (European chip-and-PIN cards are embedded with an electronic security chip, and require the purchaser to punch in a PIN rather than sign a receipt.) If you happen to encounter chip and PIN, it will probably be at automated payment machines, such as those at toll roads or self-serve gas pumps. On the outside chance that a machine won't take your card, find a cashier who can make your card work (they can print a receipt for you to sign), or find a machine that takes cash. But don't panic. Most travelers who are carrying only magnetic-stripe cards never encounter any problems. You can always use an ATM to withdraw cash with your magnetic-stripe card, even in countries where people predominantly use chip-and-PIN cards.

Dynamic Currency Conversion: If merchants offer to convert your purchase price into dollars (called dynamic currency conversion, or "DCC"), refuse this "service." You'll pay even more in fees for the expensive convenience of seeing your charge in dollars.

Damage Control for Lost Cards

If you lose your credit, debit, or ATM card, you can stop people from using it by reporting the loss immediately to the respective global customer-assistance centers. Call these 24-hour US numbers collect: Visa (tel. 303/967-1096), MasterCard (tel. 636/722-7111), or American Express (tel. 336/393-1111). In the Czech Republic, to make a collect call to the US, dial 00-800-222-55288. Press zero or stay on the line for an English-speaking operator. European toll-free numbers (listed by country) can be found at the websites for Visa and MasterCard.

Providing the following information will allow for a quicker cancellation of your missing card: full card number, whether you are the primary or secondary cardholder, the cardholder's name exactly as printed on the card, billing address, home phone number, circumstances of the loss or theft, and identification verification (your birth date, your mother's maiden name, or your Social Security number—memorize this, don't carry a copy). If you are the secondary cardholder, you'll also need to provide the primary cardholder's identification-verification details. You can generally receive a temporary card within two or three business days in Europe (see www.ricksteves.com/help for more).

If you report your loss within two days, you typically won't be responsible for any unauthorized transactions on your account, although many banks charge a liability fee of $50.

Tipping

Tipping in the Czech Republic isn't as automatic and generous as it is in the US, but for special service, tips are appreciated, if not expected. As in the US, the proper amount depends on your resources, tipping philosophy, and the circumstances, but some general guidelines apply.

Restaurants: Tipping is an issue only at restaurants that have table service. If you order your food at a counter, don't tip. At Czech restaurants that have a waitstaff, service is included, although it's common to round up the bill after a good meal (usually 5-10 percent; e.g., for a 370-Kč meal, pay 400 Kč). If you warm up the waiter with a few Czech words, such as "please" (*prosím;* PROH-zeem) and "thank you" (*děkuji;* DYACK-khuyi), you'll get better service and won't be expected to tip more than a local. But if you greet your waiter in English, he'll want a 15 percent tip. Believe me: The slightest attempt at speaking Czech (see phrases on page 360) will turn you from a targeted tourist into a special guest, even in the most touristy restaurants.

Taxis: To tip the cabbie, round up about 5 percent. If the cabbie hauls your bags and zips you to the airport to help you catch your flight, you might want to toss in a little more. But if you feel like you're being driven in circles or otherwise ripped off, skip the tip. Again, if you use some Czech words, your cabbie will be less likely to try to scam you.

Services: In general, if someone in the service industry does a super job for you, a small tip (about 50 Kč) is appropriate...but not required. If you're not sure whether (or how much) to tip for a service, ask your hotelier or the TI.

Getting a VAT Refund

Wrapped into the purchase price of your Czech souvenirs is a Value-Added Tax (VAT) of 21 percent. You're entitled to get most of that tax back if you purchase more than 2,001 Kč (about $100) of goods at a store that participates in the VAT-refund scheme. Typically, you must ring up the minimum at a single retailer—you can't add up your purchases from various shops to reach the required amount.

Getting your refund is usually straightforward and, if you buy a substantial amount of souvenirs, well worth the hassle. If you're lucky, the merchant will subtract the tax when you make your purchase. (This is more likely to occur if the store ships the goods to your home.) Otherwise, you'll need to:

Get the paperwork. Have the merchant completely fill out the necessary refund document. You'll have to present your passport. Get the paperwork done before you leave the store to ensure you'll have everything you need (including your original sales receipt).

Get your stamp at the border or airport. Process your VAT document at your last stop in the Czech Republic (such as at the airport) with the customs agent who deals with VAT refunds. (For the location of customs desks at Prague's Václav Havel Airport, see page 195). Arrive an additional hour before you need to check in for your flight, to allow time to find the customs office—and to stand in line. It's best to keep your purchases in your carry-on. If they're too large or dangerous to carry on (such as knives), pack them in your checked bags and alert the check-in agent. You'll be sent (with your tagged bag) to a customs desk outside security, which will examine your bag, stamp your paperwork, and put your bag on the belt. You're not supposed to use your purchased goods before you leave. If you show up at customs wearing your new chic Czech outfit, officials might look the other way—or deny you a refund.

Collect your refund. You'll need to return your stamped document to the retailer or its representative. Many merchants work with a service, such as Global Blue, Premier Tax Free, or Travelex, that has offices at major airports, ports, or border crossings (either before or after security, probably strategically located near a duty-free shop). These services, which extract a 4 percent fee, can refund your money immediately in your currency of choice or credit your card (within two billing cycles). If the retailer handles VAT refunds directly, it's up to you to contact the merchant for your refund. You can mail the documents from home or, more quickly, from your point of departure (using an envelope you've prepared in advance or one that's been provided by the merchant). You'll then have to wait—it can take months.

Customs for American Shoppers

You are allowed to take home $800 worth of items per person duty-free, once every 30 days. You can also bring in one liter of alcohol duty-free. As for food, you can take home many processed and packaged foods: vacuum-packed cheeses, dried herbs, jams, baked goods, candy, chocolate, oil, vinegar, and honey. Fresh fruits and vegetables and most meats are not allowed. Any liquid-containing foods must be packed in checked luggage, a potential recipe for disaster. To check customs rules and duty rates, visit http://help.cbp.gov.

Sightseeing

Sightseeing can be hard work. Use these tips to make your visits to the Czech Republic's finest sights meaningful, fun, efficient, and painless.

Plan Ahead

Set up an itinerary that allows you to fit in all your must-see sights. For a one-stop look at opening hours in Prague, see "Prague at a Glance" (page 52; also see "Daily Reminder" on page 54). Most sights keep stable hours, but you can easily confirm the latest by checking with the TI or visiting museum websites.

Don't put off visiting a must-see sight—you never know when a place will close unexpectedly for a holiday, strike, or restoration. Many museums are closed or have reduced hours at least a few days a year, especially on holidays such as Christmas, New Year's, and Labor Day (May 1). A list of holidays is on page 354; check museum websites for possible closures during your trip.

Going at the right time helps avoid crowds. This book offers tips on the best time to see specific sights. Try visiting popular sights very early or very late. Evening visits are usually peaceful, with fewer crowds.

Study up. To get the most out of the self-guided walks and sight descriptions in this book, read them before your visit.

Czech Place Names

Here's a rough pronunciation key for places mentioned in this book. For pronunciation help for specific sights and neighborhoods in Prague, see the "Prague Essentials" sidebar in the Orientation chapter.

Beskydy (mountains)	*BEH-skih-dee*
Brno	*BURR-noh*
České Budějovice	*CHESS-keh BOO-dyeh-yoh-vee-tseh*
Český Krumlov	*CHESS-key KROOM-loff*
Karlštejn (castle)	*KARL-shtayn*
Konopiště (castle)	*KOH-noh-peesh-tyeh*
Křivoklát (castle)	*KREE-vohk-laht*
Kroměříž	*KROH-myehr-eezh*
Kutná Hora	*KOOT-nah HO-rah*
Lednice	*LEHD-nee-tseh*
Litoměřice	*LEE-toh-myer-zhee-tseh*
Mikulov	*MEE-kuh-lohv*
Olomouc	*OH-loh-moats*
Pálava (hills)	*PAH-lah-vah*
Pavlov	*PAHV-lohv*
Pustevny	*POO-stehv-nee*
Rožnov	*ROHZ-nohv*
Slavonice	*SLAH-voh-neet-seh*
Šumava (mountains)	*SHOO-mah-vah*
Telč	*telch*
Terezín	*TEH-reh-zeen*
Třebíč	*TREH-beech*

At Sights

Here's what you can typically expect:

Entering: Be warned that you may not be allowed to enter if you arrive 30 to 60 minutes before closing time. And guards start ushering people out well before the actual closing time, so don't save the best for last.

Some important sights have a security check, where you must open your bag or send it through a metal detector. Some sights require you to check daypacks and coats. (If you'd rather not check your daypack, try carrying it tucked under your arm like a purse as you enter.)

Photography: If the museum's photo policy isn't clearly posted, ask a guard. Generally, taking photos without a flash or tripod is allowed (although some Czech sights charge a photography fee). Some sights ban photos altogether.

Temporary Exhibits: Museums may show special exhibits in addition to their permanent collection. Some exhibits are included in the entry price, while others come at an extra cost (which you may have to pay even if you don't want to see the exhibit).

Expect Changes: Artwork can be on tour, on loan, out sick, or shifted at the whim of the curator. To adapt, pick up a floor plan as you enter, and ask museum staff if you can't find a particular item.

Audioguides: Some sights include or rent audioguides, which generally offer good recorded descriptions in English ($3-12). If you bring your own earbuds, you can enjoy better sound and avoid holding the device to your ear. To save money, bring a Y-jack and share one audioguide with your travel partner. Increasingly, museums are offering apps (often free) that you can download to your mobile device.

Services: Important sights may have an on-site café or cafeteria (usually a handy place to rejuvenate during a long visit). The WCs at sights are usually free and generally clean.

Before Leaving: At the gift shop, scan the postcard rack or thumb through a guidebook to be sure you haven't overlooked something that you'd like to see.

Every sight or museum offers more than what is covered in this book. Use the information in this book as an introduction—not the final word.

Sleeping

I favor hotels and restaurants that are handy to your sightseeing activities. Rather than list lodgings scattered throughout a city, I choose my favorite neighborhoods and recommend the best accommodation values in each, from dorm beds to fancy doubles with all the comforts.

A major feature of this book is its extensive and opinionated listing of good-value rooms. I like places that are clean, central, relatively quiet at night, reasonably priced, friendly, small enough to have a hands-on owner and stable staff, run with a respect for Czech traditions, and not listed in other guidebooks. (In the Czech Republic, for me, meeting six out of these eight criteria means it's a keeper.) I'm more impressed by a convenient location

Sleep Code

(20 Kč = about $1)

Price Rankings

To help you sort easily through the listings, I've divided the accommodations into three categories based on their price for a double room with bath during high season:

$$$	**Higher Priced**
$$	**Moderately Priced**
$	**Lower Priced**

I always rate hostels as $, whether or not they have double rooms, because they have the cheapest beds in town. Prices can change without notice; verify the hotel's current rates online or by email.

Abbreviations

To pack maximum information into minimum space, I use the following code to describe accommodations in this book. Prices listed are per room, not per person. When a price range is given for a type of room (such as "Db-1,800-2,000 Kč"), it means the price fluctuates with the season, size of room, or length of stay; expect to pay the upper end for peak-season stays.

- **S** = Single room (or price for one person in a double).
- **D** = Double or twin room.
- **T** = Triple (often a double bed with a single).
- **Q** = Quad (usually two double beds; adding an extra child's bed to a T is usually cheaper).
- **b** = Private bathroom with toilet and shower or tub.
- **s** = Private shower or tub only (the toilet is down the hall).

According to this code, a couple staying at a "Db-2,700 Kč" hotel would pay a total of 2,700 Czech crowns (about $135) for a double room with a private bathroom. Unless otherwise noted, breakfast is included, hotel staff speak basic English, and credit cards are accepted.

There's almost always Wi-Fi and/or a guest computer available, either free or for a fee.

and a fun-loving philosophy than flat-screen TVs and a pricey laundry service.

Book your accommodations well in advance if you'll be traveling during busy times. See page 354 for a list of major holidays and festivals in the Czech Republic; for tips on making reservations, see page 22.

Rates and Deals

I've described my recommended accommodations using a Sleep Code (see sidebar). Prices listed are for one-night stays in peak season, include breakfast, and assume you're booking directly (not through an online hotel-booking engine or TI). Booking services extract a commission from the hotel, which logically closes the door on special deals. Book direct.

For most of the hotels I list, I provide a website (which often has a built-in booking form) and an email address; you can expect a response in English within a day (and often sooner).

If you're on a budget, it's smart to email several hotels to ask for their best price. Comparison-shop and make your choice. This is especially helpful when dealing with larger hotels that use "dynamic pricing," a computer-generated system that predicts the demand for particular days in advance and sets prices accordingly: High-demand days will often be more than double the price of low-demand days. This makes it impossible for a guidebook to list anything more accurate than a wide range of prices. I regret this trend. While you can assume that hotels listed in this book are good, it's very difficult to say which are the better value unless you email to confirm the price.

As you look over the listings, you'll notice that some accommodations promise special prices to Rick Steves readers who book directly with the hotel. To get these rates, you must book direct (that is, not through a booking site like TripAdvisor or Booking. com), mention this book when you reserve, and then show the book upon arrival. Rick Steves discounts apply to readers with ebooks as well as printed books. Because we trust hotels to honor this, please let me know if you don't receive a listed discount. Note, though, that discounts understandably may not be applied to promotional rates.

In general, prices can soften if you do any of the following: offer to pay cash, stay at least three nights, or mention this book. You can also try asking for a cheaper room or a discount, or offer to skip breakfast.

Types of Accommodations

Hotels

Hotel prices in Prague are at Western European levels, but once you get out of the city, you'll pay half as much for a similar room. Plan on spending $150-225 per hotel double in Prague and $50-100 in smaller towns. In general, a triple room is cheaper than the cost of a double and a single. Traveling alone can be expensive: A single room can be close to the cost of a double. Breakfast is generally included (sometimes continental, but often buffet). Hotel el-

Making Hotel Reservations

Reserve your rooms several weeks in advance—or as soon as you've pinned down your travel dates—particularly if you'll be traveling during peak times. Note that some national holidays jam things up and merit your making reservations far in advance (see "Holidays and Festivals" on page 354).

Requesting a Reservation: It's usually easiest to book your room through the hotel's website. Many have a reservation-request form built right in. (For the best rates, be sure to use the hotel's official site and not a booking agency's site.) Simpler websites will generate an email to the hotelier with your request. If there's no reservation form, or for complicated requests, send an email (see next page for a sample request). Most recommended hotels are accustomed to guests who speak only English.

The hotelier wants to know:
- the number and type of rooms you need
- the number of nights you'll stay
- your date of arrival
- your date of departure
- any special needs (such as bathroom in the room or down the hall, cheapest room, twin beds vs. double bed, crib, air-conditioning, quiet, view, ground floor or no stairs, and so on)

If you request a room by email, use the European style for writing dates: day/month/year. For example, for a two-night stay in July of 2014, ask for "1 double room for 2 nights, arrive 16/07/14, depart 18/07/14." Make sure you mention any discounts—for Rick Steves readers or otherwise—when you make the reservation.

Confirming a Reservation: When the hotel replies with its room availability and rates, just email back to confirm your reservation. Most places will request a credit-card number to hold your room. While you can email it (I do), it's safer to share that confidential info via a phone call, two emails (splitting your number between them), or the hotel's secure online reservation form. On the small chance that a hotel loses track of your reservation, bring along a hard copy of their confirmation.

Canceling a Reservation: If you must cancel your reservation, it's courteous—and smart—to do so with as much notice as possible, especially for smaller family-run places. Simply make a

evators, while becoming more common, are often very small—pack light, or you may need to send your bags up separately.

If you're arriving early in the morning, your room probably won't be ready. You can safely drop your bag at the hotel and dive right into sightseeing.

Hoteliers can be a great help and source of advice. Most know their city well, and can assist you with everything from public tran-

From:	rick@ricksteves.com
Sent:	Today
To:	info@hotelcentral.com
Subject:	Reservation request for 19-22 July

Dear Hotel Central,

I would like to reserve a room for 2 people for 3 nights, arriving 19 July and departing 22 July. If possible, I would like a quiet room with a double bed and a bathroom inside the room.

Please let me know if you have a room available and the price.

Thank you!
Rick Steves

quick phone call or send an email. Request confirmation of your cancellation in case you are accidentally billed.

Be warned that cancellation policies can be strict; read the fine print or ask about these before you book. For example, if you cancel on short notice, you could lose your deposit, or be billed for one night or even your entire stay. Internet deals may require prepayment, with no refunds for cancellations.

Reconfirming a Reservation: Call to reconfirm your room reservation a few days in advance. Smaller hotels and B&Bs appreciate knowing your estimated time of arrival. If you'll be arriving late (after 17:00), let them know.

Reserving Rooms as You Travel: You can make reservations as you travel, calling hotels a few days to a week before your arrival. If you'd rather travel without any reservations at all, you'll have greater success snaring rooms if you arrive at your destination early in the day. When you anticipate crowds (weekends are worst), call hotels at about 9:00 or 10:00 on the day you plan to arrive, when the receptionist knows who'll be checking out and which rooms will be available. If you encounter a language barrier, ask the fluent receptionist at your current hotel to call for you.

Phoning: For tips on how to call hotels overseas, see page 332.

sit and airport connections to finding a good restaurant, the nearest launderette, or an Internet café. Even at the best places, mechanical breakdowns occur: Air-conditioning malfunctions, sinks leak, hot water turns cold, and toilets gurgle and smell. Report your concerns clearly and calmly at the front desk. For more complicated problems, don't expect instant results.

If you suspect night noise will be a problem (if, for instance, your room is over a pub), ask for a quiet room in the back or on an upper floor. To guard against theft in your room, keep valuables out of sight. Some rooms come with a safe, and other hotels have safes at the front desk. I've never bothered using one.

Checkout can pose problems if surprise charges pop up on your bill. If you settle your bill the afternoon before you leave, you'll have time to discuss and address any points of contention (before 19:00, when the night shift usually arrives).

Above all, keep a positive attitude. Remember, you're on vacation. If your hotel is a disappointment, spend more time out enjoying the city you came to see.

Private Rooms

A cheap option in the Czech Republic is a room in a private home (called a "pension," sometimes advertised with the German phrase *Zimmer frei,* "room free," meaning vacancy). These places are inexpensive, at least as comfortable as a cheap hotel, and a good way to get some local insight. The boss changes the sheets, so people staying several nights are most desirable—and stays of less than three nights are often charged up to 30 percent more.

Hostels

You'll pay about $20-25 per bed to stay at a hostel. Travelers of any age are welcome if they don't mind dorm-style accommodations and meeting other travelers. Most hostels offer kitchen facilities, guest computers, Wi-Fi, and a self-service laundry. Nowadays, concerned about bedbugs, hostels are likely to provide all bedding, including sheets. Family and private rooms may be available on request. Unlike in Western Europe, many hostels in the Czech Republic are in university dorms where two- or three-person rooms are the norm.

Independent hostels tend to be easygoing, colorful, and informal (no membership required); hostelworld.com is the standard way backpackers search and book hostels these days, but also try-hostelz.com, hostels.com, and hostelbookers.com.

Official hostels are part of Hostelling International (HI) and share an online booking site (www.hihostels.com). HI hostels typically require that you either have a membership card or pay extra per night.

Other Options

Whether you're in a city or the countryside, renting an apartment, house, or villa can be a fun and cost-effective way to delve into Europe. Websites such as HomeAway.com and its sister site VRBO.com let you correspond directly with European property owners or managers.

Airbnb.com makes it reasonably easy to find a place to sleep in someone's home. Beds range from air-mattress-in-living-room basic to plush-B&B-suite posh. If you want a place to sleep that's free, Couchsurfing.com is a vagabond's alternative to Airbnb. It lists millions of outgoing members, who host fellow "surfers" in their homes.

Eating

You'll find that the local cafés, cuisine, beer, and wine are highlights of your Czech adventure. This is affordable sightseeing for your palate.

When restaurant-hunting, choose a spot filled with locals, not the place with the big neon signs boasting "We Speak English and Accept Credit Cards." Incredible deals abound in the Czech Repub-

lic, where locals routinely eat well for $5. Venturing even a block or two off the main drag leads to authentic, higher-quality food for less than half the price of the tourist-oriented places. Most restaurants tack a menu onto their door for browsers and have an English menu inside.

In general, Czech restaurants are open Sunday through Thursday 11:00-22:00, and Friday and Saturday 11:00-24:00. Only a rude waiter will rush you. Good service is relaxed (slow to an American). You can stay in a pub as long as you want—no one will bring you the *účet* (bill) until you ask for it: *"Pane vrchní, zaplatím!"* (PAH-neh VURCH-nee zah-plah-TEEM; "Mr. Waiter, now I pay!"). The service charge is included in the bill, but it's customary to tip 5-10 percent (explained earlier, under "Tipping"). In Prague, it's smart to pay cash for your meals rather than let your credit card leave your sight; for more on scams in Prague, see page 41.

When you're in the mood for something halfway between a restaurant and a picnic, look for take-out food stands, bakeries (with sandwiches and small pizzas to go), delis with stools or a table, department-store cafeterias, salad bars, or simple little eateries for fast and easy sit-down restaurant food.

Venues are required to post stickers on the exterior of their premises indicating whether they allow smoking, prohibit it, or provide a nonsmoking section.

Czech Dumplings

Czech dumplings *(knedlíky)* resemble steamed white bread. They come in plain or potato *(bramborové)* varieties; are meant to be drowned in gravy (dumplings never accompany sauceless dishes); and are eaten with a knife and fork. Sweet dumplings, listed in the dessert section on a menu, are a tempting option during summer, when they are loaded with fresh strawberries, blueberries, apricots, or plums, and garnished with custard and melted butter. Beware, though, that many restaurants like to cheat by filling the sticky dough with a smattering of jam or fruit preserve; before ordering, ask the waiter for details, or discreetly inspect that plate at your neighbor's table. Dumplings with frozen fruit lose some of the flavor, but are still good to try.

Czech Food

The Czechs have one of Europe's most stick-to-your-ribs cuisines. Heavy on meat, potatoes, and cabbage, it's hearty and tasty—designed to keep peasants fueled through a day of hard work. Some people could eat this stuff forever, while others seek a break in the form of ethnic restaurants (bigger towns such as Prague, Český Krumlov, and Kutná Hora have several options).

A Czech restaurant is a social place where people come to relax. Tables are not private. You can ask to join someone, and you will most likely make some new friends. After a sip of beer, ask for the *jídelní lístek* (menu).

Soups: *Polévka* (soup) is the most essential part of a meal. The saying goes: "The soup fills you up, the dish plugs it up." Some of the thick soups for a cold day are *zelná* or *zelňačka* (cabbage), *čočková* (lentil), *fazolová* (bean), and *dršťková* (tripe—delicious if fresh, chewy as gum if not). The lighter soups are *hovězí* or *slepičí vývar s nudlemi* (beef or chicken broth with noodles), *pórková* (leek), and *květáková* (cauliflower).

Bread: *Pečivo* (bread) is either delivered with the soup, or you need to ask for it; it's always charged separately depending on how many *rohlíky* (rolls) or slices of *chleba* (yeast bread) you eat.

Main Dishes: These can either be *hotová jídla* (quick, ready-to-serve standard dishes, in some places available only during lunch hours, generally 11:00-14:30) or the more specialized *jídla na objednávku* or *minutky* (plates prepared when you order). Even the supposedly quick *hotová jídla* will take longer than the fast food you're used to back home.

Hotová jídla come with set garnishes. The standard menu across the country includes *smažený řízek s bramborem* (fried pork

How Was Your Trip?

Were your travels fun, smooth, and meaningful? If you'd like to share your tips, concerns, and discoveries, please fill out the survey at www.ricksteves.com/feedback. I value your feedback. Thanks in advance—it helps a lot.

fillet with potatoes), *svíčková na smetaně s knedlíkem* (beef tenderloin in cream sauce with dumplings), *vepřová s knedlíkem a se zelím* (pork with dumplings and cabbage), *pečená kachna s knedlíkem a se zelím* (roasted duck with dumplings and cabbage), *maďarský guláš s knedlíkem* (the Czech version of Hungarian goulash), and *pečené kuře s bramborem* (roasted chicken with potatoes).

In this landlocked country, fish options are typically limited to *kapr* (carp) and *pstruh* (trout), prepared in a variety of ways and served with potatoes or fries—although recently, Czech perch and Norwegian salmon have cropped up on many local menus. Vegetarians can go for the delicious *smažený sýr s bramborem* (fried cheese with potatoes) or default to *čočka s vejci* (lentils with fried egg). If you are spending the night out with friends, have a beer and feast on the huge *vepřové koleno s hořčicí a křenem* (pork knuckle with mustard and horseradish sauce) with *chleba* (yeast bread).

The range of the *jídla na objednávku* (meals prepared to order) depends on the chef. You choose your starches and garnishes, which are charged separately.

Salad: *Šopský salát*, like a Greek salad, is usually the best salad option (a mix of tomatoes, cucumbers, peppers, onion, and feta cheese with vinegar and olive oil). The waiter will bring it with the main dish, unless you specify that you want it before.

Dessert: For *moučník* (dessert), there are *palačinka* (crêpes served with fruit or jam), *lívance* (small pancakes with jam and curd), *zmrzlinový pohár* (ice-cream sundae), or fruit-filled dumplings. Many restaurants will offer different sorts of *koláče* (pastries) and *štrůdl* (apple strudel), but it's much better to get these directly from a bakery.

Beverages: No Czech meal is complete without a cup of strong *turecká káva* (Turkish coffee—finely ground coffee that only partly dissolves, leaving "mud" on the bottom, highly caffeinated and drunk without milk). Although espressos and instant coffees have made headway in the past few years, some Czechs regard them as a threat to tradition.

Czech mineral waters *minerálka* have a high mineral content. They're naturally carbonated because they come from the springs in the many Czech spas (Mattoni, the most common brand, is from

Carlsbad). If you want still water, ask for *voda bez bublinek* (water without bubbles). Tap water is generally not served. Water comes bottled and generally costs more than beer.

Bohemia is beer country, with Europe's best and cheapest brew (for all the details, see the sidebar on page 162). Locals also like the herb liquor *becherovka*. Moravians prefer wine and *slivovice*

(SLEE-voh-veet-seh)—a plum brandy so highly valued that it's the de facto currency of the Carpathian Mountains (often used for bartering with farmers and other mountain folk). *Medovina* ("honey wine") is mead.

In bars and restaurants, you can go wild with memorable liqueurs, most of which cost about a dollar a shot. Experiment. *Fernet,* a bitter drink made from many herbs, is the leading Czech aperitif. Absinthe, made from wormwood and herbs, is a watered-down version of the hallucinogenic drink that's illegal in much of Europe. It's famous as the muse of many artists (including Henri de Toulouse-Lautrec in Paris more than a century ago). *Becherovka,* made of 13

herbs and 38 percent alcohol, was used to settle upset aristocratic tummies and as an aphrodisiac. This velvety drink remains popular today. *Becherovka* and tonic mixed together is nicknamed *beton* ("concrete"). If you drink three, you'll find out why.

Traveling as a Temporary Local

We travel all the way to the Czech Republic to enjoy differences—to become temporary locals. You'll experience frustrations. Certain truths we find "God-given" or "self-evident," such as cold beer, ice in drinks, bottomless cups of coffee, hot showers, and bigger being better, are suddenly not so true. One of the benefits of travel is the eye-opening realization that there are logical, civil, and even better alternatives. A willingness to go local ensures that you'll enjoy a full dose of Czech hospitality.

Europeans generally like Americans. But if there is a negative aspect to the Czech image of Americans, it's that we are loud, wasteful, ethnocentric, too formal (which can seem disrespectful), and a bit naive.

While Czechs look bemusedly at some of our Yankee excesses—and worriedly at others—they nearly always afford us individual travelers all the warmth we deserve.

Judging from all the happy feedback I receive from travelers who have used this book, it's safe to assume you'll enjoy a great, affordable vacation—with the finesse of an independent, experienced traveler.

Thanks, and happy travels!

Back Door Travel Philosophy

From *Rick Steves' Europe Through the Back Door*

Travel is intensified living—maximum thrills per minute and one of the last great sources of legal adventure. Travel is freedom. It's recess, and we need it.

Experiencing the real Europe requires catching it by surprise, going casual..."through the Back Door."

Affording travel is a matter of priorities. (Make do with the old car.) You can eat and sleep—simply, safely, and enjoyably—anywhere in Europe for $120 a day plus transportation costs. In many ways, spending more money only builds a thicker wall between you and what you traveled so far to see. Europe is a cultural carnival, and time after time, you'll find that its best acts are free and the best seats are the cheap ones.

A tight budget forces you to travel close to the ground, meeting and communicating with the people. Never sacrifice sleep, nutrition, safety, or cleanliness to save money. Simply enjoy the local-style alternatives to expensive hotels and restaurants.

Connecting with people carbonates your experience. Extroverts have more fun. If your trip is low on magic moments, kick yourself and make things happen. If you don't enjoy a place, maybe you don't know enough about it. Seek the truth. Recognize tourist traps. Give a culture the benefit of your open mind. See things as different, but not better or worse. Any culture has plenty to share.

Of course, travel, like the world, is a series of hills and valleys. Be fanatically positive and militantly optimistic. If something's not to your liking, change your liking.

Travel can make you a happier American, as well as a citizen of the world. Our Earth is home to seven billion equally precious people. It's humbling to travel and find that other people don't have the "American Dream"—they have their own dreams. Europeans like us, but with all due respect, they wouldn't trade passports.

Thoughtful travel engages us with the world. In tough economic times, it reminds us what is truly important. By broadening perspectives, travel teaches new ways to measure quality of life.

Globetrotting destroys ethnocentricity, helping us understand and appreciate other cultures. Rather than fear the diversity on this planet, celebrate it. Among your most prized souvenirs will be the strands of different cultures you choose to knit into your own character. The world is a cultural yarn shop, and Back Door travelers are weaving the ultimate tapestry. Join in!

CZECH REPUBLIC

Česká Republika

The Czech Republic is geographically small. On a quick visit, you can enjoy a fine introduction while still packing in plenty of surprises.

Despite their difficult 20th-century experience, the Czechs have managed to preserve their history. In Czech towns and villages, you'll find a simple joy of life—a holdover from the days of the Renaissance. The deep spirituality of the Baroque era still shapes the national character. The magic of Prague, the beauty of Český Krumlov, and the lyrical quality of the countryside relieve the heaviness caused by the turmoil that passed through here. Get beyond Prague and explore the country's medieval towns. These rugged woods and hilltop castles will make you feel as if you're walking through the garden of your childhood dreams.

Of the Czech Republic's three main regions—Bohemia, Moravia, and small Silesia—the best-known is Bohemia. It has nothing to do with beatnik bohemians, but with the Celtic tribe of Bohemia that inhabited the land before the coming of the Slavs. A longtime home of the Czechs, Bohemia, with Prague as its capital, is circled by a naturally fortifying ring of mountains and cut down the middle by the Vltava River. The winegrowing region of Moravia (to the east) is more Slavic and colorful, and more about the land.

Tourists often conjure up images of Bohemia when they think of the Czech Republic. But the country consists of more than rollicking beer halls and gently rolling landscapes. It's also about dreamy wine cellars and fertile Moravian plains, with the rugged Carpathian Mountains on the horizon. Politically and geologically, Bohemia and Moravia are two distinct regions. The soils and climates in which the hops and wine grapes grow are very different... and so are the two regions' mentalities. The boisterousness of the

CZECH REPUBLIC

Czech Republic Almanac

Official Name: It's the Česká Republika, born on January 1, 1993, along with Slovakia, when the nation of Czechoslovakia—formed after World War I and dominated by the USSR after World War II—split into two countries.

Population: 10.2 million people. About 64 percent are ethnic Czechs, who speak Czech. Unlike some of their neighbors (including the very Catholic Poles and Slovaks), Czechs are inclined to be agnostic: One in 10 is Roman Catholic, but the majority (55 percent) list their religion as unaffiliated.

Latitude and Longitude: 50°N and 15°E (similar latitude to Vancouver, British Columbia).

Area: 31,000 square miles (similar to South Carolina or Maine).

Geography: The Czech Republic comprises three regions—Bohemia (Čechy), Moravia (Morava), and a small slice of Silesia (Slezsko). The climate is generally cool and partly cloudy.

Biggest Cities: Prague (the capital, 1.2 million), Brno (380,000), Ostrava (300,000), and Plzeň (167,000).

Economy: The gross domestic product equals about $292 billion (similar to Indiana). The GDP per capita is approximately $28,000 (just over half that of the average American). Major moneymakers for the country include machine parts, cars and trucks (VW subsidiary Škoda has become a highly respected automaker), and beer (leading brands are Pilsner Urquell and the original Budweiser—called "Czechvar" in the US). Industrial production declined during the recent economic crisis, but not beer consump-

Czech polka contrasts with the melancholy of the Moravian ballad; the political viewpoint of the Prague power broker is at odds with the spirituality of the Moravian bard.

Only a tiny bit of Silesia—around the town of Opava—is part of the Czech Republic today; the rest of the region is in Poland and Germany. (The Habsburgs lost traditionally Czech Silesia to Prussia in the 1740s, and 200 years later, Germany in turn ceded most of it to Poland.) People in Silesia speak a wide variety of dialects that mix Czech, German, and Polish. Perhaps due to their diverse genes and cultural heritage, women from Silesia are famous for being intelligent and beautiful.

Since 1989, the year the Czechs won their independence from Soviet control, people have been working harder—but the average monthly wage is still only about $1,500. Roads have been patched up, facades have gotten facelifts, and supermarkets have been pushed out by hypermarkets.

Ninety percent of the tourists who visit the Czech Republic see only Prague. But if you venture outside the capital, you'll enjoy

tion, which dropped only minimally (the vast majority of Czech beer is consumed domestically). More than a third of trade is with next-door-neighbor Germany; as a result, Germany's economic health one year generally predicts the Czech Republic's fortunes the next.

Currency: 20 Czech crowns (*koruna,* Kč) = about $1.

Government: From 1948 to 1989, Czechoslovakia was a communist state under Soviet control. Today, the Czech Republic is a member of the European Union (since 2004) and a vibrant democracy, with about a 60 percent turnout for elections. Its parliament is made up of 200 representatives elected every four years and 81 senators elected for six years. No single political party dominates. Although the left-of-center Social Democrats technically won the 2010 election with a little over one-fifth of the vote, a coalition government was formed by three right-of-center parties united in their emphasis on fiscal responsibility. The fifth party in the parliament, the Communists, joined the Social Democrats in opposition. The president is selected every five years by popular vote. President Miloš Zeman, a populist elected in 2013, appears intent on remaking the country's parliamentary system in order to expand the power of his office.

Flag: The Czech flag is red (bottom), white (top), and blue (a triangle along the hoist side).

The Average Czech: The average Czech has 1.3 kids (slowly rising after the sharp decline that followed the end of communism), will live 77 years, and has one television in the house.

traditional towns and villages, great prices, a friendly and gentle countryside dotted by nettles and wild poppies, and almost no Western tourists. Since the time of the Habsburgs, fruit trees have lined the country roads for everyone to share. Take your pick.

Freedom Versus Babies

In communist times, it was routine to be married and start a family by age 22. Once a Czech finished training school and (for men) the compulsory two-year military service, there was little else to aspire to. Everyone was assigned essentially the same mediocre job ("They pretended to pay us, we pretended to work"), with little hope of career progress—unless you were willing to cut ties with your friends by entering the Communist Party or working for the secret police. Children (and summer homes) were the only way for people to project their dreams. Parenting was subsidized. In the countryside, young families were guaranteed housing, and in cities, flats were allocated according to long waiting lists that gave priority to married couples with children.

But after the fall of communism in 1989, many more options became available to young people who, as children or teenagers, had not even dreamed of such possibilities. Young Czechs embraced the new freedoms: Everyone wanted to travel—to the West to study law, or to the East to meditate in a cave. And everyone wanted to work—for big bucks at a multinational investment bank, or for pennies at a nonprofit organization in Afghanistan. Marriage was no longer the expected "next step." And shacking up was no longer a problem; you needed money, rather than a marriage certificate, to get a place to live. More and more young adults waited until after 30 to get married, and those already married reconsidered their choices in the light of new circumstances. Fewer Czechs had children, and many divorced.

By 2004, the falling birthrate and shrinking size of the Czech nation was a regular topic in newspaper columns. To stimulate production, the socialist government began paying new parents a baby bonus—one month's wages—in addition to the standard three years of paid maternity leave already promised to one parent.

Ironically—as if to prove that Czechs will never listen to what the government tells them to do—as soon as the newly elected conservatives revoked the monthly baby bonus in 2006, everyone between the ages of 25 and 35 suddenly decided to have children. The biggest baby boom in a generation is still on: Maternity wards are overflowing, signs regulating stroller traffic are popping up in public parks, and politicians are blaming each other for imprudently closing down many state-run nurseries.

Yet, even though they're faced with a bright and baby-filled future, some Czechs maintain a healthy dose of pessimism and seem reluctant to dive headlong into the Western rat race. Life still goes a little slower here, and people find pleasure in simple things.

PRAGUE
Praha

ORIENTATION TO PRAGUE

Few cities can match Prague's over-the-top romance, evocative Old World charm...and tourist crowds. Prague has always been historic—but it's fun, too. No other place in Europe has become popular so quickly. And for good reason: Prague—the only Central European capital to escape the bombs of the last century's wars— is one of Europe's best-preserved cities. It's filled with sumptuous Art Nouveau facades, offers tons of cheap Mozart and Vivaldi concerts, and brews the best beer in Europe. Cross the famous Charles Bridge, communing with vendors, artists, tourists, and a stoic lineup of Czech saints in stone. Hike up to the world's biggest castle for a lesson in Czech history and sweeping views across the city's spires and domes. Escape the crowds into the back lanes and pretend you're strolling through the 18th century. Delve into one of Europe's top stops.

Planning Your Time

A week in Prague is plenty of time to get a solid feel for the city and enjoy excursions to Český Krumlov and Kutná Hora. If you're in a rush, you need a minimum of two full days (with three nights, or two nights and a night train) for a good introduction to the city. From Munich, Berlin, or Vienna, Prague is a four- to six-hour daytime train ride away; from Budapest, Warsaw, Kraków, Vienna, Amsterdam, or Zürich, you can reach Prague on a handy overnight train.

With two days in Prague, I'd spend one morning seeing the castle and another morning in the Jewish Quarter. Use your afternoons to loiter around the Old Town, Charles Bridge, and the Little Quarter, and see Alfons Mucha's *Slav Epic*. Split your nights between beer halls and live music.

Keep in mind that Jewish Quarter sights close on Saturday

and Jewish holidays. Some museums, mainly in the Old Town, are closed on Monday, as is Veletržní Palace (which houses the *Slav Epic*).

Prague Overview

Prague unnerves many travelers—it's behind the former Iron Curtain, and you've heard stories of rip-offs and sky-high hotel prices (both are real problems, but avoidable if you're smart). Despite your fears, Prague is charming, safe, and ready to show you a good time. The language barrier is tiny. It seems like every well-educated young person speaks English.

Residents call their town "Praha" (PRAH-hah). It's big, with 1.2 million people, but during a quick visit, you'll focus on its relatively compact old center. As you wander, take advantage of brown street signs directing you to tourist landmarks. Self-deprecating Czechs note that while the signs are designed to help tourists (locals never use them), they're only printed in Czech. Still—thanks to the little icons—the signs can help smart visitors who are sightseeing on foot.

The Vltava River divides the west side (Castle Quarter and Little Quarter) from the east side (New Town, Old Town, Jewish Quarter, Main Train Station, and most of the recommended hotels).

Prague addresses come with references to a general zone: Praha 1 is in the old center on either side of the river; Praha 2 is in the New Town, southeast of Wenceslas Square; Praha 3 (and higher) indicates a location farther from the center.

Tourist Information

TIs are at several key locations, including: **Old Town Square** (in the Old Town Hall, just to the left of the Astronomical Clock; Easter-Oct Mon-Fri 9:00-19:00, Sat-Sun 9:00-18:00; Nov-Easter Mon-Fri 9:00-18:00, Sat-Sun 9:00-17:00); on the castle side of **Charles Bridge** (Easter-Oct daily 10:00-18:00, closed Nov-Easter); and in the Old Town, around the corner from **Havelská Market** (at Rytířská 31, April-Oct Mon-Sat 9:00-19:00, closed Nov-March). For general tourist information in English, dial 221-

ORIENTATION

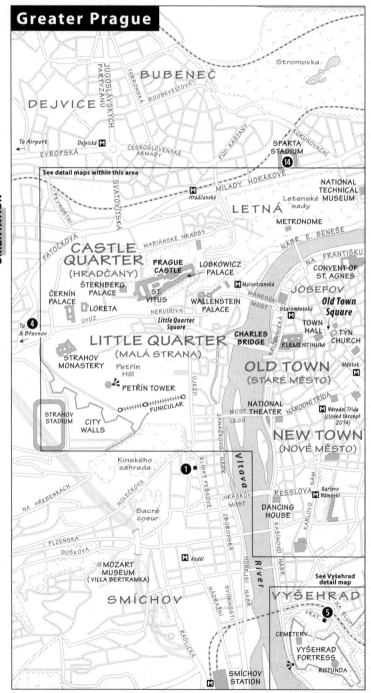

Greater Prague

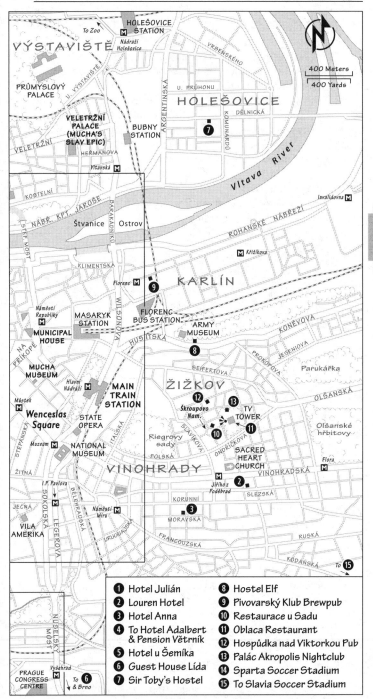

1 Hotel Julián
2 Louren Hotel
3 Hotel Anna
4 To Hotel Adalbert & Pension Větrník
5 Hotel u Šemíka
6 Guest House Lída
7 Sir Toby's Hostel
8 Hostel Elf
9 Pivovarský Klub Brewpub
10 Restaurace u Sadu
11 Oblaca Restaurant
12 Hospůdka nad Viktorkou Pub
13 Palác Akropolis Nightclub
14 Sparta Soccer Stadium
15 To Slavia Soccer Stadium

ORIENTATION

714-444 (Mon-Fri 8:00-19:00), or check the useful TI website: www.praguewelcome.cz.

The TIs offer maps, a helpful transit guide, and information on guided walks and bus tours. They can book local guides, concerts, and occasionally hotel rooms.

Monthly event guides—all of them packed with ads—include the *Prague Guide* (29 Kč), *Prague This Month* (free), and *Heart of Europe* (free, summer only). The English-language weekly *Prague Post* newspaper is handy for entertainment listings and current events (60 Kč at newsstands).

Arrival in Prague

For a comprehensive rundown on Prague's train stations, bus connections, airport, and hiring your own driver, see the Prague Connections chapter.

No matter how you arrive, your first priority is buying a city map, with trams and Metro lines marked and tiny sketches of the sights drawn in for ease in navigating (30-70 Kč, many different brands; sold at kiosks, exchange windows, and tobacco stands). It's a mistake to try doing Prague without a good map—you'll refer to it constantly. The *Kartografie Praha* city map, which shows all the tram lines and major landmarks, includes a castle diagram and a street index. It comes in two versions: 1:15,000 covers the city center, and 1:25,000 includes the whole city. The city center map is easier to navigate, and is sufficient unless you're sleeping in the suburbs.

Helpful Hints

Medical Help: A 24-hour **pharmacy** is at Palackého 5 (a block from Wenceslas Square, tel. 224-946-982). For standard assistance, there are two state hospitals in the center: the **General Hospital** (open daily 24 hours, moderate wait time, right above Karlovo Náměstí at U Nemocnice 2, Praha 2, use entry G, tel. 224-962-564) and the **Na Františku Hospital** (on the embankment next to Hotel InterContinental, Na Františku 1, go to the main entrance, for English assistance call Mr. Juřina between 7:30-16:30 on weekdays, tel. 222-801-278—serious problems only). The reception staff may not speak English, but the doctors do.

For above-standard assistance in English (including den-

Rip-Offs in Prague

There's no particular risk of violent crime in Prague, but green, rich tourists do get taken by con artists. Simply be on guard, particularly when traveling on trains (thieves thrive on overnight trains), changing money (tellers with bad arithmetic and inexplicable pauses while counting back your change), dealing with taxis (see "Getting Around Prague—By Taxi," later), paying in restaurants (see the Eating in Prague chapter), and wandering through seedy neighborhoods after dark. Wenceslas Square draws a rough crowd at night.

Anytime you pay for something, make a careful mental note of how much it costs, how much you're handing over, and how much you expect back. Count your change. Someone selling you a phone card marked 190 Kč might first tell you it's 790 Kč, hoping to pocket the difference. If you call his bluff, he'll pretend that it never happened.

Plainclothes policemen "looking for counterfeit money" are con artists. Don't show them any cash or your wallet. If you're threatened with an inexplicable fine by a "policeman," conductor, or other official, you can walk away, scare him away by saying you'll need a receipt (which real officials are legally required to provide), or ask a passerby if the fine is legit. On the other hand, do not ignore the plainclothes inspectors on the Metro and trams who show you their badges.

Pickpockets target Western tourists, and they can be little children or adults dressed as professionals—sometimes even as tourists. Many thieves drape jackets over their arms to disguise busy fingers. Thieves work the crowded and touristy places in teams. They use mobile phones to coordinate their bumps and grinds. Be careful if anyone creates a commotion at the door of a Metro or tram car (especially around the Národní Třída and Vodičkova tram stops, or on the made-for-tourists tram #22)—it's a smokescreen for theft.

Car theft is also a big problem in Prague (many Western European car-rental companies don't allow their rentals to cross the Czech border). Never leave anything valuable in your car—not even in broad daylight on a busy street.

The sex clubs on Skořepka and Melantrichova streets, just south and north of Havelská Market, routinely rip off naive tourists and can be dangerous. They're filled mostly with young Russian women and German and Asian men. Lately this district has become the rage for British "stag" parties, for guys who are happy to take a cheap flight to Prague to get to the city's cheap beer and cheap thrills.

This all sounds intimidating. But Prague is safe. It has its share of petty thieves and con artists, but very little violent crime. Don't be scared—just be alert.

Prague's Four Towns

Until about 1800, Prague was actually four distinct towns with four town squares, all separated by fortified walls. Each town had a unique character, which came from the personality of the people who initially settled it. Today, much of Prague's charm survives in the distinct spirit of each of its towns.

Castle Quarter (Hradčany): Since the ninth century, when the first castle was built on the promontory overlooking a ford across the Vltava River, Castle Hill has been occupied by the ruling class. When Christianity arrived in the Czech lands, this hilltop—oriented along an east-west axis—proved a perfect spot for a church and, later, the cathedral (which, according to custom, had to be built with the altar pointing east). Finally, the nobles built their representative palaces in proximity to the castle to compete with the Church for influence on the king. Even today, you feel like clip-clopping through this neighborhood in a fancy carriage. The Castle Quarter—which hosts the offices of the president and the foreign minister—has high art and grand buildings, little commerce, and few pubs.

Little Quarter (Malá Strana): This Baroque town of fine palaces and gardens rose from the ashes of a merchant settlement that burned down in the 1540s. The Czech and European nobility who settled here took pride in the grand design of their gardens. In the 1990s, after decades of decay, the gardens were carefully restored. While some are open only to the successors of the former nobility—including the Czech Parliament and the American, German, and Polish Embassies—many are open to visitors.

Old Town (Staré Město): The Charles Bridge connects the Little Quarter with the Old Town. A boomtown since the 10th century, this area has long been the busy commercial quarter—filled with merchants, guilds, and supporters of the Church reformer Jan Hus (who wanted a Czech-style Catholicism). Trace the walls of this town in the modern road plan (the Powder Tower is a remnant of a wall system that completed a fortified ring, the other half of which was formed by the river). The marshy area closest to the bend—least habitable and therefore allotted to the Jewish community—became the ghetto (today's Josefov, or Jewish Quarter).

New Town (Nové Město): The New Town rings the Old Town—cutting a swath from riverbank to riverbank—and is fortified with Prague's outer wall. In the 14th century, the king created

tal service), consider the top-quality **Hospital Na Homolce** (less than 1,000 Kč for an appointment, from 8:00 to 16:00 call 252-922-146, for after-hours emergencies call 257-211-111; bus #167 from Anděl Metro station, Roentgenova 2, Praha 5). The **Canadian Medical Care Center** is a small, private clinic with an English-speaking Czech staff at Veleslavínská 1 in

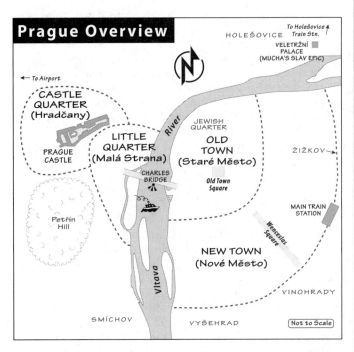

Prague Overview

HOLEŠOVICE — To Holešovice Train Stn.

VELETRŽNÍ PALACE (MUCHA'S SLAV EPIC)

← To Airport

CASTLE QUARTER (Hradčany)

PRAGUE CASTLE

LITTLE QUARTER (Malá Strana)

River

JEWISH QUARTER

OLD TOWN (Staré Město)

ŽIŽKOV →

CHARLES BRIDGE

Old Town Square

Petřín Hill

MAIN TRAIN STATION

Wenceslas Square

NEW TOWN (Nové Město)

Vltava

VINOHRADY

SMÍCHOV

VYŠEHRAD

Not to Scale

ORIENTATION

this town, tripling the size of what would become Prague. Wenceslas Square was once the horse market of this busy working-class district. Even today, the New Town is separated from the Old Town by a "moat" (the literal meaning of the street called Na Příkopě). As you cross bustling Na Příkopě, you leave the glass and souvenir shops behind, and enter a town of malls and fancy shops that cater to locals and visitors alike.

The Royal Way: Cutting through the four towns—from St. Vitus Cathedral down to the Charles Bridge, and then from the bridge to the Powder Tower—is the Royal Way (Královská Cesta), the ancient path of coronation processions. Today, this city spine is marred by tacky trinket shops and jammed by tour groups. Use it for orientation only—try to avoid it if you want to see the real Prague.

Praha 6 (3,000 Kč for an appointment, 4,500 Kč for a house call, halfway between the city and the airport, tel. 235-360-133, after-hours emergency tel. 724-300-301).

If a **massage** is all you need to cure your aches and pains, walk into one of the numerous Thai massage parlors around the Old Town. For a more professional fix, contact **Patrick**

Kočica, an experienced Hoshino therapist (1,000 Kč/hour, mobile 722-070-703, patrick.kocica@hoshino.cz).

Internet Access: Internet cafés are well-advertised and scattered through the Old and New Towns. Consider **Bohemia Bagel** near the Jewish Quarter at Masná 2.

Bookstores: Shakespeare and Sons is a friendly English-language bookstore with a wide selection of translations from Czech, the latest publications, and a reading space downstairs overlooking a river channel (daily 11:00-19:00, one block from Charles Bridge on Little Quarter side at U Lužického Semináře 10, tel. 257-531-894, www.shakes.cz).

Laundry: A **full-service laundry** near most of the recommended hotels is at Karolíny Světlé 11 (200 Kč/8-pound load, wash and dry in 3 hours, Mon-Fri 7:30-19:00, closed Sat-Sun, 200 yards from Charles Bridge on Old Town side, mobile 721-030-446); another laundry is at Rybná 27 (290 Kč/8-pound load, same-day pickup, Mon-Fri 8:00-18:00, Mon and Wed from 7:00, closed Sat-Sun, tel. 224-812-641). Or surf the Internet while your undies tumble-dry at the **self-service launderette** at Korunní 14 (160 Kč/load wash and dry, Internet access-2 Kč/minute, daily 8:00-20:00, near Náměstí Míru Metro stop, Praha 2).

Vietnamese Mini-Markets: These corner convenience stores, generally open daily until midnight and run by hardworking immigrants, cleverly stock their shelves to fill most of your grocery needs. The Vietnamese started coming to the former Czechoslovakia in the 1980s to train in textile factories as part of a communist government program. After the fall of communism, they stayed on. Prices are generally fair. Locals figure if the beer costs less than a Coke, it's a good place to shop.

Bike Rental: Prague has improved its network of bike paths, making bicycles a feasible option for exploring the center of the town and beyond (see http://doprava.praha-mesto.cz for a map). Two bike-rental shops located near the Old Town Square are **Praha Bike** (daily 9:00-22:00, Dlouhá 24, mobile 732-388-880, www.prahabike.cz) and **City Bike** (daily 9:00-19:00, Králodvorská 5, mobile 776-180-284, www.citybike-prague.com). They rent bikes for about 300 Kč for two hours or 500 Kč per day (with a 1,500-Kč deposit), and also organize guided bike tours. Or try an **electric bike** (590 Kč/half-day, 890 Kč/day, April-Oct daily 9:00-19:00, tours available, just above American Embassy in Little Quarter at Vlašská 15, mobile 604-474-546, www.ilikeebike.com).

Car Rental: All the biggies have offices in Prague (check each company's website, or ask at the TI). For a locally operated alternative, consider **Prima Rent** (Mon-Fri 8:00-16:30, closed

Sat-Sun, Kolbenova 40, Metro: Kolbenova, mobile 602-608-494, www.car-rental-czech.com). The cheaper models are a great value (900 Kč/day with basic insurance and limited mileage, plus 250 Kč/day for full theft and damage insurance; 350 Kč for hotel or airport delivery).

Local Help: Magic Praha is a tiny travel service run by Lída Jánská. A Jill-of-all-trades, she can help with accommodations and transfers throughout the Czech Republic, as well as private tours and side-trips to historic towns (mobile 604-207-225, www.magicpraha.cz, magicpraha@magicpraha.cz).

Best Views: Enjoy the "Golden City of a Hundred Spires" during the early evening, when the light is warm and the colors are rich. Good viewpoints—from highest to lowest—include the Strahov Monastery's garden terrace (above the castle), the many balconies and spires at Prague Castle, the Villa Richter restaurants overlooking the city (just below the castle past the Golden Lane), the top of either tower on Charles Bridge, the Old Town Square clock tower (has an elevator), Hotel u Prince's rooftop dining terrace overlooking the Old Town Square (also with an elevator), and the steps of the National Museum overlooking Wenceslas Square.

If you're in the Žižkov/Vinohrady neighborhood, consider taking the elevator up the Žižkov TV tower for spaceship views of the city (150 Kč to reach observatory 300 feet above the ground, free access to Oblaca restaurant and café at 200-foot-level when you buy a drink or meal—see page 174, tel. 210-320-086, www.towerpark.cz).

Updates to this Book: For news about changes to this book's coverage since it was published, see www.ricksteves.com/update.

Getting Around Prague

You can walk nearly everywhere. But after you figure out the public transportation system, the Metro is slick, the trams fun, and the taxis quick and easy. Prague's tram system is especially wonderful—trams rumble by every 5-10 minutes and take you just about anywhere. Be bold and you'll swing through Prague like Tarzan with a transit pass. For details, pick up the transit guide at the TI. City maps show the Metro, tram, and bus lines.

By Metro, Tram, and Bus

Excellent, affordable public transit is perhaps the best legacy of the communist era (locals ride all month for 550 Kč). The three-line Metro system is handy and simple, but doesn't always get you right to the tourist sights (landmarks such as the Old Town Square and Prague Castle are several blocks from the nearest Metro stops). While construction has closed the Národní Třída Metro stop in the New Town through 2014, the adjacent tram stop remains open.

Tickets: The Metro, trams, and buses all use the same tickets:

- 30-minute **short-trip ticket** *(krátkodobá)*—24 Kč, which allows transfers
- 90-minute **standard ticket** *(základní)*—32 Kč
- **24-hour pass** *(jízdenka na 24 hodin)*—110 Kč
- **3-day pass** *(jízdenka na 3 dny)*—310 Kč

Buy tickets from your hotel, at Metro stops, newsstand kiosks, or from automated machines (select ticket price, then insert coins). For convenience, buy all the tickets that you think you'll need— but estimate conservatively. Remember, Prague is a great walking town, so unless you're commuting from a hotel far outside the center, you'll likely find that individual tickets work best. Be sure to validate your ticket as you board the tram or bus, or in the Metro station, by sticking it in the machine (which stamps a time on it; watch locals and imitate). Inspectors routinely ambush ticketless riders (including tourists) and fine them 700 Kč on the spot. You can also be fined for using counterfeit tickets, even if you thought they were authentic when you bought them.

Tips: Navigate by signs that list the end stations. When you come to your stop, push the yellow button if the doors don't automatically open. Although it seems that all Metro doors lead to the neighborhood of Výstup, that's simply the Czech word for "exit." Tram tracks are not always marked very clearly, so carefully follow along with a map to be sure you get off at the right place. Further confusing matters, when a tram pulls up to a stop, two different names are announced: the name of the stop you're currently at, followed by the name of the stop that's coming up next. Confused

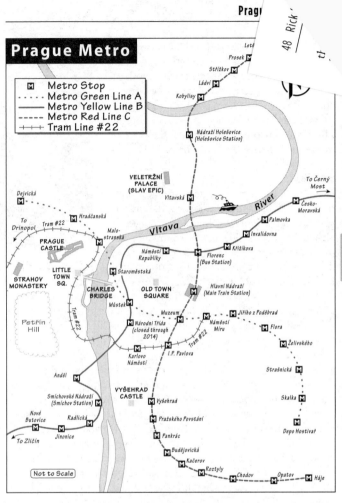

Prague Metro

M — Metro Stop
···· — Metro Green Line A
—— — Metro Yellow Line B
- - - — Metro Red Line C
++++ — Tram Line #22

Letá
Prosek
Střížkov
Ládví
Kobylisy

Nádraží Holešovice
(Holešovice Station)

VELETRŽNÍ
PALACE
(SLAV EPIC)

Vltavská

Dejvická

Hradčanská

To Drinopol   Tram #22

Malo-
stranská

PRAGUE
CASTLE

Náměstí
Republiky

Florenc
(Bus Station)

Křižíkova

LITTLE
TOWN
SQ.

Staroměstská

STRAHOV
MONASTERY

CHARLES
BRIDGE

OLD TOWN
SQUARE

Hlavní Nádraží
(Main Train Station)

Můstek

Petřín
Hill

Muzeum

Národní Třída
(closed through
2014)

Náměstí
Míru

Jiřího z Poděbrad

Flora

Želivského

Tram #22

I. P. Pavlova

Karlovo
Náměstí

Strašnická

Anděl

VYŠEHRAD
CASTLE

Vyšehrad

Skalka

Smíchovské Nádraží
(Smíchov Station)

Pražského Povstání

Nové
Butovice

Radlická

Pankrác

Depo Hostivař

To Zličín

Jinonice

Budějovická

Kačerov

Roztyly   Chodov   Opatov   Háje

Not to Scale

To Černý
Most

Česko-
Moravská

Palmovka

Invalidovna

Vltava

River

ORIENTATION

tourists, thinking they've heard their stop, are notorious for rushing off the tram one stop too soon.

Schedules and Frequency: Trams run every 5-10 minutes in the daytime (a schedule is posted at each stop). The Metro closes at midnight, and the nighttime tram routes (identified with white numbers on blue backgrounds at tram stops) run all night at 30-minute intervals. You can find more information and a complete route planner in English at www.dpp.cz/en.

Handy Tram: Tram #22 is practically made for sightseeing, connecting the New Town with the Castle Quarter (see my "Self-Guided Tram Tour," later, and find the line marked on the Prague Metro map). The tram uses some of the same stops as the Metro (making it easy to get to—or travel on from—the tram route). Of the many stops this tram makes, the most convenient are two in

New Town (Národní Třída, between the bottom of Wenceslas Square and the river; and Národní Divadlo, at the National Theater), two in the Little Quarter (Malostranské Náměstí and Malostranská Metro stop), and three above Prague Castle (Královský Letohrádek, Pražský Hrad, and Pohořelec; for details, see "Getting to Prague Castle—By Tram" on page 111).

By Taxi

Prague's taxis—notorious for hyperactive meters—are being tamed. New legislation is in place to curb crooked cabbies, and police will always take your side in an argument. Still, many cabbies are crooks who consider it a good day's work to take one sucker for a ride. You'll make things difficult for a dishonest cabbie by challenging an unfair fare.

While most hotel receptionists and guidebooks advise that you avoid taxis, I find Prague to be a great taxi town and use them routinely. With the local rate, they're cheap (read the rates on the door: drop charge starts at 40 Kč; per-kilometer charge—30 Kč; waiting time per minute—5 Kč). The key is to be sure the cabbie turns on the meter at the #1 tariff (look for the word *sazba*, meaning "tariff," on the meter). Avoid cabs waiting at tourist attractions and train stations. To improve your odds of getting a fair meter rate—which starts only when you take off—call for a cab (or have your hotel or restaurant call one for you). **AAA Taxi** (tel. 14-014) and **City Taxi** (tel. 257-257-257) are the most likely to have English-speaking staff and honest cabbies. I also find that hailing a passing taxi usually gets me a decent price, although at a slightly higher rate than when reserving by phone. If a cabbie surprises you at the end with an astronomical fare, simply pay 300 Kč, which should cover you for a long ride anywhere in the center. Then go into your hotel. On the minuscule chance that he follows you, the receptionist will back you up.

Tours in Prague

Walking Tours

Many small companies offer walking tours of the Old Town, the castle, and more (for the latest, pick up the walking tour fliers at the TI). Since guiding is a routine side-job for university students, you'll generally get hardworking young guides at good prices. While I'd rather go with my own local guide (described later), public walking tours are cheaper (about 450 Kč for a 4-hour tour), cover themes you might not otherwise consider, connect you with other English-speaking travelers, and allow for spontaneity. The quality

ORIENTATION

Rick Steves Audio Europe

If you're bringing a mobile device, be sure to check out **Rick Steves Audio Europe,** where you can download free audio tours and hours of travel interviews (via the Rick Steves Audio Europe smartphone app, www.ricksteves.com/audioeurope, iTunes, or Google Play).

My self-guided **audio tours** are user-friendly, easy to follow, fun, and informative. With the help of this book's co-author, Honza Vihan, we've created a Prague audio tour that guides you (with an enhanced version of what's already in this guidebook) from the top of Wenceslas Square through the best of the New and Old Towns to Charles Bridge. Compared with live tours, my audio tours are hard to beat: Nobody will stand you up, the quality is reliable, you can take the tour exactly when you like, and they're free.

Rick Steves Audio Europe also offers a far-reaching library of intriguing **travel interviews** with experts from around the globe.

ORIENTATION

depends on the guide rather than the company. Your best bet is to show up at the Astronomical Clock a couple of minutes before 8:00, 10:00, or 11:00, then chat with a few of the umbrella-holding guides there. Choose the one you click with. Guides also have fliers advertising additional walks.

"Free" Tours: As is the case all over Europe these days, you'll find "free" tours that are not really free; you're expected to tip your guide (with paper bills rather than coins) when finished. While these tours are fine for the backpacker and hostel crowd (for whom they're designed), the guides are really just ex-pat students (generally from the US or Australia) who memorize a script and give an entertaining performance, with little respect for serious history as you walk through the Old Town. When it comes to guided tours, nothing is free (except for my self-guided audio tour; see the sidebar).

▲▲Local Guides

In Prague, hiring a guide is particularly smart—they're twice as helpful for half the price compared with guides in Western Europe. Because prices are usually per hour (not per person), small groups can hire an inexpensive guide for several days. Guides meet you wherever you like and tailor the tour to your interests. Visit their websites in advance for details on various walks, airport transfers, countryside excursions, and other services offered, and then make arrangements by email.

Small Companies: PragueWalker is run by Katka Svobodová, a hardworking historian-guide who knows her stuff and

Prague Essentials

English	Czech	Pronounced
Main Train Station	Hlavní Nádraží	*hlav-nee nah-drah-zhee*
Old Town	Staré Město	*stah-reh MYEHS-toh*
Old Town Square	Staroměstské Náměstí	*star-roh-myehst-skeh nah-myehs-tee*
New Town	Nové Město	*noh-vay myehs-toh*
Little Quarter	Malá Strana	*mah-lah strah-nah*
Jewish Quarter	Josefov	*yoo-zehf-fohf*
Castle Quarter	Hradčany	*hrad-chah-nee*
Charles Bridge	Karlův Most	*kar-loov most*
Wenceslas Square	Václavské Náměstí	*vaht-slahf-skeh nah-myehs-tee*
Vltava River	Vltava	*vul-tah-vah*

manages a team of enthusiastic and friendly guides (600 Kč/hour for individuals, families, and small groups; mobile 603-181-300, www.praguewalker.com, katerina@praguewalker.com). **Personal Prague Guide Service**'s Šárka Kačabová uses her teaching background to help you understand Czech culture, and has picked a team of personable and knowledgeable guides for her company (600 Kč/hour for 2-3 people, 800 Kč/hour for 4-8 people, fifth hour free, mobile 777-225-205, www.personalpragueguide.com, sarka@me.com). **Athos Travel**'s licensed guides can lead you on a general sightseeing tour or fit the walk to your interests: music, Art Nouveau, architecture, and more (600-700 Kč/hour for 1-5 people, tel. 277-004-677, www.a-prague.com/tours, info@a-prague.com).

Individual Guides: These generally young guides (which is good, because they learned their trade post-communism) typically charge about 2,000-2,500 Kč for a half-day tour. **Jana Hronková** has a natural style—a welcome change from the more strict professionalism of some of the busier guides—and a penchant for the Jewish Quarter (mobile 732-185-180, www.experience-prague.info, janahronkova@hotmail.com). **Zuzana Tlášková** speaks English as well as Hebrew (mobile 774-131-335, tlaskovaz@seznam.cz). **Martin Bělohradský,** who guides on the side when not doing his organic chemistry work, is particularly enthusiastic about fine arts and architecture (mobile 723-414-565, martinb5666@gmail.

com). **Kamil and Petra Vondrouš** design tours to fit individual interests; they also guide/drive beyond Prague, as far as Vienna or Dresden (mobile 605-701-861, www.prague-extra.com, info@ prague-extra.com).

My readers have also had good experiences with these guides: **Renata Blažková,** who has a special interest in the history of Prague's Jewish Quarter (tel. 222-716-870, mobile 602-353-186, blazer@volny.cz); **Václav Štorek,** who specializes in history (mobile 603-743-523, www.storek.guide-prague.cz, vaclavstorek@post. cz); **Petr Zídek** (mobile 721-286-869, www.bohemiantours.cz, petr@bohemiantours.cz); **Andrea Řezníčková** (mobile 777-930-024, www.mypraguetours.com, andrea@mypraguetours.com); and **Darina Krajakova** (krajakova@hotmail.com).

For more specialized tours, consider Aaron John's **Taste Local Beer** or Radim Prahl's **Running Tours Prague.** Aaron, an ex-pat with a passion for local brews, is up-to-date on the evolving Prague microbrew scene (1,200 Kč per person, includes six beers at three pubs and a one-day transportation pass, www.tastelocalbeer.com). Radim, a local with an appetite for ultra-marathons, will run you past monuments, through parks, and down back alleys at your own pace (1,500 Kč for two people; mobile 777-288-862, www.runningtoursprague.com).

The **TI** also has plenty of local guides (3-hour tour: 1,200 Kč/1 person, 1,400 Kč/2 people, 1,600 Kč/3 people, 2,000 Kč/4 people; desk at Old Town Square TI, arrange and pay in person at least 2 hours in advance, tel. 236-002-562, guides@pis.cz). For a list of more guides, see www.guide-prague.cz.

Jewish Quarter Tours

Jewish guides (of varying quality) meet small groups twice daily in season for three-hour tours in English of the Jewish Quarter. **Wittmann Tours** charges a 880-Kč fee that includes entry to the Old-New Synagogue and the six other major Jewish Quarter sights (which cost 480 Kč total), so the tour actually costs only 400 Kč (May-Oct Sun-Fri at 10:30 and 14:00, Nov-Dec and mid-March-April Sun-Fri at 10:30 only, no tours Sat and Jan-mid-March, minimum 3 people). Tours meet in the little park (just beyond the café), directly in front of Hotel InterContinental at the end of Pařížská street (tel. 603-168-427 or 603-426-564, www. wittmann-tours.com).

Weekend Tours for Students in Prague

Andy Steves (Rick's son) runs Weekend Student Adventures, offering active and experiential three-day weekend tours from €199, designed for American students studying abroad (www.wsaeurope. com for details on tours of Prague and other great cities).

Prague at a Glance

Rather than a checklist of museums, Prague is a fine place to wander around and just take in the fun atmosphere. Plan some worthwhile outdoor activities—take a self-guided tram tour (page 57), hire a local guide (page 49), enjoy a concert (page 182), or go for a scenic paddle on the river (page 56).

In the Old Town

▲▲▲Old Town Square Magical main square of Old World Prague, with dozens of colorful facades, the dramatic Jan Hus Memorial, looming Týn Church, and fanciful Astronomical Clock. **Hours:** Týn Church generally open to sightseers Tue-Sat 10:00-13:00 & 15:00-17:00, Sun 10:30-12:00; clock strikes on the hour daily 9:00-21:00, until 20:00 in winter; clock tower open Tue-Sun 9:00-22:00, Mon 11:00-22:00. See page 60.

▲▲▲Charles Bridge An atmospheric, statue-lined bridge that connects the Old Town to the Little Quarter and Prague Castle. **Hours:** Always open and crossable. See page 74.

▲▲▲Jewish Quarter The best collection of Jewish sights in Europe, featuring various synagogues and an evocative cemetery. **Hours:** The quarter can be visited any time; museum sights open April-Oct Sun-Fri 9:00-18:00, Nov-March Sun-Fri 9:00-16:30, always closed Sat and on Jewish holidays. See page 78.

▲▲Museum of Medieval Art The best Gothic art in the land, at St. Agnes Convent. **Hours:** Tue-Sun 10:00-18:00, closed Mon, may close sporadically due to budget cuts. See page 68.

▲Havelská Market Colorful open-air market that sells crafts and produce. **Hours:** Daily 9:00-18:00. See page 69.

▲Klementinum National Library's lavish Baroque Hall and Observatory Tower (with views), open by 45-minute tour only. **Hours:** Mon-Fri 14:00-19:00, Sat-Sun 10:00-19:00, shorter hours off-season. See page 74.

In the New Town

▲▲Wenceslas Square Lively boulevard at the heart of modern Prague. **Hours:** Always open. See page 85.

▲▲Mucha Museum Easy-to-appreciate collection of Art Nouveau works by Czech artist Alfons Mucha. **Hours:** Daily 10:00-18:00. See page 93.

▲▲Municipal House Pure Art Nouveau architecture, including Prague's largest concert hall and several eateries. **Hours:** Daily 10:00-18:00. See page 93.

▲▲**Museum of Communism** The rise and fall of the regime, from start to Velvet finish. **Hours:** Daily 9:00-21:00. See page 95.

▲**National Memorial to the Heroes of the Heydrich Terror** Tribute to members of the resistance, who assassinated a notorious Nazi architect of the Holocaust. **Hours:** Tue-Sun 9:00-17:00, closed Mon. See page 101.

In the Little Quarter
▲**Petřín Hill** Little Quarter hill with public art, a funicular, and a replica of the Eiffel Tower. **Hours:** Funicular—daily 8:00-22:00; tower—daily 10:00-22:00. See page 109.

Church of St. Nicholas Jesuit centerpiece of Little Quarter Square, with ultimate High Baroque decor and a climbable bell tower. **Hours:** Church—daily 9:00-17:00, until 16:00 Nov-Feb; tower—April-Oct daily 10:00-18:00, closed Nov-March. See page 103.

Wallenstein Palace Garden Largest and beautiful Renaissance palace garden. **Hours:** April-Oct Mon-Fri 7:30-18:00, Sat-Sun 10:00-18:00, daily until 19:00 June-Sept; closed Nov-March. See page 106.

In the Castle Quarter
▲▲▲**St. Vitus Cathedral** The Czech Republic's most important church, featuring a climbable tower and a striking stained-glass window by Art Nouveau artist Alfons Mucha. **Hours:** Daily April-Oct 9:00-17:00, Nov-March 9:00-16:00, closed Sunday mornings year-round for Mass. See page 117.

▲▲**Prague Castle** Traditional seat of Czech rulers, with St. Vitus Cathedral (see above), Old Royal Palace, Basilica of St. George, shop-lined Golden Lane, and lots of crowds. **Hours:** Castle sights—daily April-Oct 9:00-17:00, Nov-March 9:00-16:00; castle grounds—daily 5:00-24:00. See page 112.

▲▲**Lobkowicz Palace** The most entertaining palace in town. **Hours:** Daily 10:00-18:00. See page 125.

▲**Strahov Monastery and Library** Baroque center of learning, with ornate reading rooms and old-fashioned science exhibits. **Hours:** Daily 9:00-11:45 & 13:00-17:00. See page 127.

Beyond the Core
▲▲▲**Alfons Mucha's *Slav Epic*** Twenty enormous canvases at Veletržní Palace depicting momentous events of Slavic history. **Hours:** Tue-Sun 10:00-18:00, closed Mon. See page 132.

ORIENTATION

Daily Reminder

Monday: Veletržní Palace, which houses Alfons Mucha's *Slav Epic,* is closed. Most of the other major sights—such as Prague Castle and the Jewish Quarter—are open, but a number of the lesser sights, including the Bethlehem Chapel (in winter), House of the Golden Ring, Loreta Church, Sternberg Palace, and Museum of Medieval Art, are closed.

If you're day-tripping today, Terezín and Kutná Hora's Sedlec Bone Church are open. The three castles—Konopiště, Karlštejn, and Křivoklát—are closed.

In Prague's Old Town, classical musicians have a jam session at 17:00 at St. Martin in the Wall, and the cover is free at the Roxy music club, where concerts start at 20:00.

Tuesday-Friday: All sights are open.

Saturday: The Jewish Quarter sights are closed. In nearby Terezín, the Crematorium and Columbarium are closed.

Sunday: St. Vitus Cathedral at Prague Castle is closed Sunday morning for Mass. Some stores have shorter hours or are closed.

Crowd-Beating Tips: Visit Prague Castle either first thing in the morning (be at St. Vitus Cathedral right at 9:00—except Sun morning, when it's closed for Mass) or midafternoon (closes at 17:00 in summer, 16:00 in winter). Hiring your own guide for a historic walk is relatively cheap and allows you to choose a time (evening or early morning) and route to avoid crowds.

Summer Activities: Outdoor movies on the Střelecký Ostrov island are shown nightly at about 21:00 from mid-July through early September (see page 100). And a paddle down the river is always fun in warm weather.

Evening Activities: Prague Castle's grounds stay open until 24:00 and provide a fanciful people-free zone to wander in the evening. Concerts in the National Theater, Smetana Hall at the Municipal House, and Rudolfinum feature superb artists at bargain prices (see the Entertainment in Prague chapter).

Tours Outside of Prague

To get beyond the sights listed in most guidebooks, call Tom and Marie Zahn from **P.A.T.H. Finders International.** Tom is American, Marie is Czech, and together they organize and lead family-friendly day excursions (in Prague and throughout the country). Their tours are creative and affordable, and they teach travelers how to find off-the-beaten-track destinations on their own. Their specialty is Personal Ancestral Tours & History (P.A.T.H.)—with sufficient notice, they can help Czech descendants find their ancestral homes, perhaps even a long-lost relative. Tom and Marie can also help with other parts of your Eastern European travel by linking you with associates in other countries, especially Germany, Hunga-ry, Poland, Romania, Slovakia, and Ukraine (US tel. 360-450-5959, Czech tel. 257-940-113, www.pathfinders.cz, info@pathfinders.cz).

Reverend Jan Dus, an enthusiastic pastor who lived in the US for several years, now serves a small congregation about 100 miles east of Prague. Jan can design itineraries, and likes to help travel-ers connect with locals in little towns, particularly in northeastern Bohemia and Moravia. He also has an outstanding track record in providing genealogical services (toll-free US tel. 800-807-1562, www.revjan.com, rev.jan.services@gmail.com).

Bus Tours

Although I generally recommend cheap big-bus orientation tours for an efficient, once-over-lightly look at great cities, Prague's sight-seeing core (Castle Quarter, Charles Bridge, and the Old Town) is not accessible by bus. In fact, most bus tours of the city are basically walking tours that use buses for pickups and transfers. So if you insist on a bus, you're playing basketball with a catcher's mitt.

Bus tours make more sense for day trips out of Prague. Several companies have kiosks on Na Příkopě, where you can comparison-shop. **Premiant City Tours** offers 20 different tours, including one to Karlštejn and Konopiště castles (1,950 Kč, 8.5 hours) and a river cruise. The tours feature live guides and depart from near the bottom of Wenceslas Square at Na Příkopě 23. Get tickets at an AVE travel agency, your hotel, on the bus, or at Na Příkopě 23 (tel. 224-946-922, mobile 606-600-123, www.premiant.cz). **Wittmann Tours,** listed earlier in "Jewish Quarter Tours," offers an all-day minibus tour to the Terezín Memorial (www.wittmann-tours.com).

Tour salespeople are notorious for telling you anything to sell a ticket. Some tours, especially those heading into the countryside, can be in as many as four different languages. Hiring a guide, many of whom can drive you around in their car, can be a much better value (described earlier, under "Local Guides").

More Tours

Tram Tours

Prague's tram #22 is a cheap and easy way to get familiar with the city (see "Self-Guided Tram Tour"). Handy tram stops for this tour are located near the intersection of Národní Třída and Spálená streets in the New Town, and near the Malostranská Metro stop in the Little Quarter.

Hop-On, Hop-Off Bus Tours

In Prague, hop-on, hop-off bus tours give ticket holders 24 hours to hop on and off tour buses that come by every half-hour or so as they circulate through town, stopping at the major attractions. An uninspired recorded narration plays along the way. Tickets cost

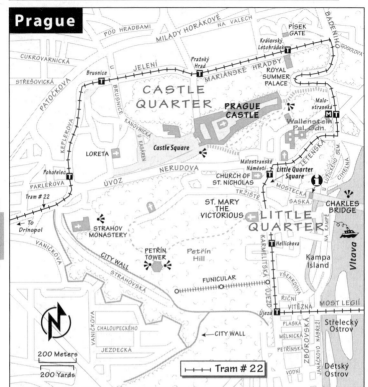

about 450 Kč and may include a one-hour riverboat cruise (described next). While this type of tour works great in some European cities, Prague—which is so delightful on foot—really doesn't lend itself to the hop-on, hop-off bus-tour formula.

Cruises

Prague isn't ideal for a boat tour because you might spend half the time waiting to go through the locks. Still, the hour-long Vltava River cruises, which leave from near the castle end of Charles Bridge about hourly, are scenic and relaxing, though not informative (150-200 Kč).

▲Rowboat or Paddleboat Cruises

Renting a rowboat or paddleboat on the island by the National Theater is a better way to enjoy the river. You'll float at your own pace among the swans and watch local lovers cruise by in their own boats (40 Kč/hour for rowboats, 60 Kč/hour for paddleboats, bring photo ID for deposit).

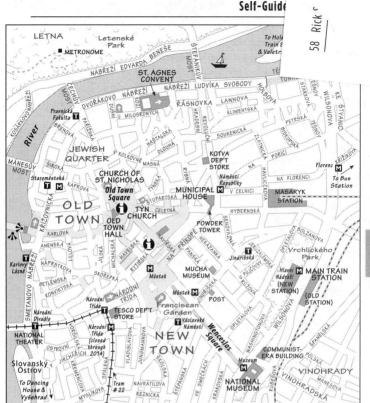

Self-Guided Tram Tour

▲▲Welcome to Prague: Tram #22

Tram #22 makes a good Prague orientation joyride. It runs roughly every 5-10 minutes, and you can hop on and off as you like (32-Kč standard ticket valid for 1.5 hours—described on page 46). Be warned: Thieves and plainclothes ticket-checkers like this route as much as the tourists.

Catch the tram in the New Town and ride it over the river, through the Little Quarter, and up to the castle (stop: Pohořelec). You'll see how easy it is to use the trams, get the lay of the land, and zip effortlessly up to the castle (saving lots of sweat or a 200-Kč taxi ride).

Start by catching the tram at the **Národní Třída** stop on the same side of Spálená street as the Tesco department store (a Metro stop of the same name is nearby, but is closed through 2014). The tram will turn and rattle along National Street (Národní Třída). Or, since several recommended places to eat and sleep are near the Náměstí Míru stop (four stops before Národní Třída), you could start the tour from there.

At the next stop, **Národní Divadlo,** you'll see Café Slavia facing the National Theater, just before the tram crosses the river. Survey the boat-rental scene (island with rental wharfs) and the romantic beach island, and enjoy a great castle view. The Dancing House (designed by Frank Gehry), while hard to see, is 400 yards upstream.

The next stop, **Újezd,** faces a park. See the Monument to Victims of Communism—the bronze spectral figures descending the steps into the park at the corner (described on page 110). A funicular leads to the Eiffel-like Petřín Tower.

The tram then heads north from the **Hellichova** stop, paralleling Kampa Island on the river side (to the right). On the left side, the tram passes St. Mary the Victorious Church, popular with pilgrims for its Infant Jesus of Prague. As the tram gradually goes uphill, it enters Little Quarter Square. You'll catch a peek-a-boo view of the Charles Bridge off to the right at the end of the street.

The tram stops next at **Malostranské Náměstí** (closest stop to the Charles Bridge), on the Little Quarter's main square, dominated by the Church of Saint Nicholas. From here you can hike up Nerudova street to Prague Castle.

Fifteen yards beyond the **Malostranská** stop, on the left, is the entry to the Wallenstein Palace Garden. Behind you, on the right in the park, is a modern memorial to World War II freedom fighters. (Beyond that, a bridge leads across the Vltava River to Josefov, the Jewish Quarter.) The tram now enters the longest stretch between stations—perfect for ticket-checkers to reveal themselves and catch anyone traveling without a valid ticket. Just after the tram completes its climb up the hill and makes a sharp left turn, you'll see the **Písecká Brána** (Písek Gate, or Sand Gate) on your right, one of the few preserved gates of Prague's Baroque fortification system.

The next stop is **Královský Letohrádek.** Immediately across the street is the Royal Summer Palace, the Royal Gardens leading fragrantly to Prague Castle, and a public WC.

If you're in a hurry to hit the castle sights, jump out at the **Pražský Hrad** stop for the most direct route to the castle entrance. If you've got more time, stay on board for my favorite approach from Pohořelec, coming up soon.

The next stop is **Brusnice,** from which you can explore the Nový Svět (New World) neighborhood, a time capsule of cobblestone streets and tiny houses with no shops or tourists (to reach this area from the stop, walk across the small park that has a statue— just ahead on the left—then go down the steps).

The tram now winds through a greenbelt built along the remains of the city wall. The stop at **Pohořelec** is my preferred approach to the castle and the closest stop to the Strahov Monastery.

Hop out here, and it's all downhill (see directions to the monastery, page 112). Or catch a tram going the opposite direction to do this trip in reverse.

Extending the Route: If you want to experience workaday Prague without a hint of tourism, stay on the tram three more stops to **Drinopol.** Browse all the organic shops and French cheese stores indicating that this 1930s neighborhood is now populated by cosmopolitan young families. Sit down for a fine, relatively inexpensive meal at the **U Bílého Lva** ("By the White Lion," daily 11:00-24:00, Bělohorská 79, tel. 233-355-909), just on the left as you get off the tram, or choose from a wide array of poppy-seed pastries in the tiny bakery-cum-café across the street. You can also walk or take the tram two stops farther to Břevnovský Klášter (five stops after Pohořelec), a peaceful Benedictine monastery built in a pleasantly simple Baroque style with a garden, low-key restaurant, and the recommended Hotel Adalbert (see page 153). To get back to the Strahov Monastery and the castle at any point, simply take tram #22 back in the other direction.

ORIENTATION

THE OLD TOWN

Staré Město

From Prague's dramatic centerpiece, the Old Town Square, sight-seeing options fan out in all directions. Get oriented on the square before venturing onward. You can learn about Jewish heritage in the Jewish Quarter (Josefov), a few blocks from the Old Town Square. Closer to the square, you'll find the quaint and historic Ungelt courtyard and Celetná street, which leads to the Cubist House of the Black Madonna and the landmark Estates Theater. If you're intrigued by Jan Hus, the preacher and martyr, look for his pulpit in the chapel on Bethlehem Square. Nearby, Karlova street funnels all the tourists to the famous Charles Bridge. All the sights described here are within a five-minute walk of the magnificent Old Town Square.

▲▲▲Old Town Square (Staroměstské Náměstí)

The focal point for most visits, Prague's Old Town Square is one of the city's top sights. This has been a market square since the 11th

century. It became the nucleus of the Old Town (Staré Město) in the 13th century, when its Town Hall was built. Today, the old-time market stalls have been replaced by outdoor cafés and touristy horse buggies. But under this shallow surface, the square hides a magic power to evoke the history that has passed through here. The square's centerpiece is a memorial to Jan Hus.

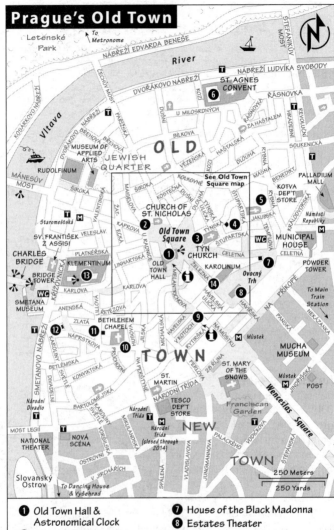

Prague's Old Town

1. Old Town Hall & Astronomical Clock
2. Church of St. Nicholas
3. Týn Church
4. Ungelt Courtyard & House of the Golden Ring
5. Church of St. James
6. Museum of Medieval Art
7. House of the Black Madonna
8. Estates Theater
9. Havelská Market
10. Bethlehem Chapel
11. Family Museum of Postcards
12. Theater on the Balustrade
13. Klementinum (National Library)
14. Charles University

THE OLD TOWN

Jan Hus and Martin Luther

The word *catholic* means "universal." The Roman Catholic Church—in many ways the administrative ghost of the Roman Empire—is the only organization to survive from ancient times. For more than a thousand years, it enforced its notion that the Vatican was the sole interpreter of God's word on earth, and the only legitimate way to be a Christian was as a Roman Catholic.

Jan Hus (c. 1369-1415) lived and preached a century before Martin Luther. Both were college professors as well as priests. Both drew huge public crowds as they preached in their university chapels. Both condemned Church corruption and promoted a local religious autonomy. Both helped establish their national languages. (Hus gave the Czech alphabet its unique accent marks so that the letters could fit the sounds.) And both got in big trouble.

While Hus was burned at the stake as a heretic, Luther survived. Thanks to the new printing press, invented by Gutenberg, Luther was able to spread his message cheaply and effectively. Since Luther was high-profile and German, killing him would have caused major political complications. While Hus may have loosened Rome's grip on Christianity, Luther orchestrated the Reformation that finally broke it. Today, both are honored as national heroes as well as religious reformers.

Jan Hus Memorial

This monument, erected in 1915 (500 years after the Czech reformer's martyrdom by fire), symbolizes the long struggle for Czech freedom. Walk around the memorial. Jan Hus stands tall between two groups of people: victorious Hussite patriots,  and Protestants defeated by the Habsburgs in 1620. One patriot holds a chalice (cup)—in the medieval Church, only priests could drink the wine at Communion. Since the Hussites fought for their right to take both the wine and the bread, the cup is their symbol. Hus looks proudly at Týn Church (described later), which became the headquarters and leading church of his followers. A golden chalice once filled the now-empty niche under the gold bas-relief of the Virgin Mary on the church's facade. After the Habsburg (Catholic) victory over the Czechs in 1620, the Hussite chalice was melted down and made into the image of Mary that shines from that spot high over the square today.

Behind the statue of Jan Hus, the bronze statue of a mother

with her children represents the ultimate rebirth of the Czech nation. Because of his bold advocacy for the participation of common people in worship rituals (and his challenges to the state-church hierarchy), Hus was excommunicated and burned in Germany, a century before the age of Martin Luther. For more about Jan Hus, see sidebar.

Old Town Square Orientation Spin-Tour

Get your bearings with this quick orientation to the square. Most important sights are described in greater detail later.

Whirl clockwise to get a look at Prague's diverse architectural styles: Gothic, Renaissance, Baroque, Rococo, and Art Nouveau. Start with the green domes of the Baroque **Church of St. Nicholas.** Originally Catholic, now Hussite, this church is a popular venue for concerts. (Another green-domed Church of St. Nicholas, by the same architect, is across the Charles Bridge in the Little Quarter. It, too, often hosts concerts.) The Jewish Quarter (Josefov) is a few blocks behind the church, down the uniquely tree-lined Pařížská—"Paris street." Pařížská, an eclectic cancan of mostly Art Nouveau facades, leads to a bluff that once sported a 100-foot-tall stone statue of Stalin. Demolished in 1962 after Khrushchev exposed Stalin's crimes, it was replaced in 1991 by a giant ticking

metronome—partly to commemorate Prague's centennial exhibition (the 1891 exhibition is remembered by the Little Quarter's Eiffel-esque Petřín Tower), and partly to send the message that for every power, there's a time to go.

Spin to the right, past the Hus Memorial and the fine yellow Art Nouveau building. The large Rococo building on the right with a public WC in the courtyard, known as **Kinský Palace,** is part of the National Gallery, but it's generally closed.

To the right, you can't miss the towering Gothic **Týn Church** (pronounced "teen"), with its fanciful spires flanking the gold bas-relief of Mary. For 200 years after Hus' death,  this was Prague's leading Hussite church. A lane just to the left leads behind Týn Church to a gorgeously restored medieval courtyard called **Ungelt.** Straight ahead, the narrow lane leading to the church's entrance passes the **Via Musica,** the most convenient ticket office in town—an essential stop if you want to understand all of your concert options (for details, see page 180. The row of pastel houses in front of Týn Church has a mixture of Gothic, Renaissance, and Baroque facades. To the right of these buildings, shop-lined **Celetná street** leads to the Czech Cubist House of the Black Madonna and, beyond that, to the Municipal House and Powder Tower in the New Town.

Continue spinning right, taking in more gloriously colorful architecture, until you reach the pointed 250-foot-tall spire marking  the 14th-century **Old Town Hall** (with the famous Astronomical Clock and the only elevator-accessible tower in town). The chunk of dark purple building attached to the tower of the Neo-Gothic City Hall is the town's "memorial" to sore losers. The building once stretched all the way to the Church of St. Nicholas (notice the broken Gothic arch). Then, in the last days of World War II (May 1945), German tanks knocked off this landmark—to the joy of many Prague citizens who considered it an ugly, oversized 19th-century stain on the medieval square. Across the square from the Old Town Hall (opposite the Astronomical Clock), touristy **Melantrichova street** leads directly to the New Town's Wenceslas Square, passing the craft-packed Havelská Market along the way.

Twenty-Seven Crosses

Embedded in the pavement at the base of the Old Town Hall tower (near the snack stand), you'll see white inlaid crosses marking the spot where 27 Protestant nobles, merchants, and intellectuals were beheaded in 1621 after rebelling against the Catholic Habsburgs. The execution ended Czech independence for 300 years and is still one of the grimmest chapters in the country's history.

▲▲Astronomical Clock

Join the gang for the striking of the hour on the Town Hall clock (daily 9:00-21:00, until 20:00 in winter). As you wait, see if you can figure out how the clock works.

With revolving discs, celestial symbols, and sweeping hands, this clock keeps several versions of time. Two outer rings show the

hour: Bohemian time (gold Gothic numbers on black background, counts from sunset—find the zero, between 23 and 1...supposedly the time of tonight's sunset) and modern time (24 Roman numerals, XII at the top being noon, XII at the bottom being midnight). Five hundred years ago, everything revolved around the earth (the fixed middle background—with Prague marking the center, of course).

To indicate the times of sunrise and sunset, arcing lines and moving spheres combine with the big hand (a sweeping golden sun) and the little hand (a moon that spins to show various stages). Look for the orbits of the sun and moon as they rise through day (the blue zone) and night (the black zone).

If this seems complex to us, it must have been a marvel in the early 1400s, when the clock was installed here. The clock was heavily damaged during World War II, and much of what you see today is a reconstruction. The circle below (added in the 19th century) shows the signs of the zodiac, scenes from the seasons of a rural peasant's life, and a ring of saints' names—one for each day of the year, with a marker showing today's special saint (at top).

Four statues flanking the clock represent the 15th-century outlook on time and prejudices. A Turk with a mandolin symbolizes hedonism, a Jewish moneylender is greed, and the figure staring into a mirror stands for vanity. All these worldly goals are vain in the face of Death, whose hourglass reminds us that our time is unavoidably running out.

At the top of the hour (don't blink—the show is pretty quick): First, Death tips his hourglass and pulls the cord, ringing the bell; the windows open and the 12 apostles parade by, acknowledging the gang of onlookers; the rooster crows; and, finally, the hour is rung. The hour is often off because of Daylight Saving Time (completely senseless to 15th-century clockmakers). At the top of the next hour, stand under the tower—protected by a line of banner-wielding concert salespeople in powdered wigs—and watch the tourists.

Clock Tour and Tower Climb: The most straightforward entry to the tower is through the orange TI building to the left of the Astronomical Clock; take the elevator to the third floor, buy your ticket, then take another elevator to the top (100 Kč, Tue-Sun 9:00-22:00, Mon 11:00-22:00, good views). You can add a 45-minute tour of the Old Town Hall, which includes a Gothic chapel and a close-up look at the inner guts of the Astronomical Clock, plus its statues of the 12 apostles (160-Kč combo-ticket, 2 tours/hour, buy at ground-floor TI desk).

▲Týn Church

Though this church has a long history, it's most notable for its 200-year stint as the leading church of the Hussite movement. It was Catholic before the Hussites, and was returned to Catholicism after the Hussites were defeated. As if to insult the Hussite doctrine of simplicity, the church's once elegant and pure Gothic columns are now encrusted with noisy Baroque altars. The church interior is uncharacteristically bright for a Gothic building because of its clear Baroque windowpanes and whitewash. Read the Catholic spin on the church's history—told with barely a mention of Hus (rear-left side, in English). The fine 16th-century carved John the Baptist altar (right aisle) is worth a look. As you enjoy this church, try to ignore its unwelcoming signs telling you what not to do.

Outside, on the side of the church facing Celetná street, find a statue of the Virgin Mary resting on a temporary column in an ignored niche. Catholics are still waiting for a chance to re-install Mary in the middle of the Old Town Square, where she stood for about 250 years until being torn down in 1918 by a mob of anti-Habsburg (and therefore anti-Catholic) demonstrators.

Cost and Hours: Free but 20 Kč donation suggested, generally open to sightseers Tue-Sat 10:00-13:00 & 15:00-17:00, Sun 10:30-12:00, closed Mon.

Behind Týn Church

▲Ungelt Courtyard (Týnský Dvůr)

This fortified courtyard was the commercial nucleus of medieval Prague. Step through its stout gate (immediately behind Týn Church). The Ungelt courtyard once served as a hostel for foreign merchants, much like a Turkish caravanserai. Here the merchants (usually German) would store their goods and pay taxes before setting up stalls on the Old Town Square (where two old trade routes crossed). Notice that, for the purpose of guaranteeing the safety of goods and merchants, there are only two entrances to the complex. After decades of disuse, the courtyard had fallen into such disrepair by the 1980s that authorities considered demolishing it. But now, marvelously restored, the Ungelt courtyard is the most pleasant area in the Old Town for dining outdoors (such as at the recommended Indian Jewel). Although Prague has undoubtedly lost some of its dreamy character to the booming tourist industry, places such as Ungelt stand as testimony to the miracles that money can work. Had the communists stayed in power for a few more years, Ungelt would have been a black hole by now. Ungelt also reminds us that Prague, for most of its history, has been a cosmopolitan center.

House of the Golden Ring (Dům u Zlatého Prstenu)

This medieval townhouse is the home of the City of Prague Gallery and its delightful collection of 20th-century Czech art. Since 1900, Czech artists have been refining the subtle differences between dream, myth, and ideal. The English descriptions in each room psychoanalyze this demanding art and recall Prague's role at the forefront of the European avant-garde in the 1930s and again in the 1960s. Notice the absence of Socialist Realism (the state-sanctioned propaganda art of the communist era): The artists exhibited here chose deeply personal means of expression over regime-sponsored proclamations of universal optimism.

Cost and Hours: 120 Kč, Tue-Sun 10:00-18:00, closed Mon, just left of the entry into Ungelt courtyard as you approach it from the Old Town Square, Týnská 6, tel. 224-827-0224, www.citygalleryprague.cz. The house's courtyard is home to a lively-with-students café.

Church of St. James (Kostel Sv. Jakuba)

Perhaps the most beautiful church in the Old Town, the Church of St. James is just behind the Ungelt courtyard. The Minorite Order has occupied this church and the adjacent monastery almost as long as merchants have occupied Ungelt. A medieval city was a complex phenomenon: Commerce, prostitution, and a life of contemplation existed side by side. (I guess it's not that much different from today.) Artistically, St. James (along with the Church of the Ascension of St. Mary at Strahov Monastery) is a stunning example of how simple medieval spaces could be rebuilt into sumptuous feasts of Baroque decoration. The original interior was destroyed by fire in 1689; what's here now is an early 18th-century remodel. The blue light in the altar highlights one of Prague's most venerated treasures—the bejeweled Madonna Pietatis. Above the *pietà*, as if held aloft by hummingbird-like angels, is a painting of the martyrdom of St. James.

Proceed grandly up the central aisle, enjoying a parade of gild-ed statues and paintings under a colorfully frescoed ceiling telling stories of Virgin Mary's life. When you reach the altar at the front, turn around and notice how the church suddenly becomes simpler without all that ornamentation. Prague's grandest pipe organ fills the back wall.

As you leave, look for the black, shriveled-up arm with clenched fingers (hanging by a chain from a metal post 15 feet above and to the left of the door). According to legend, a thief at-tempted to rob the Madonna Pietatis from the altar, but his hand was frozen the moment he touched the statue. The monks had to cut off his arm to get the hand to let go. The desiccated arm now hangs here as a warning.

Cost and Hours: Free, Tue-Sun 9:30-12:00 & 14:00-16:00, closed Mon.

North of the Old Town Square, near the River
▲▲Museum of Medieval Art
(Středověké umění v Čechách a Střední Evropě)

The St. Agnes Convent houses the Museum of Medieval Art in Bohemia and Central Europe (1200-1550). The 14th century was Prague's Golden Age, and the religious art displayed in this Gothic space is a testament to the rich cultural life of the period. Each exquisite piece is well-lit and thoughtfully described in English. Follow the arrows for a chronological sweep through Gothic art history. The various Madonnas and saints were gathered here from churches all over Central Europe.

Princess Agnes founded this Clarist convent in the 13th cen-tury as the first hospital in Prague. Agnes was canonized by Pope John Paul II (who loved to promote the Slavic faithful) in 1989. Since local celebrations of her sainthood on November 26 coin-cided with the Velvet Revolution (the peaceful overthrow of the Communist government in 1989), Agnes has since been regarded as the patron of the renascent Czech democracy (you'll see her on the rare 50-Kč bill).

Cost and Hours: 150 Kč, Tue-Sun 10:00-18:00, closed Mon, two blocks northeast of the Spanish Synagogue, along the river at Anežská 12, tel. 224-810-628, www.ngprague.cz/en.

On Celetná Street, Toward the New Town

Celetná, a pedestrian-only street, is a convenient and relatively un-touristy way to get from the Old Town Square to the New Town (specifically the Municipal House and Powder Tower, described on page 93). Along the way, at the square called Ovocný Trh, you'll find these sights.

House of the Black Madonna (Dům u Černé Matky Boží)

Cubism was a potent force in Prague in the early 20th century. This fascinating house combines Cubist architecture (stand back and see how masterfully it makes its statement while mixing with its neighbors...then get up close and study the details) and a great café (the recommended Grand Café Orient, one flight up) that plays on the Cubist theme with cube-shaped chairs and square-shaped vanilla rolls. This building is an example of what has long been considered the greatest virtue of Prague's architects: the ability to adapt grandiose plans to the existing cityscape.

Estates Theater (Stavovské Divadlo)

Built by a nobleman in the 1770s, this Classicist building—gently opening its greenish walls onto Ovocný Trh—was the prime opera venue in Prague at a time when an Austrian prodigy was changing the course of music. Wolfgang Amadeus Mozart premiered *Don Giovanni* in this building (with a bronze statue of Il Commendatore duly flanking the main entrance on the left), and he directed many of his works here. Prague's theatergoers would whistle arias from Mozart's works on the streets the morning after they premiered. Today, the Estates Theater (part of the National Theater group) continues to produce *The Marriage of Figaro, Don Giovanni,* and occasionally *The Magic Flute.* This building is generally seen as a German theater. In fact, for a time the Habsburgs forbid plays here in the Czech language. In the late 1800s, the Czechs built the National Theater in the New Town to celebrate Czech culture—with no regard for their German-speaking rulers (see page 98).

On Melantrichova Street

Skinny, tourist-clogged Melantrichova street leads directly from the Old Town Square's Astronomical Clock to the bottom of Wenceslas Square. But even along this most crowded of streets, a genuine bit of Prague remains.

▲Havelská Market

This open-air market, offering crafts and produce, was first set up in the 13th century for the German trading community. Though heavy on souvenirs these days, the market still feeds hungry locals and vagabonds cheaply. It's ideal for a healthy snack—merchants are happy to sell a single vegetable or piece of fruit—and

Czechs and Indians

The German writer Karl May used the time he spent in prison for fraud in the 1860s to write stories about the fictional noble Apache chief Winnetou and his German friend Old Shatterhand (although May did not visit America until 1908, very late in his life). Ever since, the Czechs have been obsessed with Native Americans. Most kids spend summers in camps (as Boy Scouts and Girl Scouts), where they learn about the Native Americans' respect for nature, survival skills in the wilderness, courage, and the idealized noble spirit. A tune celebrating the Native Americans' victory at Little Bighorn is one of the most popular sagas sung around Czech campfires. When cancer survivor and cyclist Lance Armstrong visited Prague's oncology ward in July 2004, child cancer patients rewarded him with the Native American name "Fast Wind." Prague's Náprstek Museum of Asian, African, and American Cultures displays attire worn by Lakota Chief Sitting Bull (Betlémské Náměstí 1).

THE OLD TOWN

you'll find a washing fountain and plenty of inviting benches midway down the street. The market is also a fun place to browse for crafts. It's a homegrown, homemade kind of place; you'll often be dealing with the actual artist or farmer. The many cafés and little eateries circling the market offer a relaxing vantage point from which to view the action.

Hours: Market open daily 9:00-18:00, produce best on weekdays; more souvenirs, puppets, and toys on weekends.

Bethlehem Square (Betlémské Náměstí)

The charming, relatively quiet Bethlehem Square is a pleasantly untouristy chunk of Old Town real estate.

Bethlehem Chapel (Betlémská Kaple)

Holy Roman Emperor Charles IV founded the first university in Prague—and Central Europe—in 1348, and this was its chapel. In about 1400, priest and professor Jan Hus preached from the pulpit here (see the "Jan Hus and Martin Luther" sidebar, earlier). While meant primarily for students and faculty, services were open to the public, and standing-room-only crowds of more than 3,000 were the norm when Hus preached. He proposed that the congregation should be more involved in worship (for example, be allowed to drink the wine at Communion) and have better access to the word of God through services and scriptures written in the people's language, not in Latin. The stimulating, controversial ideas debated at the university spread throughout the city and, after Hus' death at the stake, sparked the bloodiest civil war in Czech history.

Each subsequent age has interpreted Hus to its liking: For Protestants, Hus was the founder of the first Protestant church (though he was actually an ardent Catholic); for revolutionaries, this critic of the Church's power was a proponent of social equality; for nationalists, this Czech preacher was the defender of the language; and for communists, Hus was the first ideologue to preach the gospel of socialism.

Today's chapel is a 1950s reconstruction of the original. Try the unbelievably bad acoustics inside—they demonstrate the sloppy restoration work sponsored by the communists. English info sheets are available for the tiny upstairs exhibit and big chapel.

Cost and Hours: 60 Kč; April-Oct daily 10:00-18:30; Nov-March Tue-Sun 10:00-17:30, closed Mon and during frequent university functions; Betlémské Náměstí, tel. 224-248-595.

Eating: The recommended **Klub Architektů** restaurant, across from the chapel's entry, has a cave-like atmosphere inside, straw-chair seating outside, and good food in and out.

Sights near Bethlehem Square

The tiny **Family Museum of Postcards,** inside Choco Café, is around the corner on Liliová street, which connects Bethlehem Square with Karlova. After learning how the Austro-Hungarian Empire invented the postcard, you can buy your own early-20th-century specimen (40 Kč, Tue-Sun 11:00-19:00, closed Mon, Liliová 4, tel. 222-222-519).

Walk down Liliová street for 30 yards and then turn left into a narrow corridor leading past a church-like structure into the quiet Anenské Náměstí (St. Anne Square), with a black iron grill covering a medieval well in the middle. On the opposite side of the square is the avant-garde **Theater on the Balustrade** (Divadlo Na zábradlí) with a handy café inside (Mon-Fri 10:00-1:00, Sat-Sun 16:00-1:00). It was here that Václav Havel found a job as a stagehand in the early 1960s, and wrote and staged the first Czech plays of the absurd (for more on Havel see page 352). The copper drainpipe in the shape of an embryo on the corner of the building symbolizes the traditionally experimental nature of the art performed inside.

If you were to turn and go around the corner with the embryo, you'd pass the second-floor balustrade, after which the theater was named, and head down to the Vltava River. From here you could go to the right along the tram tracks to the Charles Bridge, or go to the left to the National Theater.

Or, instead of heading to the river, you can turn right (as you face the front of the theater), walk to the far end of the square,

Prague's Charles University

Back in the 1300s, Charles University students studied the arts first, and only then proceeded to one of the other three faculties (medicine, law, and theology), of which theology was the most prestigious. Classes were taught in Latin, and the student body was cosmopolitan—Czechs made up only a fourth of all students.

During the chaotic period of Hussite reforms in the early 1400s, the university's policies were changed to give more power to the Czechs. In protest, many foreign students and professors left Prague and founded the first German university in Leipzig. Celebrated by Czech nationalists as a victory over foreigners, the new policies reduced Charles University from a European center of learning to a provincial institution.

In the 1600s, the predominantly Protestant university was handed over to the Jesuits. But in the 1780s, Habsburg Emperor Josef II abolished the Jesuit order, opened the university to non-Catholics, and changed the language of instruction from Latin to German. Czechs did not win the freedom to study in their own language until 1882, when the university split into two separate schools (the German school ceased to exist in 1945).

Today, the Old Town continues to live a double life as both a commercial center and a university campus. Though lined with souvenir stalls outside, many buildings hold classrooms that have been animated by lecturers for centuries. Some of the Old Town's most hidden courtyards have provided Czech scholars with their two most essential needs: good beer and space for inspiring conversation.

Charles University, always a center of Czech political thinking, has incited trouble and uprisings. It's where Jan Hus called for reform of the Church; the revolutions of 1618 and 1848 were sparked by university minds; and in the modern era, students rose up against totalitarian regimes in 1939, 1948, and 1968. The Germans closed down all Czech universities for the duration of World

THE OLD TOWN

and enter a passageway. This leads to two connected courtyards and busy Karlova street. The bronze sculpture in the first courtyard, depicting a planet with elliptical orbits modeled around it, is a reminder that Johannes Kepler occupied the adjacent house in the early 1600s. The Czech Astronomical Society runs the small **Kepler Museum** here (60 Kč, Tue-Sun 10:00-18:00, closed Mon, Karlova 4, tel. 608-971-236, www.keplerovomuzeum.cz).

From Old Town Square to the Charles Bridge
Karlova Street
This street winds through medieval Prague from the Old Town Square to the Charles Bridge (it zigzags—just follow the crowds). The touristy feeding-frenzy of Prague is at its ugliest along this

War II. Later, the communists fired professors unwilling to follow the party line and replaced them with applicants chosen on the basis of class background rather than ability. The Velvet Revolution, which swept communists out of power in November 1989, started as a student demonstration.

Although many professors returned to their classrooms after 1989, the education system itself has yet to fully escape the legacy of the authoritarian regimes. From an early age, students are taught to memorize rather than to think independently; knowledge is measured by facts rather than by the ability to use them; and even at the university level, few students dare to challenge the professor's view. Another problem is the small size of the Czech Republic: The only employment opportunities for Ph.D. graduates are in the same departments in which they studied. Each department functions much like a self-contained world, doing things its own way, and unwilling to open itself to influences from outside. University teachers receive a basic salary, supplemented by grants. Funding varies greatly across the departments: Those with capable scholars are well-funded, while departments with teachers who lack the initiative to seek grants barely get by.

Charles University still attracts the best Czech and Slovak students. There has been some talk about charging tuition, but the move is highly controversial, as Czechs are accustomed to university educations being free of charge. On the other hand, free admission hasn't made education any more accessible to students from poorer backgrounds. Demand for seats exceeds the supply, so only a third of the people who apply to state high schools ("gymnasium") are accepted, and only half of applicants to state universities get in. Those from well-educated (and well-off) families tend to do better in a system that begins selecting students from the age of 10.

commercial gauntlet. Locals look with disdain on the many Russian-owned shops selling Matryoshka dolls, furry hats, and other things that have nothing to do with Czech culture. Obviously, you'll find few good values on this drag.

But the street's got plenty of historic charm—if you're able to ignore the 21st-century tourism. Look up. Notice the historic symbols and signs from the original shops; these advertised who lived there or what they sold. Cornerstones, designed to protect buildings from careening carriages, also date from centuries past. Street signs keep you on track, and *Karlův most* signs point to the bridge.

Two favorite places providing a quick break from the crowds are just a few steps off Karlova on Husova street: **Cream and Dream Ice Cream** (Husova 12) and the recommended **U Zlatého**

Tygra, a colorful pub that serves great, cheap beer in a classic and untouristy setting (Husova 17).

▲Klementinum

The Czech Republic's massive National Library borders touristy Karlova street. The contrast could not be starker: Step out of the most souvenir-packed stretch of Eastern Europe, and enter the meditative silence of Eastern Europe's biggest library. Jesuits built the Klementinum in the 1600s to house a new college; they had been invited to Prague by the Catholic Habsburgs to offset the influence of the predominantly Protestant Charles University nearby. The building was transformed into a library in the early 1700s, when the Jesuits took firm control of the university. Their books, together with the collections of several noble families (written in all possible languages...except Czech), form the nucleus of the National and University Library, which is now six million volumes strong. (Note that the Klementinum's Chapel of Mirrors is a popular venue for evening concerts.)

While much of the Klementinum building is simply a vast library, its magnificent original Baroque Hall and Observatory Tower are open to the public by tour only (45 minutes, in English). You'll belly up to a banister at the end of the ornate library with its many centuries-old books, fancy ceilings with Jesuit leaders and saints overseeing the pursuit of knowledge, and Josef II—the enlightened Habsburg emperor—looking on from the far end. Then you'll climb the Observatory Tower, learning how early astronomers charted the skies over Prague. The tour finishes with a grand Prague view from the top.

Cost and Hours: Tour—220 Kč, departs on the hour Mon-Fri 14:00-19:00, Sat-Sun 10:00-19:00, shorter hours off-season, tel. 221-663-165, mobile 603-231-241, www.klementinum.com; strolling down Karlova, turn at the intersection with Liliová through an archway into the Klementinum's courtyard.

▲▲▲Charles Bridge (Karlův Most)

Among Prague's defining landmarks, this much-loved bridge offers one of the most pleasant and entertaining 500-yard strolls in Europe. Enjoy the bridge at different times of day; it's most memorable early—before the crowds—and late, during that "magic hour" for photographers, when the sun is low in the sky.

At the Old Town end of the bridge, in a little square, is a statue of the bridge's namesake, **Charles IV** (Karlo Quatro—the guy on

the 100-Kč bill), the Holy Roman Emperor who ruled his vast empire from Prague in the 14th century. This statue was erected in 1848 to celebrate the 500th anniversary of Prague's university. Charles is holding a contract establishing the university, the first in this part of Europe. The women around the pedestal symbolize the school's four subjects: the arts, medicine, law, and theology. (From the corner by the busy street, many think the emperor's silhouette makes it appear as if he's peeing on the tourists. Which reminds me, public WCs are in the passageway opposite the statue.)

The magically aligned spot on the Old Town side (see sidebar, next page) is occupied by the **bridge tower,** considered one of the finest Gothic gates anywhere. Contemplate the fine sculpture on the Old Town side of the tower, showing the 14th-century hierarchy of bishops above kings, and kings above the people on the street. Climbing the tower rewards you with wonderful views over the bridge (75 Kč, daily 10:00-19:00, as late as 22:00 in summer).

Originally, there were no statues on the bridge—only a **cross,** which you can still see as part of the third sculpture on the right. With the Habsburg attempt to convert Czechs back to Catholicism in the 17th and 18th centuries, the many preachy statues were added. These religious figures overlooked the town folk each day as they crossed this, the only bridge over the river until the 19th century. The gilded Hebrew inscription from the Book of Isaiah celebrates Christ ("Holy, holy, holy is the Lord of hosts"). The inscription was paid for by a fine imposed on a Prague Jew—the result of a rivalry within the Jewish community (fellow Jews turned him in for mocking the cross).

In the space between the third and fourth statues after the cross, look for a small **brass relief** depicting a floating figure with a semicircle of stars above him. This marks the spot where St. John of Nepomuk, the national saint of the Czech people, was tossed off the bridge into the river (I'll tell you that story a bit later). The relief is a replica of a Baroque original that was badly damaged by a flood in 1890, marred by protesters in the 1920s, and finally removed by the communists. In May of 2009, this replacement was installed by Prague's archbishop to help revive traditional celebrations of the saint.

The relief is the ideal location from which to survey your surroundings. Looking **downstream** from right to left, you'll see the modern Four Seasons Hotel (with the black roof, doing a pretty good job of fitting in). Farther down (look for a green roof), a large Neo-Renaissance facade hides the concert hall of the Czech

Charles Bridge: Past and Present

Bridges had previously been built at this location, as the tower from the earlier Judith Bridge attests (it's the smaller of the two bridge towers at the far end), but all were washed away by floods. After a major flood in 1342, Emperor Charles IV decided against repairing the old bridge and instead commissioned an entirely new structure. Initially called the Stone Bridge, it was Prague's only bridge across the Vltava River for more than 400 years.

The bridge has long fueled a local love of legends—including one tied to numbers. According to medieval records, the bridge's foundation was laid in 1357. In the late 1800s, an amateur astronomer noticed a curious combination of numbers, leading to a popular theory about Charles IV. Charles is known to have been interested in numerology and astrology, and was likely aware of the significance of this date: the ninth of July at 5:31 in the morning. Written out in digits—as the year, month, day, hour, and minute—it's a numerical palindrome: 135797531. It's said that Charles must have chosen that precise moment (which also coincides with a favorable positioning of the earth and Saturn) to lay the foundation stone of the bridge. Further "corroboration" of this remarkable hypothesis was provided by the discovery that the end of the bridge on the Old Town side aligns perfectly with the tomb of St. Vitus (in the cathedral across the river) and the setting sun at summer solstice. In the absence of accurate 14th-century records, this intriguing proposition has delighted the modern Czech imagination. The number "135797531" is bound to remain celebrated as the adopted birthday of Prague's most beloved structure.

But even the most auspicious numbers could not protect the bridge from periodic damage caused by floods, ice, and inept repairs. A long-overdue reconstruction project began in the summer of 2007, with the first two stages completed in December of 2010. Some work remains to be done, but is unlikely to affect the bridge's appearance or traffic.

Philharmonic. Across the river and up the hill, the red needle of a metronome ticks at the spot where a 50-foot-tall granite Joseph Stalin—flanked by eight equally tall deputies—stood from 1955 to 1962. To the right of Stalin's former perch (hiding under the trees and worth the climb on a hot summer day) is Prague's most popular beer garden. Visible between the trees to the left of the metronome is the small but attractive Art Nouveau Havana pavilion, now a fancy restaurant peeking above. To the left of it is a yellow villa in the trees, the residence of the Czech prime minister. The little green roof in the shape of an upturned ship along the tree-lined horizon belongs to the Royal Summer Palace, an exquisite Renaissance structure (see page 131). Finally, capping the hill, a line of noble palaces leads to the cathedral.

Looking **upstream,** notice the icebreakers protecting the abutments upon which the bridge sits (ice flow has historically threatened the very sur-

vival of the bridge). Look farther upstream for the tiny locks on the right side of the weir. While today's river traffic is limited to tourist boats, in earlier times traders floated timber, lashed like rafts, down the river. The building with the gilded crown atop its black dome on the left (by the next upstream bridge) is the National Theater. The rentable paddleboats plying the water (easy and affordable) are a romantic way to get a little exercise.

Pause for a moment to enjoy the musicians, artisans, and parade of people on the bridge itself—my favorite strolling bridge in all of Europe.

Continue along the bridge, passing two more statue groups. You'll reach the bronze Baroque statue depicting **St. John of**

Nepomuk (look for the guy with the five golden stars around his head, near the Little Quarter end of the bridge on the right). This statue always draws a crowd. John was a 14th-century priest to whom the queen confessed all her sins. According to a 17th-century legend, the king wanted to know his wife's secrets, but Father John dutifully refused to tell. He was tortured and eventually killed by being thrown off the bridge. When he hit the water, five stars appeared. The shiny plaque at the base of the statue depicts the heave-ho. Notice the date on the inscription: This oldest statue on the bridge was unveiled in 1683, on the supposed 300th anniversary of the martyr's death. Devout pilgrims believe that touching the St. John plaque will make a wish come true. But you get only one chance in life to make this wish, so think carefully before you touch the saint.

The reason for John of Nepomuk's immense Baroque popularity and 1729 canonization remains contested. Some historians claim that at a time when the Czechs were being forcibly converted to Catholicism, Nepomuk became the rallying national symbol

THE OLD TOWN

("We will convert, but our patron must be Czech"). Others argue that Nepomuk was a propaganda figure used by Catholic leaders to give locals an alternative to Jan Hus. You'll find statues like this one on squares and bridges throughout the country.

Most of the other Charles Bridge statues date from the late 1600s and early 1700s and are impressively expressive. Today, half of them are replicas—the originals are in city museums, out of the polluted air. At the far end of the Charles Bridge, you reach the **Little Quarter.** For sights in this neighborhood, see the Little Quarter chapter.

▲▲▲Jewish Quarter (Josefov)

Prague's Jewish Quarter neighborhood and its well-presented, profoundly moving museum tell the story of this region's Jews. For me, this is the most interesting collection of Jewish sights in Europe, and well worth seeing. The Jewish Quarter is an easy walk from Old Town Square, up delightful Pařížská street (next to the green-domed Church of St. Nicholas).

As the Nazis decimated Jewish communities in the region, Prague's Jews were allowed to collect and archive their treasures here. Though the archivists were ultimately killed in concentration camps, their work survives. Seven sights scattered over a three-block area make up the tourists' Jewish Quarter. Six of the sights—all except the Old-New Synagogue—are part of the Jewish Museum in Prague (Židovské Muzeum v Praze) and are covered by one admission ticket. Your ticket comes with a map that locates the sights and lists admission appointments—the times you'll be let in if it's very busy. (Ignore the times unless it's really crowded.) You'll notice plenty of security.

Going from sight to sight in the Jewish Quarter, you'll walk through perhaps Europe's finest Art Nouveau neighborhood. Make a point to enjoy the circa-1900 buildings with their marvelous trimmings and oh-wow entryways. While today's modern grid plan has replaced the higgledy-piggledy medieval streets of old, Široká ("Wide Street") was and remains the main street of the ghetto.

Cost and Hours: A discount ticket covering all seven Jewish Quarter sights is 480 Kč (ticket available at any of the sights; separately, you'd pay 300 Kč for the six sights that make up the Jewish Museum, and 200 Kč for the Old-New Synagogue). The **museum** sights are open April-Oct Sun-Fri 9:00-18:00; Nov-March Sun-Fri 9:00-16:30; closed year-round on Sat—the Jewish Sabbath—and on Jewish holidays; check the website for a complete list of holiday closures, especially if you are visiting in the fall (tel. 222-317-191, www.jewishmuseum.cz). The **Old-New Synagogue** is open Sun-Thu 9:30-18:00, Fri 9:30-17:00 or until sunset, closed Sat and on

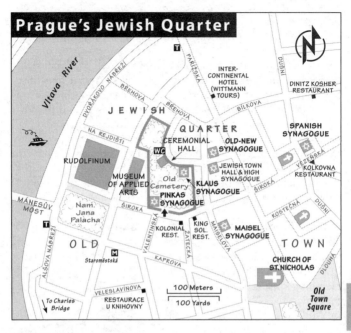

Prague's Jewish Quarter

Jewish holidays (admission includes worthwhile 10-minute tour, tel. 222-317-191, www.synagogue.cz).

Avoiding Lines: The Pinkas Synagogue is the Jewish Quarter's most popular sight—and has the longest ticket-buying lines. Before making your way to the Pinkas, consider buying your ticket at one of the other sights (such as the Maisel Synagogue).

Free View of Cemetery: The Old Jewish Cemetery—with its tightly packed, topsy-turvy tombstones—is, for many, the most evocative part of the experience. Unfortunately, you can't get a ticket just to see the cemetery, and most of the formerly free viewpoints have been closed off. If the museum ticket is too steep and you just want a free glimpse of the famous cemetery, climb the steps to the covered porch of the Ceremonial Hall (but don't rest your chin on the treacherous railing).

Photos: While *No Photo* signs are posted everywhere, photos without flash seem to be allowed (except during prayer times at the Old-New Synagogue). Photography is permitted in the cemetery if you pay a 50-Kč fee.

Tours: Because the Jewish Museum sights are scattered throughout the neighborhood, many tourists think they need a guide, but for most, a private guided tour is unnecessary. Group tours flow like chain gangs through the congested and emotional museum sights. Instead, use the descriptions in this guidebook, and rely on the helpful commentary thoughtfully posted in English throughout the quarter. The 250-Kč audioguide is slow-moving and not worth the time or expense (rent and return at Pinkas Synagogue, ID required).

Touring on Your Own: This plan works well: Buy your ticket at the museum-like Maisel Synagogue, and start your tour there. (Avoid buying your ticket at the Pinkas Synagogue, which is usually overcrowded.) Next, visit the Pinkas Synagogue and the adjacent Old Jewish Cemetery, which leads you to the Ceremonial Hall and Klaus Synagogue (at the far side of the cemetery; cemetery entry only possible through the Pinkas). Break for coffee, then visit the Old-New Synagogue and the Spanish Synagogue. (Note that Prague's fine Museum of Medieval Art, described on page 68, is only a few blocks from the Spanish Synagogue.)

Maisel Synagogue (Maiselova Synagóga)

This synagogue was built as a private place of worship for the Maisel family during the 16th-century Golden Age of Prague's Jews. Maisel, the wealthy financier of the Habsburg king, lavished his riches on the synagogue's Neo-Gothic interior. In World War II, it served as a warehouse for the accumulated treasures of decimated Jewish communities, a collection that Hitler planned to use for his Jewish museum (see later). Before entering, notice the facade featuring the Ten Commandments top and center  (standard in synagogues). Below that is the symbol for Prague's Jewish community: the Star of David, with the pointed hat local Jews wore here through medieval times. The one-room exhibit shows a thousand years of Jewish history in Bohemia and Moravia. Well-explained in English, topics include the origin of the Star of David, Jewish mysticism, the history of discrimination, and the creation of Prague's ghetto. Notice the eastern wall, with the Holy Ark containing the scroll of the Torah. The central case shows the silver ornamental Torah crowns that capped the scroll.

Pinkas Synagogue (Pinkasova Synagóga)

A site of Jewish worship for 400 years, this synagogue (built in 1535) is a poignant memorial to the victims of the Nazis. The walls are covered with the handwritten names of 77,297 Czech Jews who were sent from here to the gas chambers at Auschwitz and other camps. (As you ponder this sad sight, you'll hear the somber reading of the names alternating with a cantor singing the Psalms.) The names are carefully organized by hometown (in gold, listed alphabetically). Family names are in red, followed in black by the individual's first name, birthday, and last date known to be alive. Notice that families generally perished together. Extermination camps are listed on the east wall. Climb eight steps into the women's gallery. When the communists moved in, they closed the synagogue and erased virtually everything. With freedom, in 1989, the Pinkas Synagogue was reopened and the names were rewritten. (The names in poor condition near the ceiling are original.) Note that large tour groups may disturb this small memorial's compelling atmosphere between 10:00 and 12:00.

Upstairs is the **Terezín Children's Art Exhibit** (very well-described in English), displaying art drawn by Jewish children who were imprisoned at Terezín Concentration Camp and later perished. Terezín makes an emotionally moving day trip from Prague; it's easily accessible by local bus (see page 209) or tour bus (see page 55).

Old Jewish Cemetery (Starý Židovský Hřbitov)

From the Pinkas Synagogue, you enter one of the most wistful scenes in Europe—Prague's Old Jewish Cemetery. As you wander

among 12,000 evocative tombstones, remember that from 1439 until 1787, this was the only burial ground allowed for the Jews of Prague. Guides claim the tombs are layered seven or eight deep, and say there are close to 100,000 tombs here. The tombs were piled atop each other because of limited space, the sheer number of graves, and the Jewish belief that the body should not be moved once buried. With its many layers, the cemetery became a small plateau. And as things settled over time, the tombstones became crooked. The Hebrew word for cemetery means "House of Life." Many Jews believe that death is the gateway into the next world. Pebbles on the tombstones are "flowers of the desert," reminiscent of the old days when rocks were placed upon a sandy gravesite to keep the body covered. Wedged under some of the pebbles are scraps of paper that contain prayers.

Ceremonial Hall (Obřadní Síň)

Leaving the cemetery, you'll find a Neo-Romanesque mortuary house (on the left) built in 1911 for the purification of the dead. It's filled with a worthwhile exhibition, described in English, on Jewish medicine, death, and burial tradi-

Prague's Jewish Heritage

The Jewish people from the Holy Land (today's Israel) were dispersed by the Romans 2,000 years ago. Over the centuries, their culture survived in enclaves throughout the world: "The Torah was their sanctuary which no army could destroy." Jews first came to Prague in the 10th century. The Jewish Quarter's main intersection (Maiselova and Široká streets) was the meeting point of two medieval trade routes.

During the Crusades in the 12th century, the pope declared that Jews and Christians should not live together. Jews had to wear yellow badges, and their quarter was walled in and became a ghetto. In the 16th and 17th centuries, Prague had one of the biggest ghettos in Europe, with 11,000 inhabitants. Within its six gates, Prague's Jewish Quarter was a gaggle of 200 wooden buildings. It was said that "Jews nested rather than dwelled."

These "outcasts" of Christianity relied mainly on profits from moneylending (forbidden to Christians) and community solidarity to survive. While their money bought them protection (the kings taxed Jewish communities heavily), it was often also a curse. Throughout Europe, when times got tough and Christian

tions. A series of crude but instructive paintings (hanging on walls throughout the house) show how the "burial brotherhood" took care of the ill and buried the dead. As all are equal before God, the rich and poor alike were buried in embroidered linen shrouds similar to the one you'll see on display.

Klaus Synagogue (Klauzová Synagóga)

This 17th-century synagogue (also near the cemetery exit) is the final wing of a museum devoted to Jewish religious practices. Exhibits on the ground floor explain the Jewish calendar of festivals. The central case displays a Torah (the first five books of the Bible) and the solid silver pointers used when reading it—necessary since the Torah is not to be touched. Upstairs is an exhibit on the rituals of Jewish life (circumcisions, bar and bat mitzvahs, weddings, kosher eating, and so on).

Old-New Synagogue (Staronová Synagóga)

For more than 700 years, this has been the most important syna-

debts to the Jewish community mounted, entire Jewish communities were evicted or killed.

In the 1780s, Emperor Josef II, motivated more by economic concerns than by religious freedom, eased much of the discrimination against Jews. In 1848, the Jewish Quarter's walls were torn down, and the neighborhood—named Josefov in honor of the emperor who provided this small measure of tolerance—was incorporated as a district of the Old Town.

In 1897, ramshackle Josefov was razed and replaced by a new modern town—the original 31 streets and 220 buildings became 10 streets and 83 buildings. This is what you'll see today: an attractive neighborhood of pretty, mostly Art Nouveau buildings, with a few surviving historic Jewish structures. By the 1930s, Prague's Jewish community was hugely successful, thanks largely to their ability to appreciate talent—a rare quality in small Central European countries whose citizens, as the great Austrian novelist Robert Musil put it, "were equal in their unwillingness to let one another get ahead."

Of the 120,000 Jews living in the area in 1939, just 10,000 survived the Holocaust to see liberation in 1945. Today there are only 3,000 "registered" Jews in the Czech Republic, and of these, only 1,700 are in Prague. (There are probably more Jewish people here, but after their experiences with the Nazis and communists, you can understand why many choose not to register.) Today, in spite of their tiny numbers, the legacy of Prague's Jewish community lives on.

gogue and the central building in Josefov. Standing like a bomb-hardened bunker, it feels as though it has survived plenty of hard times. Stairs take you down to the street level of the 13th century and into the Gothic interior. Built in 1270, it's the oldest synagogue in Eastern Europe. Snare an attendant, who is likely to love showing visitors around. The separate, steep, 200-Kč admission keeps many away, but even if you decide not to pay, you can see the exterior and a bit of the interior. (Go ahead...pop in and crane your cheapskate neck.)

The lobby (down the stairs, where you show your ticket) has two fortified old lockers—in which the most heavily taxed community in medieval Prague stored its money in anticipation of the taxman's arrival. As 13th-century Jews were not allowed to build, the synagogue was erected by Christians (who also built the St. Agnes Convent nearby). The builders were good at four-ribbed vaulting, but since that resulted in a cross, it wouldn't work for a synagogue. Instead, they made the ceiling using clumsy five-ribbed vaulting.

The interior is pure 1300s. The Shrine of the Ark in front is the focus of worship. The holiest place in the synagogue, it holds the sacred scrolls of the Torah. The old rabbi's chair to the right remains empty (notice the thin black chain) out of respect. The red banner is a copy of the one that the Jewish community carried through town during medieval parades. On the banner, within the Star of David, is pictured the yellow-pointed hat that the pope ordered all Jewish men to wear in 1215. Twelve is a popular number (e.g., windows), because it symbolizes the 12 tribes of Israel. The horizontal slit-like windows are an 18th-century addition, allowing women to view the male-only services. While Nazis routinely destroyed synagogues, this most historic synagogue in the country survived because the Nazis intended it to be part of their "Museum of the Extinct Jewish Race."

Spanish Synagogue (Španělská Synagóga)

Displays of Jewish history through the 18th, 19th, and tumultuous 20th centuries continue in this ornate, Moorish-style synagogue built in the 1800s. The upstairs is particularly intriguing, with circa-1900 photos of Josefov, an exhibit on the fascinating story of this museum and its relationship with the Nazi regime, and life in Terezín. The Winter Synagogue (also upstairs) shows a trove of silver—Kiddush cups, Hanukkah lamps, Sabbath candlesticks, Torah ornaments—gathered from countryside Jewish neighborhoods that were depopulated in the early 1940s, giving you a glimpse of the treasures the Nazis stole and stockpiled.

THE NEW TOWN

Nové Město

Enough of pretty, medieval Prague—let's leap into the modern era. The New Town, with Wenceslas Square as its focal point, is today's urban Prague. This part of the city offers bustling boulevards and interesting neighborhoods. The New Town is one of the best places to view Prague's remarkable Art Nouveau art and architecture, and to learn more about its communist past.

▲▲Wenceslas Square (Václavské Náměstí)

More a broad boulevard than a square (until recently, trams rattled up and down its park-like median strip), this city landmark is named for King Wenceslas—featured both on the 20-Kč coin and the equestrian statue that stands at the top of the boulevard. Wenceslas Square functions as a stage for modern Czech history: The creation of the Czechoslovak state was celebrated here in 1918; in 1968, the Soviets suppressed huge popular demonstrations at the square; and, in 1989, more than 300,000 Czechs and Slovaks converged here to claim their freedom.

❷ **Self-Guided Walk:** Let's take a stroll down Prague's urban centerpiece.
• *Starting near the Wenceslas statue (Metro: Muzeum), look to the building crowning the head of the square.*

National Museum (Národní Muzeum)

This museum—closed for renovation through 2014—stands grandly at the top of Wenceslas Square. While its collection is dull (a skippable assemblage of Czech fossils and animals), the interior is richly decorated in the Czech Revival Neo-Renaissance style that heralded the

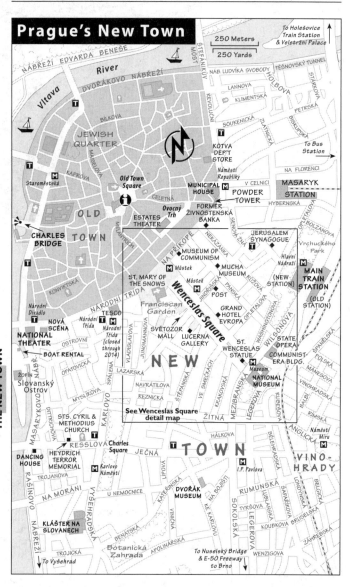

19th-century rebirth of the Czech nation. A grand, purpose-built national museum made perfect sense in 19th-century Europe. As different political powers wrangled over territory, some groups would end up with countries and others would become "nations without states." During this tumultuous time, people did their best to prove their distinctive identities and affirm their right to exist. The light-colored patches in the museum's columns fill holes where

Soviet bullets hit during the crackdown against the 1968 Prague Spring uprising. Masons—defying their communist bosses, who wanted the damage to be forgotten—showed their Czech spirit by intentionally mismatching their patches.

The nearby Metro stop (Muzeum) is the crossing point of two Metro lines built with Russian know-how in the 1970s.

• *To the left of the National Museum (as you face it) is a...*

Communist-Era Building

Because there was almost no WWII bombing in the city center, the communists had little opportunity to rebuild and scar Prague's

cityscape with their brutal "aesthetics" (as they did in heavily bombed cities such as Dresden and Warsaw). This structure, a rare exception, housed the rubber-stamp Czechoslovak Parliament back when it voted with Moscow. A Socialist Realist statue showing triumphant workers still stands at its base.

Between 1994 and 2008, this building was home to Radio Free Europe. After communism fell, RFE lost some of its funding and could no longer afford its Munich headquarters. In gratitude for its broadcasts—which had kept the people of Eastern Europe in touch with real news—the Czech government offered this building to RFE for 1 Kč a year. But as RFE energetically beamed its American message deep into the Muslim world from here, it drew attention—and threats—from Al-Qaeda. In 2009, RFE moved to a new fortress-like headquarters at an easier-to-defend locale farther from the center.

Today, this building is run by the National Museum and hosts temporary exhibits.

• *In front of the National Museum is the equestrian...*

St. Wenceslas Statue

Wenceslas (Václav) is the "good king" of Christmas-carol fame. He was the wise and benevolent 10th-century Duke of Bohemia. A rare example of a well-educated and literate ruler, King Wenceslas I was credited by his people for Christianizing his nation and lifting the culture. He astutely allied the Czechs with Saxony, rather than Bavaria, giving the Czechs a vote when

THE NEW TOWN

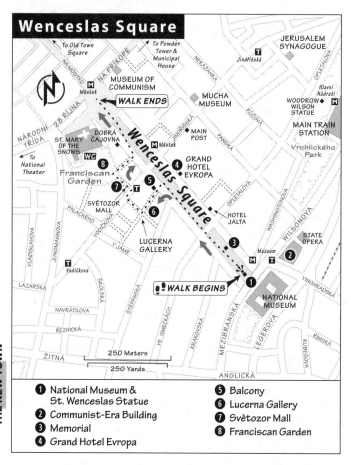

Wenceslas Square

① National Museum &
St. Wenceslas Statue
② Communist-Era Building
③ Memorial
④ Grand Hotel Evropa
⑤ Balcony
⑥ Lucerna Gallery
⑦ Světozor Mall
⑧ Franciscan Garden

THE NEW TOWN

the Holy Roman Emperor was selected (and therefore more political clout).

After his murder in 935, Wenceslas was canonized as a saint. He became a symbol of Czech nationalism and statehood, and remains an icon of Czech unity whenever the nation has to rally. Legend has it that when the Czechs face their darkest hour, Wenceslas will come riding out of Blaník Mountain (east of Prague) with an army of knights to rescue the nation. In 1620, when Austria stripped the Czechs of their independence, many people went to Blaník Mountain to see whether it had opened up. They've done the same at other critical points in their history (in 1938, 1948, and 1968), but Wenceslas never emerged. Although the Czech Republic is now safely part of NATO and the European Union, Czechs remain realistic: If Wenceslas hasn't come out yet, the worst times must still lie ahead...

Study the statue. Wenceslas, on the horse, is surrounded by the four other Czech patron saints. Notice the focus on books. A small nation without great military power, the Czech Republic chose national heroes who enriched the culture by thinking, rather than fighting. This statue is a popular meeting point. Locals say, "I'll see you under the tail."

Take a moment at this spot to survey the square. You'll see businesspeople, families, Dumpster divers, security guards, the Pepsi generation, and students. The scene sums up the transformation of society here since 1968 and the ultimate triumph of private enterprise.

The long-term vision for the square is a matter of controversy among locals. The city plans to turn it into a long, tree-lined pedestrian mall, with trams running up and down the middle (as they once did), and to hide the busy freeway underground (currently it separates the museum from the square). This freeway originated as part of a 1970s plan by communists to connect the city with inner and outer freeway rings, while running the busiest thoroughfare into the heart of the city—but they completed only a small portion of the grandiose plan. After 1989, the project moved forward again, thanks to the aid of EU funds and a boost in local car production, as manufacturers hoped to realize the dream of a car for every person. (This project is a good illustration of how decision makers have continued the trends and policies started under the communists rather than breaking from them.)

Prague's tunnel-to-tunnel inner circle (the city's "Big Dig") is scheduled to be completed by 2016, at an astronomical price. In keeping with the current era of austerity, parts of the tunnel not already begun have been eliminated from the plan, meaning that automobiles will continue to spit their fumes on the museum's facade (the most polluted spot in the city) for decades to come.

• *Begin walking down the square. Thirty yards below the big horse is a small garden with a low-key...*

Memorial

This commemorates victims of communism such as Jan Palach. In 1969, a group of patriots decided that an act of self-immolation would stoke the fires of independence. Palach, a philosophy student who loved life—but wanted to live in freedom—set himself on fire on the steps of the National Museum for the cause of Czech independence. He died a few days later in a hospital ward. Czechs are keen on anniversaries, and huge

THE NEW TOWN

demonstrations swept the city on the 20th anniversary of Palach's death. These protests led, 10 months later, to the overthrow of the Czech communist government in 1989.

This grand square is a gallery of modern architectural styles. As you wander downhill, notice the fun mix, all post-1850: Romantic Neo-Gothic, Neo-Renaissance, and Neo-Baroque from the 19th century; Art Nouveau from about 1900; ugly Functionalism from the mid-20th century (the "form follows function" and "ornamentation is a crime" answer to Art Nouveau); Stalin Gothic from the 1950s "communist epoch" (a good example is the Hotel Jalta building, halfway downhill on the right); and the glass-and-steel buildings of the 1970s.

• *Walk a couple of blocks downhill through the real people of Prague (not tourists) to Grand Hotel Evropa, with its dazzling yellow Art Nouveau exterior and plush café interior full of tourists. Stop for a moment to consider the events of...*

November 1989

This huge square was filled every evening with more than 300,000 ecstatic Czechs and Slovaks who believed freedom was at hand. Assembled on the balcony of the building opposite Grand Hotel Evropa (look for the *Marks & Spencer* sign) were a priest, a rock star (famous for his unconventional style, which constantly unnerved the regime), Alexander Dubček (hero of the 1968 revolt), and Václav Havel (the charismatic playwright, newly released from prison, who was every freedom-loving Czech's Nelson Mandela). Through a sound system provided by the rock star, Havel's voice boomed over the gathered masses, announcing the resignation of the Politburo and the imminent freedom of the Republic of Czechoslovakia. Picture that cold November evening, with thousands of Czechs jingling their key chains in solidarity, chanting at the government, "It's time to go now!" (To quell this revolt, government tanks could have given it the Tiananmen Square treatment, which had spilled protesters' blood in China just six months earlier. Locals believe that the Soviet head of state, Mikhail Gorbachev, must have made a phone call recommending a nonviolent response.) For more on the events leading up to this climactic rally, see the sidebar on page 97.

• *Immediately opposite Grand Hotel Evropa is the Lucerna Gallery (use entry marked* Pasáz Rokoko *and walk straight in).*

Lucerna Gallery

This grand mall retains some of its Art Deco glamour from the 1930s, with shops, theaters, a ballroom in the basement, and the fine Lucerna Café upstairs. You'll see a sculpture—called **Wenceslas Riding an Upside-Down Horse**—hanging like a swing from a glass dome. David Černý, who created the statue in 1999, is one of the Czech Republic's most original contemporary artists. Always aspiring to provoke controversy, Černý has painted a menacing Russian tank pink, attached crawling babies to the rocket-like Žižkov TV tower, defecated inside the National Gallery to protest the policies of its director, and sunk a shark-like Saddam Hussein inside an aquarium. His art hoax *Entropa* was created to commemorate the Czech presidency of the European Union in 2009. But when it was unveiled in Brussels, it insulted many EU nations with its satirical symbolism (Bulgaria was represented by squat toilets, Germany consisted of twisted autobahns hinting at a swastika, and so on). The piece is now housed in a museum in Plzeň.

Inside the gallery, you'll find a **Ticketpro box office** (with a line on concerts and events, daily 9:00-20:00, 30 Kč fee), a lavish 1930s Prague cinema (under the upside-down horse, shows films in original language with Czech subtitles, 115 Kč), and the popular **Lucerna Music Bar** in the basement ('80s and '90s video parties, 100-Kč cover, from 21:00 on Fri and Sat, concerts on other nights; see listing on page 186).

Leave the mall from the side of the gallery, then cross busy Vodičkova street (with a handy tram stop) and enter **Světozor mall** (a few steps to the right). The 1930s glass window advertising Tesla, a defunct Czech radio manufacturer (not the Bay Area electric car company), lends a retro brightness to the place. The busy place in front of the sign is the **World of Fruit Bar Světozor,** every local's favorite ice-cream joint (banana-strawberry is the top choice). They also sell cakes, milkshakes, and "little breads"—delightful Czech-style open-face sandwiches (20 Kč each). Ask at the counter for an English menu.

• *Walk under the* Tesla *sign to exit the mall. To the right, a lane leads to Wenceslas Square. But first, side-trip to your left, into the peaceful...*

Franciscan Garden (Františkánská Zahrada)

Its white benches and spreading rosebushes are a universe away from the fast beat of the city, which throbs behind the buildings that surround the garden. The garden's peacefulness reflects its Franciscan origin. Enjoy its herb garden and children's playground. This is a popular place for discreet rendezvous; it's famous among locals for kicking off romances. (If you need a WC, there's one just out the far side of the garden, and another in the tiny wine bar coming up on this walk.)

Back on Wenceslas Square, if you're in the mood for a mellow hippie teahouse, consider a break at the recommended **Dobrá Čajovna** ("Good Teahouse") near the bottom of the square (#14).

The bottom of Wenceslas Square is called **Můstek,** which means "Bridge"; a bridge once crossed a moat here, allowing en-

Art Nouveau

Prague is the best Art Nouveau town in Europe, with fun fa-cades gracing streets all over the city. Art Nouveau, born in Paris, is "nouveau" because it wasn't inspired by Rome. It's neo-nothing...a fresh answer to all the revival styles of the later 19th century and an organic response to the Eiffel Tower art of the Industrial Age. The style liberated the artist in each architect. Notice the unique curves and motifs expressing original-ity on each Art Nouveau facade. Art-ists such as Alfons Mucha believed that the style should apply to all facets of daily life. They designed everything from buildings and furniture to type-faces and cigarette packs.

Prague's three top Art Nouveau architects are Jan Koula, Josef Fanta, and Osvald Polivka (whose last name sounds like the Czech word for "soup"). Think "Cola, Fanta, and Soup"—easy to re-member and a good way to impress your local friends.

Prague's Art Nouveau highlights include the facades lining the streets of the Jewish Quarter, the Jerusalem Syn-agogue, the Mucha window in St. Vitus Cathedral, and the Grand Hotel Evropa on Wenceslas Square. The top two sights for Art Nouveau fans are the Mucha Museum and the Munici-pal House.

trance into the Old Town (you can still see the original Old Town entrance down in the Metro station).

• *Your Wenceslas Square walk ends here, but there's more to see. From the bottom of the square, you can either head right, to Prague's top Art Nou-veau sights (described next) or left, toward the river and the National Theater (described later).*

Na Příkopě: Art Nouveau Prague

At the bottom of Wenceslas Square, the street running to the right is called Na Příkopě. Meaning "On the Moat," this busy boule-vard follows the line of the Old Town wall, leading to one of the wall's former gates, the Powder Tower (the black tower spire in the distance). Along the way, it passes the Museum of Communism (nestled awkwardly between the McDonalds and a casino) and two of Prague's best Art Nouveau sights: the Mucha Museum (featur-ing the work of my favorite Art Nouveau artist) and the Municipal House (with my favorite Art Nouveau interior anywhere). As you walk, look up at the parade of fine facades.

City tour buses (see page 55) leave from along this street,

which offers plenty of shopping temptations (including these modern malls: Slovanský Dům at Na Příkopě 22 and Černá Růže at Na Příkopě 12, next door to Mosers, which has a crystal showroom upstairs).

• *Start strolling up Na Příkopě. Turn right at Panská to reach the...*

▲▲Mucha Museum (Muchovo Museum)

This enjoyable little museum features a small selection of the insistently likeable art of Alfons Mucha (MOO-kah, 1860-1939), a founding father of the Art Nouveau movement. See the crucifixion scene he painted as an eight-year-old boy. Read how his popular posters, filled with Czech symbols and expressing his people's ideals and aspirations, were patriotic banners that aroused the national spirit. Enjoy decorative posters from his years in Paris, including his celebrated posters for the French actress Sarah Bernhardt. And check out the photographs of his models (to get the most from his sessions with models, he photographed them from all angles). Partly overseen by Mucha's grandson, the museum is two blocks off Wenceslas Square, and its collection is displayed on one comfortable floor.

The included 30-minute video is worthwhile (in English, generally at the top and bottom of each hour—check the starting time); it describes the main project of Mucha's life—the *Slav Epic,* housed across town at Veletržní Palace. (For more about Mucha and his masterpiece, see the Beyond the Core chapter.)

Cost and Hours: 180 Kč, daily 10:00-18:00, good English descriptions, Panská 7, tel. 224-233-355, www.mucha.cz.

• *Backtrack to Na Příkopě and turn right. Continue a couple blocks to the...*

▲▲Municipal House (Obecní Dům)

The Municipal House, which celebrated its centennial birthday in 2011, is the "pearl of Czech Art Nouveau." Stand in front and study the *Homage to Prague* mosaic on the building's striking facade. Featuring a goddess-like Praha presiding over a land of peace and high culture, the image stoked cultural pride and nationalist sentiment.

The building (1905-1911) is Neo-Baroque with a dusting of Art Nouveau. The cultural and artistic leaders who financed it wanted a ceremonial palace to reinforce self-awareness of the Czech nation. Built under Catholic Habsburg rule, it was drenched in patriotic Czech themes to emphasize how the Protestant Czechs were a distinct culture. In 1918, Czechoslovakia's independence was declared from the building's balcony.

While the exterior is impressive, the highlight is inside—arguably Europe's finest

Art Nouveau interior. The Municipal House features Prague's largest concert hall, a recommended Art Nouveau café (Kavárna Obecní Dům), and two other restaurants. Downstairs is a gift shop offering a look at delightful Art Nouveau jewelry (and a handy WC). While you can poke around its entrance halls (daily 10:00-18:00) or wander around the lobby of the concert hall, to really appreciate the building you must attend a concert or take a tour.

Tours: Daily one-hour tours give you a guided look at all the sumptuous halls and banquet rooms (English-only, 290 Kč, usually 3/day, leaving between 11:00 and 17:00). Tours are limited to 35 people so buy your ticket as soon as you can from the ground-floor shop where tours depart (and pay 55 Kč extra to take photos).

Information: Tel. 222-002-101, www.obecnidum.cz.

Concerts: Performances are held regularly in the lavish Smetana Hall (see the schedule at www.obecnidum.cz/web/en/programme). Note that many concerts brag they are held in the Municipal House, but are performed in a smaller, less impressive hall in the same building.

Powder Tower

Next to the Municipal House, the big, black Powder Tower was the Gothic gate of the town wall, built to house the city's gunpowder. The interior is not worth touring, but the decoration on the outside of the tower is some of the best 15th-century sculpture in town. This is the only surviving bit of the wall that was built to defend the city in the 1400s. Look at your city map and conceptualize medieval Prague's smart design. The city was encircled by the river and its wall (now a main street), which arced from a bend in the river. The only  river crossing back then was the fortified Charles Bridge. The road from Vienna arrived here at the foot of the Powder Tower—it was the city's formal front door. When Empress Maria Theresa was crowned the Queen of Bohemia here, she came down that road and through this gate. Go back 500 years and look up at the impressive welcoming committee, reminding all of the hierarchy of our mortal existence: from artisans flanking Prague's coat of arms, up to a pair of Czech kings with seals of alliance with neighboring regions, and finally to angels heralding the heavenly zone with Saints Peter and Paul flanking Jesus.

• *OK, got it...let's go in. Pass through the tower to reach commercial and touristy Celetná Street, which leads directly to the Old Town Square (see page 60). Or consider a side-trip to visit another of Prague's Art Nouveau buildings, the...*

Prague: Pre-1989

It's hard to imagine the gray and bleak Prague of the communist era. Before 1989, the city was a wistful jumble of unrealized possibility. Cobbled lanes were shadowed by decrepit, crusty buildings. Timbers—strung across the lanes like laundry lines—held crumbling buildings apart. Consumer goods were plain and uniform, stacked like Legos on thin shelves in shops where customers waited in line for a tin of pineapple or a bottle of ersatz Coke. The Charles Bridge and its statues were black with soot, and there was no commerce, except for a few shady characters trying to change money. Hotels had two price schedules: one for people from the Warsaw Pact nations, and another (6-8 times more expensive) for capitalists. This made the run-down, Soviet-style hotels as expensive as fine Western ones. At the train station, frightened but desperate folks would meet arriving foreigners and offer to rent them a room in their apartment, hoping to earn enough Western cash to buy batteries or Levi's at one of the hard-currency stores.

Jerusalem Synagogue (Jeruzalémské Synagóga)

This colorful synagogue, also known as the Jubilee Synagogue, is a fascinating combination of Moorish Renaissance and Viennese Art Nouveau styles. It was built from 1905 to 1906 in commemoration of the first 50 years of Franz Josef's liberal, relatively Jewish-friendly rule. Recently restored, still serving the Prague Jewish community, and sparsely visited, this is the most contemplative as well as visually stunning of Prague's synagogues.

Cost and Hours: 80 Kč, April-Oct Sun-Fri 13:00-17:00, closed Sat, closed in winter and on Jewish holidays, between Powder Tower and Main Train Station at Jeruzalémská 7, tel. 222-319-002, www.synagogue.cz/Jerusalem.

Národní Třída: Communist Prague

From Můstek at the bottom of Wenceslas Square, you can head west on Národní Třída (in the opposite direction from Na Příkopě and the Art Nouveau sights) for an interesting stroll through urban Prague to the National Theater and the Vltava River. But first, consider dropping into the Museum of Communism, a few steps down Na Příkopě (on the right).

▲▲Museum of Communism (Muzeum Komunismu)

This museum traces the story of communism in Prague: the origin, dream, reality, and nightmare; the cult of personality; and, finally, the Velvet Revolution—all thoughtfully described in English. Along the way, it gives a fascinating review of the Czech Republic's 40-year stint with Soviet economics, "in all its dreariness and puffed-up glory." You'll find propaganda posters, busts of communist All-Stars (Marx, Lenin, Stalin), and a photograph of the massive stone Stalin that overlooked Prague until 1962.

Slices of communist life are re-created here (complete with period music to stir your soul), from a bland store counter to a typical classroom, with textbooks using Russia's Cyrillic alphabet—no longer studied—and a poem on the chalkboard that extols the virtues of the tractor. Don't miss the Jan Palach exhibit and the 20-minute video (plays continuously, English subtitles) that shows how the Czech people chafed under the big Red yoke from 1969 through 1989.

Cost and Hours: 190 Kč, daily 9:00-21:00, Na Příkopě 10, above a McDonald's and next to a casino—Lenin is turning over in his Red Square mausoleum, tel. 224-212-966, www.muzeum-komunismu.cz.

Národní Třída and the Velvet Revolution

Národní Třída (National Street) is where you feel the pulse of the modern city. The street, which connects Wenceslas Square with the National Theater and the river, is a busy thoroughfare running through the heart of urban Prague. In 1989, this unassuming boulevard played host to the first salvo of a Velvet Revolution that would topple the communist regime.

Make your way down Národní Třída until you hit the tram tracks (just beyond the Tesco department store). On the left, look for the photo of Bill Clinton playing saxophone, with Václav Havel on the side (this is the entrance to **Reduta,** Prague's best jazz club—see page 186; next door are two recommended eateries, **Café Louvre** and **Le Patio**). Just beyond that, you'll come to a short corridor with white arches. Inside this arcade is a simple **memorial** to the hundreds of students injured here by the police in the Velvet Revolution, which took place on November 17, 1989. The monument's open hands and peace signs are a reminder that the terrified students corralled in here by the burly "Red Berets" that night were unarmed and entirely nonviolent.

Sights near the Vltava River

I've listed these sights from north to south, beginning at the grand, Neo-Renaissance National Theater, which is five blocks south of the Charles Bridge and stands along the riverbank at the end of Národní Třída.

The Velvet Revolution of 1989

On the afternoon of November 17, 1989, 30,000 students gathered in Prague's New Town to commemorate the 50th anniversary of the suppression of student protests by the Nazis, which had led to the closing of Czech universities through the end of World War II. The 1989 demonstration—initially planned by the Communist Youth as a celebration of the communist victory over fascism—spontaneously turned into a protest *against* the communist regime. "You are just like the Nazis!" shouted the students. The demonstration was supposed to end in the National Cemetery at Vyšehrad (the hill just south of the New Town). But when the planned events concluded in Vyšehrad, the students, making history, decided to march on toward Wenceslas Square.

As they worked their way north along the Vltava River toward the New Town's main square, the students were careful to keep their demonstration peaceful. Any hint of violence, the demonstrators knew, would incite brutal police retaliation. Instead, as the evening went on, the absence of police became conspicuous. (In the 1980s, the police never missed a chance to participate in any demonstration...preferably outnumbering the demonstrators.) At about 20:00, as the students marched down this very stretch of street toward Wenceslas Square, three rows of policemen suddenly blocked the demonstration at the corner of Národní and Spálená streets. A few minutes later, military vehicles with fences on their bumpers (having crossed the bridge by the National Theater) appeared behind the marching students. This new set of cops compressed the demonstrators into the stretch of Národní Třída between Voršilská and Spálená. The end of Mikulandská street was also blocked, and policemen were hiding inside every house entry. The students were trapped.

At 21:30, the "Red Berets" (a special anti-riot commando force known for its brutality) arrived. The Red Berets lined up on both sides of this corridor. To get out, the trapped students had to run through the passageway as they were beaten from the left and right. Police trucks ferried captured students around the corner to the police headquarters (on Bartolomějská) for interrogation.

The next day, university students throughout Czechoslovakia decided to strike. Actors from theaters in Prague and Bratislava joined the student protest. Two days later, the students' parents—shocked by the attacks on their children—marched into Wenceslas Square. Sparked by the events of November 17, 1989, the wave of peaceful demonstrations ended later that year on December 29, with the election of Václav Havel as the president of a free Czechoslovakia.

The Assassination of Reinhard Heydrich

In September 1941, Reinhard Heydrich, the SS second-in-command, Hitler's personal favorite, and one of the masterminds behind the Holocaust, volunteered to replace the ineffective Otto Neurath as the governor of the occupied Czech lands. Heydrich acutely understood the role that the Nazi-established Protectorate of Bohemia and Moravia played in the German war effort, as the heavily industrialized territory was home to two of Europe's largest armaments factories—one in Plzeň, the other in Brno.

As a wave of sabotage threatened to disrupt supply lines to the eastern front, a determined Heydrich arrived in Prague, armed with a sinister carrot-and-stick strategy. While increasing worker benefits—bribing the Czech proletariat with meat, shoes, and spa vacations—he also violently lashed out against any hint of resistance or illegal economic activity.

At the same time, the Czechoslovak government-in-exile was suffering a crisis of legitimacy in Britain's eyes. Following the British signing of the Munich Pact (an act of appeasement that would annex Czechoslovakia's Sudetenland area to the Nazis), thousands of Czechs and Slovaks went abroad to fight, and few of those left in the occupied lands were cut out for underground resistance. Moreover, rather than occupying Czechoslovakia, the Nazis were able to rule through a cabinet of willing Czech helpers. Edvard Beneš, the exiled prime minister, appeared to the Allies to be a self-proclaimed spokesperson for a complicit nation.

It was under these circumstances that two paratroopers, Jozef Gabčík and Jan Kubiš, were chosen by British Special Operations and trained in Scotland for a secret and—as they were made to understand from the start—potentially suicidal mission to eliminate Heydrich.

On the morning of May 27, 1942, Heydrich was coming down Kobylisy hill on his daily commute. Just as the unaccompanied open car slowed down at a hairpin turn, Gabčík jumped in front of the car and pointed his Sten machine gun at Heydrich, and pulled the trigger. But nothing happened (the gun probably jammed). Heydrich, ordering his driver to stop, pulled out his revolver. At

National Theater (Národní Divadlo)

Opened in 1883 with Smetana's opera *Libuše,* this theater was the first truly Czech venue in Prague. From the very start, it was nicknamed the "Cradle of Czech Culture." The building is a key symbol of the Czech national revival that began in the late 18th century. In 1800, "Prag" was predominantly German. The Industrial Revolution brought Czechs from the countryside

that moment, Kubiš, coming in from behind, threw a handmade grenade that missed and exploded outside the car. But the explosion was enough to wound Heydrich, who was transported to a nearby hospital, where he died a few days later. At his funeral—the Nazis' most elaborate funeral ceremony ever—Hitler appeared genuinely distressed, and Heydrich was eulogized as the model for all SS men.

The Nazi response in the Protectorate was brutal. Martial law was declared, two villages were summarily razed to the ground, and in the ensuing months, 5,000 individuals were executed. A reward was announced for tips leading to the capture of the assassins. Karel Čurda, a member of another paratrooper unit, betrayed his comrades. On June 18, at 4:15 in the morning, the Gestapo surrounded the Sts. Cyril and Methodius Church on Resslova street, where the two paratroopers were hiding. After a two-hour battle, Kubiš, on guard in the nave of the church, was killed along with two other defenders. Gabčík and three other paratroopers committed suicide in the crypt below.

For years, feelings about the Heydrich assassination were mixed. Many regretted the lives lost, and some felt it effectively wiped out Czech underground resistance. The fact that the operation stemmed from British (rather than native or Soviet) roots also became problematic following the communist takeover. The act was officially depicted as shortsighted and symbolic.

Today, historians praise the sacrifice. Days after the assassination, the British government revoked its signature on the Munich Pact, recognizing Czechoslovakia's prewar boundaries; the French followed two months later. Heydrich—whose elimination was one of the most significant acts of resistance in occupied Europe—remains the highest-ranked Nazi official killed while in office. During anniversaries, Czech politicians cover the pavement outside the crypt with wreaths and flowers. And in 2009, the spot of Heydrich's assassination (next to the freeway to Terezín, in the northern part of town) was finally marked with a thoughtful monument.

THE NEW TOWN

into the city, their new urban identity defined by patriotic teachers and priests. By 1883, most of the city spoke Czech, and the opening of this theater represented the birth of the modern Czech nation. It remains an important national icon: The state annually pours more subsidies into this theater than into all of Czech film production. It's the most beautiful venue in town for opera and ballet, often with world-class singers (for more details on performances, see page 184).

Next door (just inland, on Národní Třída) is the boxy, glassy facade of the **Nová Scéna.** This "New National Theater" building, dating from 1983 (the 100th anniversary of the original National Theater building), reflects the bold and stark communist aesthetic.

Across the street from the National Theater is the former haunt of Prague's intelligentsia, the recommended **Kavárna Slavia,** a Viennese-style coffee house that is fine for a meal or drink with a view of the river.

• *Just south of the National Theater, in the Vltava you'll find...*

Prague's Islands

From the National Theater, the Bridge of Legions (Most Legií) leads across the island called **Střelecký Ostrov.** Covered with chestnut trees, this island boasts Prague's best beach (on the sandy tip that points north to Charles Bridge). You might see a fisherman pulling trout out of a river that's now much cleaner than it used to be. Bring a swimsuit and take a dip just a stone's throw from Europe's most beloved bridge. In summer, the island hosts open-air movies (most in English or with English subtitles, nightly mid-July-early Sept at about 21:00, www.strelak.cz).

In the mood for boating instead of swimming? On the next island up, **Slovanský Ostrov,** you can rent a boat (40 Kč/hour for rowboats, 60 Kč/hour for paddleboats, bring a picture ID as deposit). A lazy hour paddling around Střelecký Ostrov—or just floating sleepily in the middle of the river surrounded by this great city's architectural splendor—is a delightful experience on a sunny day. It's cheap, easy fun (and it's good for you).

• *A 10-minute walk (or one stop on tram #17) south from the National Theater, beyond the islands, is Jirásek Bridge (Jiráskův Most), where you'll find the...*

Dancing House (Tančící Dům)

If ever a building could get your toes tapping, it would be this one, nicknamed "Fred and Ginger" by American architecture buffs. This metallic samba is the work of Frank Gehry (who designed the equally striking Guggenheim Museum in Bilbao, Spain, and Seattle's Experience Music Project). Eight-legged Ginger's wispy dress and Fred's metal mesh head are easy to spot. Some Czechs prefer to think that the two "figures" represent the nation's greatest 20th-century heroes, Jozef Gabčík and Jan Kubiš (see the sidebar on the previous two pages).

The building's top-floor restaurant, **Céleste,** is a fine place for a fancy French meal. Whether you go up for lunch (reasonable, 12:00-14:30), a drink (16:00-18:00), or an expensive dinner, you'll be a louse in the Gehry haircut (tel. 221-984-160).

• *Two blocks up Resslova street is the Sts. Cyril and Methodius Church, which contains in its crypt the...*

▲National Memorial to the Heroes of the Heydrich Terror (Národní Památník Hrdinů Heydrichiády)

In 1942, WWII paratroopers Jozef Gabčík and Jan Kubiš assassinated the SS second-in-command Reinhard Heydrich, who controlled the Nazi-occupied Czech lands and was one of the main architects of the Holocaust (see sidebar). In the weeks following his assassination, the two paratroopers hid, along with other freedom fighters, in the crypt of the Greek Orthodox Sts. Cyril and Methodius Church on Resslova street. Today, a modest exhibition in the church's crypt retells their story, along with the history of the Czech resistance movement. Outside, notice the small memorial, including bullet holes, plaque, and flowers on the street. Around the corner is the entry into the museum and the crypt.

Cost and Hours: 75 Kč, full history explained in small 25-Kč booklet, Tue-Sun 9:00-17:00, closed Mon, 2 blocks up from the Dancing House at Resslova 9A, tel. 224-916-100.

• *Farther up Resslova street is...*

Charles Square (Karlovo Náměstí)

Prague's largest square is covered by lawns, trees, and statues of Czech writers. It's a quiet antidote to the bustling Wenceslas and Old Town squares. The Gothic New Town Hall at the top-left corner of the square has excellent views and labeled panoramic photographs that help you orient yourself. The little parlor across the street has some of the best gelato in town.

THE NEW TOWN

THE LITTLE QUARTER

Malá Strana

This charming neighborhood, huddled under the castle on the west bank of the river, is low on blockbuster sights but high on ambience. The most enjoyable approach from the Old Town is across the Charles Bridge. From the end of the bridge (TI in tower), Mostecká street leads two blocks up to the Little Quarter Square (Malostranské Náměstí) and the huge Church of St. Nicholas. But before you head up there, consider a detour to Kampa Island.

Between Charles Bridge and Little Quarter Square

Kampa Island

One hundred yards from the castle end of the Charles Bridge, stairs on the left lead down to the main square of Kampa Island (mostly created from the rubble of the Little Quarter, which was destroyed in a 1540 fire). The island features relaxing pubs, a breezy park, hippies, lovers, a fine contemporary art gallery, and river access. From the main square, Hroznová lane (on the right) winds around to a little bridge. The high-water mark at the end of the bridge dates from 1890. The **old water wheel** is the last survivor of many mills that once lined the canal here. Each mill had its own protective water spirit *(vodník)*. The padlocks adorning the bridge are the scourge of romantic spots throughout Europe these days, popular with not-very-creative Romeos who think that clinching a lock onto something (mill, bridge, whatever) proves their enduring love.

• Fifty yards beyond the bridge (on the right, under the trees) is the...

Lennon Wall (Lennonova Zeď)

While V. I. Lenin's ideas hung like a water-soaked trench coat upon the Czech people, rock singer John Lennon's ideas gave many locals hope and a vision. When Lennon was killed in 1980, a large wall was spontaneously covered with memorial graffiti. Night after night, the police would paint over the "All You Need Is Love" and "Imagine" graffiti. And day after day, it would reappear. Until independence came in 1989, travelers, freedom lovers, and local hippies gathered here. Silly as it might seem, this wall is remembered as a place that gave hope to locals craving freedom. Even today, while the tension and danger associated with this wall are gone, people come here to imagine. *"John žije"* is Czech for "John lives."

• From here, continue up to the Little Quarter Square.

On or near Little Quarter Square

The focal point of this neighborhood, the Little Quarter Square (Malostranské Náměstí) is dominated by the huge Church of St. Nicholas. Note that there's a handy Via Musica ticket office across from the church (on the uphill side).

Church of St. Nicholas (Kostel Sv. Mikuláše)

When the Jesuits came to Prague, they found the perfect piece of real estate for their church and its associated school—right on

Little Quarter Square. The church (built 1703-1760) is the best example of High Baroque in town.

Cost and Hours: 70 Kč, daily 9:00-17:00, until 16:00 Nov-Feb, opens at 8:30 for prayer.

Visiting the Church: The church's interior is giddy with curves and illusions. Stand directly under the tallest dome and look up. Spin slowly around, greeting four giant statues—the fathers of the Eastern Church. Pan up and see the earthly world merging with heaven above.

The **altar** features a lavish gold-plated Nicholas, flanked by the two top Jesuits: the founder, St. Ignatius Loyola, and his missionary follower, St. Francis Xavier.

Climb up the **gallery** through the staircase in the left transept

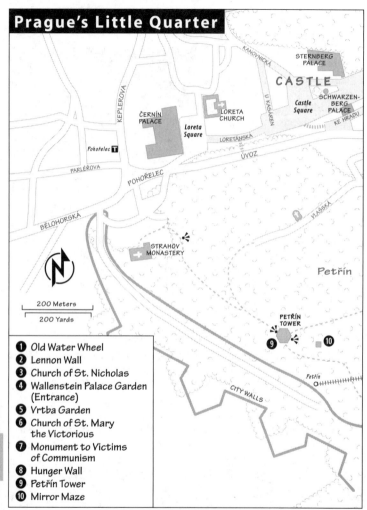

Prague's Little Quarter

CASTLE

STERNBERG PALACE

SCHWARZEN-BERG PALACE

Castle Square

KE HRADU

ČERNÍN PALACE

LORETA CHURCH

Loreta Square

U KASÁREN

KANOVNICKÁ

KEPLEROVA

Pohořelec T

LORETÁNSKÁ

ÚVOZ

PARLÉŘOVA

POHOŘELEC

VLAŠSKÁ

BĚLOHORSKÁ

STRAHOV MONASTERY

Petřín

200 Meters
200 Yards

PETŘÍN TOWER

9

10

Petřín

CITY WALLS

1 Old Water Wheel
2 Lennon Wall
3 Church of St. Nicholas
4 Wallenstein Palace Garden (Entrance)
5 Vrtba Garden
6 Church of St. Mary the Victorious
7 Monument to Victims of Communism
8 Hunger Wall
9 Petřín Tower
10 Mirror Maze

THE LITTLE QUARTER

for a close-up look at a collection of large canvases and illusion-ary frescoes by Karel Škréta, who is considered the greatest Czech Baroque painter. Notice that at first glance the canvases are utterly dark, but as sunbeams shine through the window, various parts of the painting brighten up. Like a looking glass, the image reflects the light, creating a play of light and dark. This painting technique represents a central Baroque belief: The world is full of darkness, and the only hope that makes it come alive emanates from God. The church walls seem to nearly fuse with the sky, suggesting that happenings on earth are closely connected to heaven.

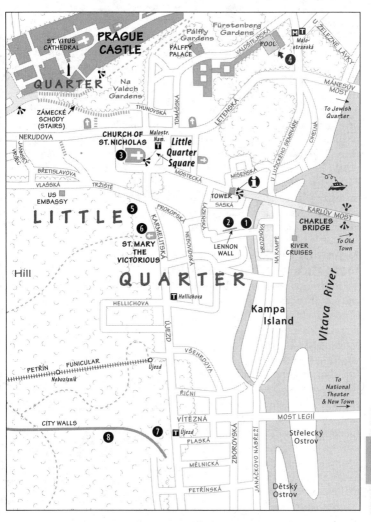

Tower Climb: For a good look at the city and the church's 250-foot dome, climb 215 steps up the bell tower (50 Kč, April-Oct daily 10:00-18:00, closed Nov-March, tower entrance is outside the right transept).

Concerts: The church is also an evening concert venue; tickets are usually on sale at the door (490 Kč, generally nightly at 18:00 except Tue, www.stnicholas.cz).

• *From here, you can hike 10 minutes uphill to the castle (and 5 more minutes to the Strahov Monastery). For information on these sights, see the next chapter. If you're walking up to the castle, consider going via...*

Nerudova Street

This steep, cobbled street, leading from Little Quarter Square to the castle, is named for Jan Neruda, a gifted 19th-century journalist (and somewhat less-talented fiction writer). It's lined with old buildings still sporting the characteristic doorway signs (such as the lion, three violinists, house of the golden suns) that once served as street addresses. The surviving signs are carefully restored and protected by law. They represent the family name, the occupation, or the various passions of the people who once inhabited the houses. (If you were to replace your house number with a symbol, what would it be?) In the 1770s, in order to collect taxes more effectively, Habsburg empress Maria Theresa decreed that numbers be used instead of these quaint house names. This neighborhood is filled with old noble palaces, now generally used as foreign embassies and as offices of the Czech Parliament.

North of Little Quarter Square, near Malostranská Metro Station

Twenty yards from the Malostranská Metro station (go left from the top of the escalator and turn right when you get outside), a few blocks north of Little Quarter Square, is a lovely palace and garden. If you want to reach Little Quarter Square from here, follow Valdštejnská street.

Wallenstein Palace Garden (Valdštejnská Palac Zahrada)

Of the neighborhood's many impressive palace gardens, this is by far the largest and most beautiful. The complex—consisting of a palace (generally closed) and the surrounding garden (generally open)—was commissioned during the Thirty Years' War by the Habsburg general and Czech nobleman Albrecht z Valdštejna (or, in German, Albrecht von Wallenstein). It's a testimony to how war can be such a great business for the unscrupulous. For 16 years (1618-1634), the mercenary Albrecht conspired with all sides involved in the war. He was the banker of the Czech Estates Uprising until he ran off to Vienna with the money to join the Habsburgs. Plundering territories in the name of the Catholic faith, Albrecht followed his own simple rule: half for the emperor, half for me. When Habsburg favors waned, Albrecht secretly negotiated with the Swedes. When desperate Habsburgs put him in charge of their armies once again, he continued to play both sides. Finally, somebody had enough: Albrecht was murdered in his bedroom in 1634.

Cost and Hours: Garden—free; April-Oct Mon-Fri 7:30-

18:00, Sat-Sun 10:00-18:00, daily until 19:00 June-Sept; closed Nov-March. Palace—usually closed to the public.

Visiting the Palace Garden: The inconspicuous entry to the palace's Wallenstein Garden is by the Malostranská Metro station. The garden, renovated in the late 1990s, features a large pool surrounded by peacocks. The statues that line the central walkway (inspired by Greek mythology) were created by the Danish artist Adriaen de Vries—arguably the best Renaissance sculptor outside of Italy. Notice the elegant classical shapes, a sharp contrast to the chubbiness of the Baroque figures on the Charles Bridge and elsewhere in the city. The original statues were stolen by invading Swedish armies in 1648 and are still in Sweden; the present replicas were cast in the early 1900s.

The Renaissance garden and the palace were built by Italian architects, just like most of the Little Quarter. The theatrical loggia—the *sala terena*—is a stage for drama and music inspired by Greek amphitheaters. Notice the unusual pairing of columns—at the time, a trendy invention of the Italian architect Andrea Palladio. Inside, the gory depictions of the Trojan War tell you about the taste and character of the owner. (A handy WC is to the left of the amphitheater.) The bizarre grotto wall farther on the left was an expression of an uncertain age. It creates the illusion of caves and holes, stalagmites and stalactites, interspersed with partially hidden stone goblins, frogs, and snakes (count how many you can find). The wall continues into a cage with live owls, completing the transition from dead to living nature. The twisted cries of the owls deepen the surreal sensation of the place.

Exit through the door in the right corner of the garden by the *sala terena*. You'll pass into a small courtyard surrounded by what once was the residential part of the palace. Today, the upper chamber of the Czech Parliament meets inside.

South of Little Quarter Square, to Petřín Hill

The following sights lie along Karmelitská street, which leads south (along the tram tracks) from Little Quarter Square.

Vrtba Garden (Vrtbovská Zahrada)

This terraced Baroque garden makes for an interesting comparison to the Renaissance garden at Wallenstein Palace, described earlier.

Cost and Hours: 60 Kč, April-Oct 10:00-18:00, closed Nov-March, just south of Little Quarter Square at Karmelitská 25, www.vrtbovska.cz.

• *Continue past the gardens to the...*

Church of St. Mary the Victorious
(Kostel Panny Marie Vítězné)

This otherwise ordinary Carmelite church displays Prague's most worshipped treasure, the Infant of Prague (Pražské Jezulátko).

Jára Cimrman: Czech Genius

"I am such a complete atheist that I am afraid God will punish me." Such is the pithy wisdom of Jára Cimrman, the man overwhelmingly voted the "Greatest Czech of All Time" in a 2005 national poll. Who is Jára Cimrman? A philosopher? An explorer? An inventor? He is all these things, yes, and much more.

Born in the mid-19th century to a Czech tailor of Jewish descent and an Austrian actress, Cimrman studied in Vienna before starting off on his journeys around the world. He traversed the Atlantic in a steamboat he designed himself, taught drama to peasants in Peru, and drifted across the Arctic Sea on an iceberg. Other astounding feats soon followed. Cimrman was the first to come within 20 feet of the North Pole. He was the first to invent the lightbulb (unfortunately, Edison beat him to the patent office by five minutes). It was he who suggested to the Americans the idea for a Panama Canal, though, as usual, he was never credited. Indeed, Cimrman surreptitiously advised many of the world's greats: Eiffel on his tower, Einstein on his theories of relativity, Chekhov on his plays. ("You can't just have *two* sisters," Cimrman told the playwright. "How about three?") In 1886, long before the world knew of Sartre or Camus, Cimrman was writing tracts such as *The Essence of the Existence,* which would become the foundation for his philosophy of "Cimrmanism," also known as "nonexistentialism." (Its central premise: "Existence cannot not exist.")

This man of unmatched genius would have won the honor of "Greatest Czech of All Time" if not for the bureaucratic narrowmindedness of the poll's sponsors, who had a single objection to Cimrman's candidacy: He's not real. Jára Cimrman is the brainchild of two Czech humorists—Zdeněk Svěrák and Jiří Šebánek—who brought their patriotic Renaissance Man to life in 1967 in a satirical radio play. So, even though Cimrman handily won the initial balloting in January 2005, Czech TV officials—blatantly biased against his nonexistentialism—refused to let him into the final rounds of the competition.

How should we interpret the fact that the Czechs would rather choose a fictional character as their greatest countryman

Kneel at the banister in front of the tiny lost-in-gilded-Baroque altar, and find the prayer in your language (of the 13 in the folder). Brought to Czech lands during the Habsburg era by a Spanish noblewoman who came to marry a Czech nobleman, the Infant has become a focus of worship and miracle tales in Prague and Spanish-speaking countries. South Americans come on pilgrimage to Prague just to see this one statue. An exhibit upstairs shows tiny embroidered robes given to the Infant, including ones from Habsburg Empress Maria Theresa of Austria (1754) and the country of Vietnam (1958), as well as a video showing a nun lovingly dressing the doll-like sculpture.

over any of their flesh-and-blood national heroes—say, Charles IV (the 14th-century Holy Roman Emperor who established Prague as the cultural and intellectual capital of Europe), Jan Hus (the 15th-century religious reformer who challenged the legitimacy of the Catholic Church), Comenius (the 17th-century educator and writer, considered one of the fathers of modern education), or Martina Navrátilová (someone who plays a sport with bright green balls)? The more cynically inclined—many Czechs among them—might point out that the Czech people have largely stayed behind their mountains for the past millennia, with little interest in, or influence on, happenings elsewhere in the world. Perhaps Cimrman is so beloved because he embodies that most prickly of ironies: a Czech who was greater than all the world's greats, but who for some hiccup of chance has never been recognized for his achievements.

I like to think that the vote for Cimrman says something about the country's rousing enthusiasm for blowing raspberries in the face of authority. Throughout its history—from the times of the Czech kings who used crafty diplomacy to keep the German menace at bay, to the days of Jan Hus and his questioning of the very legitimacy of any ruler's power, to the flashes of anticommunist revolt that at last sparked the Velvet Revolution in 1989—the Czechs have maintained a healthy disrespect for those who would tell them what is best or how to live their lives. Other countries soberly choose their "Greatest" from musty tomes of history, but the Czechs won't play this silly game. Their vote for a fictional personage, says Cimrman's co-creator Svěrák, shows two things about the Czech nation: "That it is skeptical about those who are major figures and those who are supposedly the 'Greatest.' And that the only certainty that has saved the nation many times throughout history is its humor."

Cimrman would agree. A man of greatness, he was always a bit skeptical of those who saw themselves as great, or who marched forward under the banner of greatness. As Cimrman liked to say, "There are moments when optimists should be shot."

Cost and Hours: Free, Mon-Sat 9:30-17:30, Sun 13:00-18:00, English-language Mass Sun at 12:00, Karmelitská 9, www.pragjesu.info.

• *Continue a few more blocks down Karmelitská to the south end of the Little Quarter (roughly where the street, now called Újezd, intersects with Vítězná). Here you find yourself at the base of...*

▲Petřín Hill (Petřínské Sady)

This hill, topped by a replica of the Eiffel Tower, features several unusual sights.

Monument to Victims of Communism (Pomník Obětem Komunismu)

The sculptural figures of this poignant memorial, representing victims of the totalitarian regime, gradually atrophy as they range up the hillside steps. They do not die but slowly disappear, one limb at a time. The statistics inscribed on the steps say it all: From 1948 until 1989, in Czechoslovakia alone, 205,486 people were imprisoned, 248 were executed, 4,500 died in prison, 327 were shot attempting to cross the border, and 170,938 left the country. For further information, see the "Czechs After Communism" sidebar on page 324.

• *To the left of the monument is the...*

Hunger Wall (Hladová Zed')

This medieval defense wall was Charles IV's 14th-century equivalent of FDR's work-for-food projects.

• *On the right (50 yards away) is the base of a handy **funicular**—hop on to reach Petřín Tower (uses tram/Metro ticket, runs daily every 10-15 minutes 8:00-22:00).*

Summit and Tower

The summit of Petřín Hill is considered the best place in Prague to take your date for a romantic city view. Built for an exhibition in 1891, the 200-foot-tall **Petřín Tower** is one-fifth the height of its Parisian big brother, which was built two years earlier. But, thanks to this hill, the top of the tower sits at the same elevation as the real Eiffel Tower. Climbing the 400 steps rewards you with amazing views of the city. Czech wives drag their men to Petřín Hill each May Day to reaffirm their love with a kiss under a blooming sour-cherry tree.

Cost and Hours: 105 Kč, daily 10:00-22:00, shorter hours off-season; the mirror maze next door is nothing special, but fun to wander through quickly since you're already here—75 Kč, daily 10:00-22:00, shorter hours off-season.

• *To the left of the tower as you face Prague Castle, stairs lead down to a path that swirls left along the hill's contour and takes you directly to the Strahov Monastery, described in the next chapter.*

THE LITTLE QUARTER

THE CASTLE QUARTER

Hradčany

Looming above Prague, dominating its skyline, is the Castle Quarter. Prague Castle and its surrounding sights are packed with Czech history, as well as with tourists. In addition to the castle, I enjoy visiting the nearby Strahov Monastery—which has a fascinating old library and beautiful views over all of Prague.

Castle Square (Hradčanské Náměstí)—right in front of the castle gates—is at the center of this neighborhood. Stretching along the promontory away from the castle is a regal neighborhood that ends at the Strahov Monastery. Above the castle are the Royal Gardens, and below the castle are more gardens and lanes leading down to the Little Quarter (see previous chapter).

Visit the castle early or late to minimize crowds. If you plan to see both the castle and the monastery, start with the castle if you can get there early. For an afternoon visit, begin at the monastery, then hike down to the castle.

Getting to Prague Castle

If you're not up for a hike, the tram offers a sweat-free ride up to the castle.

By Taxi: If you just tell your driver to take you to "the castle," the taxi ride is a long way around—and expensive. Instead, have the cab drop you off just under the castle at the top of Nerudova street (described on page 106) and climb the cobblestones from there.

By Foot: Begin in the Little Quarter, just across Charles Bridge from the Old Town. Hikers can follow the main cobbled road (Mostecká) from Charles Bridge to Little Quarter Square, marked by the huge, green-domed Church of St. Nicholas. (The nearest Metro stop is Malostranská, from which Valdštejnská street leads down to Little Quarter Square.) From Little Quarter Square, hike uphill along Nerudova street. After about 10 minutes, a steep lane on the right leads to the castle. (If you continue straight, Nerudova becomes Úvoz and climbs to the Strahov Monastery.)

By Tram: Tram #22 takes you up to the castle (see page 57 for my self-guided tram tour, which ends at the castle). While you can catch the tram in various places, these three stops are particularly convenient: the Národní Třída stop (between Wenceslas Square and the National Theater in the New Town); in front of the National Theater (Národní Divadlo, on the riverbank in the New Town); and at Malostranská (the Metro stop in the Little Quarter).

Which Tram Stop for the Castle? After rattling up the hill, the tram makes three stops near the castle.

The first stop, **Královský Letohrádek,** allows a scenic but slow approach through the Royal Gardens.

For the quickest commute to the castle, stay on the tram one more stop to get off at **Pražský Hrad,** then simply walk along U Prašného Mostu over the bridge into the castle.

If you'd like to start with the Strahov Monastery, stay on the tram for two more stops—passing the Brusnice stop—to the **Pohořelec** stop. Tour the monastery, then hike down to the castle.

Note: If you plan to take the tram back to town after visiting Prague Castle, bring an extra ticket with you, as there is no handy place to buy one at the castle. If you ride with an expired ticket you risk being caught—and fined—by inspectors who patrol the tram regularly.

▲▲Prague Castle (Pražský Hrad)

For more than a thousand years, Czech leaders have ruled from Prague Castle. Today, Prague Castle is, by some measures, the biggest on earth.

Cost: Admission to the grounds is free, but you need a ticket to enter the sights. Choose the short-tour ticket (250 Kč), which covers the highlights: St. Vitus Cathedral (entry to the vestibule is free, but to go farther requires a ticket), the Old Royal Palace, the Basilica of St. George, and the Golden Lane. The comprehensive long-tour ticket (350 Kč) includes a few additional sights that aren't worth visiting. A separate ticket (300 Kč) covers the St. Vitus Treasury exhibit (in the recently renovated Chapel of the Holy Cross).

There are three places to buy tickets (each marked by a green "*i*"): two in the second courtyard and one in front of the cathedral. Lines can be long at one and nonexistent at the next, so if it's crowded check all three. Hang on to your ticket; you must present it at each sight.

Hours: Castle sights—daily April-Oct 9:00-17:00, Nov-March 9:00-16:00, last entry 15 minutes before closing; grounds—daily 5:00-24:00; St. Vitus Treasury exhibit—daily 10:00-18:00. St. Vitus Cathedral is closed Sunday mornings for Mass. Be warned that the cathedral can be closed unexpectedly due to special services—consider calling ahead to confirm (tel. 224-371-111 or 724-933-441).

Tours: Hour-long **tours** in English depart from the main ticket office near the cathedral entrance about three times a day, but they cover only the cathedral and Old Royal Palace (100 Kč plus entry ticket, tel. 224-371-111). You can rent an **audioguide** at the main desk (350 Kč plus 500-Kč deposit). It's perfectly shareable if you have a cheek-to-cheek partner and not much money.

Crowd-Beating Tips: Huge throngs of tourists turn the grounds into a sea of people during peak times (9:30-12:30). The small, free entrance area in St. Vitus Cathedral is the most crowded part of the castle complex. If you're visiting in the morning, be at the cathedral entrance promptly at 9:00, when the doors open. For 10 minutes you'll have the sacred space to yourself (after about 9:15, tour guides cram unwieldy groups into the free entrance area, forming a noisy human traffic jam). I'd avoid the castle entirely in midmorning.

Even if you do hit crowds, keep in mind that most groups stick to the free areas. For fewer crowds, head for the sights that require a ticket: St. Vitus Cathedral (past the free entrance area), the Old Royal Palace, the Basilica of St. George, and the Golden Lane.

Late afternoon is least crowded; tour groups are napping and the castle grounds are relatively uncrowded. If you're not interested in entering the sights, you could try a nighttime visit—the castle grounds are free, safe, peaceful, floodlit, and open late (see www. hrad.cz for more information).

Eateries: The castle complex has several forgettable cafés scattered within it, but good eateries are nearby: between the castle and Strahov Monastery, and also near the castle-complex exit (see map on page 170, with listings on page 172). I like the scenic, creative café at Lobkowicz Palace (see page 126).

Sightseeing Plan: Begin at Castle Square, then tour St. Vitus Cathedral, the Old Royal Palace, the Basilica of St. George, the Golden Lane, and Lobkowicz Palace (a non-castle sight, requiring a separate admission fee, at the bottom of the castle complex).

Note that if you're planning to visit the Strahov Monastery and Loreto Church, which sit above the castle, the most efficient plan is to begin at the monastery (tram stop: Pohořelec) and work your way downhill through the castle sights. However, if you're

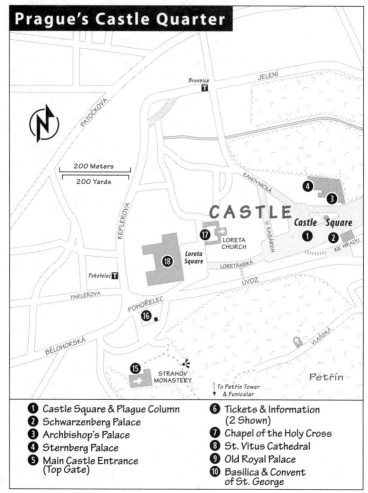

Prague's Castle Quarter

200 Meters
200 Yards

CASTLE

Castle Square

Brusnice

JELENÍ

PATOČKOVA

KANOVNICKÁ

U KASÁREN

KEPLEROVA

LORETA CHURCH

Loreta Square

LORETÁNSKÁ

KE HRADU

ÚVOZ

Pohořelec

PARLEŘOVA

POHOŘELEC

BĚLOHORSKÁ

VLAŠSKÁ

STRAHOV MONASTERY

Petřín

To Petřín Tower & Funicular

1 Castle Square & Plague Column
2 Schwarzenberg Palace
3 Archbishop's Palace
4 Sternberg Palace
5 Main Castle Entrance (Top Gate)
6 Tickets & Information (2 Shown)
7 Chapel of the Holy Cross
8 St. Vitus Cathedral
9 Old Royal Palace
10 Basilica & Convent of St. George

rushing to reach the castle by 9:00 (to avoid crowds), it may be worth backtracking uphill to Strahov and Loreto later.

Castle Square (Hradčanské Náměstí)

This is the central square of the Castle Quarter. Enjoy the awesome city view and the two entertaining bands that play regularly at the gate. (If the Prague Castle Orchestra is playing, say hello to friendly, mustachioed Josef, and consider buying the group's terrific CD.) From the square, stairs lead down to the Little Quarter.

Castle Square was the focal point of medieval power—the king, the most powerful noblemen, and the archbishop lived here. Look uphill from the gate. The Renaissance-era **Schwarzenberg Palace**

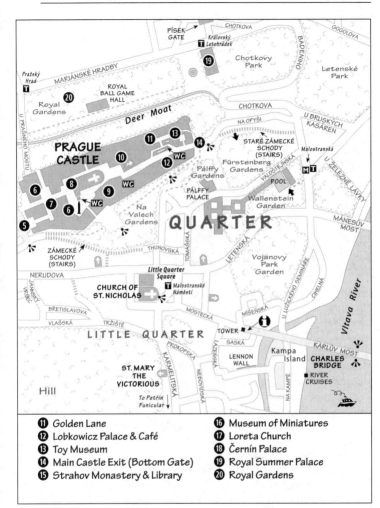

11 Golden Lane
12 Lobkowicz Palace & Café
13 Toy Museum
14 Main Castle Exit (Bottom Gate)
15 Strahov Monastery & Library

16 Museum of Miniatures
17 Loreta Church
18 Černín Palace
19 Royal Summer Palace
20 Royal Gardens

(Schwarzenberský Palác, on the left, with the big, envelope-like rectangles scratched on the wall) was where the Rožmberks "humbly" stayed when they were in town visiting from their Český Krumlov estates. The Schwarzenberg family inherited the Krumlov estates and aristocratic prominence in Bohemia, and stayed in the palace until the 20th century. The palace now houses the National Gallery's collection of Czech Baroque paintings, displayed in restored rooms that have great views of the city (200 Kč, cheaper after 16:00, open Tue-Sun 10:00-18:00, closed Mon, www.ngprague.cz).

The archbishop still lives in the yellow Rococo **palace** across the square (with the three white goose necks in the red field—the coat of arms of Prague's archbishops).

Through the portal on the left-hand side of the palace, a lane leads to the **Sternberg Palace** (Šternberský Palác), filled with the

National Gallery's collection of European paintings—including minor works by Albrecht Dürer, Peter Paul Rubens, Rembrandt, and El Greco (200 Kč, Tue-Sun 10:00-18:00, closed Mon, www.ngprague.cz).

The black Baroque sculpture in the middle of the square is a **plague column.** Erected as a token of gratitude to the saints who saved the population from the epidemic, these columns are an integral part of the main square of many Habsburg towns.

The statue marked *TGM* honors **Tomáš Garrigue Masaryk** (1850-1937), a university prof and a pal of Woodrow Wilson. At the end of World War I, Masaryk united the Czechs and the Slovaks into one nation and became its first president (see sidebar, page 320). Considered the father of Czechoslovakia, he was the only 20th-century leader to actually live inside Prague Castle.

Castle Gate and Courtyards

Standing in the square, survey the castle—the tip of a 1,500-foot-long series of courtyards, churches, and palaces. The guard changes on the hour from 5:00-23:00 at every gate: top, bottom, and side. The best ceremony and music occurs at noon, at the top gate.

Walk under the fighting giants. The modern green awning with the golden-winged cat (just to the right of the fountain) across the next courtyard marks the **of-**

fices of the Czech president. Beginning in 2013, the Czech president has been elected by popular vote rather than by the Parliament. The first to be elected in this way was Miloš Zeman, who quickly took advantage of a parliamentary crisis by attempting to change the country's par-

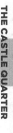

liamentary/prime-minister system into one wh
the most power.

In the corner of the square to the right is
Chapel of the Holy Cross. This holds the St
hibit, which displays precious reliquaries and liturgical objects dating as far back as the reign of Charles IV. (Maximum capacity is 45 visitors.)

• *As you walk through another passageway, you'll find yourself facing...*

▲▲▲St. Vitus Cathedral (Katedrála Sv. Víta)

The Roman Catholic cathedral symbolizes the Czech spirit—it contains the tombs and relics of the most important local saints and kings, including the first three Habsburg kings.

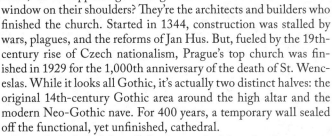

Note that even without a ticket, tourists can go inside the cathedral and, with a bit of neck craning, even jostle to get a peek at the popular Mucha window, described later. But it's worth paying to enter the whole church.

❷ **Self-Guided Tour:** Before entering, check out the **facade.** What's up with the guys in suits carved into the stone, as if supporting the big round window on their shoulders? They're the architects and builders who finished the church. Started in 1344, construction was stalled by wars, plagues, and the reforms of Jan Hus. But, fueled by the 19th-century rise of Czech nationalism, Prague's top church was finished in 1929 for the 1,000th anniversary of the death of St. Wenceslas. While it looks all Gothic, it's actually two distinct halves: the original 14th-century Gothic area around the high altar and the modern Neo-Gothic nave. For 400 years, a temporary wall sealed off the functional, yet unfinished, cathedral.

• *Enter the cathedral through the door on the left and make your way through the crowds in the vestibule. If you have a ticket, pass through the turnstile (at the left of the roped-off area), and find the third window just beyond the ticket check.*

Mucha Stained-Glass Window: This masterful 1931 Art Nouveau window was designed by Czech artist Alfons Mucha and executed by a stained-glass craftsman (if you like this, you'll love the Mucha Museum in the New Town—see page 93—and Mucha's masterpiece, the *Slav Epic*—described on page 132).

Notice Mucha's stirring nationalism: Methodius and Cyril, widely considered the

THE CASTLE QUARTER

. Vitus Cathedral

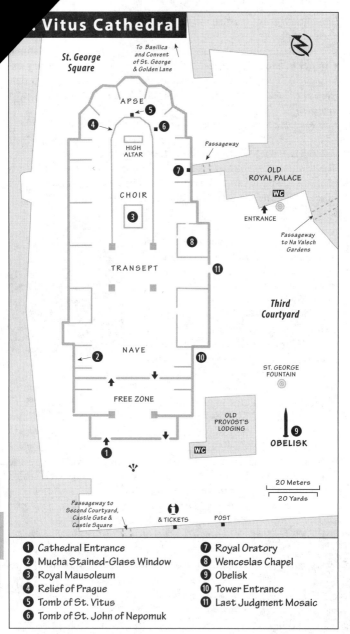

St. George Square

To Basilica
and Convent
of St. George
& Golden Lane

APSE

5

4

6

HIGH
ALTAR

Passageway

7

OLD
ROYAL PALACE

CHOIR

WC

ENTRANCE

3

*Passageway
to Na Valech
Gardens*

8

TRANSEPT

11

*Third
Courtyard*

NAVE

ST. GEORGE
FOUNTAIN

2

10

FREE ZONE

OLD
PROVOST'S
LODGING

OBELISK **9**

1

WC

20 Meters

20 Yards

*Passageway to
Second Courtyard,
Castle Gate &
Castle Square*

& TICKETS

POST

THE CASTLE QUARTER

1 Cathedral Entrance	**7** Royal Oratory
2 Mucha Stained-Glass Window	**8** Wenceslas Chapel
3 Royal Mausoleum	**9** Obelisk
4 Relief of Prague	**10** Tower Entrance
5 Tomb of St. Vitus	**11** Last Judgment Mosaic
6 Tomb of St. John of Nepomuk	

fathers of Slavic-style Christianity, are top and center. Cyril—the monk in black holding the Bible—brought the word of God to the Slavs. They had no written language in the ninth century, so he designed the necessary alphabet (Glagolitic, which later developed into Cyrillic). Methodius, the bishop, is shown baptizing a mythic, lanky, long-haired Czech man—a reminder of how he brought Christianity to the Czech people.

Scenes from the lives of Cyril (on the left) and Methodius (on the right) bookend the stirring and epic Slavic story. In the center are a kneeling boy and a prophesying elder—that's young St. Wenceslas and his grandmother, St. Ludmila. In addition to being specific historical figures, these characters are also symbolic: The old woman, with closed eyes, stands for the past and memory; the young boy, with a penetrating stare, represents the hope and future of a nation. Notice how master designer Mucha draws your attention to these two figures through the use of colors—the dark blue on the outside gradually turns into green, then yellow, and finally the gold of the woman and the crimson of the boy in the center. In Mucha's color language, blue stands for the past, gold for the mythic, and red for the future. Besides all the meaning, Mucha's art is simply a joy to behold. (And on the bottom, the tasteful little ad for *Banka Slavie*, which paid for the work, is hardly noticeable.)

Royal Mausoleum: Continue circulating around the church. A slight incline near the middle takes you into the older, 14th-century section. The big royal tomb (within the black iron fence) contains the remains of the first Habsburgs to rule Bohemia, including Ferdinand I, his wife Anne, and Maximilian II. The tomb dates from 1590, when Prague was a major Habsburg city.

Relief of Prague: As you walk around the high altar (Neo-Gothic, circa 1900), study the fascinating carved-wood relief of Prague. It depicts the action after the Battle of White Mountain, when the Protestant King Frederic escaped over the Charles Bridge (before it had any statues). Carved in 1630, 10 years after the famous event occurred, the relief gives you a peek at Prague in 1620, stretching from the Týn Church (far left) to the cathedral (half-built at that time, up to where you are now). Notice that back then, the Týn Church was Hussite, so the centerpiece of its facade is not the Virgin Mary, but a chalice, a symbol of Jan Hus' ideals. The old city walls—now replaced by the main streets of the city—stand strong. The Jewish Quarter (the slummy, muddy zone along the riverside below the bridge on the left) fills land no one else wanted. Notice the weir system on the river—it survives to this day.

Apse: Circling around the high altar, you pass graves of medieval kings and bishops, including (in the center) the tomb of **St. Vitus** (with a rooster at his feet). A few steps further, the big silvery tomb is that of **St. John of Nepomuk.** Locals claim it has more

The Battle Between Church and State for St. Vitus Cathedral

There's no question that St. Vitus Cathedral is close to the hearts of Czechs. But in recent years controversy has erupted over just what aspect of the national spirit the cathedral embodies.

The cathedral was nationalized in the 1950s and was managed by the Czech government for the next several decades. But in 1993—after the fall of communism—the Church began vying with the state for property rights. Since this building holds such symbolic value for the Czechs, it's not just the keys to the country's most precious artwork at stake. Those who wanted the cathedral to remain state-owned argued that it was the king, not the Church, who commissioned the cathedral, and that its completion in the 19th century was inspired more by patriotism than by religious fervor. The Church, however, pointed out the cathedral's role as a pilgrimage site, claiming that it should be dedicated to prayer. In 2006, the Czech courts ruled in the Church's favor (and against public opinion).

The Church has been cash-strapped since the fall of communism. While the state returned thousands of deteriorating chapels throughout the country to the Church, it didn't return ownership of the lands that once provided the revenue for their maintenance. So, perhaps understandably, once the keys changed hands, the Church looked for an easy source of cash. Hoping that the throngs of cathedral visitors would help them bring new life to neglected rural chapels, Church leaders immediately imposed a 100-Kč entrance fee. Some accused them of greediness. In 2008, before the coins had filled a single coffer, the Supreme Court overruled the decision and returned the cathedral to the state (which made the entrance free).

In 2010, the new archbishop, Dominik Duka, proposed a compromise, which was promptly accepted. The cathedral is now administered jointly by the state and the Church. Visitors can enter for free, stay within a roped-off area, and get a look at the cathedral's impressive interior. To walk through the cathedral—to see its stained-glass windows and historic tombs close up—requires a ticket.

than a ton of silver (for more on St. John of Nepomuk, see page 77). About three yards after the tomb (above on the right) is a finely carved wood relief, circa 1630. It gives a Counter-Reformation spin on the Wars of Religion, showing the "barbaric" Protestant nobles destroying the Catholic icons here in the cathedral after their short-lived victory.

Ahead on the left, look up at the **royal oratory,** a box supported by busy late-Gothic, vine-like ribs. This is where the king would go to attend Mass in his jammies (an elevated corridor connected his private apartment with his own altar-side box pew).

• *From here, walk 25 paces and look left through the crowds and door to see the richly decorated chapel containing the tomb of St. Wenceslas. The best views are around the corner, ahead and to the left.*

Wenceslas Chapel: A fancy chapel (right transept) houses the tomb of St. Wenceslas, surrounded by walls encrusted with precious and semiprecious stones. (There are two roped-off doorways giving visitors a look inside. The best view is the second one, around the corner in the transept.) Above the altar is St. Wenceslas, flanked by angels and the four patron saints of the Czech people. The scene evokes heavenly Jerusalem to anyone entering with a 14th-century mind-set. Above are circa-1590 frescoes showing scenes of the saint's life (for more on Wenceslas, see page 87). The door leads to the crown jewels. Get as close as you can. Notice the jewel-toned stained-glass windows from the 1950s. The Czech kings used to be crowned right here in front of the coffin, draped in red.

Back Outside the Cathedral: Leaving the cathedral, turn left (past the public WC). The **obelisk** was erected in 1928—a single piece of granite celebrating the 10th anniversary of the establishment of Czechoslovakia and commemorating the soldiers who

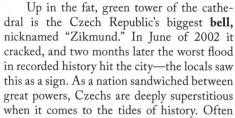

fought for its independence. It was originally much taller, but broke in transit—an inauspicious start for a nation destined to last only 70 years.

Up in the fat, green tower of the cathedral is the Czech Republic's biggest **bell,** nicknamed "Zikmund." In June of 2002 it cracked, and two months later the worst flood in recorded history hit the city—the locals saw this as a sign. As a nation sandwiched between great powers, Czechs are deeply superstitious when it comes to the tides of history. Often feeling unable to influence their own destiny, they helplessly look at events as we might look at the weather and other natural phenomena—trying to figure out what fate has in store for them next. You can view the bell as you climb up the 287 steps of the **tower** to the observation deck at the top (150 Kč, daily 10:00-18:30, until 16:30 in winter, enter near sculpture of St. George—a 1960s replica of the 13th-century original). A few steps to the left you can survey the ruins of the first basilica of St. Vitus from the 11th century, protected under a green roof.

Find the 14th-century **mosaic** of the Last Judgment outside on the right transept (above the church's "golden gate"). It was commissioned in the Italian style by King Charles IV, who, in 1370 was modern, cosmopolitan, and ahead of his time. Jesus oversees the action, as some go to heaven and some go to hell. The Czech king and queen kneel directly beneath Jesus and six patron saints. On coronation day, they would walk under this arch, a reminder to them (and their subjects) that even those holding great power are not above God's judgment. The royal crown and national jewels are kept in a chamber (see the grilled windows) above this entry-way, which was the cathedral's main entry for centuries while the church remained uncompleted.

• *Across the square and 20 yards to the right, a door leads into the Old Royal Palace (in the lobby, there's a WC with a window shared by the men's and women's sections—meet your partner to enjoy the view).*

Old Royal Palace (Starý Královský Palác)

Starting in the 12th century, this was the seat of the Bohemian princes. While extensively rebuilt, the **large hall** is late Gothic, designed as a multipurpose hall for the old nobility. It was big enough for jousts—even the staircase (which you'll use as you exit) was designed to let a mounted soldier gallop in. It was filled with market stalls, giving nobles a chance to shop without actually going into town. In the 1500s, the nobility met here to elect their king. The tradition survived until

modern times, as the parliament crowded into this room into the late 1990s to elect the president of Czechoslovakia, and later, of the Czech Republic. Look up at the flower-shaped, vaulted ceiling.

On your immediate right, enter the two small Renaissance rooms known as the **"Czech Office."** From these rooms (empty today except for their 17th-century porcelain heaters), two governors used to oversee the Czech lands for the Habsburgs in Vienna. In 1618, angry Czech Protestant nobles poured into these rooms and threw the two Catholic governors out the window. An old law actually permits this act—called defenestration—which usually targets bad politicians. Old prints on the wall show the second of Prague's many defenestrations. The two governors landed—fittingly—in a pile of horse manure. Even though they suffered only broken arms and bruised egos, this event kicked off the huge and lengthy Thirty Years' War.

At the far end of the large hall, go out on the balcony for a sweeping view of Prague. Is that Paris' Eiffel Tower in the distance? No, it's Petřín Tower, a fine place for a relaxing day at the park, offering expansive views over Prague.

As you re-enter the main hall, head for the door immediately

The Catholic Church in Prague

In stark contrast to the Poles, the freedom-loving Czechs never fully accepted the powerful Catholic Church—traditionally closely allied with the Habsburgs and Austria. The communists took advantage of this popular sentiment, and in their Marxist zeal did everything short of banning the Church to uproot the faith of the relatively few practicing Catholics. In the early 1950s, most monks and priests, including the archbishop, were arrested and sent to prisons, from which they were not released until the thawing that came with the Khrushchev era. A wise old priest remembers his 13 years in a labor camp as "a fascinating, well-spent time in the company of some truly great minds."

During the communist era, Church property was confiscated, churches quickly deteriorated, churchgoers were persecuted, and many priests had to become confidants of the secret police in order to continue their service. Ironically, by persecuting Catholics, the communists gave the Church the opportunity to improve its reputation with the Czechs. In the 1980s, the charismatic archbishop of Prague, Cardinal Tomášek, became a local hero by frequently standing up to the regime. By 1989, Tomášek was a main symbol of anticommunist opposition (along with Václav Havel).

After 1989, many Czechs returned to the Catholic faith. The trend peaked in 1992 when Tomášek died (he's now buried under the Mucha window in St. Vitus Cathedral). Since then, the Church's hold has steadily declined for various reasons, including the media's depiction of the Church as greedy; questions about the status of former Church property (see earlier sidebar); and the uninspiring archbishop of Prague who served from 1991 until 2010, Miloslav Vlk (Wolf)—a name his critics found fitting.

But things are starting to look up for the Church. In 2010, the Vatican smartly replaced the withered Vlk with the bubbly Dominik Duka, who shot to the top of popularity rankings (thanks in part to his compromise proposal on the status of the cathedral). Whether Duka's rising star will help recruit Czechs to the priesthood remains to be seen. As for now, many parishes are served by Polish missionaries with heavy accents.

The Church is also facing challenges from "new" and fashionable spiritual movements, such as Buddhism, which are drawing Czechs in moderate numbers, partly due to sympathy for the Tibetan cause (the Dalai Lama has been a frequent visitor to Prague). But even within these movements, the Czechs remain on the skeptical side.

THE CASTLE QUARTER

opposite. It opens into a room with a fine Gothic ceiling, a crimson throne, and benches for the nobility who once served as the high court. Notice the balcony on the left where scribes recorded the proceedings (without needing to mix with the aristocrats). The portraits on the walls depict Habsburg rulers, including Maria Theresa and Joseph II dressed up as George Washington (both wore the 18th-century fashions of the times), and the display case on the right contains replicas of the Czech crown jewels. The originals are locked up.

Return to the main hall; the next door to your right is the exit. As you leave, pause at the door to consider the subtle yet racy little Renaissance knocker. Go ahead—play with it for a little sex in the palace (be gentle).

• *Across from the palace exit is the...*

Basilica and Convent of St. George (Bazilika Sv. Jiří)

Step into the beautiful-in-its-simplicity Basilica of St. George to see Prague's best-preserved Romanesque church and the burial

place of Czech royalty. Notice the characteristic thick walls and round arches. In those early years, building techniques were not yet advanced, and the ceiling is made of wood, rather than arched with stone. Climb the stairs to study the area around the apse. St. Wenceslas' grandmother, St. Ludmila, was reburied here in 925. Her stone tomb is in the space just to the right of the altar. Look for her portrait—looking quite cultured for a 10th-century woman—in the arch above her tomb.

The fine curved green facade opposite the basilica decorates Maria Theresa's Institute for Noblewomen, created in the 1750s to empower and educate aristocratic ladies.

• *Continue walking downhill through the castle grounds. To the left were the residences of soldiers and craftsmen, to the right, tucked together, were the palaces of Catholic nobility who wanted both to be close to power and able to band together should the Protestants grab the upper hand. The next street on the left leads to the popular...*

Golden Lane (Zlatá Ulička)

The tiny old buildings of this picturesque street originally housed castle servants, and perhaps goldsmiths. Well-written English texts explain the history of the lane and its cannon towers, which served as prisons. The houses themselves were occupied until World War

II—Franz Kafka lived briefly at #22. These days, the dwellings are filled with a mix of shops and reconstructions (including a pub and a goldsmith's workshop) portraying life through the ages. At the top end of the lane there's a fascinating alchemy exhibit. From there you can climb to the upper corridor, which displays armor and painted shields. There's also a deli/bistro at the top end of the lane. During the day the street is jammed with tourists. At night (after 17:00 in summer, 16:00 in winter), the tiny street is open to those without a ticket, empty and romantic. Exit the lane through a corridor at the last house (#12).

More Castle-Area Sights

Extend your visit by dropping by a nobleman's palace and a toy museum with an entire floor devoted to the Barbie doll. Each sight requires a separate admission ticket; they're not included in any castle tickets.

▲▲Lobkowicz Palace (Lobkowiczký Palác)

This palace, at the bottom of the castle complex, displays the private collection of a prominent Czech noble family, including paintings, ceramics, and musical scores. The Lobkowiczes' property was confiscated twice in the 20th century: first by the Nazis at the beginning of World War II, and then by the communists in 1948. In 1990, William Lobkowicz, then a Boston investment banker, returned to Czechoslovakia to fight a legal battle to reclaim his family's property and, eventually, to restore the castles and palaces to their former state.

Cost and Hours: 275 Kč, includes audioguide, daily 10:00-18:00, last entry one hour before closing, tel. 233-312-925, www.lobkowicz.cz.

Visiting the Palace: A conscientious host, William Lobkowicz himself narrates the delightful, included audioguide. As you pass by the portraits of his ancestors, listen to their stories, including that of Polyxena, whose determination saved the two Catholic governors defenestrated next door (according to family legend, she hid the bruised officials under the folds of her skirt). The museum's highlights are Pieter Bruegel the Elder's magnificently preserved *Haymaking,* from 1565, one of the earliest entirely secular landscape paintings in Europe (showing an idyllic and almost heroic connection between peasants and nature), along with the manuscript of Beethoven's *Eroica* (dedicated to his sponsor, Prince Lobkowicz), displayed near Mozart's reorchestration of Handel's *Messiah.* While the National Gallery may seem a more logical choice for the art enthusiast, the obvious care that went into creating this museum, the collection's variety, and the personal insight that it opens into the past and present of Czech nobility make the Lobkowicz worth an hour of your time.

THE CASTLE QUARTER

Eating: The Lobkowicz Palace Café by the exit has a creative cosmopolitan menu and stunning panoramic views of the city (daily 10:00-18:00). If a charming young man is selling ice cream out front, it may be William's son, Will.

Toy Museum (Muzeum Hraček)

Across the street from Lobkowicz Palace, a courtyard and a long wooden staircase lead to two entertaining floors of old toys and dolls, thoughtfully described in English. You'll see a century of teddy bears, some 19th-century model train sets, old Christmas decor, and an incredible Barbie collection. Find the buxom 1959 first edition, and you'll understand why these capitalistic sirens of material discontent weren't allowed here until 1989.

Cost and Hours: 70 Kč, 120 Kč family ticket, daily 9:30-17:30, WC next to entrance.

Leaving the Castle Complex

Tourists squirt slowly through a fortified door at the bottom end of the castle. A scenic rampart just below the lower gate offers a commanding view of the city. From there, you can head to the nearest Metro/tram station, the Strahov Monastery, the Little Quarter, or Castle Square.

To the Malostranská Metro/Tram Station: You can follow the steep lane directly back to the riverbank...or turn right about halfway down the steps to visit the Fürstenberg Gardens, with 3,500 flowering plants and 2,200 rose bushes (80 Kč, April-Oct daily from 10:00 until one hour before sunset). For a gentler descent, start heading down the steep lane. About 40 yards below the castle exit, a gate on the left leads you through a scenic vineyard and past the Villa Richter restaurants (see page 172 of the Eating chapter) to the station.

To the Strahov Monastery by Tram: Follow directions to the Malostranská Metro/tram station (above), then catch tram #22 up to the Pohořelec stop.

To the top of the Little Quarter or Castle Square (and Monastery): As you leave the castle gate, take a hard right and stroll through the long, delightful park (free, April-Oct 10:00-18:00 or later, closed Nov-March). Along the way, notice the Modernist layout of the Na Valech Gardens, designed by the 1920s court architect, Jože Plečnik of Slovenia. Halfway through the long park is a viewpoint overlooking the terraced Pálffy Gardens (80 Kč, same hours as park). You can zigzag down through these gardens into the Little Quarter. Or, if you want to walk to Castle Square, continue uphill along the castle wall and through the garden to the square. You can hike up to the monastery from here.

Strahov Monastery and Nearby

Twin Baroque domes high above the castle mark the Strahov Monastery. It's best reached from the Pohořelec stop on tram #22 (from the stop, follow the tram tracks uphill for 50 yards, enter the fancy gate on the left near the tall red-brick wall, and you'll see the twin spires of the monastery; the library entrance is in front of the church on the right). If you're coming on foot from the Little Quarter, allow 15 minutes for the uphill hike. After seeing the monastery, hike down to the castle (a 10-minute walk), or detour into the tiny Museum of Miniatures (described later).

▲Strahov Monastery and Library
(Strahovský Klášter a Knihovna)

As you enter the grounds, consider that medieval monasteries were a mix of industry, agriculture, and education, as well as worship and theology. In its heyday, the **monastery** had a booming economy of its own, with vineyards, a brewery, and a sizeable beer hall—all open once again.

Cost and Hours: Grounds—free and always open; library—80 Kč, daily 9:00-11:45 & 13:00-17:00, last entry 15 minutes earlier, www.strahovskyklaster.cz.

Visiting the Monastery and Library: The monastery's **main church,** dedicated to the Assumption of St. Mary, is an originally Romanesque structure decorated by the monks in textbook Baroque (usually closed, but look through the gate inside the front door to see its interior). Notice the grand effect of the Baroque architecture—both rhythmic and theatric. Go ahead, inhale. That's the scent of Baroque.

The adjacent **library** offers a peek at how enlightened thinkers in the 18th century influenced learning. Cases in the library gift

shop show off illuminated manuscripts, described in English. Some are in old Czech, but because the Enlightenment promoted the universality of knowledge (and Latin was the universal language of Europe's educated elite), there was little place for regional dialects—therefore, few books here are in the Czech language.

Two rooms (seen only from the door) are filled with 10th- to 17th-century books, shelved under elaborately painted ceilings. The theme of the first and bigger hall is philosophy, with the history of Western man's pursuit of knowledge painted on the ceiling. The second hall focuses on theology. As the Age of Enlightenment began to take hold in Europe at the end of the 18th century, monasteries still controlled the books. Notice the gilded, locked case containing the *libri prohibiti* (prohibited books) at the end of the room. Only the abbot had the key, and you had to have his blessing to read these books—by writers such as Nicolas Copernicus and Jan Hus, and even including the French encyclopedia. The hallway connecting the two library rooms was filled with cases illustrating the new practical approach to natural sciences. Find the dried-up elephant trunks (flanking the narwhal or unicorn horn), baby dodo bird (which became extinct in the 17th century; in case at far right), and one of the earliest models of an electricity generator.

Nearby Views: Just downhill from the monastery, past the venerable linden trees (a symbol of the Czech people) and through the gate, the views from the **monastery garden** are among the finest in Prague. The Bellavista Restaurant, with perhaps the city's best view tables, serves quality food at reasonable prices, given the location. From the public perch beneath the tables, you can see St. Vitus Cathedral (the heart of the castle complex), the green dome of the Church of St. Nicholas (marking the center of the Little Quarter), the two dark towers fortifying both ends of Charles Bridge, and the fanciful black spires of the Týn Church (marking the Old Town Square). On the horizon is the modern Žižkov TV and radio tower (conveniently marking the liveliest nightlife zone in town—see page 188). Begun in the 1980s, the tower was partly meant to jam Radio Free Europe's broadcast from Munich. By the time it was finished, communism was dead, and Radio Free Europe's headquarters had moved to Prague.

Getting from the Monastery to the Castle: From the monastery, take Loretánská (the upper road, passing Loreta Square, with Loreta Church and Černín Palace—both described later) to the castle. This is a more interesting route than the lower road, Úvoz, which takes you down a steep hill, below Castle Square.

• *Or, for one more little sight, consider visiting the Museum of Miniatures. From the monastery garden viewpoint, backtrack through the gate to the big linden trees and leave through a passage on your right. At the door is the minuscule...*

Museum of Miniatures (Muzeum Miniatur)

You'll see 40 teeny exhibits, each under a microscope, crafted by an artist from a remote corner of Siberia. Yes, you could fit the entire museum in a carry-on-size suitcase, but good things sometimes come in very, very small packages—it's fascinating to see minutiae such as a padlock on the leg of an ant. Notice how the Russian staff has a certain gentility.

Cost and Hours: 100 Kč, kids-50 Kč, daily 9:00-17:00, tel. 233-352-371.

Loreta Square, Between the Monastery and Castle

From the monastery, take Loretánská street to Loreta Square (Loretánské Náměstí).

Loreta Church

This church has been a hit with pilgrims for centuries, thanks to its dazzling bell tower, peaceful yet plush cloister, sparkling treasury, and much-venerated Holy House.

Cost and Hours: 130 Kč, audioguide-150 Kč, daily 9:00-12:15 & 13:00-17:00, closes at 16:00 Nov-March, tel. 220-516-740, www.loreta.cz.

Visiting the Church: Inside, follow the one-way clockwise route. While you stroll along the cloister, notice that the ceiling is painted with the many places Mary has miraculously appeared to the faithful in Europe.

In the garden-like center of the cloister stands the ornate **Santa Casa (Holy House),** considered by some pilgrims to be part of Mary's home in Nazareth. Because many pilgrims returning from the Holy Land docked at the Italian port of Loreto, it's called the Loreta Shrine. The Santa Casa is the "little Bethlehem" of Prague. It is the traditional departure point for Czech pilgrims setting out on the long, arduous journey to Europe's most important pilgrimage site, Santiago de Compostela, in northwest Spain. Inside, on the left wall, hangs what some consider to be an original beam from the house of Mary. It's overseen by a much-venerated statue of the Black Virgin. The Santa Casa itself might seem like a bit of a letdown, but generations of believers have considered this to be the holiest spot in the country.

The small **Baroque church** behind the Santa Casa is one of the most beautiful in Prague. The decor looks rich—but the marble and gold are all fake. From the window in the back, you can see a stucco relief on the Santa Casa that shows angels rescuing the house from a pagan attack in Nazareth and making a special delivery to Loreto in Italy.

Continue around the cloister. In the last corner is **"St. Bearded Woman"** (Svatá Starosta). This patron saint of unhappy marriages is a woman whose family arranged for her to marry a pagan man. She prayed for an escape, sprouted a beard...and the guy said, "No way." While she managed to avoid the marriage, it angered her father, who crucified her. The many candles here are from people suffering through unhappy marriages.

European Flags Fly in the Czech Republic

Today, the blue flag of the European Union flies alongside the Czech flag on the roof of government buildings, such as the Černín Palace (housing the Ministry of Foreign Affairs). The Czech Republic entered the EU along with nine other countries on May 1, 2004. Most Czechs are disappointed they weren't admitted much earlier.

But there also are Euro-skeptics, including the right wing, the communists, and former Czech president Václav Klaus (2003-2013), who argued that the country has surrendered too much of its autonomy to Brussels. From 2004 to 2009, Klaus never flew the European flag, but current President Miloš Zeman flies it daily by the castle's main entry—deliberately setting himself apart from Klaus. Most Czechs are optimistic about their membership in the EU, and the majority of the government feels that it benefits the country. The year following Czech entry into the EU saw the largest GDP growth since 1989, as well as growing foreign investment. Japanese and Korean companies now find it advantageous to produce goods in the Czech Republic (or Slovakia), since assembling their final products within these member countries exempts them from EU tariffs.

During the first half of 2009, the Czech Republic assumed the rotating presidency of the European Union. Halfway through its term, however, the opposition pushed through a no-confidence vote, forcing the administration to step down.

The Czech Republic currently has no plans to adopt the euro: The recent financial downturn seems to support those economists who argue that using the euro is actually a disadvantage for the small-country economies of Central and Eastern Europe. Czech exporters, the majority of whose customers use the euro, disagree.

THE CASTLE QUARTER

Take a left just before the exit and head upstairs, following signs to the **treasury**—a room full of jeweled worship aids (well-described in English). The highlight here is a monstrance (Communion wafer holder) from 1699, with more than 6,000 diamonds.

Enjoy the short **carillon concert** at the top of the hour; from the lawn in front of the main entrance, you can see the racks of bells being clanged. (At the exit, you'll see a schedule of upcoming *pout'*—pilgrimages—departing from here.)

• *On the opposite side of the square (just uphill from the Loreta Church) is the...*

Černín Palace (Černínsky Palác)

This palace once belonged to one of the most cosmopolitan Czech families, and so, in 1918, it was turned into the Ministry of Foreign

Affairs. In May of 2005, a memorial to the first secretary of state of Czechoslovakia, Edvard Beneš, was unveiled in front of the Ministry. This second president of Czechoslovakia, who led the country as an exile in London during World War II, is controversial (see sidebar on page 234). The tiny size of the statue expresses the nation's present uncertainty about the legacy of the man.

Beneš faces the bronze portrait bust of Hana Benešová, Edvard's wife, on the house across the street, where she lived for a brief period. Hana has long been regarded as the force behind many of Edvard's crucial decisions. Czechs often measure statesmen by their wives, since many Czechs regard men as pathologically ambitious and imprudent creatures, whose success and apparent political wisdom are due to the sensible judgment of their out-of-sight better halves.

Royal Summer Palace and Royal Gardens

These minor sights, above Prague Castle, are only worth visiting if you get off tram #22 at Královský Letohrádek (the Royal Summer Palace is across the street from this stop, WC at gate).

Royal Summer Palace (Královský Letohrádek)

This gift of love is like a Czech Taj Mahal, presented by Emperor Ferdinand I to his beloved Queen Anne. It's the purest Renaissance building in town. You can't go inside, but the building's detailed reliefs are worth a close look. In good Renaissance style, they're based on classical, rather than Christian, stories. The one depicted here is Virgil's *Aeneid*. The fountain in front of the palace features the most elaborate bronze work in the country. (For a trip to Tibet, stick your head under the bottom of the fountain. The audio rainbow you hear is the reason it's called the Singing Fountain.)

• *From here, set your sights on the cathedral's lacy, black spires marking the castle's entrance. Stroll through the...*

Royal Gardens (Královská Zahrada)

Once the private grounds and residence (you'll see the building) of the communist presidents, these were opened to the public with the coming of freedom under Václav Havel (free, April-Oct daily 10:00-18:00, closed Nov-March). Walk through these gardens (with lovely views of St. Vitus Cathedral) to the gate, which leads you over the moat and into Castle Square, the entrance to the vast castle complex.

BEYOND THE CORE

Slav Epic • Vyšehrad Walk

While the tourist's Prague is mostly contained to the Old Town, New Town, Little Quarter, and Castle Quarter, one of the city's most important sights sits just outside this core. The *Slav Epic*—Alfons Mucha's 20-canvas ode to his nation and its history—is a must-see while you're in Prague and is on display at Veletržní Palace, north of the New Town (across the river).

In the opposite direction, south of the New Town, is the peaceful park at Vyšehrad. With a 17th-century fortress and views overlooking the city, Vyšehrad provides a welcome break from the Prague bustle and a wonderful setting for a contemplative stroll any time of day.

Alfons Mucha's *Slav Epic*

This collection of 20 massive canvases, painted by the great Czech Art Nouveau artist Alfons Mucha, depicts momentous events in Slavic history. Located at Veletržní Palace, the *Slav Epic* is one of the most powerful artistic experiences in Europe. It's easily worth ▲▲▲—don't miss it. Allow two hours to appreciate the work.

Orientation

Cost: 180 Kč. The 240-Kč ticket also includes the National Gallery's huge modern art collection.

Hours: Tue-Sun 10:00-18:00, closed Mon.

Information: An excellent 10-Kč English guide to the *Slav Epic* is available right in the gallery with the paintings. Tel. 224-301-122, www.ngprague.cz.

While You're There: Upstairs from the *Slav Epic* is the National Gallery's modern art collection, with works by Monet, Van

Gogh, Picasso, and Czech contemporaries such as František Kupka.

Getting There: Veletržní Palace is located near Holešovice Station at Dukelských Hrdinů 47 (Praha 7). To get there, take any of the following **trams** to the Veletržní stop: tram #17 from the Staroměstská Metro stop (four stops); tram #24 from Náměstí Republiky (three stops); or tram #12 from Malostranská (three stops). The nearest **Metro** stop is Vltavská; exiting the Metro, walk through the underpass to the right of tram tracks, continue to the first tram intersection, turn right, and walk for two blocks. The gallery is the huge, gray, concrete building towering above the tram stop.

Background

Alfons Mucha (1860-1939) was born in the small Moravian town of Ivančice. Like most artists of his generation, he went to Paris to seek his fortune. After suffering as a starving artist, he was hired to design a poster for a play starring the well-known French actress Sarah Bernhardt. Overnight, Mucha was famous. He forged an instantly recognizable style—willowy maidens with flowing hair amid flowery designs and backed with a halo-like circle. His pastel pretties appeared on magazine covers, wallpaper, carpets, and ad campaigns hawking everything from biscuits to beer. Mucha's florid style helped define what became known as Art Nouveau.

But even as he pursued a lucrative (if superficial) career in Paris and the US, Mucha was always thinking about his native land. While preparing a piece for the Paris Exposition of 1900, he traveled widely through Slavic lands. He soaked up the culture, history, and proud traditions. He conceived a plan to immortalize great moments in Slavic history on a grand, epic scale. Mucha convinced the Chicago industrialist Charles Crane to sponsor his project. They both believed art could inspire understanding and bring humanity closer together.

At age 50, Mucha returned to Prague and started work. For his studio, he rented a castle that was big enough to accommodate the huge canvases. For the next 16-plus years, he cranked out these enormous works. At the same time, he was juggling fatherhood and the worries of World War I. The year 1918 brought a watershed in Czech history, as World War I ended and the modern self-governing nation of Czechoslovakia was created. Mucha was immediately tapped by the new government to design the nation's currency and stamps.

In 1928, on the 10th anniversary of modern Czechoslovakia, Mucha's lifework was finally unveiled. The response was lukewarm. In the experimental age of Picasso, Mucha's representational style was out of fashion. And with the rise of fascism in the 1930s, Mucha's overt Slavic nationalism came under attack.

In 1939, German tanks rumbled into Czechoslovakia. The Nazis considered Slavs an inferior race. They arrested the patriot Mucha—now 79 years old—and he was interrogated by the Gestapo. He died a few weeks later.

During World War II, Mucha's canvases were rolled up and hidden away from the Nazis and, in the process, damaged. In 1963, after years of restoration, the paintings were put on display in the obscure Czech town of Moravský Krumlov, near Mucha's birthplace.

After Mucha's death, the city of Prague moved to reclaim the lost masterpiece. In 2011, after a decades-long legal battle, the *Slav Epic* was brought to Prague's Veletržní Palace. Mucha's work is finally in an accessible place where Czechs and tourists alike can appreciate his grand vision.

Self-Guided Tour

In these 20 panels, Mucha traces the 1,500-year history of the Slavic people. The panels are roughly chronological, but Mucha isn't above veering from the facts to emphasize the people's spiritual journey. The canvases are mindbogglingly big—some are 25 by 20 feet, and together they total 6,800 square feet, which is more than Michelangelo's

Sistine ceiling. Mucha's magnum opus has been scorned by many Czech intellectuals for its style and overt patriotism. But the work goes beyond the style of the time, beyond Art Nouveau, and beyond Slavic nationalism.

1. The Slavs in Their Original Homeland (1912)

Two desperate refugees (at bottom) huddle for safety as their homeland is ravaged by invading armies (in the distance). But from these humble beginnings, the Slavic people will someday rise to greatness—as symbolized by the vision of a pagan Slavic priest (upper right).

Historically, it's 500 A.D. Nomadic tribes are sweeping across the European landscape—Huns from the East and Germans from the West. Caught in the crossfire is a small population of peace-loving farmers in (today's) Ukraine—the Slavs. They share a com-

Viewing the Paintings

Contemplate the *Slav Epic* on several levels. First, figure out what's being depicted. (My descriptions are a start; buy the excellent pamphlet for more detail.) With his ad-man expertise, Mucha sucks you right into the scene, using strong composition and a sense of color.

Next, read the symbolism: Red is the color of war, white is peace, blue is the past, and orange is the future. (Freemasons will find even more occult symbolism.) Study Mucha's painting technique. He employs egg-based tempera paint for the low-resolution background, then finishes with sharp-focus oil paint to make the details pop. Appreciate Mucha's unique ability to crystalize entire historical epochs into a single scene, expressed in the emotions of individuals and condensed into the expressions on their faces.

Finally, step back and consider the paintings as the works of an Impressionist or abstract artist. The fusion of colors stands far beyond any particular meaning. Like the tones of a 19th-century symphony, Mucha's visual concert has the power to stir the deepest emotions.

mon language, culture, and DNA, but have no country to call their own.

Mucha begins his 20-canvas story with this Slavic Adam and Eve driven from paradise. Over the centuries, the Slavs would roam from their Ukrainian epicenter, searching for a homeland in places as far away as (today's) Russia, Poland, the Balkans, and—on the western perimeter—Prague.

Mucha (an avid photographer) uses a double-exposure technique to show two realities: the historical/earthly events (e.g., the terrified couple and army) and the mythic otherworld (the priest flanked by "war" and "peace"). Also notice how Mucha highlights crucial details (like the couple's terrified faces) by using sharp-focus oil paints on top of the foggy base of egg tempera.

2. The Celebration of Svantovit (1912)

The Slavs—originally a pagan people—dress in white to celebrate the harvest by sacrificing bulls to their fertility god, Svantovit (who hovers above with other gods, holding a drinking horn). But their peace is about to be shattered, in the form of Thor (upper left), who arrives with wolves. It's the Slavs' eternal enemy—the Germans. When you gaze into the eyes of the forlorn-looking young mother (at bottom, echoing the woman in the first painting), it seems that the Slavs are forever destined to be refugees.

3. Introduction of the Slavonic Liturgy in Great Moravia (1912)

The Slavs are converted to Christianity, thanks to Saint Methodius (standing just left of center, with long white beard) and Saint Cyril (in the background at left, leading a parade of men). Recall that Mucha also featured these two founding fathers in his stained-glass window at St. Vitus Cathedral (see page 117).

Floating above the earthly scene are the rulers who welcomed the new religion of Christianity. At top, the Catholic pope and the Orthodox patriarch—representing the two strains of Slavic Christianity—embrace. Back on earth, the boy with the ring symbolizes how Christianity will bring the Slavs together in never-ending union.

4. Tsar Simeon I of Bulgaria (1923)

The enlightened Slavic ruler dictates the Christian message to his scribes. The wisdom seems to radiate out from the center of this essentially circular composition. This is the first of several paintings in the series immortalizing the great Slavic rulers of the Middle Ages who established sophisticated kingdoms of art and literature across Eastern Europe.

5. King Přemysl Otakar II of Bohemia (1924)

In an elaborate tent set up for an outdoor wedding, King Otakar (in shining gold, with a red cap) welcomes royal guests from around Europe. By sealing political alliances with this marriage, Otakar (c. 1233-1278) ushers in the Golden Age of Bohemia (i.e., the Czech Republic). Under Otakar, the Slavic influence dominated Austria and Hungary.

6. Coronation of Serbian Tsar Stefan Dušan (1923)

A parade of happy Slavs leaves the palace after watching Stefan Dušan (c. 1308-1355) be crowned ruler of Serbia. Dušan established a constitution—a kind of Slavic Magna Carta for basic rights throughout Eastern Europe.

Unfortunately, the golden days of Slavic self-rule were num-

bered. By the 14th century, Slavic lands were increasingly dominated by German colonizers and by the Catholic Church of Rome.
Who could stand up to them?

The Triptych:
7. Jan Milič of Kroměříž (1916)
8. Master Jan Hus Preaching at the Bethlehem Chapel (1916)
9. The Meeting at Křížky (1916)
This three-paneled work—the kind normally seen as a church al-
tarpiece—is dedicated to the life and influence of the great Czech
reformer who spoke truth to power, Jan Hus. (For more on Hus,
see page 62.)

    Central panel (#8): The scene is Bethlehem Chapel (which
was rebuilt in the 1950s using supposedly the original design—
see page 70). The year is 1414. Hus preaches from the pulpit (left),
leaning out to make his point. He's been excommunicated by the
pope for his heretical views. But here in Prague he's a rock star.
Among the rapt listeners are the queen (far right, seated under
the red canopy) and loyal General Jan Žižka (far left, against the
wall; he's the guy with an eye patch depicted in several Hus-related
scenes). But there's a weasel in their midst—at the far right behind
the queen's entourage. In a few short weeks, Hus would be arrested,
imprisoned, and eventually burned at the stake.

    But his legacy lived on...

    Left panel (#7): Hus inspired concern for society's downtrod-
den. Here, a notorious brothel in Prague's Old Town is dismantled,
to be replaced with a convent for reformed prostitutes.

    Right panel (#9): On a remote hill outside Prague, Hus' fol-
lowers gather as they prepare to defend their beliefs. The Hussite
Wars are coming. The sky darkens.

10. After the Battle of Grunwald (1924)
A quarter-million men squared off on a battlefield in Poland, pitting
Slavs against German invaders who tried to impose the pope's will.
The Slavs held out. Here, the battlefield is littered with the blood-
stained tunics (white with black crosses) of the German Teutonic
Knights. Notice how the winners don't revel in victory; instead their
faces express sorrow over the destruction and loss of life.

11. After the Battle of Vítkov Hill (1923)
War comes to Prague. In this battle (1420), on a hill east of Prague's
Old Town, the Hussites drove off the pope's forces. Now a priest
holds a monstrance and says Mass—a service that will include
both the bread and the wine, affirming the fundamental right the
Hussites were fighting for. Amid the gloom, a glimmer of heav-

enly light shows through and illuminates General Jan Žižka, who thanks God for the victory.

12. Petr of Chelčický (1918)

Refugees from the wars—in this case, victims of Hussite atrocities—flee their village. One angry man (near the center) turns and vows revenge, but he's restrained by peace-loving Petr (in hat and scarf and clutching a Bible), whose pacifist ideas—rather than those of Hus—would later inspire the Unity of the Brethren, Comenius, and Mucha himself.

13. The Hussite King Jiří z Poděbrad (1923)

At war's end, the pope and Hussites signed a peace treaty allowing the Czechs to choose their own king. But the long fight for Slavic autonomy wasn't over. In this scene, set in Prague's Old Town, the pope's ambassador (in red, framed by the window) tries to weasel out of the deal. The proud Czech king (far right) stands up and defies the pope by kicking over the ambassador's chair. The king is so mighty that he bows to no one, not even the pope's representative.

14. The Defense of Szigetvár by Nikola Zrinski (1914)

The Slavs also had to defend their lands on the Eastern front, against Muslim Ottomans (from today's Turkey). Szigetvár—a small town in the south of Hungary—was a Slavic Alamo. Outnumbered 50 to 1, the defenders vowed to go up in flames for their cause. They did. A column of black smoke rises up ominously in the foreground.

15. The Printing of the Bible of Kralice in Ivančice (1914)

This painting of a garden outside a city wall is set in Ivančice, Mucha's hometown (near Brno, 150 miles southeast of Prague). The teenager at lower right (in white shirt, carrying a sheaf of papers) is Mucha himself.

Mucha's birthplace was home to a band of Hussite followers called the Unity of the Brethren. They helped bring literacy to the Slavic lands by translating the Latin Bible into the language of the people. The wooden lean-to on the right is the Bible print shop. Mucha is bringing in fresh paper to help spread the good word. Rich and poor alike intermingle, showing the leveling effect of education.

16. Jan Amos Komenský (1918)

On a lonely seashore sits a solitary figure. It's the famous Czech teacher Jan Amos Komenský (a.k.a. Comenius, 1592-1670), the man who virtually invented textbooks and modern education. (For more on Comenius, see page 284.) Now at the end of his days—

having lived as an exile for his beliefs—he faces death alone. His followers huddle nearby. Will they ever regain their homeland? The tiny lantern holds out "A Flicker of Hope" (Mucha's subtitle for the work).

17. The Holy Mount Athos (1926)
Now in his sixties and nearing completion of the cycle, Mucha returns to the double-exposure mysticism of early works. Pilgrims fill the church below while holy presences inhabit the sunlit atmosphere above.

Before this piece, Mucha had visited the Orthodox monastery of Mount Athos, Greece—a pilgrimage center for Orthodox Slavs. Mucha—though very much a worldly, modern man—was fascinated with occult forms of Christianity. He saw Christianity as a unifying and enlightening element for the Slavic people.

18. The Oath of the Youth under the
Slavic Linden Tree (1926)
But Mucha never neglected the Slavs' pagan origins. Here, young people join hands to sing "Kumbaya" to the goddess of their people—Slávia. Men in 19th-century clothes join in. They're part of the movement in the 1800s to revive Slavic language and culture, and create a national homeland (see page 317). Many faces remain unfinished, but they could easily be men like Antonín Dvořák and Bedřich Smetana, who composed symphonies from folk songs to remind the Slavic peoples of their common heritage. By the way, the two allegorical figures sitting on the wall are Mucha's son and daughter.

19. The Abolition of Serfdom in Russia (1914)
The Russian Emancipation Proclamation has just been issued (1861). Stunned by the news that their slaves are now free, the populace wanders dumbfounded across a snowy field. The symbols of

Russian oppression—the Kremlin and St. Basil's Cathedral—loom behind. Emancipation is a first step for a few Slavs, but true freedom for all remains a dream. But soon, the dream would become a reality...

20. The Apotheosis of the Slavs (1926)
In the final panel, Mucha tries to sum up the whole thing—the 1,500-year journey of the Slavic people, and where they're headed. Take a deep breath and dive in.

Start in the lower right. In blue, we

BEYOND THE CORE

see the huddled, oppressed people of the sixth century longing for a peaceful homeland. Poor Slavs. In the upper left (the band of red), it's the Middle Ages, and the Slavs rise to prominence under a series of strong kings (like the man on his throne to the right).

In the center (joyous yellow), it's 1918. World War I has ended, and gaily clad Slavs rejoice, waving flags of the victorious nations (including the Stars and Stripes) and olive branches to salute the troops. Emerging from the war is a new Slavic nation—Czechoslovakia—symbolized by the torso of a strong young man who rises up from the chaos, clutching the wreaths of freedom and Slavic unity. Behind him, Christ blesses the new nation, and a rainbow signals a new era of peace.

Today, the Slavic community is almost 400 million strong. They inhabit the Czech Republic, Slovakia, Poland, much of the Balkans, Ukraine, Belarus, Russia, and beyond. Some are Catholic, some Orthodox; some write in Cyrillic script, some Latin. But they share a common heritage, which Mucha has celebrated in the audacious artistic endeavor known as the *Slav Epic*.

Vyšehrad Walk

For a park-like break from the big city, fine views, and a special insight into Czech culture and history, consider this easy walk through Vyšehrad (VEE-sheh-rahd), a park just south of the New Town with a 17th-century fortress overlooking Prague. You'll ride the Metro to the top of the park and stroll through ramparts and trees with locals, past monuments and commanding views, then gradually head downhill, eventually ending up in the area known as Výtoň. From here, an easy walk along the river or a tram ride takes you back into the tourist action.

Orientation

Length of This Walk: Allow two hours.
When to Go: This walk works during the day but is also appealing in the evening, as most everything (except the basilica and casemates) is open 24/7, romantic, and lit at night.
Getting There: Take the Metro to the Vyšehrad stop.
Information: Tel. 241-410-348, www.praha-vysehrad.cz.
Vyšehrad Gallery: 30 Kč, daily 10:00-18:00 except closed Jan-Feb.
Basilica of Sts. Peter and Paul: 30 Kč, daily 10:00-18:00.
Casemates: Only viewable by 20-minute tour, 60 Kč, tours depart daily 10:00-17:00 at the top of the hour.

The Walk Begins

• *The Vyšehrad Metro exit leads directly to a terrace with a balcony overlooking the city. Take a moment to appreciate the...*

❶ View of Prague

Survey the scene. The tall, modern bridge was built in the 1970s to accommodate both the Metro and cars. To test whether it could carry its designed load, the first vehicles to cross the bridge were a battalion of tanks. Along the opposing slopes you can discern the brick fortifications of the New Town (one of the last places in Prague that these fortifications have been preserved). Now turn around. The gigantic glass and concrete building is the Congress Center. Finished in the early 1980s, it was originally designed to house Communist Party conventions but quickly came to be considered the ugliest building in town. In 1999, several former Warsaw Pact countries (including the Czech Republic) joined NATO, and the Congress Center became the first place in Eastern Europe to host a NATO summit.

• *Walk along the granite bannister the length of the Congress Center building, angling down the ramp and following the brown signs down to the actual Vyšehrad fortress walls. Once you reach the walls, notice the combination of red brick and white* opuka, *Prague's native limestone. Enter through a gate on the right, and stop at the map of the park on an info post.*

❷ Old Vyšehrad

The map shows the layout of this 17th-century fortress, built in the shape of a pentagon with a bastion at every corner. The only access was from the east, along a fortified corridor with double gates. You are standing just inside the outer one, called the Tábor Gate.

Archaeological records show that Vyšehrad once housed a royal palace and an astounding number of churches. By the 10th century, this place had become a Slavic alternative to the more Latin Prague Castle. Unfortunately, much of what was once here was destroyed by looters in 1420 during the Hussite Wars.

Two and a half centuries later, the Habsburgs chose this more-or-less empty site to serve as the city garrison. Despite the high construction costs, the fortress never saw real fighting. The Austrians remained at Vyšehrad until the 1840s.

Once the soldiers departed, another gate was blasted through the walls on the north side to create an easier connection to the New Town (this walk will take you around the ramparts and out through that gate). The fortress was eventually turned into a park that became popular with Romantic Czech artists, who walked the ramparts daydreaming about their nation's mythic past. The

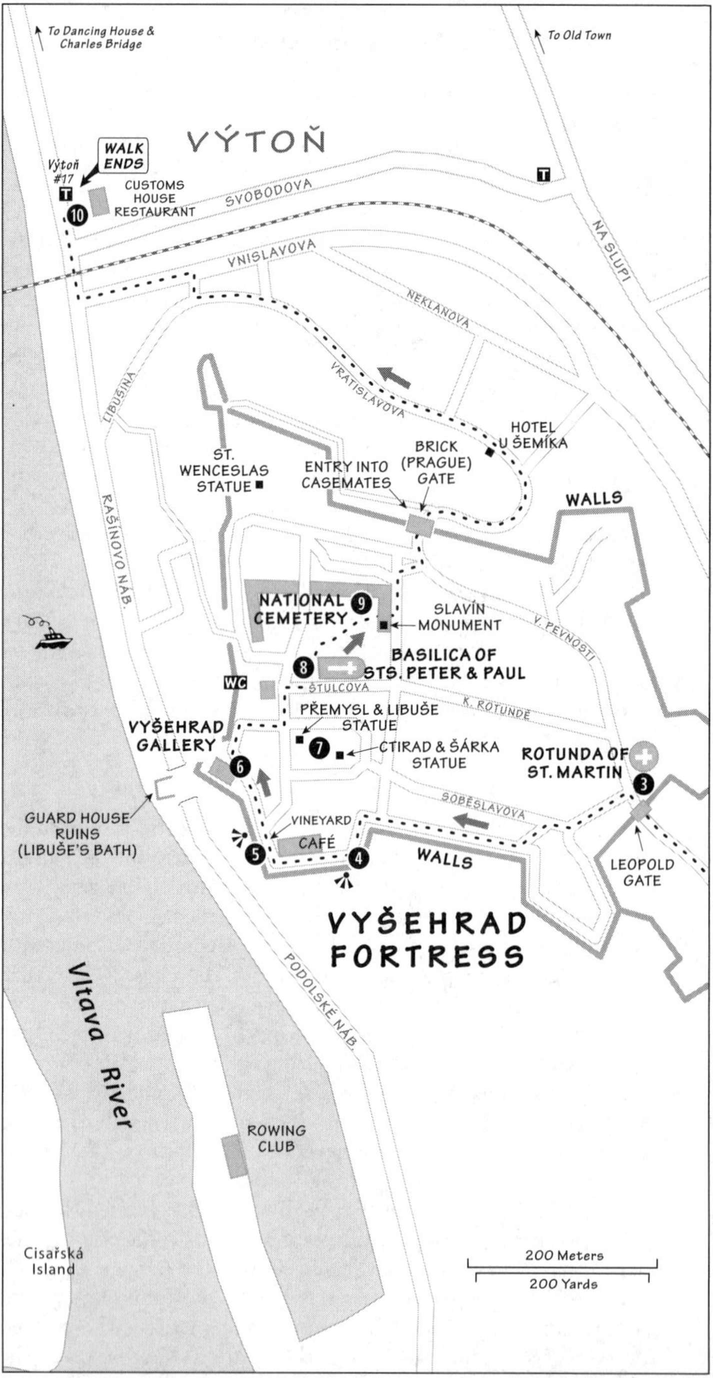

To Dancing House & Charles Bridge

To Old Town

VÝTOŇ

Výtoň #17

WALK ENDS

CUSTOMS HOUSE RESTAURANT

10

SVOBODOVA

NA SLUPI

VNISLAVOVA

NEKLANOVA

LIBUŠINA

VRATISLAVOVA

HOTEL U ŠEMÍKA

ST. WENCESLAS STATUE

ENTRY INTO CASEMATES

BRICK (PRAGUE) GATE

WALLS

RAŠÍNOVO NÁB.

NATIONAL CEMETERY

9

SLAVÍN MONUMENT

V. PEVNOSTI

8

BASILICA OF STS. PETER & PAUL

WC

ŠTULCOVA

K. ROTUNDĚ

VYŠEHRAD GALLERY

PŘEMYSL & LIBUŠE STATUE

7

ČTIRAD & ŠÁRKA STATUE

ROTUNDA OF ST. MARTIN

3

6

GUARD HOUSE RUINS (LIBUŠE'S BATH)

5

VINEYARD CAFÉ

4

SOBĚSLAVOVA

WALLS

LEOPOLD GATE

VYŠEHRAD FORTRESS

Vltava River

PODOLSKÉ NÁB.

ROWING CLUB

Cisařská Island

200 Meters

200 Yards

BEYOND THE CORE

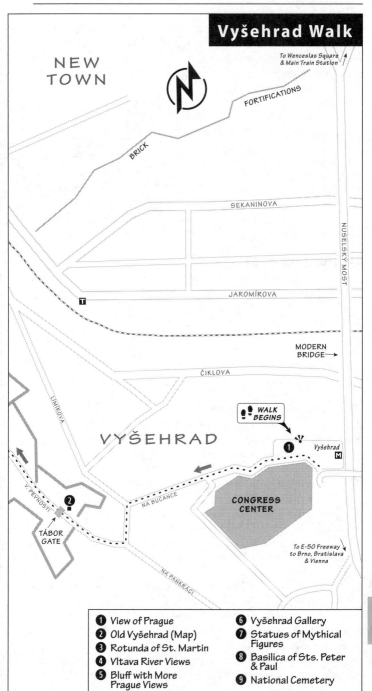

Vyšehrad Walk

NEW TOWN

FORTIFICATIONS

To Wenceslas Square & Main Train Station

BRICK

SEKANINOVA

JAROMÍROVA

NUSELSKÝ MOST

MODERN BRIDGE →

ČIKLOVA

WALK BEGINS

Vyšehrad M

❶

VYŠEHRAD

V PEVNOSTI

LUMÍROVA

NA BUČANCE

CONGRESS CENTER

❷

TÁBOR GATE

To E-50 Freeway to Brno, Bratislava & Vienna

NA PANKRÁCI

❶ View of Prague
❷ Old Vyšehrad (Map)
❸ Rotunda of St. Martin
❹ Vltava River Views
❺ Bluff with More Prague Views

❻ Vyšehrad Gallery
❼ Statues of Mythical Figures
❽ Basilica of Sts. Peter & Paul
❾ National Cemetery

BEYOND THE CORE

less that remained of the Romanesque and Gothic past, the better, leaving that much more to the imagination and stirring the Czech soul inside artists like the composer Bedřich Smetana. Just as it had centuries before, Vyšehrad became the Slavic alternative to the more Germanic town.

• *Continue along the cobbled street. On the right, notice a tiny piece of a Gothic gate, a reminder of the pre-Hussite period. As you pass through a second gate (the Leopold Gate), look up at the double-headed eagle—the coat of arms of the Habsburgs, who ruled in Prague for 300 years. Once through the gate, stop on the corner under a horse-chestnut tree to survey the little round...*

❸ Rotunda of St. Martin

This 11th-century Romanesque rotunda, constructed out of Prague's native limestone, is named for St. Martin, patron saint of soldiers, horses, riders, geese, and vintners. St. Martin's feast day falls on November 11 and is celebrated with roast goose and the year's first wine. On this day, St. Martin arrives on a white horse, signifying snow and the coming of winter.

• *Turn left and walk up the lane under the chestnut tree. Turn right, left, and right again to reach the ramparts. This is a good spot to enjoy...*

❹ Vltava River Views

You are looking south, or upstream. Bohemia, one of three regions that make up the Czech Republic (the others are Moravia and Silesia), is defined by its watershed. The region is essentially a big basin with mountains at its edges and Prague right in the middle. The Vltava originates in the south at the border with Germany and collects the waters from the south, east, and west before it flows into the Elbe River about 30 miles north of Prague. The Elbe breaks its way through the sandstone formations at the northern Czech/German border, marking the only place where water leaves Bohemia. It then flows through Dresden, on to Hamburg, and empties into the North Sea.

The TV tower on the horizon marks the spot where the Vltava meets up with two big rivers, one from the east and one from the west. The hill above the confluence was once the largest Celtic settlement in the country (Bohemia derives its name from the Celtic tribe that used to inhabit the area). Celts were the first to recognize Prague's strategic location at a time when waterways were the main or only means of transportation. The two main products that traveled downstream were Austrian salt (Bohemia lacks its own salt) and wood from the border mountains.

The name of the river, Vltava, comes from the old Germanic for "wild awa," meaning wild waters. Moldau—what Germans call the river today—is a variant of the same word. The rapids that gave the river its name disappeared in the 1950s and '60s under a series of dams that were, among other things, built to protect Prague from flooding. But in 2002, the dams were unable to rein in massive flood waters during what was the country's biggest recorded flood.

• *Turn right and follow the ramparts to the end, where you'll find yourself on a bluff overlooking the river.*

❺ Bluff with More Prague Views

Down below, find the wooden house flanked by yachts. This is Prague's oldest rowing club. Next, locate the island across the way. In 1896, the first soccer match between Sparta and Slavia was played on the island's meadow, marking the start of the biggest sports rivalry in the country. The large mansion on top of the hill belongs to Karel Gott (literally "God" in German), the never-fading pop star whose fame has persisted from the 1950s to today (imagine if Elvis was still alive). The mansion is just a little uphill from Villa Bertramka, where Mozart stayed with friends during his visits to Prague.

Down below, perched on a cliff, are the ruins of a guard house for customs collectors. Popular legend has reinvented it as the bathhouse of Princess Libuše, Prague's mythic founder. As the tale goes, Libuše led her Slavic people down from the plains north of Prague and decided to build a castle at Vyšehrad. Upon reaching the rocky hill, Libuše sent her men into the valley to ask about the name of the place where they had just arrived. The men encountered some charcoal makers. While standing in the doorway, they were told that they were "on the threshold" *(práh)*. This popular interpretation of the etymology of the city's name is symbolic of the way locals perceive Prague: They view the city as a place of encounter between East and West and between Latin culture and Slavic heritage.

• *Walk downhill through the tiny vineyard. To the right is a delightful park café—good for a beer and a sandwich (indoor and outside seating). Carry on to the left to...*

BEYOND THE CORE

❻ Vyšehrad Gallery

Vyšehrad Gallery has small exhibits featuring local artists. It also boasts more city views. From here study the sprawling Prague Castle in the distance, with its five noble palaces crowned by a cathedral. Just across the river is the smokestack of the Staropramen brewery (marked with a big *A*). Depending on the direction of the wind, you may be able to smell the malt. High up on the hill is a 200,000-seat stadium that has hosted mass calisthenics gatherings (called Sokol) since the 1930s. During the communist years, these were adapted into even more grandiose gatherings that took place every five years.

• *Walk through a park dotted with deciduous trees typical of the Czech Republic: linden, oak, alder, and ash. This is where you'll find a few...*

❼ Statues of Mythical Figures

These 19th-century statues give shape to some old Slavic legends. The one on the left depicts **Princess Libuše** with an outstretched hand and closed eyes, prophesizing the great future of the city. To her right is her husband, **Přemysl the Plower** (holding, of course, a plow in his hands). Together they founded a historic dynasty that ruled from Prague for more than four centuries.

Diagonally across from the couple is a statue of a stout man with a mustache kneeling in front of a beautiful girl. These are **Ctirad** (the honor-loving one) and **Šárka** (the twilight girl), the main protagonists of a legend that retells a 1,500-year-old battle of the sexes. The women knew that they would be unable to beat Ctirad—the most powerful fighter—and his men on the battlefield. So instead, they used trickery: One summer day, they tied the beautiful Šárka to a tree, naked, and hid in the woods to await Ctirad and his men. When they arrived, Ctirad stopped to help the girl, who told him that she had been left there to die as a traitor. Ctirad untied her, gave her some clothes, and sent his men to a nearby meadow to drink honey mead. Ctirad asked Šárka about the golden horn around her neck, and she encouraged him to try it. The sound of the horn signaled the women, who jumped out of the woods, killed the drunk men, and took Ctirad as their prisoner, eventually torturing him to death by tearing his limbs apart on a large wheel. The men lost the war, and ever since women have ruled most Czech households. As for Šárka, she eventually went mad and jumped off a cliff into a rocky valley on the western edge of town (which now bears her name).

• *Continue on to the nearby...*

❽ Basilica of Sts. Peter and Paul

The Neo-Gothic Basilica of Sts. Peter and Paul was built on the site of earlier Romanesque and Baroque churches. Until the 18th century, Vyšehrad was so important that this church and its priest answered directly to the pope (not to the bishops and archbishops of Prague). On the front facade are statues of Peter and Paul, along with mosaics depicting Cyril and Methodius, the Macedonian saints who first brought Christianity to the Slavs in their own language (rather than in Latin). The interior features circa-1900 Art Nouveau frescoes and richly decorated Neo-Gothic windows. Most of the chapels hold Baroque altars; the most precious of these is the first one on the right by Karel Škréta, dedicated to the patrons of Czech lands.

• *Leaving the church, turn right and enter the...*

❾ National Cemetery

Since the 1870s, major Czech cultural figures have been buried here, including Mucha, Smetana, and Dvořák (a map at the cemetery gate shows the locations of their graves). The most important tomb is Slavín (meaning "ground of glory"), a large monument capped by angels and dedicated to many cultural VIPs, including Mucha. The word *Rodina*, which you'll see inscribed on gravestones, means family.

• *Leave the graveyard through a gate just after the Slavín monument, turn left, and follow the cemetery wall. At the corner, continue straight down the steps, which lead out of the fortress through a big brick gate. Built into the gate are impressive 18th-century military casemates. These passageways lead to a chapel-like space (designed for ammunition storage), with six original statues from the Charles Bridge (viewable by tour only).*

Follow the cobbled lane as if you were arriving from Austria 150 years ago. You'll exit the park onto a street that leads downhill, under a railway trestle, to the river and the ❿ stop for tram #17.

Within a few steps of the tram stop are the interesting customs house restaurant and a Saturday morning farmers' market along the riverbank (8:00-14:00). From here you can walk or ride the tram to Frank Gehry's Dancing House (two stops). Tram #17 also goes to Charles Bridge, or all the way to Veletržní Palace, where you can view Mucha's Slav Epic.

SLEEPING IN PRAGUE

Peak months for hotels in Prague are May, June, and September. Easter and New Year's are the most crowded times, when prices are jacked up a bit. I've listed peak-time prices—if you're traveling in July or August, you'll find rates generally 15 percent lower, and from November through March, about 30 percent lower. It's often possible to negotiate a discount off the official rack rate (a hotel's highest, published rate). Most rack rates are given in euros, so the listed prices in crowns may differ somewhat due to currency fluctuations.

Old Town Hotels and Pensions

You'll pay higher prices to stay in the Old Town, but for many travelers, the convenience is worth the expense. These places are all within a 10-minute walk of the Old Town Square.

$$$ Hotel Metamorphis is a splurge, with solidly renovated rooms in Prague's former caravanserai (hostel for foreign merchants). Its breakfast room is in a spacious medieval cellar with modern artwork. Some of the street-facing rooms, located above two popular bars, are noisy at night (Db-3,800 Kč on average, check website for special rates and last-minute discounts, guest computer, free Wi-Fi, Malá Štupartská 5, tel. 221-771-011, www.hotelmetamorphis.cz, hotel@metamorphis.cz).

$$ Hotel Maximilian is a sleek, mod, 70-room place with Art Deco black design; big, plush living rooms; and all the business services and comforts you'd expect in a four-star hotel. It faces a church on a perfect little square just a short walk from the action (Db-3,300 Kč, extra bed-1,200 Kč; online deal sometimes offered: stay 3 days and pay for 2; guest computer, free Wi-Fi, Haštalská 14, tel. 225-303-111, www.maximilianhotel.com, reservation@maximilianhotel.com).

Sleep Code

(20 Kč = about $1, country code: 420)
S = Single, **D** = Double/Twin, **T** = Triple, **Q** = Quad, **b** = bathroom, **s** = shower only. Unless otherwise noted, credit cards are accepted, and breakfast and tax are included. Everyone listed here speaks English.

To help you sort easily through these listings, I've divided the accommodations into three categories based on the price for a standard double room with bath:

$$$ **Higher Priced**—Most rooms 3,500 Kč or more.
$$ **Moderately Priced**—Most rooms between 2,500-3,500 Kč.
$ **Lower Priced**—Most rooms 2,500 Kč or less.

Prices can change without notice; verify the hotel's current rates online or by email. For the best prices, always book direct.

$$ Pension u Medvídků ("By the Bear Cubs") has 31 comfortably renovated rooms in a big, rustic, medieval shell with dark wood furniture. Upstairs, you'll find lots of beams—or, if you're not careful, they'll find you (Sb-2,000 Kč, Db-3,000 Kč, Tb-4,000 Kč, extra bed-500 Kč, "historical" rooms-10 percent more, apartment-20 percent more, manager Vladimír promises my readers a 10 percent discount with cash if you book direct, guest computer, Na Perštýně 7, tel. 224-211-916, www.umedvidku.cz, info@umedvidku.cz). The pension runs a popular beer-hall restaurant with live music most Fridays and Saturdays until 23:00—request an inside room for maximum peace.

$$ Design Hotel Jewel Prague (U Klenotníka), with 11 modern, comfortable rooms in a plain building, is three blocks off the Old Town Square (Sb-2,250 Kč, small double-bed Db-3,000 Kč, bigger double or twin-bed Db-3,400 Kč, Tb-3,750 Kč, 10 percent off when you book direct and mention this book, no elevator, free Wi-Fi, Rytířská 3, tel. 224-211-699, www.hoteljewelprague.com, info@jewelhotel.cz).

$ Green Garland Pension (U Zeleného Věnce), on a central cobbled lane, has a warm and personal feel rare for the Old Town. Located in a thick 14th-century building with open beams, it has a blond-hardwood charm decorated with a woman's touch. The nine clean and simply furnished rooms are two and three floors up, with no elevator (big Sb-2,100 Kč, Db-2,400 Kč, bigger Db-2,700 Kč, Tb-3,000 Kč, family suite, 5 percent cash discount, Wi-Fi, Řetězová 10, tel. 222-220-178, www.uzv.cz, pension@uzv.cz).

SLEEPING

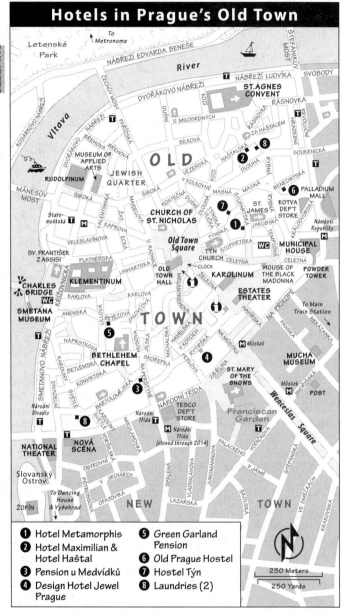

Hotels in Prague's Old Town

1. Hotel Metamorphis
2. Hotel Maximilian & Hotel Haštal
3. Pension u Medvídků
4. Design Hotel Jewel Prague
5. Green Garland Pension
6. Old Prague Hostel
7. Hostel Týn
8. Laundries (2)

250 Meters

250 Yards

$ Hotel Haštal is next to Hotel Maximilian (listed earlier) on the same quiet, hidden square in the Old Town. A popular hotel back in the 1920s, it has been renovated to complement the neighborhood's vibrant circa-1900 architecture. Its 24 rooms are comfortable, and its thin walls have recently been insulated against noise (Sb-1,500 Kč, Db-2,000 Kč, extra bed-550 Kč; manager Patrick promises my readers a 20 percent discount off their lowest online price, book via email to get the discount and avoid their online booking fee; air-con, free Wi-Fi, Haštalská 16, tel. 222-314-335, www.hastal.com, info@hastal.com).

Under the Castle, in the Little Quarter

The first and third listings below are buried on quiet lanes deep in the Little Quarter, among cobbles, quaint restaurants, rummaging tourists, and embassy flags. Hotel Julián is a 10-minute walk up the river on a quiet and stately street, with none of the intense medieval cityscape of the others. For locations, see the map on page 170.

$$$ Vintage Design Hotel Sax's 22 rooms are decorated in a retro, meet-the-Jetsons fashion. With a fruity atrium and a distinctly modern, stark feel, this is a stylish, no-nonsense place (Sb-3,800-4,300 Kč, Db-3,800-4,500 Kč, Db suite-5,000 Kč, extra bed-750 Kč, 10 percent off with this book—cannot be combined with other discounts, elevator, guest computer, free Wi-Fi, Jánský Vršek 3, tel. 257-531-268, www.sax.cz, hotel@sax.cz).

$$$ Hotel Julián is an oasis of professional, predictable decency in an untouristy neighborhood. Its 32 spacious, fresh, well-furnished rooms and big, homey public spaces hide behind a noble Neoclassical facade. The staff is friendly and helpful. Their official "rack rates" are ridiculous, but with the Rick Steves discount, you can generally get a double here for around 2,200 Kč (Sb-3,725 Kč, Db-3,975 Kč, suites and bigger rooms available, check website for discounts, 15 percent discount off best website price when you book direct and mention this book, half of the rooms have air-con—request when you reserve, elevator, free guest computer and Wi-Fi, plush and inviting lobby, summer roof terrace, parking lot; Metro: Anděl, then take tram #6, #9, #12, or #20 to the left as you leave Metro station for two stops; Elišky Peškové 11, Praha 5, reservation tel. 257-311-150, reception tel. 257-311-145, www.julian.cz, info@julian.cz). Free lockers and a shower are available for those needing a place to stay after checkout (while waiting for an overnight train, for example).

$$ Dům u Velké Boty ("House at the Big Boot"), on a quiet square in front of the German Embassy, is the rare quintessential family hotel in Prague: homey, comfy, and extremely friendly. Charlotta, Jan, and their two sons treat every guest as a (thirsty) friend, and the wellspring of their stories never runs dry. Each of their 12 rooms is uniquely decorated, most in a tasteful, 19th-century Biedermeier style (tiny Sb-2,100 Kč, two D rooms that share a bathroom-2,250 Kč each, Db-2,900-3,600 Kč, extra bed-725 Kč, 10 percent off with advance reservation and this book, prices can be soft when slow, cash only, children up to age 10 sleep free—toys provided, free guest computer and Wi-Fi, Vlašská 30, tel. 257-532-088, www.bigboot.cz, info@bigboot.cz). There's no hotel sign on the house—look for the splendid geraniums that Jan nurtures in the windows.

Away from the Center

Sleeping just outside central Prague saves you money—and gets you away from other tourists and into more workaday residential neighborhoods. The following listings are great values compared with the downtown hotels listed previously, and are all within a 5- to 15-minute tram or Metro ride from the center. Unless otherwise noted, for locations see the map on page 38.

Beyond Wenceslas Square

These hotels are in urban neighborhoods on the outer fringe of the New Town, beyond Wenceslas Square. But they're still within several minutes' walk of the sightseeing zone and are well-served by trams.

$$ Louren Hotel, with 20 rooms, is a quality four-star, business-class hotel in an upscale, circa-1900 residential neighborhood (Vinohrady) that has recently become popular with Prague's expat community. They do a good job of being homey and welcoming (Sb-2,900 Kč, Db-3,200 Kč, extra bed-1,600 Kč, fourth night free, 20 percent discount when you book direct and mention this book, 30 percent discount for last-minute reservations, air-con, elevator, guest computer, free Wi-Fi, 3-minute walk to Metro: Jiřího z Poděbrad, or tram #11, Slezská 55, Praha 3, tel. 224-250-025, www.louren.cz, reservations@louren.cz).

$$ Hotel 16 is a sleek and modern business-class place with an intriguing Art Nouveau facade, polished cherry-wood elegance, high ceilings, and 14 fine rooms (Sb-2,300 Kč, Db-2,900 Kč, Tb-3,500 Kč, 10 percent discount when you book direct and mention this book, check website for last-minute discounts, triple-paned windows, complimentary tea, back rooms facing the garden are quieter, air-con, elevator, free guest computer and Wi-Fi, limited free parking, 10-minute walk south of Wenceslas Square, Metro: I.P. Pavlova, Kateřinská 16, Praha 2, for location see the map on page 167, tel. 224-920-636, www.hotel16.cz, hotel16@hotel16.cz).

$ Hotel Anna offers 26 bright, simple, pastel rooms and basic service. It's a bit closer to the action—just 10 minutes by foot east of Wenceslas Square (Sb-1,600 Kč, Db-1,900 Kč, Tb-2,100 Kč, check website for discounts, elevator, free Wi-Fi, Budečská 17, Praha 2, Metro: Náměstí Míru, tel. 222-513-111, www.hotelanna. cz, sales@hotelanna.cz).

The Best Values, Farther from the Center

These accommodations are a 10- to 20-minute tram ride from the center, but once you make the trip, you'll see it's no problem—and you'll feel pretty smug saving $50-100 a night per double by not sleeping in the Old Town. Hotel Adalbert is on the grounds of an ancient monastery, and Pension Větrník is adjacent, with two of Prague's best-preserved natural areas (Star Park and Šárka) just a short walk away. Hotel u Šemíka and Guest House Lída are within a stone's throw of peaceful Vyšehrad Park, with its legendary castle on a cliff overlooking the Vltava River.

$$ Hotel Adalbert occupies an 18th-century building in the Břevnov Monastery (one of the Czech Republic's oldest monastic institutions, founded in 993). Meticulously restored after the return of the Benedictine monks in the 1990s, the monastery complex is the ultimate retreat for those who come to Prague for soul-searching or just wanting a quiet place away from the bustle. Join the monks for morning (7:00) and evening (18:00) Mass in the St. Margaret Basilica, a large and elegant Baroque church decorated with unusual simplicity. You can help yourself in the monastery fruit orchard and eat in the atmospheric monastery pub (Klášterní Šenk). The hotel itself caters primarily to business clientele and takes ecology seriously: recycling, water conservation, and free tram tickets for guests. I prefer the first-floor rooms, as some of the attic rooms—room numbers in the 200s—feel a bit cramped (Sb-1,800 Kč, Db-2,600 Kč, extra bed-1,000 Kč, less on weekends, check website for special rates and last-minute discounts, free Wi-Fi, free parking, halfway between city and airport at Markétská 1, Praha 6, tram #22 to Břevnovský Klášter; 5 minutes by tram beyond the castle, 20 minutes from Old and New Towns; tel. 220-406-170, www.hoteladalbert.cz, info@hoteladalbert.cz).

$$ Hotel u Šemíka, named for a heroic mythical horse, offers 25 rooms in a quiet residential neighborhood just below Vyšehrad Castle and the Slavín cemetery where Dvořák, Mucha, and Čapek are buried. It's a 10-minute tram ride south of the Old Town (Sb-2,000 Kč, Db-2,650 Kč, apartment-3,350-3,700 Kč for 2-4 people, extra bed-600 Kč, ask for the "direct booking" Rick Steves 10 percent discount when you reserve, guest computer and Wi-Fi; from the center, take tram #3, #17, or #21 to Výtoň, go under rail bridge, and walk 3 blocks uphill to Vratislavova 36; Praha 2, tel. 221-965-610, www.usemika.cz, usemika@usemika.cz).

$ Pension Větrník fills an attractive white-and-orange former 18th-century windmill in one of Prague's most popular residential

SLEEPING

areas, right next to the Břevnov Monastery and midway between the airport and the city. The talkative owner, Miloš Opatrný, is a retired prizewinning Czech chef whose culinary work took him as far as Japan. On request, he will gladly prepare a meal you won't forget. The six rooms here are the pride of the Opatrný family, who live on the upper floors. The garden has a red-clay tennis court—rackets and balls are provided (Db-1,800 Kč, suite-2,300 Kč, extra bed-500 Kč, guest computer, U Větrníku 1, Praha 6; airport bus #179 stops near the house, tram #18 goes straight to Charles Bridge, both take 20 minutes; tel. 220-513-390, www.vetrnik1722. cz, pension@vetrnik1722.cz).

$ **Guest House Lída,** with 12 homey and spacious rooms, fills a big house in a quiet residential area farther inland, a 15-minute tram ride from the center. Jan, Jitka, Jiří, and Jana Prouzas—who run the place—are a wealth of information and know how to make people feel at home (Sb-1,380 Kč, small Db-1,440 Kč, Db-1,760 Kč, Tb-2,110 Kč, Qb-2,530 Kč, cash only, family rooms, top-floor family suite with kitchenette, guest computer, free Wi-Fi, parking garage-200 Kč/day, Metro: Pražského Povstání; exit Metro and turn left on Lomnického between the Metro station and big blue-glass ČSOB building, follow Lomnického for 500 yards, then turn left on Lopatecká, go uphill and ring bell at Lopatecká 26; Praha 4, tel. 261-214-766, www.lidabb.eu, lidabb@seznam.cz). The Prouzas brothers also rent two **apartments** across the river, an equal distance from the center (Db-1,400 Kč, Tb-1,700 Kč, Qb-2,000 Kč).

Hostels in the Center

It's tough to find a double for less than 2,500 Kč in the old center. But Prague has an abundance of fine hostels—each with a distinct personality, and each excellent in its own way for anyone wanting a 300-500-Kč dorm bed or an extremely simple twin-bedded room for about 1,300 Kč. With travelers seeking cheaper options these days, it's good to keep in mind that hostels are no longer the exclusive domain of backpackers. The first two hostels are centrally located, but lack care and character; the last two are found in workaday neighborhoods and have atmospheric interiors.

$ **Old Prague Hostel** is a small place with 70 beds on the second and third floors of an apartment building on a back alley near the Powder Tower. The spacious rooms were once apartment bedrooms, so it feels less institutional than most hostels, but older travelers might feel a bit out of place. You can hang out in the comfy TV lounge/breakfast room (D-1,400 Kč, bunk in 4- to 8-person room-400-500 Kč; includes breakfast, sheets, towels, lockers, and free Wi-Fi; in summer reserve 2 weeks ahead for doubles, a few days ahead for bunks; Benediktská 2, see map on page 150 for location, tel. 224-829-058, www.oldpraguehostel.com, info@oldpraguehostel.com).

$ Hostel Týn is a quiet, mature, and sterile place hidden in a silent courtyard two blocks from the Old Town Square. The management is very aware of its valuable location, so they don't have to bother being friendly (D-1,240 Kč, T-1,410 Kč, bunk in 4- to 5-bed co-ed room-420 Kč, lockers, guest computer, free Wi-Fi, kitchen, no breakfast, reserve one week ahead, Týnská 19, see map on page 150 for location, tel. 224-808-301, www.hostelpraguetyn.com, info@hostelpraguetyn.com).

$ Sir Toby's is in a 1930s working-class neighborhood—a newly popular residential and dining-out area that's a 12-minute tram ride from the center. The owners have taken great pains to stamp the place with character: restored hardwood floors, a back garden with tables made out of sewing machines, and rooms filled with vintage 1930s furniture and photographs. Amenities include self- and full-service laundry, an on-site pub, and a friendly staff (120 beds, Sb-1,400 Kč, D-1,300 Kč, Db-1,700 Kč, Tb-1,840 Kč, bunk in 4- to 6-bed co-ed room-450 Kč, bunk in 8- to 10-bed co-ed room-350 Kč, free guest computer and Wi-Fi, take tram #5 from the Main Train Station or tram #3 from the middle of Wenceslas Square to Dělnická, at Dělnická 24, Praha 7, see map on page 38 for location, tel. 246-032-610, www.sirtobys.com, info@sirtobys.com). The owners also run two contemporary-design hostels in Vinohrady.

$ Hostel Elf, a 10-minute walk from the Main Train Station or one bus stop from the Florenc Metro station, is fun-loving, ramshackle, covered with noisy, self-inflicted graffiti, and the wildest of these hostels. They offer cheap, basic beds, a helpful staff, and lots of creative services—kitchen, free luggage room, free guest computer and Wi-Fi, laundry, no lockout, free tea, cheap beer, a terrace, and lockers (120 beds, D-1,100 Kč, bunk in 6- to 11-person room-320 Kč, includes sheets and breakfast, cash only, reserve four days ahead, Husitská 11, Praha 3, take bus #133 or #207 from Florenc Metro station for one stop to U Památníku, see map on page 38 for location, tel. 222-540-963, www.hostelelf.com, info@hostelelf.com).

Room-Booking Services

Prague is awash with fancy rooms on the push list; private, small-time operators with rooms to rent in their apartments; and roving agents eager to book you a bed and earn a commission. You can save about 30 percent by showing up without a reservation and finding accommodations upon arrival. However, it can be a hassle, and you won't necessarily get your ideal choice. If you're coming in by train or car, you'll encounter booking agencies. They can almost always find you a reasonable room, and, if it's in a private guesthouse, your host can even come and lead you to the place.

Athos Travel has a line on 200 properties (ranging from hostels to five-star hotels), 90 percent of which are in the Old Town. To book a room, call them or use their handy website, which allows you to search for a room, based on various criteria (best to arrange in advance during peak season, can also help with last-minute booking off-season, tel. 241-440-571, www.a-prague.com, info@a-prague.com). Readers report that Athos is aggressive with its business policies—although there's no fee if you cancel well in advance, they strictly enforce penalties on cancellations within 48 hours.

Touristpoint, at the Main Train Station (Hlavní Nádraží), is another booking service (daily 8:00-22:00). They have a slew of hotels and small pensions available (2,000-Kč pension doubles in the Old Town, 1,500-Kč doubles a Metro ride away). You can reserve online, using your credit card as a deposit (tel. 224-946-010, www.touristpoint.cz, info@touristpoint.cz), or just show up at the office and request a room. Be clear on the location before you make your choice.

Lída Jánská's **Magic Praha** can help with accommodations (mobile 604-207-225, www.magicpraha.cz, magicpraha@magicpraha.cz; see "Helpful Hints" on page 45). Lída rents a well-situated apartment with a river view near the Jewish Quarter.

EATING IN PRAGUE

A big part of Prague's charm is found in wandering aimlessly through the city's winding old quarters, marveling at the architecture, watching the people, and sniffing out fun restaurants. You can eat well here for very little money. What you'd pay for a basic meal in Vienna or Munich will get you a feast in Prague. In addition to meat-and-potatoes Czech cuisine, you'll find trendy, student-oriented bars and lots of fine ethnic eateries. For ambience, the options include traditional, dark Czech beer halls; elegant Art Nouveau dining rooms; and hip, modern cafés.

Watch out for scams. Many restaurants put more care into ripping off green tourists (and even locals) than into their cooking. Tourists are routinely served cheaper meals than what they ordered, given a menu with a "personalized" price list, charged extra for things they didn't get, or shortchanged. Speak Czech. Even saying "Hello" in Czech (*Dobrý den;* also see "Czech Survival Phrases" in the appendix) will get you better service. Avoid any menu without clear and explicit prices. Be careful of waiters padding the tab. Closely examine your itemized bill and understand each line (a 10 percent service charge is sometimes added—in that case, there's no need to tip extra). Tax is always included in the price, so it shouldn't be tacked on later.

Make it a habit to pay for your meals with cash. Part with very large bills only if necessary, and deliberately count your change. If you pay with a credit card, never let it out of your sight.

Remember, there are two parallel worlds in Prague: the tourist town and the real city. Generally, if you walk two minutes away from the tourist flow, you'll find better value, atmosphere, and service. (For more on scams, see "Rip-Offs in Prague" on page 41.)

I've listed eating and drinking establishments by neighborhood. The most options—and highest prices—are in the Old

Town. For a light meal, consider one of Prague's many cafés (see page 174). Many of the places listed here are handy for an efficient lunch, but may not offer fine evening dining. Others make less sense for lunch, but are great for a slow, drawn-out dinner. Read the descriptions to judge which is which.

Fun, Touristy Neighborhoods: Several areas are pretty and well-situated for sightseeing, but lined only with touristy restaurants. While these places are not necessarily bad values, I've listed only a few of your many options—just survey the scene in these spots and choose whatever looks best. **Kampa Square,** just off the Charles Bridge, feels like a small-town square. **Havelská Market** is surrounded by colorful little eateries, any of which offer a nice perch for viewing the market scene while you munch. The massive **Old Town Square** is the place to nurse a drink or enjoy a meal while watching the tide of people, both tourists and locals, sweep back and forth. There's often some event on this main square, and its many restaurants provide tasty and relaxing vantage points.

Traditional Czech Places: With the inevitable closing of cheap student pubs (replaced by shops and hotels that make more money), it's getting difficult to find a truly Czech pub in the historic city center. Most Czechs no longer go to "traditional" eateries, preferring the cosmopolitan taste of the world to the mundane taste of sauerkraut. As a result, ancient institutions with "authentic" Czech ambience have become touristy—but they're still great fun, a good value, and respected by locals. Expect wonderfully rustic spaces, smoke, surly service, and reasonably good, inexpensive food. Understand every line on your bill. I've listed several of these characteristically Czech eateries throughout this chapter.

Dining with a View: For great views, consider these options, all described in detail in the following pages: **Hotel u Prince's terrace** (rooftop dining above a fancy hotel, completely touristy but with awesome views); **Villa Richter** (next to Prague Castle, above Malostranská Metro stop); **Bellavista Restaurant** at the Strahov Monastery; **Petřínské Terasy** and **Nebozízek** next to the funicular stop halfway up Petřín Hill and **Čertovka** in the Little Quarter (superb views of the Charles Bridge). For the best cheap riverside dinner, have a picnic on a paddleboat (see page 56). There's nothing like drifting down the middle of the Vltava River as the sun sets, while munching on a picnic meal and sipping a beer with your favorite travel partner.

Cheap-and-Cheery Sandwich Shops: All around town you'll find modern little sandwich shops (like the Panería chain) offering inexpensive fresh-made sandwiches (grilled if you like), pastries, salads, and drinks. You can get the food to go, or eat inside at simple tables.

In the Old Town

Traditional Czech

Restaurace u Provaznice ("By the Ropemaker's Wife") has all the Czech classics, peppered with the story of a once-upon-a-time-faithful wife. (Check the menu for details of the gory story.) Natives congregate under bawdy frescoes for the famously good "pig leg" with horseradish and Czech mustard (100-300-Kč main dishes, daily 11:00-24:00, a block into the Old Town from the bottom of Wenceslas Square at Provaznická 3, tel. 224-232-528).

U Medvídků ("By the Bear Cubs") started out as a brewery in 1466 and is now a flagship beer hall of the Czech Budweiser. The one large room is bright, noisy, touristy, and a bit smoky (100-300-Kč main dishes, daily 11:30-23:00, a block toward Wenceslas Square from Bethlehem Square at Na Perštýně 7, tel. 224-211-916). The small beer bar next to the restaurant (daily 16:00-3:00 in the morning) is used by university students during emergencies—such as after most other pubs have closed.

U Zlatého Tygra ("By the Golden Tiger") has long embodied the proverbial Czech pub, where beer turns strangers into kindred spirits, who cross the fuzzy line between memory and imagination as they tell their hilarious life stories to each other. Today, "The Tiger" is a buzzing shrine to one of its longtime regulars, the writer Bohumil Hrabal, whose fictions immortalize many of the colorful characters that once warmed the wooden benches here. Only regulars have reserved tables. If you find a rare empty spot, you'll be treated as a surprise guest rather than as a customer—and likely will wait quite a while to land a beer (38-Kč pints of Pilsner, 50-Kč beer cheese, daily 15:00-23:00, just south of Karlova at Husova 17, tel. 222-221-111).

Jan Paukert is a traditional Czech deli that has been in business for a century, specializing in open-face sandwiches *(chlebíčky)*, cakes, and desserts. They also serve warm, ready-made meals in the seating area in back (30-Kč open-face sandwiches, 110-Kč main dishes, Mon-Fri 9:00-19:00, Sat 10:00-18:00, closed Sun, Národní 17, tel. 224-222-615).

Restaurace u Betlémské Kaple, behind Bethlehem Chapel, is not "ye olde" Czech. It has light wooden decor, cheap lunch deals, and fish specialties that attract natives and visitors in search of a good Czech bite for good Czech prices (100-200-Kč main dishes, daily 11:00-23:00, Betlémské Náměstí 2, tel. 222-221-639).

Česká Kuchyně ("Czech Kitchen") is a blue-collar cafeteria serving steamy old Czech cuisine. It's fast, practical, cheap, and traditional as can be. Pick up your tally sheet as you enter, grab a tray, point to whatever you'd like, and keep the paper to pay as you exit. It's extremely cheap...unless you lose your paper. As you

EATING

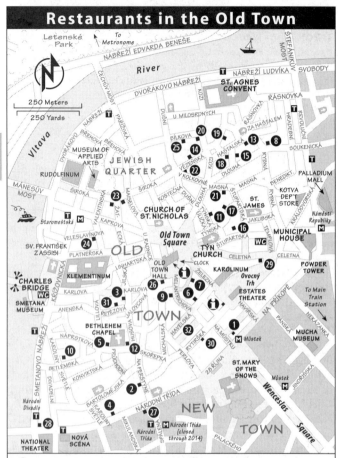

Restaurants in the Old Town

1. Restaurace u Provaznice
2. U Medvídků Beer Hall
3. U Zlatého Tygra Pub
4. Jan Paukert Deli
5. Restaurace u Betlémské Kaple
6. Česká Kuchyně
7. Restaurace Mlejnice
8. Lokál Restaurant
9. Country Life Vegetarian Rest.
10. Lehká Hlava Vegetarian Rest.
11. Vegetarian Rest. Maitrea
12. Klub Architektů
13. Chez Marcel
14. Amici Miei Restaurant
15. Ariana Afghan Restaurant
16. Indian Jewel
17. Beas Indian Cafeteria
18. Orange Moon
19. James Joyce Irish Pub
20. La Casa Blú
21. Bohemia Bagel
22. Kolkovna Restaurant
23. Kolonial & King Solomon Restaurants
24. Restaurace u Knihovny
25. Dinitz Kosher Restaurant
26. Hotel/Rest. u Prince Terasa
27. Le Patio & Café Louvre
28. Kavárna Slavia
29. Grand Café Orient
30. Café Café
31. Café Montmartre & Ebel Coffee House
32. Havelská Market

enter, you'll come across serving stations in this order: salads, fruit dumplings and sweets, soups, main dishes, and finally, drinks (60-150-Kč main dishes, daily 9:00-20:00, very central, across from Havelská Market at Havelská 23, tel. 224-235-574).

Restaurace Mlejnice ("The Mill") is a fun little pub strewn with farm implements and happy eaters, located just out of the tourist crush two blocks from the Old Town Square. They serve hearty traditional and modern Czech plates for 150-180 Kč. Reservations are smart in the evening (150-300-Kč main dishes, daily 11:00-24:00, between Melantrichova and Železná at Kožná 14, tel. 224-228-635).

Lokál ("The Dump") is a hit with residents for its good-quality Czech classics at low prices. Filling a long, arched space, the restaurant plays on customers' nostalgia: The stark interior is a deliberate 1980s retro design, and the waiters have been instructed to be curt (but not impolite)—just as if they were serving in one of Prague's notorious train station "dumps" (100-300-Kč main dishes, daily 11:00-1:00 in morning, ask for English menu at the front by the tap, Dlouhá 33, tel. 222-316-265). The same group has a smaller branch, **Lokál u Bílé Kuželky,** in the Little Quarter (see listing later).

Vegetarian and Modern

These hip and trendy places have a fun, youthful vibe.

Country Life Vegetarian Restaurant is a bright, easy, non-smoking cafeteria with a well-displayed buffet of salads and hot veggie dishes. It's midway between the Old Town Square and the bottom of Wenceslas Square. They're serious about their vegetarianism, serving only plant-based, unprocessed, and unrefined food. Its quiet dining area is elegant for a cafeteria, with a few tables outside in the courtyard (pay by weight, expect 150-200 Kč per meal, Sun-Thu 9:00-20:30, Fri 9:00-17:00, closed Sat, through courtyard at Melantrichova 15/Michalská 18, tel. 224-213-366).

Lehká Hlava Vegetarian Restaurant ("Clear Head"), tucked away on a cul-de-sac, has a mission to provide a "clear atmosphere for enjoying food." Sitting in an enchanted-forest setting, diners enjoy dishes from around the world. Reserve in advance for evenings (115-Kč two-course daily special, 150-185-Kč plates, no eggs, no smoke, lots of vegan dishes, daily 11:30-23:30, between Bethlehem Chapel and the river at Boršov 2, tel. 222-220-665, www.lehkahlava.cz).

Vegetarian Restaurant Maitrea, just off the Old Town Square alongside the Týn Church, serves imaginative dishes in a swoopy modern interior where every inch is curved to ensure the "unobstructed flow of energy." Its organic woody basement is even more seductive than the ground floor. The 105-Kč lunch special is

EATING

Czech Beer

Czechs are among the world's most enthusiastic beer *(pivo)* drinkers—adults drink an average of 80 gallons a year. The pub is a place to have fun, complain, discuss art and politics, talk hockey, and chat with locals and visitors alike. The *pivo* that was drunk in the country before the Industrial Revolution was much thicker, providing the main source of nourishment for the peasant folk.

Even today, it doesn't matter whether you're in a *restaurace* (restaurant), *hostinec* (pub), or *hospoda* (bar)—a beer will land on your table upon the slightest hint to the waiter, and a new pint will automatically appear when the old glass is almost empty. (You must tell the waiter not to bring more.) Order beer from the tap (*točené* means "draft," *sudové pivo* means "keg beer"). A *pivo* is large (0.5 liter—17 oz); a *malé pivo* is small (0.3 liter—10 oz). Men invariably order the large size. *Pivo* for lunch has me sightseeing for the rest of the day on Czech knees.

The Czechs invented Pilsner-style lager in nearby Plzeň ("Pilsen" in German), and the result, Pilsner Urquell, is on tap in many local pubs. But be sure to venture beyond this famous beer. The Czechs produce plenty of other good beers, including Krušovice, Gambrinus, Staropramen, and Kozel. Budvar, from the town of Budějovice ("Budweis" in German), is popular with Anheuser-Busch's attorneys. (The Czech and the American breweries for years disputed the "Budweiser" brand name. The solution: The Czech Budweiser is sold under its own name in Europe, China, and Africa, while in America it is marketed as Czechvar.)

The big degree symbol on bottles does not indicate the per-

a great value (150-250-Kč main dishes, Mon-Fri 11:30-23:30, Sat-Sun 12:00-23:30, Týnská ulička 6, tel. 221-711-631).

Klub Architektů, next to Bethlehem Chapel, is a modern hangout in a medieval cellar with a fun menu offering excellent original dishes, hearty salads, Moravian wines, and Slovak beer (150-300-Kč main dishes, daily 11:30-24:00, Betlémské Náměstí 169, tel. 224-401-214).

Ethnic Eateries and Bars
Dlouhá, the wide street leading away from the Old Town Square behind the Jan Hus Memorial, is lined with ethnic restaurants catering mostly to cosmopolitan locals. Within a couple of blocks, you can eat your way around the world. From Dlouhá, wander the

centage of alcohol content. Instead, it is a measurement used by brewers to track the density of certain ingredients. As a rough guide, 10 degrees is about 3.5 percent alcohol, 12 degrees is about 4.2 percent alcohol, and 11 and 15 degrees are dark beers.

The most popular Czech beers are about as potent as German beers and only slightly stronger than typical American beers.

Each establishment has only one kind of beer on tap; to try a particular brand, look for its sign outside. A typical pub serves only one brand of 10-degree beer, one brand of 12-degree beer, and one brand of dark beer. Czechs do not mix beer with anything, and they do not hop from pub to pub (in one night, it is said, you must stay loyal to one woman and to one beer). *Na zdraví* means "to your health" in Czech.

Microbrews are gaining in popularity. While the trend for much of the last 20 years has been for the three biggest beer corporations—SABMiller (maker of Pilsner Urquell, Gambrinus, and Kozel), StarBev (makes Staropramen), and Heineken (makes Krušovice)—to buy up or edge out the smaller companies, more recently Czechs have begun moving beyond "eurotaste" beers to creative microbrews. Consequently, more and more restaurants are making their own beer or serving beer only from independent breweries. In 2011, SABMiller—which holds 50 percent of the Czech beer market—suddenly decided to cut its supply of beer yeast to microbrewers (the production of beer yeast is beyond the means of small breweries). But microbrewers quickly found a new supplier in Bernard, the largest of independent breweries, and celebrated a small victory—the biggies are beginning to take them seriously.

Rámová/Haštalská/Vězeňská area to survey a United Nations of eateries: You'll find French (**Chez Marcel** at Haštalská 12); Italian (the expensive **Amici Miei** at Vězeňská 5, which prides itself on fresh *pesci* and *frutti di mare*); and Afghan (**Ariana** at Rámová 6).

These places deserve special consideration:

Indian: **Indian Jewel,** in the Ungelt courtyard behind the Týn Church, is the best place in Prague to find a full Indian menu that actually tastes Indian. Located in a pleasant, artfully restored courtyard, this is my choice for outdoor dining, with seriously executed sub-Continental classics and good-value lunch specials (110-Kč daily specials, 300-Kč main dishes, daily 11:00-23:00, Týn 6, tel. 222-310-156). For something trendier, head over to **Beas Indian Cafeteria.** This spartan little vegetarian restaurant is ruled by

EATING

a Punjabi chef, while diners grab a steel tray and point to whatever looks good. The food is sold by weight—you'll likely spend 150 Kč for lunch. Tucked away in a courtyard behind the Týn Church, this place is popular with university students (Mon-Fri 11:00-20:00, Sat 12:00-20:00, Sun 12:00-18:00, Týnská 19, mobile 608-035-727).

Thai: **Orange Moon** specializes in Thai curries, but you'll also find dishes from Myanmar (Burma) and India, served in a space delightfully decorated with artwork from Southeast Asia. This restaurant attracts a mixture of locals, expats, and tourists (120-200-Kč lunch specials, 200-350-Kč main dishes, daily 11:30-23:30, reservations recommended, Rámová 5, tel. 222-325-119, www.orangemoon.cz).

Irish: **James Joyce Irish Pub** may seem like a strange recommendation in Prague—home of some of the world's best beer—but it has the kind of ambience that locals (and few tourists) seek out. Expats have favored this pub (formerly known as Molly Malone's) for Guinness ever since the Velvet Revolution enabled the Celts to return to one of their homelands. Worn wooden floors, dingy walls, and the Irish manager transport you right into the heart of blue-collar Dublin, which was, after all, a popular place for young Czechs to seek jobs in the high-tech industry—before the recession hit (daily 11:00-1:00, U Obecního Dvora 4, tel. 224-818-851).

Latin American: **La Casa Blů,** with cheap lunch specials, Mexican plates, Staropramen beer, and greenish mojitos, is your own little pueblo in Prague. It's one of the last student bastions in the Old Town. Painted in warm oranges and reds, energized by upbeat music, and guarded by creatures from Mayan mythology, La Casa Blů attracts a fiesta of happy eaters and drinkers (120-Kč specials, 170-Kč burritos and quesadillas, Mon-Sat 11:00-23:00, Sun 14:00-23:00, non-smoking, on the corner of Kozí and Bílkova, tel. 224-818-270).

North American: **Bohemia Bagel** is hardly authentic—exasperated Czechs insist that bagels have nothing to do with Bohemia. Owned by an American, this practical café caters mostly to youthful tourists, offering good sandwiches (100-125 Kč), a little garden out back, and Internet access. If homesick, you'll love the menu, with everything from Philly cheesesteaks to bacon and eggs (daily 8:00-21:00, Masná 2, tel. 224-812-560). Outside of meal times, it's a quiet and comfy hangout.

In the Jewish Quarter

These eateries are well-located to break up a demanding tour of the Jewish Quarter—all within two blocks of each other on or near Široká (see map on page 79). Also consider the nearby ethnic eateries listed above.

Kolkovna, the flagship restaurant of a chain allied with Pilsner Urquell, is big and woody yet modern, serving a fun mix of Czech and international cuisine—ribs, salads, cheese plates, and beer. It feels a tad formulaic...but not in a bad way (a bit overpriced, 200-400-Kč main dishes, daily 11:00-24:00, across from Spanish Synagogue at V Kolkovně 8, tel. 224-819-701).

Kolonial ("Bicycle Place"), across the street from the Pinkas Synagogue, has a modern interior playing on the bicycle theme, six beers on tap, and an imaginative menu drawing from Czech, French, Italian, and Spanish cuisine (100-150-Kč daily specials, 150-400-Kč main dishes, daily 9:00-24:00, Široká 6, tel. 224-818-322).

Restaurace u Knihovny ("By the Library"), situated steps away from the City and National libraries as well as the Pinkas Synagogue, is a favorite lunch spot for locals who work nearby. The cheap daily lunch specials consist of seven variations on traditional Czech themes. The service is friendly, and the stylish red-brick interior is warm (80-150-Kč main dishes, daily 11:00-23:00, smoke-free at lunch, on the corner of Veleslavínova and Valentinská, mobile 732-835-876).

Dinitz Kosher Restaurant, around the corner from the Spanish Synagogue, is the most low-key and reasonably priced of the kosher restaurants in the Jewish Quarter (350-550-Kč main dishes, 800-Kč Shabbat meals by prepaid reservation only, Sun-Thu 11:30-22:30, Fri 11:30-14:30, Bílkova 12, tel. 222-244-000, www.dinitz.cz). For Shabbat meals, the fancier **King Solomon Restaurant** is a better value (Široká 8, tel. 224-818-752, www.kosher.cz).

Dining with an Old Town Square View

The **Hotel u Prince Terasa,** atop the five-star hotel facing the Astronomical Clock, is designed for foreign tourists. A sleek elevator takes you to the rooftop terrace, where every possible inch is used to serve good food (international with plenty of fish) from their open-air grill. The view is arguably the best in town—especially at sunset. The menu is a fun but overpriced mix, with photos that make ordering easy. Being in such a touristy spot, waiters are experts at nicking you with confusing menu charges; don't be afraid to confirm exact prices before ordering. This place is also great for a drink at sunset or late at night (240-300-Kč plates, fine salads, daily until 24:00, brusque staff, outdoor heaters when necessary, Staroměstské Náměstí 29, tel. 224-213-807, no reservations possible).

In the New Town
Traditional Czech

Restaurace u Pinkasů, founded in 1843, is known among locals as the first place to serve Pilsner beer. You can sit in its traditional interior, in front to watch the street action, or out back in a garden shaded by the Gothic buttresses of the St. Mary of the Snows Church. While the prices are straightforward, some of the waiters could win the rudest-service award (150-300-Kč main dishes, daily 9:00-24:00, 90-Kč lunch special, near the bottom of Wenceslas Square, between Old and New Towns, Jungmannovo Náměstí 16, tel. 221-111-150).

Hospoda u Nováka, behind the National Theater, is emphatically Czech, with few tourists. It takes good care of its regulars (you'll see the old monthly beer tabs in a rack just inside the door). Nostalgic communist-era signs are everywhere. During that time, pubs like this were close-knit communities where regulars escaped from the depression of daily life. Today, the U Nováka is a bright and smoky hangout where you can still happily curse whatever regime you happen to live under. While the English menu lists the well-executed Czech classics, it doesn't list the cheap daily specials (100-200-Kč main dishes, daily 10:00-23:00, V Jirchářích 2, tel. 224-930-639).

Pivovarský Dům ("The Brewhouse"), on the corner of Ječná and Lípová, is popular with locals for its rare variety of fresh beers (yeast, wheat, and fruit-flavored), fine classic Czech dishes, and an inviting interior that mixes traditional and modern (100-300-Kč main dishes, daily 11:00-23:00, reservations recommended in the evenings, variety of beer mugs sold; walk up Štěpánská street from Wenceslas Square for 10 minutes, or take tram #22 for two stops from Národní to Štěpánská; Lípová 15, tel. 296-216-666, www. pivovarskydum.com).

Modern and Ethnic

Pivovarský Klub ("The Brew Club," related to Pivovarský Dům, above) serves the widest selection of Czech microbrews in town in a modern, blond-wood restaurant. Every week different beers are featured on tap on the ground floor, while small breweries hold regular presentations in the basement (250-Kč main dishes, daily 11:30-23:30, evening reservations recommended; about 50 yards on the left along Křižíkova from Florenc Metro station, Křižíkova 17, see map on page 38 for location, tel. 222-315-7770, www.pivovarskyklub.com).

Le Patio, on the big and busy Národní Třída, has a hip, continental feel. But for a place that also sells furniture (head straight back and down the stairs), it definitely needs comfier dining chairs. Hanging lanterns and live music (Fri-Sat) contribute to the pleasant atmosphere. Dishes are from India, France, and points in between, and there's always a serious vegetarian option (200-350-Kč plates, daily 8:00-23:00, Národní 22, tel. 224-934-375).

Pasha Kebab Turkish Restaurant, near the bottom of Wenc-

Restaurants in the New Town

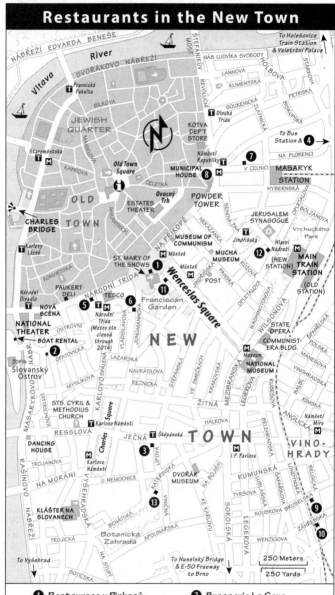

EATING

1. Restaurace u Pinkasů
2. Hospoda u Nováka
3. Pivovarský Dům
4. To Pivovarský Klub
5. Le Patio & Café Louvre
6. Pasha Kebab Turkish Restaurant
7. Brasserie La Gare
8. Municipal House Eateries
9. Café Medúza
10. Hlučná Samota
11. Dobrá Čajovna Teahouse
12. Čajový Klub
13. Hotel 16

eslas Square, has American fast-food-chain ambience, good ingredients, and wonderful, authentic ready-to-eat Turkish dishes (120-Kč meals, daily 10:00-22:00, a block from Můstek Metro stop, just beyond Franciscan garden at Jungmannova 27, tel. 224-948-481).

Brasserie La Gare, just off Náměstí Republiky, opened with the mission to prove to Czechs that French food can be simple and inexpensive. The menu includes such classics as *escargots de Bourgogne* and coq au vin. The red-hued, modern interior also contains a French bakery and a deli (89-Kč lunch specials, 250-Kč entrées, daily 11:00-24:00, V Celnici 3, tel. 222-313-712).

Art Nouveau Splendor in the Municipal House

The Municipal House (Obecní Dům), the sumptuous Art Nouveau concert hall, has three restaurants: a café, a French restaurant, and a beer cellar (all at Náměstí Republiky 5). The dressy café, **Kavárna Obecní Dům,** is drenched in chandeliered, Art Nouveau elegance and offers the best value and experience here. Light, pricey meals and drinks come with great atmosphere and bad service (280-Kč

three-course special daily for lunch or dinner, open daily 7:30-23:00, live piano or jazz trio 16:00-20:00, tel. 222-002-763). The fine and formal **French restaurant** in the next wing oozes Mucha elegance (700-1,000-Kč meals, daily 12:00-16:00 & 18:00-23:00, tel. 222-002-777). The **beer cellar** is overpriced and touristy (daily 11:30-23:00).

In the Little Quarter

These characteristic eateries are handy for a bite before or after your Prague Castle visit.

Malostranská Beseda, in the impeccably restored former Town Hall, weaves together an imaginative menu of traditional Czech dishes (both classic and little known), vegetarian fare, and fresh fish. It feels a bit sterile and formulaic, but that follows a local trend. You can choose among three settings: the non-smoking ground-floor restaurant on the left; the café on the right (serves meals, but it's OK to have only coffee or cake); or the packed beer hall downstairs, where Pilsner Urquell is served well (150-300-Kč main dishes, daily 11:00-23:00, Malostranské Náměstí 21, tel. 257-409-112). The restaurant has a recommended music club upstairs.

U Zavěšenýho Kafe ("By the Hanging Coffee"), up 20 yards on the right after Nerudova turns into Úvoz, is a creative little pub/

restaurant that has attracted a cult following among Prague's co-
gnoscenti. You can "hang" a coffee here for a local vagabond by
paying for an extra coffee on your way out (100-200-Kč main dishes, daily 11:00-24:00, Úvoz 6, look for the only house covered by
vines, mobile 605-294-595).

U Hrocha ("By the Hippo"), a small authentic pub with tar
dripping from its walls, is packed with beer drinkers. Expect
simple, traditional meals—basically meat starters with bread.
Just below the castle near Little Quarter Square (Malostranské
Náměstí), it's actually the haunt of many members of Parliament,
which is located around the corner (40 Kč for a pint of Pilsner, 120
Kč for a chunk of meat, daily 12:00-23:00, chalkboard lists daily
meals in English, Thunovská 10, tel. 257-533-389).

Lokál u Bílé Kuželky ("By the White Bowling Pin"), a branch
of the Old Town's recommended Lokál restaurant, is the best bet
for quick, cheap, well-executed Czech classics on this side of the
river (100-200-Kč main dishes, Mon-Fri 11:30-24:00, Sat-Sun
12:00-22:00, non-smoking section, Míšeňská 12; from the Charles
Bridge, turn right around the U Tří Pštrosů Hotel just before the
Little Quarter gate; tel. 257-212-014).

Vinograf Wine Bar is a small, intimate place with just eight
tables. It's run by Czech wine-lover Karel, who speaks English
and enjoys helping visitors appreciate his wines. Karel prepares a
daily list of Czech wines available by the glass and serves meat-
and-cheese plates for wine-tasters who'd like a light meal (daily
16:00-24:00, a few steps off the end of Charles Bridge at Míšeňská
8, next to Lokál, tel. 603-116-085).

Čertovka, down an alley so narrow that it requires a signal
to regulate foot traffic, offers outdoor seating on two small ter-
races right on the water, with some of the best views of the Charles
Bridge. Given the location, the prices are reasonable (400-Kč
meals, daily 11:30-23:30, off the little square at U Lužického
Semináře 24, no reservations taken, arrive early to claim a spot, tel.
257-534-524).

Cukrkávalimonáda ("Sugar, Coffee, Lemonade") is part restaurant and part patisserie, serving big salads, ciabatta sandwiches,
artful pastries, and freshly squeezed juice in a setting mixing old
and new decor. The bistro—an oasis just a block away from the
tourist crush—is 50 yards down the first street to the left after you
exit the Charles Bridge (100-Kč sandwiches, 150-Kč salads, Mon-
Sat 9:00-23:00, Sun 9:00-19:00, Lázeňská 7, tel. 257-225-396).

Campanulla Café, in the courtyard on the left side of the
Lennon Wall, is a secluded spot serving fresh sandwiches, rasp-
berry drinks, and Italian coffee next to a flower garden, an English
lawn, and one of the oldest trees in Prague (170-Kč salads and pas-
tas, daily 11:00-22:00, Velkopřevorské Náměstí 4, look for small

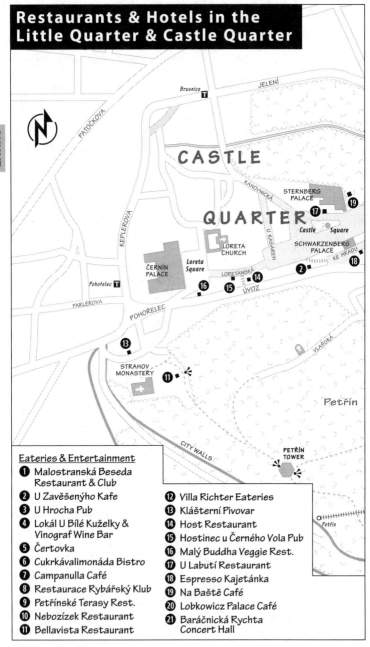

EATING

Restaurants & Hotels in the Little Quarter & Castle Quarter

Eateries & Entertainment

1 Malostranská Beseda Restaurant & Club
2 U Zavěšenýho Kafe
3 U Hrocha Pub
4 Lokál U Bílé Kuželky & Vinograf Wine Bar
5 Čertovka
6 Cukrkávalimonáda Bistro
7 Campanulla Café
8 Restaurace Rybářský Klub
9 Petřínské Terasy Rest.
10 Nebozízek Restaurant
11 Bellavista Restaurant
12 Villa Richter Eateries
13 Klášterní Pivovar
14 Host Restaurant
15 Hostinec u Černého Vola Pub
16 Malý Buddha Veggie Rest.
17 U Labutí Restaurant
18 Espresso Kajetánka
19 Na Baště Café
20 Lobkowicz Palace Café
21 Baráčnická Rychta Concert Hall

EATING

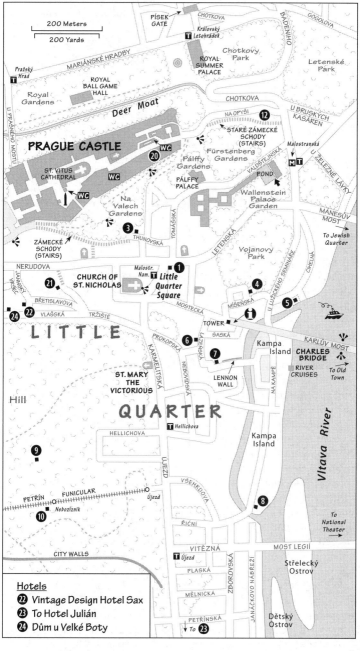

200 Meters
200 Yards

PÍSEK GATE

CHOTKOVA

BADENIHO

GOGOLOVA

Královský Letohrádek

ROYAL SUMMER PALACE

Chotkovy Park

Letenské Park

Pražský Hrad

MARIÁNSKÉ HRADBY

ROYAL BALL GAME HALL

Royal Gardens

CHOTKOVA

Deer Moat

NA OPYŠI

U BRUSKÝCH KASÁREN

STARÉ ZÁMECKÉ SCHODY (STAIRS)

⑫

PRAGUE CASTLE

WC ⑳

Fürstenberg Gardens

Pálffy Gardens

Malostranská

Ⓜ T

U ŽELEZNÉ LÁVKY

ST. VITUS CATHEDRAL

WC

PÁLFFY PALACE

POND

VALDŠTEJNSKÁ

Wallenstein Palace Garden

WC

Na Valech Gardens

TOMÁŠSKÁ

Vojanovy Park

MÁNESŮV MOST

To Jewish Quarter

③

ZÁMECKÉ SCHODY (STAIRS)

THUNOVSKÁ

LETENSKÁ

CHELINA

NERUDOVA

Malostr. Nám.

CHURCH OF ST. NICHOLAS

①

T

Little Quarter Square

④

U LUŽICKÉHO SEMINÁŘE

㉑

JÁNSKÝ VRŠEK

BŘETISLAVOVA

VLAŠSKÁ

TRŽIŠTĚ

MOSTECKÁ

MÍŠEŇSKÁ

⑤

㉔ ㉒

L I T T L E

PROKOPSKÁ

SASKÁ

TOWER

Ⓘ

Kampa Island

KARLŮV MOST

CHARLES BRIDGE

⑥

LENNÁ

⑦

RIVER CRUISES

To Old Town

ST. MARY THE VICTORIOUS

KARMELITSKÁ

NEBOVIDSKÁ

LENNON WALL

NA KAMPĚ

Hill

Q U A R T E R

HELLICHOVA

T Hellichova

Kampa Island

Vltava River

⑨

ÚJEZD

VŠEHRDOVA

PETŘÍN FUNICULAR

Újezd

⑩ Nebozízek

⑧

ŘÍČNÍ

To National Theater

CITY WALLS

VÍTĚZNÁ

T Újezd

MOST LEGII

Střelecký Ostrov

PLASKÁ

ZBOROVSKÁ

JANÁČKOVO NÁBŘEŽÍ

MĚLNICKÁ

Dětský Ostrov

PETŘÍNSKÁ

㉓ To

Hotels

㉒ Vintage Design Hotel Sax
㉓ To Hotel Julián
㉔ Dům u Velké Boty

gate at left end of Lennon Wall, entrance to indoor seating area is another 20 yards to the left, tel. 257-217-736).

Restaurace Rybářský Klub, just off the park on Kampa Island, is run by the Society of Czech Fishermen and serves a wide selection of local freshwater fish. Dine along the dock on fish-cream soup, pike, trout, carp, or catfish at a not-so-scenic part of the river—but still with a glimpse of the Charles Bridge (three-course meal about 500 Kč, daily 12:00-23:00, U Sovových Mlýnů 1, tel. 257-534-200).

Near the Funicular, on Petřín Hill: These two places are near the funicular stop halfway up Petřín Hill, and offer great views over the city. **Petřínské Terasy** has woody seating indoors, or outside on the terrace (300-Kč main dishes, daily 12:00-23:00; Petřín 393, tel. 257-320-688), while **Nebozízek** is more modern, with glassed-in seating (600-Kč tasting menu, cash only, daily 11:00-23:00, Petřín 411, tel. 257-315-329).

In the Castle Quarter

Bellavista Restaurant is in the garden of the Strahov Monastery, where the abbot himself would come to meditate in a peaceful garden setting. You'll pay for the amazing city views, but if the weather's nice, this is a good value, with traditional grilled meats, pasta, and salads (200-300-Kč main dishes, daily 11:00-24:00, tel. 220-517-274).

Villa Richter, at the end of the castle promontory (closest to the river) and surrounded by newly replanted vineyards, consists of three classy restaurants, each with killer Prague views. Forty yards below the lower castle gate, you'll see a gate leading to a vineyard. Stroll downhill through the vineyard and you'll come upon three distinct restaurants (all open daily 10:00-23:00, tel. 257-219-079). At **Panorama Pergola,** a string of outdoor tables lines a vineyard terrace overlooking the city (wine, sandwiches, cold plates, and hot views). **Piano Nobile** is more pretentious, with Italian and French dishes and romantic white-linen tables indoors and out—it's the perfect place to propose (1,000-Kč three-course meals). **Piano Terra** serves more affordable Czech dishes (200-300-Kč entrées).

Klášterní Pivovar ("Monastery Brewery"), founded by an abbot in 1628 and reopened in 2004, has two large rooms and a pleasant courtyard. This is the place to taste a range of unpasteurized beers brewed on the premises, including amber, wheat, and IPA (India Pale Ale). The wooden decor and circa-1900 newspaper clippings (including Habsburg Emperor Franz Josef's "Proclamation to My Nations," announcing the beginning of the First World War) evoke the era when Vienna was Europe's artistic capital, Prague was building its faux Eiffel Tower, and life moved much slower. To accompany the beer, try the strong beer-flavored cheese served on toasted black-yeast bread (150-300-Kč main dishes, daily 10:00-22:00, Strahovské Nádvoří 301, tel. 233-353-155). It's directly across from the entrance to the Strahov Library (don't confuse it with the enormous, tour group-oriented Klášterní Restaurace next door, to the right).

Host Restaurant is hidden in the middle of a staircase that connects Loretánská and Úvoz streets. This spot, which boasts super views of the Little Quarter and Petřín Hill, has a modern black-and-white design and an imaginative menu. Most entrées are priced around 350 Kč, but try asking for the "business lunch" menu (two courses for 145 Kč) advertised only in Czech (300-415-Kč main dishes, daily 11:30-22:00, as you go up Loretánská, watch for stairs leading down to the left at #15—just before the arcaded passageway, mobile 728-695-793).

Hostinec u Černého Vola ("By the Black Ox") is a smoky, dingy old-time pub—its survival in the midst of all the castle splendor and tourism is a marvel. It feels like a kegger on the banks of the river Styx, with classic bartenders serving up Kozel beer (traditional "Goat" brand with excellent darks) and beer-friendly gut-bomb snacks (fried cheese, local hot dogs). The pub is located on Loretánská (50 yards from Loreta Church, no sign outside, sniff for cigarette smoke and look for the only house on the block without an arcade, 35-Kč beers, 50-Kč sausages, daily 10:00-22:00, English menu on request, tel. 220-513-481).

Malý Buddha ("Little Buddha") serves delightful food—especially vegetarian—and takes its theme seriously. You'll step into a mellow, low-lit escape of bamboo and peace, where you'll be served by people with perfect complexions and almost no pulse to the no-rhythm of meditative music. Eating in their little back room is like being in a temple (100-200-Kč meals, Tue-Sun 12:00-22:30, closed Mon, non-smoking, between the castle and Strahov Monastery at Úvoz 46, tel. 220-513-894).

U Labutí ("By the Swans") offers reasonably priced, classic Czech food in a quiet courtyard, just across from the Plague Column on Castle Square (150-250-Kč main dishes, daily 10:00-22:00, Hradčanské Náměstí 11, tel. 220-511-191).

Espresso Kajetánka, just off Castle Square, has magnificent city views. It's a handy, though overpriced, place for a coffee in a plastic cup or a snack as you start or end your castle visit (daily 10:00-20:00, Ke Hradu, tel. 257-533-735).

Na Baště ("At the Bastion"), serene but not as scenic, is in a garden through the gate to the left of the main castle entry. The outdoor seating, among Jože Plečnik's ramparts and obelisks, is the castle at its most quiet (100-Kč sandwiches, 250-Kč salads, daily 10:00-18:00, tel. 281-933-010).

Away from the Center

To rub elbows with hip locals, try these spots in Vinohrady and Žižkov.

Café Medúza ("Café Jellyfish"), an authentic between-the-World-Wars café with plush sofas and pictures of 1930s movie stars, draws a crowd of dreamy young Czechs enjoying coffee, cigarettes, dark Svijany beer, and cheap lunch specials (daily 11:00-24:00, Belgická 17, Metro: Náměstí Míru; from Metro stop, walk down the street a bit and look for Belgická on your left, see map on page 167, tel. 222-515-107).

At **Hlučná Samota** ("Loud Solitude"), the wooden floor and brick walls are dedicated to the great Czech writer Bohumil Hrabal. Though he never visited here, Hrabal would surely be inspired by the rich mix of Czech and Italian cuisine (including honey duck, spinach salmon, and Prague's own Staropramen beer). On a nice day, the good sidewalk seating is a pleasure (100-200-Kč main dishes, daily 11:00-23:00, Záhřebská 14, see map on page 167, tel. 222-522-839).

Restaurace u Sadu, dark and dingy, is decorated with old typewriters, radios, meat grinders, skis, and sledges. It serves cheap beer and decent food indoors on aged green tablecloths or outside on wooden tables. The way that Czechs of all generations drink beer in this classic blue-collar pub hasn't changed a beat since the 1920s (70-150-Kč main dishes, daily 10:00-4:00 in the morning, on Škroupa Square below Žižkov TV tower at Škroupovo Náměstí 5, see map on page 38, tel. 222-727-072).

Oblaca ("The Clouds"), the restaurant 200 feet up in the Žižkov TV tower, is expensive, but it comes with a Sputnik's-eye view (400-Kč main dishes, daily 8:00-24:00, less-expensive café open 8:00-17:00, Mahlerovy sady 1, see map on page 38, tel. 210-320-086).

Hospůdka nad Viktorkou, named for this neighborhood's soccer team, is around the corner on Bořivojova street. This quintessential Žižkov pub features occasional live performances by local bands, a warm glassed-in terrace in the winter, and a little courtyard with a shady canopy of chestnut trees in the summer (80-150-Kč main dishes, daily 15:00-24:00, English menu available, Bořivojova 79, see map on page 38, tel. 222-722-557).

Cafés

Dripping with history, these places in the Old and New Towns are as much about the ambience as they are about the coffee. Most cafés also serve sweets and light meals. For locations, see the map on page 160.

Kavárna Slavia, across from the National Theater (facing the Legií Bridge on Národní street), is a fixture in Prague, famous as a hangout for its literary elite. Today, it's tired and clearly past its prime, with an Art Deco interior, lousy piano entertainment, and celebrity photos on the wall. But its iconic status makes it a fun stop for a coffee—skip the food (daily 8:00-23:00, sit as near the river as possible, Smetanovo Nábřeží 2, tel. 224-218-493). Notice the *Drinker of Absinthe* painting on the wall (and on the menu for 55 Kč)—with the iconic Czech writer struggling with reality.

Grand Café Orient is just one flight up off busy Celetná street, yet a world away from the crush of tourism below. Located in the Cubist House of the Black Madonna, the café is upstairs and fittingly decorated with a Cubist flair. With its stylish, circa-1910 decor toned to dark green, this space is full of air and light—and a good value as well. The café takes its Cubism seriously: Traditionally round desserts are served square (100-Kč sandwiches, 160-Kč salads, 40-Kč vanilla squares, other desserts about 100 Kč, great balcony seating, Mon-Fri 9:00-22:00, Sat-Sun 10:00-22:00, Ovocný Trh 19, at the corner of Celetná near the Powder Tower, tel. 224-224-240).

Café Café, just off to the right from the main drag connecting the Old Town and Wenceslas Square, serves salads, sandwiches, and cakes in a fancy setting (200-Kč salads, 100-Kč cakes, daily 9:00-23:00, Rytířská 10, tel. 224-210-597).

Café Montmartre, on a small street parallel to Karlova, combines Parisian ambience with unbeatable Czech prices for coffee (no food served). Dreamy Czech minds found their quiet asylum here after Kavárna Slavia (listed earlier) and other longtime favorites either closed down or became stuck in their past. The main room is perfect for discussing art and politics; the intimate room behind the courtyard is where you recite poetry to your partner (Mon-Fri 9:00-23:00, Sat-Sun 12:00-23:00, Řetězová 7, tel. 222-221-244).

Ebel Coffee House, next door to Café Montmartre, prides itself on its wide assortment of fresh brews from every coffee-bean-growing country in the world, inviting cakes, and a colorful setting that delights the mind as much as the caffeine does (daily 9:00-22:00, Řetězová 3, tel. 224-895-788).

Café Louvre is a longtime elegant favorite (opened in 1902 and maintaining its classic atmosphere) that still draws an energetic young crowd that's crazy about their cheesecake and hot chocolate. From the big and busy Národní street, you walk upstairs into a venerable world of newspapers on sticks (including English) and waiters in vests and aprons. The back room has long been the place for billiard tables (100 Kč/hour). An English flier tells its history (200-Kč plates, 120-Kč two-course lunch offered 11:00-15:00, good gluten-free options, open daily 8:00-23:30, Národní 22, tel. 224-930-949).

Teahouses

Many Czech people are bohemian philosophers at heart and prefer the mellow, smoke-free environs of a teahouse to the smoky, traditional beer hall. Young Czechs are much more interested in traveling to exotic destinations like Southeast Asia, Africa, or Peru than to Western Europe, so the Oriental teahouses set their minds in vacation mode.

While there are teahouses all over Prague, a fine example in a handy New Town locale is Prague's original one, established in 1991—just after freedom. **Dobrá Čajovna** ("Good Teahouse"), only a few steps off the bustle of Wenceslas Square, takes you into a very peaceful world that elevates tea to an almost religious ritual. You'll be given an English menu—which lovingly describes each tea—and a bell. The menu lists a world of tea (very fresh, prices by the small pot), "accompaniments" (such as Exotic Miscellany), and light meals "for hungry tea drinkers." When you're ready to order, ring your bell to beckon a tea monk—likely a member of the Lovers of Tea Society (80-200 Kč/teapot, Mon-Fri 10:00-21:30, Sat-Sun 14:00-21:30, near the base of Wenceslas Square, opposite McDonald's at Václavské Náměstí 14, see map on page 167, tel. 224-231-480).

For a taste of tea from Prague's newly emerging Chinese middle class (rather than from some Czech's dreams of the Orient), head to **Čajový Klub** ("Tea Club"), just down the street from the Jerusalem Synagogue. Creatively run by a cultured man from Beijing, here you'll find red cherry-wood decor, expertly served tea, and the freshest green leaves in town (80-200 Kč/teapot, Mon-Sat 10:00-21:00, closed Sun, Jeruzalémská 10, see map on page 167, tel. 222-721-072).

EATING

SHOPPING IN PRAGUE

Prague's entire Old Town seems designed to bring out the shopper in visitors. Puppets, glass, and ceramics are traditional. For information on VAT refunds (for purchases of more than 2,000 Kč—about $100) and customs regulations, see page 16.

Shopping Streets and Squares

Shop your way from the Old Town Square up Celetná street to the Powder Tower, then along Na Příkopě to the bottom of Wenceslas Square (Václavské Náměstí). The city center is tourist-oriented—most locals do their serious shopping in the suburbs.

Celetná is lined with big stores selling all the traditional Czech goodies. Tourists wander endlessly here, mesmerized by the window displays. Celetná Crystal, about midway down the street at #15, offers the largest selection of affordable crystal. You can have the glass safely shipped home directly from the shop (daily 10:00-21:00). The Manufaktura shop at #12 has a good selection of hand-made products: wooden toys, straw ornaments, ceramics, and "blueprint" Moravian fabrics (daily 10:00-20:00).

Náměstí Republiky (Republic Square) boasts Prague's newest and biggest mall, Palladium (Sun-Wed 9:00-21:00, Thu-Sat 9:00-22:00), hidden behind a pink Neo-Romanesque facade. Across the square is the communist-era brown steel-and-glass 1980s department store Kotva ("Anchor"), an obsolete beast on the verge of extinction (Mon-Fri 9:00-20:00, Sat-Sun 10:00-18:00).

Na Příkopě has a couple of good modern malls. The best is Slovanský Dům ("Slavic House," daily 10:00-20:00, Na Příkopě 22), where you'll wander past a 10-screen multiplex deep into a world of classy restaurants and designer shops surrounding a peaceful, park-like inner courtyard. Another modern mall is Černá Růže ("Black Rose," daily 10:00-20:00, Na Příkopě 12), with a great

Czech Puppets

The first puppets were born on the Indian subcontinent and soon found their way to Europe and Southeast Asia. Czechs have treasured the art of puppets for centuries; at times of heavy German influence in the 18th century, traveling troupes of puppeteers kept the Czech language and humor alive in the countryside. While the language of "legitimate theater" had to be German, Czech was tolerated if it came out of a puppet's mouth.

Until recently, most grandfathers felt obliged to bequeath to their grandsons an assembly of their own linden-wood-carved designs. The power of puppetry peaked between 1938 and 1989, when the Czechs were ruled by a series of puppet governments. Today, Špejbl and Hurvínek, who have their own permanent stage in Prague, are the greatest Czechs for kids from Japan to Patagonia. Filmmaker Jan Švankmajer (see page 354) is turning wooden characters into Oscar-winning film stars.

Most marionettes sold in the tourist shops in Prague and Český Krumlov are meant as souvenirs. It takes a rare artist to turn pieces of wood into nimble puppets, and prices for these can reach into the thousands of dollars. But given that puppets have a glorious past and vibrant present in the Czech Republic, even a simple jester, witch, or Pinocchio can make a thoughtful memento of your Czech adventure.

Japanese restaurant around a small garden. Next door is Moser, which has a museum-like crystal showroom upstairs. The Galerie Myslbek, directly across the street, has fancy stores in a space built to Prague's scale.

Národní Třída (National Street) is less touristy and lined with some inviting stores. The big Tesco department store in the middle sells anything you might need, from a pin for a broken watchband to a swimsuit (generally daily 9:00-21:00, Národní Třída 26).

Crystal, Garnets, and Beads

Crystal: You'll find crystal display rooms on shopping streets such as Na Příkopě and Celetná. A small square just off the Old Town Square, Malé Náměstí, is home to two major crystal retailers: Moser and Crystalex (which claims to have "factory-direct" prices, at #6). Among the shops in the

Ungelt courtyard is the Material Glass showroom, showcasing local artists. All are generally open daily 10:00-20:00. Or consider venturing an hour beyond Prague to the Rückl Glassworks in Nižbor (see page 221).

"**Bohemian Garnets**": These fiery red gemstone-quality garnets, with unique refractive—some claim even curative—properties, were mined from a mountainous area of Bohemia. This region was the major source of garnet gems from the Renaissance through the Victorian Age, and is now largely mined out. Traditional handcrafted designs pack many small garnets together, and much of the authentic jewelry you'll see today is Victorian-era. Of the many garnet shops in Prague's shopping districts, Turnov Granát Co-op has the largest selection (with shops at Dlouhá 28 and Panská 1, www.granat.eu). If you buy garnet jewelry, shop around, use a reputable dealer, and ask for a certificate of authenticity to avoid buying a glass imitation.

Beads: To reach Koralky, one of the best-supplied bead shops in Prague, take the Metro's green line to the Jiřího z Poděbrad stop (Vinohradská 76, www.koralky.cz).

Books and Maps

Try **Shakespeare and Sons** (offers a big selection in the Little Quarter), open daily and described on page 44.

Kiwi Map Store, near Wenceslas Square, is Prague's best source for maps and travel guides (Mon-Fri 9:00-19:00, Sat 9:00-14:00, closed Sun, Jungmanova 23, tel. 224-948-455).

For CDs and DVDs, see the sidebar on page 187.

Markets

Farmers' markets have become trendy in the past few years, cropping up around the city. Apart from vegetables, you will find quality cheeses, juices, fish, cakes, coffee, and more. The most scenic market is on the Vltava embankment just south of the Palacký Bridge (Sat 8:00-14:00).

The open-air **Havelská Market,** in the Old Town, is a touristy but enjoyable place to find fresh produce and handicrafts (daily 9:00-18:00, for details see page 69).

ENTERTAINMENT IN PRAGUE

Prague booms with live and inexpensive theater, classical music, jazz, and pop entertainment. Everything is listed in several monthly cultural events programs (free at TIs) and in the *Prague Post* newspaper (60 Kč at newsstands).

You'll be tempted to gather fliers as you wander through town. Don't bother. To really understand all your options (the street Mo-zarts are pushing only their own concerts), drop by a **Via Musica** box office. There are two: One is next to Týn Church on the Old Town Square (daily 10:30-19:30, tel. 224-826-969), and the other is in the Little Quarter across from the Church of St. Nicholas (daily 10:30-18:00, tel. 257-535-568). The event schedule posted on the wall clearly shows every-  thing that's playing today and tomorrow, including tourist concerts, Black Light Theater, and marionette shows, with photos of each venue and a map locating everything (www.viamusica.cz). If you don't see a posted list of today's events, just ask for it.

Ticketpro sells tickets for the serious concert venues and most music clubs (English-language reservations tel. 296-329-999, www. ticketpro.cz). Ticketpro has several outlets: at Rytířská 31 (daily 8:00-12:00 & 12:30-16:30, between Havelská Market and Estates Theater); in the Lucerna Gallery (daily 9:30-18:00, on Wenceslas Square, opposite Grand Hotel Evropa); and in the privately run Tourist Center at Rytířská 12 (Mon-Fri 11:00-19:00, closed Sat-Sun). As with most ticket box offices, you'll pay about 30 Kč extra per ticket.

Entertainment in Prague

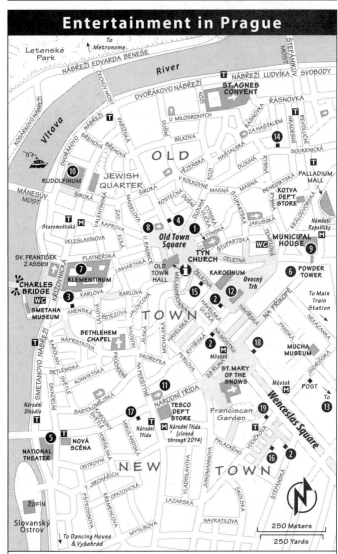

1. Via Musica Box Office
2. Ticketpro (3)
3. Ta Fantastika Theater
4. Image Theater
5. National Theater & Laterna Magica
6. Srnec Theater
7. Klementinum (Chapel of Mirrors)
8. Church of St. Nicholas
9. Municipal House (Smetana Hall)
10. Rudolfinum
11. St. Martin in the Wall
12. Estates Theater
13. To State Opera
14. Roxy Club
15. Agharta Jazz Club
16. Lucerna Music Bar
17. Reduta Jazz Club
18. Bontonland CD Shop
19. Terryho Ponožky DVD Shop

ENTERTAINMENT

Locals dress up for the more "serious" concerts, opera, and ballet, but many tourists wear casual clothes—as long as you don't show up in shorts, sneakers, or flip-flops, you'll be fine.

Black Light Theater

A kind of mime/modern dance variety show, Black Light Theater has no language barrier and is, for some, more entertaining than a classical concert. Unique to Prague, Black Light Theater originated in the 1960s as a playful and mystifying theater of the absurd. These days, aficionados and critical visitors lament that it's becoming a cheesy variety show, while others are uncomfortable with the sexual flavor of some acts. Still, it's an unusual theater experience that many enjoy. Shows last about an hour and a half. Avoid the first four rows, which get you so close that it ruins the illusion. Each theater has its own spin on what Black Light is supposed to be:

Ta Fantastika is traditional and poetic, with puppets and a little artistic nudity (680 Kč, *Aspects of Alice* nightly at 18:00 and 21:30, reserved seating, near east end of Charles Bridge at Karlova 8, tel. 222-221-366, www.tafantastika.cz).

Image Theater has more mime and elements of the absurd, with shows including *Black Box, Cabinet,* and *The Best of Image:* "It's precisely the fact that we are all so different that unites us" (480 Kč, shows nightly at 20:00, open seating—arrive early to grab a good spot, just off Old Town Square at Pařížská 4, tel. 222-314-448, www.imagetheatre.cz).

Laterna Magica, in the big, glassy building next to the National Theater, mixes Black Light techniques with film projection into a multimedia performance that draws Czech audiences (680 Kč, *Wonderful Circus, Legends of Magic, Graffiti,* shows Mon-Sat at 20:00, no shows on Sun, tel. 224-931-482, www.laterna.cz).

Srnec Theater is an ensemble run by founder Jiří Srnec (credited with inventing the Black Light Theater concept in 1961) and his son. Their show, *Anthology,* traces the development of the art over the past 50 years (380-680 Kč, generally one show weekly at 20:00, in the Broadway Passage between Celetná and Na Příkopě streets, next to the Powder Tower, Na Příkopě 31, tel. 225-113-352, www.srnectheatre.com).

The other Black Light theaters advertised around town aren't as good.

Classical Concerts

Each day, six to eight classical concerts designed for tourists fill delightful Old World halls and churches with music of the crowd-pleasing sort: Vivaldi, Best of Mozart, Most Famous Arias, and works by the famous Czech composer Antonín Dvořák. Concerts typically cost 400-1,000 Kč, start anywhere from 13:00 to 21:00, and last about an hour. Typical venues include two buildings on the Little Quarter Square (the Church of St. Nicholas and the Prague Academy of Music in Liechtenstein Palace), the Klementinum's Chapel of Mirrors, the Old Town Square (in a different Church of St. Nicholas), and the stunning Smetana Hall in the Municipal House. Musicians vary from excellent to amateurish.

To ensure a memorable venue and top-notch musicians, choose a concert in one of three places (Municipal House's Smetana Hall, Rudolfinum, or National Theater) featuring Prague's finest ensembles (such as the Prague Symphony Orchestra or Czech Philharmonic).

The **Prague Symphony Orchestra** plays in the gorgeous Art Nouveau Municipal House. Their ticket office is on the right side of the building, on U Obecního Domu street opposite Hotel Paris (Mon-Fri 10:00-18:00, tel. 222-002-336, www.fok.cz, pokladna@ fok.cz). A smaller selection of tickets is sold in the information office inside the Municipal House.

The **Czech Philharmonic** performs in the classical Neo-Renaissance Rudolfinum in the Jewish Quarter. Their ticket office is on the right side of the Rudolfinum, under the stairs (250-1,000 Kč, open Mon-Fri 10:00-18:00, and until just before the show starts on concert days, on Palachovo Náměstí on the Old Town side of Mánes Bridge, tel. 227-059-352, www.ceskafilharmonie.cz, info@cfmail.cz).

Both orchestras perform in their home venues about five nights a month from September through June. Most other nights these spaces are rented to agencies that organize tourist concerts of varying quality for double the price (as described earlier). Check first whether your visit coincides with either ensemble's performance.

You'll find tickets for tourist concerts advertised and sold on the street in front of these buildings. An advantage of such a concert is that it allows you to experience music in one of Prague's best venues on the night of your choice. This is especially worth considering if you want to enjoy classical music in the Municipal House when the Symphony Orchestra isn't in town—but make sure your concert takes place in the building's Smetana Hall rather than in the much smaller Grégr Hall.

Both the Municipal House and Rudolfinum also act as chief venues for the Prague Spring, Prague Proms, and Dvořák's Prague music festivals (see "Festivals," later).

Jam Session: A good bet is the session held every Monday at 17:00 at **St. Martin in the Wall,** where some of Prague's best musicians gather to tune in and chat with one another (400 Kč, Martinská 8, just north of the Tesco department store in the Old Town).

Mozart, Smetana, Dvořák, and More

The three major composers connected with Prague—Mozart, Smetana, and Dvořák—all have museums dedicated to their lives and work in the city.

Wolfgang Amadeus Mozart (1756-1791)

During his frequent visits to Prague, Mozart lodged with his friends in the beautiful, small Neoclassical Villa Bertramka, now the **Mozart Museum.** The Salzburg prodigy felt more appreciated in Prague than in his homeland, and this villa, set in a peaceful garden, gives one the sense of the surroundings in which Mozart stayed. But there's not much to see inside, as almost all of the original interior furnishings are now housed at the Czech Museum of Music (where some are on display). Unless you're an absolute Mozart fan, there's little reason to make the trek here (50 Kč, March-Oct daily 10:00-17:00, closed Nov-Feb; Metro: Anděl, then a 10-minute walk along a busy street to Mozartova 169; tel. 241-493-547, check www.mozartovaobec.cz for occasional concerts).

Bedřich Smetana (1824-1884)

A statue of Smetana, the father of Czech classical music, is seated in front of the **Smetana Museum,** listening intently to the rapids of the Vltava River near the Charles Bridge (museum entry-50 Kč, Wed-Mon 10:00-17:00, closed Tue, Novotného Lávka, Praha 1, tel. 224-229-075). Like Richard Wagner in Germany, Smetana aimed to stir the Romantic nationalist spirit of the Czechs. His finest work, the cycle of symphonic poems called *My Country (Má Vlast)*, was inspired by places and myths important to the Czech people. *Vltava*, the most beautiful of the poems, is played to get your attention as trains arrive in stations.

ENTERTAINMENT

Buskers: The **Prague Castle Orchestra,** one of the city's most entertaining acts, performs regularly on Castle Square. This trio—Josef on flute, Radek on accordion, and Zdeněk on bass—plays a lively Czech mélange of Smetana, swing, old folk tunes, and 1920s cabaret songs. Look for them if you're visiting the castle (see page 114), and consider picking up their fun CD. They're also available for private functions (mobile 603-552-448, josekocurek@volny.cz).

Opera and Ballet

A handy ticket office for all three of the following theaters is in the little square (Ovocný Trh) behind the Estates Theater, next to a pizzeria.

The **National Theater** (Národní Divadlo), on the New Town side of Legií Bridge, is best for opera and ballet. Enjoy its Neo-Renaissance interior (300-1,000 Kč, shows from 19:00, tel. 224-912-673, www.narodni-divadlo.cz).

Antonín Dvořák (1841-1904)

Dvořák is the Czech Republic's best-known composer. For three years, Dvořák directed the National Conservatory in New York, during which time he composed his most famous work, the *New World Symphony (Z Nového Světa)*. Dvořák's advice to his students was to look for inspiration in America's authentic melodies (African American spirituals and Native American music) rather than in European models. Dvořák's gentle opera of a water nymph, *Rusalka,* is considered by many to be the best Czech opera and is often performed in Prague's National Theater.

The **Dvořák Museum** is located in Villa America, a building designed by Prague's most prolific Baroque architect, K. I. Dientzenhofer. It was the first of his structures to be built in the city and was purchased by the Dvořák Society in 1932 (museum entry-50 Kč, Tue-Sun 10:00-17:00, closed Mon, Ke Karlovu 20, Praha 2, see map on page 86, tel. 224-923-363).

Other Composers

Two other important composers from Czech lands are the moderns, Mahler and Janáček. **Gustav Mahler** (1860-1911), a Jew from Jihlava (see page 261), was a pioneer of atonal music. His best works are *Symphony No. 1: Titan* and *The Song of the Earth,* both inspired by the sounds of the Moravian woods and fields. **Leoš Janáček** (1854-1928), arguably the most original and least accessible Czech composer, was stimulated by language—its flow and abrupt pauses. He's known for his *Symphonietta* and *Lachian Dances (Lašské Tance),* as well as the operas *Cunning Little Vixen (Příhody Lišky Bystroušky)* and my favorite, *Jenůfa*—both perennials in the National Theater's repertoire.

ENTERTAINMENT

The **Estates Theater** (Stavovské Divadlo) is where Mozart premiered and personally directed many of his most beloved works (see page 69). *Don Giovanni, The Marriage of Figaro,* and *The Magic Flute* are on the program a couple of times each month (800-1,400 Kč, shows from 20:00, between the Old Town Square and the New Town on a square called Ovocný Trh, tel. 224-214-339, www.narodni-divadlo.cz).

The **State Opera** (Státní Opera), formerly the German Theater, is not as architecturally rewarding as the National Theater. Operas by non-Czech composers are typically performed here (400-1,200 Kč, shows at 19:00 or 20:00, 101 Wilsonova, on the busy street between the Main Train Station and Wenceslas Square, see map on page 86, tel. 224-227-693, www.narodni-divadlo.cz).

Festivals

World-class musicians are in town during these musical festivals: **Prague Spring** (mid-May-early June, www.festival.cz), **Prague Proms** (mid-June-late July, www.pragueproms.cz), the newer **Dvořák Prague** (Sept, www.dvorakovapraha.cz), and the **International Jazz Festival** (autumn, www.agharta.cz).

Music Clubs

Young locals keep Prague's many music clubs in business. Most clubs are neighborhood institutions with decades of tradition, generally holding only 100-200 people. Live rock and Bob Dylan-style folk are what younger generations go for. A number of good jazz clubs attract a diverse audience, from ages 18 to 80. In the last decade, ethnic music has also become hugely popular: Roma (Gypsy) bands, Moravian poets, African drummers, Cuban boleros, and Moroccan divas often sell out even the largest venues. You can buy tickets at the club, or, for most places, at the Ticketpro offices (described earlier). If you like jazz, I've listed some fine options; avoid the Jazzboat (advertised by commission-hungry hotels), which has mediocre musicians and high prices.

In the Old Town

Roxy, a few blocks from the Old Town Square, features live bands from outside the country twice a week—anything from Irish punk to Balkan brass. On other nights, the floor is taken over by experimental DJs spinning a healthy dose of Japanese pop (cover from 100 Kč, no cover on Mon, concerts start at 20:00, disco at 22:00, easy to book online and pick up tickets at the door, Dlouhá 33, tel. 224-826-296, www.roxy.cz).

Agharta Jazz Club, which showcases some of the best Czech and Eastern European jazz, is just steps off the Old Town Square in a cool Gothic cellar. Inside they also sell a wide selection of Czech jazz CDs (250-Kč cover, shows start nightly at 21:00, Železná 16, tel. 222-211-275, www.agharta.cz).

In the New Town

Lucerna Music Bar, at the bottom of Wenceslas Square, is popular for its '80s and '90s video parties on Friday and Saturday nights. The scene is a big, noisy dance hall with a giant video screen. Young and trendy, the Lucerna is cheap, and even older visitors mix in easily with the crowd of half locals, half tourists (about 100-Kč cover, music starts around 21:00, in the basement of Lucerna Gallery, Vodičkova 36, tel. 224-217-108, www.musicbar.cz). On other nights the Lucerna often hosts concerts (tickets 300-500 Kč, starts at 21:00).

The small **Reduta Jazz Club,** with cushioned brown sofas

Buying Czech CDs and DVDs

While the most convenient places to get CDs of classical music are the shops in the **Via Musica** and **Rudolfinum** ticket offices, you'll find a larger selection and other genres at the huge **Bontonland** music and video store, at the bottom of Wenceslas Square (enter from the mall with the big *Kenvelo* sign on the outside). In the classical music section, you'll find many interpretations of Czech works. For the best renditions, look for music performed by the Czech Philharmonic.

For contemporary, lighter music, get a CD by Čechomor (*Metamorphosis* is their best). This band, which began by playing traditional Czech music at weddings and funerals, synthesized the sound of folk ballads and has since become one of the most popular groups in the country. Jiří Pavlica and Hradišťan keep the music of Moravia alive; Věra Bílá and Ida Kellarová capture the lively spirit of the Roma (Gypsies). Some cool Czech contemporary groups are Psí Vojáci, Neočekávaný Dýchánek, and Už Jsme Doma.

A handy place to get DVDs of Czech and European films is the tiny **Terryho Ponožky** shop in the Světozor mall just off Wenceslas Square (Mon-Sat 10:00-20:00, closed Sun; enter from Vodičkova 41, the store is on the right next to the Světozor Cinema; tel. 224-946-829, www.terryhoponozky.cz). Be warned that many European discs don't work in American DVD players (though they usually play on computers just fine).

ENTERTAINMENT

stretching along mirrored walls, launches you straight into the 1960s-era classic jazz scene (when jazz provided an escape for trapped freedom-lovers in communist times). The top Czech jazzmen—Stivín and Koubková—regularly perform. Bill Clinton played the sax here (about 300 Kč; live jazz, blues, swing, or big band every night from 21:30; on Národní street next to Café Louvre, tel. 224-933-486, www.redutajazzclub.cz).

In the Little Quarter

Baráčnická Rychta, with a gymnasium-like hall, saw many great polka parties in the 1920s. Rock has long since replaced waltz, but the place still feels like a village dancehall, complete with flags of bakers' and butchers' guilds and black-and-white photos of the proud Austro-Hungarian landlords. It's a great scene if the hall is full, but less popular bands look a bit lost in the large space. Try the yeasty and strong Svijany beer here (150-Kč cover, 3 shows weekly starting at 20:00 or 21:00, arrive earlier to get a seat at a table, on Tržiště, tucked away from tourists and out-of-town Czechs in a small courtyard directly across from the American Embassy, see map on page 170, tel. 257-532-461, www.baracnickarychta.cz).

Malostranská Beseda, at the bottom of the Little Quarter, was known in the communist era for playing host to underground rock bands, semi-legal bards, and daring jazzmen—a stark contrast to the regime-pampered pop stars. Following a major renovation, Beseda—with its tight, steamy, standing-room-only space—is back in action as the only club in the center with daily live performances. The crowd tends to be a bit older than at other clubs (150-300-Kč cover depending on band, shows from 21:00, Malostranské Náměstí 21, see map on page 170, www.malostranska-beseda.cz, tel. 257-409-123). The building also houses a recommended restaurant and beer hall.

In Žižkov

This hip neighborhood has Prague's highest concentration of cool pubs.

Palác Akropolis is *the* home of Czech independent music. Originally a 1920s movie theater, in the 1990s it was turned into a chill-out lounge, a literary café, and two halls that offer a mix of concerts, disco, and theater (advance ticket sales at café, Mon-Fri 10:00-24:00, Sat-Sun 16:00-24:00, corner of Kubelíkova and Fibichova, under Žižkov TV tower, Metro: Jiřího z Poděbrad, see map on page 38, tel. 296-330-913, www.palacakropolis.cz).

Sports

Prague's top sports are soccer (that's "football" here) and hockey. Surprisingly, the Czechs have often been a world power in both. You'll find the latest schedules for games in the *Prague Post* newspaper (soccer—usually late Sat, Sun, or Mon afternoons Feb-May and Aug-Nov; hockey—Tue, Fri, and Sun nights Sept-April). With the exception of matches between the top two Czech soccer teams (Sparta and Slavia), both soccer and hockey games are rarely sold out—just show up at the stadium 15 minutes before the game starts.

Soccer

The Czech national soccer team reached the semifinals of the 2004 European Cup, and the knockout stages of the 2012 Euro Cup.

Within the Czech Republic, the two oldest and most successful soccer clubs are the bitter Prague rivals AC Sparta and SK Slavia. Sparta's 1970s-era stadium is at Letná (behind the giant Metronome ticking above the river in Letenské Park). Slavia's brand-new stadium is in Vršovice (12 stops from the National Theater on tram #22). Other teams in the country occasionally challenge the supremacy of the two S's, as was the case in 2012 when Slovan Liberec won the league title, and in 2011, when FC Viktoria Plzeň (Pilsen) won the title and qualified for the highly lucrative, 32-club European Champions League—becoming only the third Czech team to do so.

Another Prague team in the top Czech league is FK Dukla—formerly an army team from the communist era—that made Czech soccer famous across the globe in the 1960s.

Hockey

Between 1996 and 2005, the Czech national hockey team won five of the annual world championships. In 1998, they won the gold medal at the Olympic Games in Nagano, Japan. However, its golden generation is retiring—and younger players have been slow to fill the gap. Following a disappointing performance at the 2010 Vancouver Olympics, it seemed the Czech team, with no big-name players, had hit rock bottom. But it managed to pull off a major upset by beating the fired-up Russians to win the 2010 World Championship. In 2011, after a very good tournament, the Czechs finished third, but few fans minded, as the team managed to beat the Russians twice en route to their bronze medal.

Currently, more than 40 Czech players take the ice in America's National Hockey League; think of Jaromír Jágr, one of the NHL's all-time leading scorers and Dominik "The Dominator" Hašek, a top goaltender (who played 16 seasons in the NHL before retiring from US hockey).

Sparta and Slavia, the traditional Czech soccer powers, also have hockey teams, but their rivalry is less intense, as the teams from smaller towns are more than their equals. Slavia plays in the state-of-the-art Sazka Arena, which was built for the 2004 World Hockey Championships (right at the Českomoravská Metro stop).

Back in the old days, ice hockey was the only battleground on which Czechoslovaks could seek revenge on their Russian oppressors (ice hockey is also the most popular sport in Slovakia). The hockey rink is still where Czechs are proudest about their nationality. If you're in town in May during the hockey championships, join locals cheering their team in front of a giant screen on the Old Town Square, as well as on other main squares around the country.

Sports on the Old Town and Wenceslas Squares

When there are sporting events of great interest (such as hockey and soccer championships), the Old Town Square plays host to huge TV screens, beer and bratwurst stands, and thousands of Czechs. The warm and friendly scene is like a big family gathering. Some fans lie on the cobblestones up front and focus on the game, while others mill around in the back and just enjoy the party.

Major running and biking events (such as the Prague International Marathon at the beginning of May) finish in the Old Town Square. The two biggest sporting events on Wenceslas Square are the Prague Pole Vault and a cycling competition that uses the square as a lap. The bottom of Wenceslas Square is sometimes set up for soccer, basketball, and beach volleyball tournaments. Both squares are also used for pop and folk concerts and for political rallies. These events are fine opportunities to feel the pulse of the Czech capital.

ENTERTAINMENT

PRAGUE CONNECTIONS

Centrally located Prague is a logical gateway between Western and Eastern Europe. It's also the hub for trains and buses in the Czech Republic—from here, rail lines and expressways fan out like spokes on a wheel. This chapter covers arrivals and departures by train, bus, plane, and car. You'll find handy Czech train and bus schedules at www.idos.cz.

By Train

Prague's **Main Station** (Hlavní Nádraží) serves all international trains; most trains within the Czech Republic, including high-speed SC Pendolino trains; and the DB (Deutsche Bahn) buses to and from Nürnberg and Munich. Trains serving Berlin also stop at the secondary **Holešovice Station** (Nádraží Holešovice, located north of the river).

Upon arrival, get money. Both stations have ATMs (best rates) and exchange bureaus (rotten rates).

Main Train Station (Hlavní Nádraží)
The station's underground two-floor hall is filled with expensive cafés and shops. It's come a long way since a communist makeover enlarged the once-classy Art Nouveau station and painted it the compulsory dreary gray with reddish trim. While the underground hall now looks great, the deteriorated above-ground complex remains untouched under scaffolding.

First named for Emperor Franz Josef, the station was later renamed for President Woodrow Wilson (see the commemorative plaque in the main exit hall leading away from the tracks and the large bronze statue in the park in front of the station), because his promotion of self-determination led to the creation of the free state of Czechoslovakia in 1918. Under the communists (who weren't big fans of Wilson), it was bluntly renamed Hlavní Nádraží—"Main Station."

Upon arrival by train, take any of the three parallel tunnels that connect the tracks to the arrival hall. The first area you reach (with low ceilings) has an **exchange office** with **Internet** booths, and two handy picnic-supply shops (**Mr. Baker** and **BioPoint**) on the right. Signs point to the "official" taxi stand to the sides (avoid these rip-off cabbies—explained later). If you turn around and go up another floor, you'll find the **Fantova Kavárna,** a decrepit café beneath an Art Nouveau cupola. Outside is the stop for the **AE bus** to the airport (buy 50-Kč ticket from driver, runs every half-hour daily 6:35-22:05, 40 minutes) and the **DB buses** to Nürnberg and Munich.

Straight down from the low-ceilinged area is the main hall, where you'll find four Metro entrances in the center (two for each direction; for more on the Metro, see "Getting from the Main Station to Your Hotel," later). One **ATM** is along the right wall, while two more are in front of the ticketing area under the central stairs. Lockers for **luggage storage** are in the corner under the stairs on the right. The **Billa supermarket** is in the corner under the stairs to the left. You can get Czech mobile-phone SIM cards at the **Vodafone** store in the main hall.

The **Czech Railways (České Dráhy) ticket office** is in the middle of the main hall under the stairs. Its tiny **ČD Travel center,** on the left as you enter the main office, sells both domestic and international tickets, and is your best bet for information in English (Mon-Fri 9:00-18:00, Sat 9:00-14:00, closed Sun, shorter hours in winter, tel. 972-241-861, www.cd.cz/en). The regular ticket desks are faster if you already know your schedule and destination, but not all attendants speak good English.

The **RegioJet travel office** (desks at both sides of the main ticket office; free Internet access to the right) sells international train tickets from the DB (Deutsche Bahn—German railways) system and offers various DB deals and discounts. RegioJet also runs its own trains to Olomouc at 220 Kč. The office, a branch of the **Student Agency bus company,** sells a variety of domestic (e.g., to Český Krumlov) and international (Vienna) bus tickets without a commission (Mon-Fri 5:00-19:45, Sat-Sun 6:45-19:45, tel. 539-000-511, www.regiojet.cz, jizdenky@regiojet.cz). Despite its name, RegioJet does not sell plane tickets.

The **Leo Express ticket office,** across the hall from Czech Railways, sells tickets for its new Swiss-made trains to Olomouc (www.le.cz).

Touristpoint (with your back to the tracks, it's on your right under the stairs) arranges last-minute rooms in hotels and pensions, as well as car rentals, sightseeing tours, and adrenaline experiences.

They accept any currency and credit cards, and also sell maps and international phone cards. A phone is available for calling a **taxi**—and the driver will come to the desk to get you (daily 8:00-22:00, tel. 224-946-010, www.touristpoint.cz, info@touristpoint.cz).

For a quiet, air-conditioned place to spend your last coins before leaving Prague, enjoy a coffee at **Leonidas** (in front of the RegioJet office, near Touristpoint).

Getting from the Main Station to Your Hotel

Even though the Main Train Station is basically downtown, getting to your hotel can be a little tricky. The biggest challenge is that the **taxi** drivers at the train station's run-down "official" stand are a gang of no-neck mafia thugs just waiting for the chance to charge an arriving tourist five times the regular rate. To get an **honest cabbie,** exit the station's main hall through the big glass doors, then cross 50 yards through a park to Opletalova street (a few taxis are usually waiting in front of the Hotel Chopin, on the corner of Jeruzalémská street). You can also call a taxi from the Touristpoint office, described earlier (AAA Taxi—tel. 14-014; City Taxi—tel. 257-257-257). Before getting into a taxi, always confirm the maximum price to your destination, and make sure the driver turns on the meter—it should cost no more than 300 Kč to get to your hotel. For more pointers on taking taxis, see page 48.

Better yet, take the **Metro.** It's dirt cheap and easy, with frequent departures. Once you're on the Metro, you'll wonder why you would ever bother with a taxi (inside the station's main hall, look for the red *M* with two directions: Háje or Letňany). To purchase tickets from the automated machine by the Metro entrance, you'll need Czech coins (get change at the change machine in the corner near the luggage lockers, or break a bill at a newsstand or grocery). Validate your ticket in the yellow machines *before* you go down the stairs to the tracks. To get to hotels in the Old Town, catch a Háje-bound train to the Muzeum stop, then transfer to the green line (direction: Dejvická) and get off at either Můstek or Staroměstská; these stops straddle the Old Town. For more information on Prague's public transit, see page 46.

Most hotels I list in the Old Town are within a 20-minute **walk** of the train station. Exit the station into a small park, walk through the park, and then cross the street on the other side. Head down Jeruzalémská street to the Jindřišská Tower and tram stop, walk under a small arch, then continue slightly to the right down Senovážná street. At the end of the street, you'll see the Powder Gate—the grand entry into the Old Town—to the left. Alternatively, Wenceslas Square in the New Town is a 10-minute walk—exit the station, cross the park, and walk to the left along Opletalova street.

CONNECTIONS

The nearest **tram** stop is to the right as you exit the station (about 200 yards away). Tram #9 (headed away from railway tracks) takes you to the neighborhood near the National Theater and the Little Quarter, but isn't useful for most Old Town hotels.

Holešovice Train Station (Nádraží Holešovice)

This station, slightly farther from the center, is suburban mellow. The main hall has the same services as the Main Train Station, in a more compact area. On the left are international and local ticket windows (open 24 hours) and an information office. On the right is an uncrowded café with Internet access (1 Kč/minute, daily 8:00-19:30). Two ATMs are just outside the first glass doors, and the Metro is 50 yards to the right (follow signs toward *Vstup,* which means "entrance"; it's three stops to Hlavní Nádraží—the Main Station—or four stops to the city-center Muzeum stop). Taxis and trams are outside to the right (allow 300 Kč for a cab to the center).

Train Connections

Direct overnight trains connect Prague to Amsterdam, Vienna, Frankfurt, Zurich, Budapest, Kraków, and Warsaw; several trains leave daily for Munich, Berlin, and Vienna. From the East, Prague is connected by convenient night trains with Budapest, Kraków, and Warsaw. All international trains pass through the Main Station (Hlavní Nádraží); some also stop at the Holešovice Station (Nádraží Holešovice). For tips on rail travel, see the appendix.

From Prague's Main Station to Domestic Destinations: **Konopiště Castle** (train to **Benešov,** 2/hour, 1 hour, then 1.5-mile walk to castle), **Karlštejn** (2/hour, 40 minutes, then a 20-minute walk to castle), **Křivoklát** (hourly, 1.5 hours total, transfer in Beroun), **Kutná Hora** (11/day, 1 hour, more with change in Kolín), **Terezín** (train to Bohušovice station, nearly hourly, 1-1.5 hours, then 5-minute taxi or bus ride—bus is better), **Český Krumlov** (8/day, 1/day direct, 4 hours—bus is faster, cheaper, and easier), **České Budějovice** (almost hourly, 2.5 hours), **Třeboň** (7/day, 2.5 hours, transfer at Veselí nad Lužnicí—get off at Třeboň-Lázně station, not Třeboň-Město), **Telč** (3/day, 4-5 hours, requires 2 changes, bus is better), **Třebíč** (nearly hourly, 4-5 hours, transfer in Brno, bus is better), **Slavonice** (must first take bus to Telč, 5/day Mon-Fri, 3/day Sat-Sun, 2-3 hours, then 1-hour train to Slavonice, 5/day), **Olomouc** (at least hourly, 2-3 hours; use Olomouc for connections to **Wallachia**), **Valtice** (hourly, 4 hours, 1 transfer), **Břeclav** (with connections to **Mikulov Wine Region**—see page 300; 9/day direct, 3 hours, most from Holešovice Station), **Brno** (every 2 hours direct, 2.5 hours, more with changes).

From Prague's Main Station to International Destinations: **Berlin** (6/day, 4.5-5 hours), **Dresden** (about hourly, 2-2.5 hours),

Nürnberg (2/day, 5-5.25 hours, bus is better—see below), **Munich** (2/day direct, 6.25 hours; bus is faster—see below, no night train), **Frankfurt** (6/day via ExpressBus to Nürnberg then train to Frankfurt, 6.5 hours total; 1 night train, 9.5 hours), **Vienna**—Vídeň in Czech (5/day direct, 4-4.5 hours, more with 1 change, 5-6 hours; 1 night train, 7.5 hours), **Amsterdam** (1 night train, 15 hours), **Zürich** (1 night train, 15 hours), **Paris** (5/day, 12.5-13.5 hours; 1 night train possible via Mannheim), **Budapest** (3/day, 7 hours; more with 2-3 changes, 8.5 hours; 1 night train, 7.5 hours), **Kraków** (1/day direct, 7.5 hours; 4/day with 1-2 changes, 8.25 hours; 1 night train, 9.5 hours), **Warsaw** (1/day direct, 8.75 hours; 3/day with 1-2 changes, 8.5-10 hours; 1 night train, 10 hours).

By Bus

Prague's main bus station is at Florenc, east of the Old Town (Metro: Florenc). But some connections use other stations, including Roztyly (Metro: Roztyly), Na Knížecí (Metro: Anděl), the Nádraží Holešovice train station (Metro: Nádraží Holešovice), Hradčanská (Metro: Hradčanská), or the Main Train Station (Metro: Hlavní Nádraží). Be sure to confirm which station your bus uses.

From Prague by Bus to: Terezín (hourly, 50 minutes, 10 more minutes to **Litoměřice,** departs from Nádraží Holešovice train station), **Český Krumlov** (7/day, 3.5 hours, some leave from Florenc station, others leave from Na Knížecí station or Roztyly station), **Třeboň** (2/day, 2.5 hours), **Telč** (5/day Mon-Fri, 3/day Sat-Sun, 2-3 hours, some from Roztyly station; more with a transfer in Jihlava, 3 hours total), **Třebíč** (7/day, 2.5 hours, some from Roztyly station), **Lány**/Kladno district (6/day, fewer on weekends, 1 hour, departs from Hradčanská station), **Brno** (2/hour from Florenc station, 2.5 hours), **Nürnberg,** Germany (6/day via ExpressBus, 3.75 hours, covered by railpasses, departs in front of Main Train Station), **Munich,** Germany (4/day via ExpressBus, 4.75-6 hours, covered by railpasses, also departs from Main Train Station), **Budapest** (1-4/day via Orange Ways, not covered by railpasses, 6.5-7.5 hours, www.orangeways.com).

By Plane

Václav Havel Airport

Prague's modern, tidy, low-key Václav Havel Airport (formerly Ruzyně Airport), located 12 miles (about 30 minutes) west of the city center, is as user-friendly as any airport in Western Europe or the US. Terminal 2 serves destinations within the EU except for Great Britain (no passport controls); Terminal 1 serves Great Britain and everywhere else. The airport has ATMs (avoid the change desks),

desks promoting their transportation services (such as city transit and shuttle buses), kiosks selling city maps and phone cards, and a TI with few printed materials. Airport info: airport code: PRG, tel. 220-113-314, operator tel. 220-111-111, www.prg.aero/en.

If you're flying out of Václav Havel Airport and need to process a VAT refund (see page 16), get your papers stamped at customs *before* you go through security. In Terminal 1, customs is located in the far left-hand corner of the departure hall, next to the oversize baggage desk. At Terminal 2, customs is immediately to the right of the security check. You can cash in your refund on the spot (minus the 4 percent fee) at a Travelex office: In Terminal 1, these are located both before and after security. In Terminal 2, Travelex has a booth *before* security only (just to the left).

Getting from the Airport to Your Hotel

Getting between the airport and downtown is easy. Leaving either airport terminal, you have four options, listed below from cheapest to priciest:

Dirt Cheap: Take bus #119 to the Dejvická Metro station, or #100 to the Zličín Metro station (20 minutes), then take the Metro into the center (32 Kč, buy tickets at info desk in airport arrival hall).

Budget: Take the airport express (AE) bus to the Main Train Station, or to the Masarykovo Nádraží station near Náměstí Republiky—Republic Square (50 Kč, runs every half-hour daily 5:46-21:16, 40 minutes, look for the *AE* sign in front of the terminal and pay the driver, www.cd.cz/en). From either station, you can take the Metro, hire a taxi, or walk to your hotel. The Masarykovo Nádraží stop is slightly closer to downtown.

Moderate: Take the Čedaz minibus shuttle (from exit F at Terminal 1 or exit E at Terminal 2) to the Náměstí Republiky station, at the entrance to the Old Town. The shuttle stop is on V Celnici street, across the street from Hotel Marriott and near the recommended Brasserie La Gare (pay 130 Kč directly to driver, daily 7:30-19:00, 2/hour, info desk in arrival hall).

Expensive: Catch a taxi. Cabbies wait at the curb directly in front of the arrival hall. Or book a yellow AAA taxi through their office in the airport hall—you'll get a 50 percent discount coupon for the trip back (book your return trip by calling 221-111-111). AAA taxis wait in front of exit D at Terminal 1 and exit E at Terminal 2 (metered rate, generally 500-600 Kč to downtown).

CONNECTIONS

By Private Car Service

Mike's Chauffeur Service is a reliable, family-run company with fair and fixed rates around town and beyond. Friendly Mike's motto is, "We go the extra mile for you" (round-trip fares, with waiting time included, guaranteed through 2014 with this book: Český Krumlov-3,800 Kč, Terezín-1,900 Kč, Karlštejn-1,700 Kč, 4 percent surcharge for credit-card payment; these prices for up to 4 people, minibus for up to 7 also available; tel. 241-768-231, mobile 602-224-893, www.mike-chauffeur.cz, mike.chauffeur@cmail.cz). On the way to Český Krumlov, Mike will stop at no extra charge at Hluboká Castle or České Budějovice, where the original Bud beer is made. For day trips from Prague, Mike can bring bicycles along and will pedal with you.

Mike also offers "Panoramic Transfers" to **Vienna** (7,000 Kč, depart Prague at 8:00, arrive Český Krumlov at 10:00, stay up to 5 hours, 1-hour scenic Czech riverside-and-village drive, then a 2-hour autobahn ride to your Vienna hotel, maximum 4 people); **Budapest** (8,900 Kč, 6 hours, Bratislava or Český Krumlov options); and **Kraków** (8,900 Kč, Auschwitz stop). Check Mike's website for special deals on last-minute transfers, including super-cheap "deadhead" rides when you travel in the opposite direction of a full-fare client.

CONNECTIONS

DAY TRIPS FROM PRAGUE

Kutná Hora • Terezín Memorial • Konopiště Castle • Karlštejn Castle • Křivoklát Castle

Prague has plenty to keep a traveler busy, but don't overlook the interesting day trips in the nearby Bohemian countryside. Within an hour of Prague (in different directions), you'll find a rich medieval town, a sobering concentration camp, and three grand castles. Descriptions and ratings follow:

▲▲Kutná Hora

Once home to the world's largest silver mine, this down-to-earth city is known for its opulent cathedral—built with riches from the mining bonanza—and a creepy church decorated with human bones.

▲▲Terezín Memorial

The walled town of Terezín served as an internment camp for Jews during World War II. Nearby, the town of Litoměřice offers charm and an opportunity to reflect on the camp.

▲Konopiště

This popular castle, with an impressive interior, provides a good look at the Czech version of this European medieval architectural form.

▲Karlštejn

Another touristy castle, this is similar to Konopiště, but has a better exterior. Advance reservations are required for Karlštejn's Chapel of the Holy Cross.

Křivoklát

One of the purest Gothic castles in the country, it's a less touristy alternative to the other two castles. En route to Křivoklát, the Rückl Glassworks in Nižbor is a worthwhile stop for a look at the traditional manufacture of Czech crystal. The nearby village of

Day Trips

Lány, with the grave of Tomáš Garrigue Masaryk, is a modern-day pilgrimage site for Czech patriots.

Kutná Hora

Kutná Hora (KOOT-nah HO-rah) is a refreshingly authentic town of 20,000 that sits on top of what was once Europe's largest silver mine. In its heyday, the mine was so productive that Kutná Hora was Bohemia's "second city" after Prague. Much of Europe's standard coinage was minted here. By about 1700, the mining and minting petered out, and the city slumbered. Once rich, then ignored, Kutná Hora is now appreciated by tourists looking for a

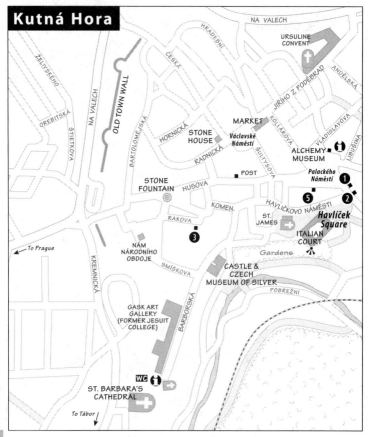

Kutná Hora

handy side-trip from Prague. Visitors are charmed by this wonderfully preserved town and its interesting sights: the fine St. Barbara's Cathedral, the fascinating silver mine, and the eerie Sedlec Bone Church.

Kutná Hora, unlike dolled-up Český Krumlov, is a typical Czech town. The shops on the main square cater to locals, and the factory between the Sedlec Bone Church and the train station—since the 1930s, the biggest tobacco processor in the country—is now Philip Morris' headquarters for Central Europe. After touristy Prague, Kutná Hora is about as close to quintessential Czech life as you can get.

Getting to Kutná Hora

The town is 40 miles east of Prague. Direct trains from Prague's Main Station stop at Kutná Hora's Main Station, two miles from the town center (11/day, 1 hour; other trains are slower and re-

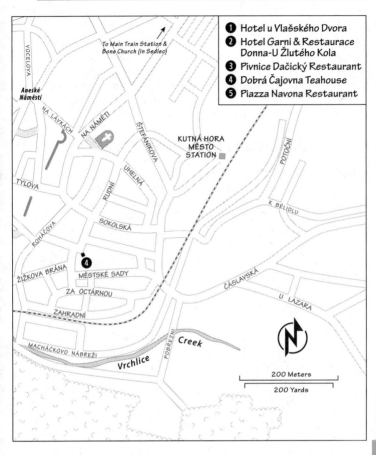

1. Hotel u Vlašského Dvora
2. Hotel Garni & Restaurace Donna-U Žlutého Kola
3. Pivnice Dačický Restaurant
4. Dobrá Čajovna Teahouse
5. Piazza Navona Restaurant

quire transfer in Kolín). From there, a local train shuttles visitors to Sedlec Station (near the Sedlec Bone Church), then to the central Město Station (near the rest of the sights). For train schedules, see www.jizdnirady.idnes.cz.

In Prague, make sure to buy a ticket to the Kutná Hora Město Station rather than its Main Station—the price is nearly the same, and this gives you the flexibility to get off and on at any of the three Kutná Hora stations.

Planning Your Time

For the most efficient visit, visit the Sedlec Bone Church first, then St. Barbara's Cathedral, and end with the Museum of Silver.

Here are the specifics: At Kutná Hora's Main Station, transfer to the local train. Get off at its first stop (Kutná Hora-Sedlec), and walk one block down the street perpendicular to the tracks, passing a large church on your right. Cross the main street and find the small Bone Church in the middle of the cemetery directly ahead. After your visit, ride the Bone Church's tourist minivan to St. Barbara's Cathedral in the town center. From the cathedral, walk to the Museum of Silver and reserve your spot on the next English-language tour (it's also possible to call the museum ahead to reserve). At the end of the day, walk to the Kutná Hora Město Station to catch the train back to Prague.

Orientation to Kutná Hora

Tourist Information

The main TI is on **Palackého Náměstí,** housed in the same building as the Alchemy Museum (April-Sept daily 9:00-18:00; Oct-March Mon-Fri 9:00-17:00, Sat-Sun 9:00-16:00; tel. 327-512-378, www.kutnahora.cz). It offers Internet access and also rents bicycles (220 Kč/day, mobile 605-802-874).

A small TI kiosk, with handy WCs, is in front of the **cathedral;** you can also hire a local guide here. Reserve ahead if you can (500 Kč/hour Tue-Sun, no tours Mon, tel. 327-516-710, mobile 736-485-408, infocentrum@kh.cz).

Sights in Kutná Hora

St. Barbara's Cathedral (Chrám Sv. Barbory)

The cathedral was founded in 1388 by miners, who dedicated it to their patron saint. The dazzling interior celebrates the town's sources of wealth, with frescoes featuring mining and minting. Even the Renaissance vault—a stunning feat of architecture by the two Gothic geniuses of Prague, Matyáš Rejsek and Benedict Ried—is decorated with miners' coats of arms. The artistic highlight is the Smíšek Chapel to the right of the altar. The late-Gothic frescoes—*The Arrival of the Queen of Sheba, The Trial of Trajan,* and especially the fresco under the chapel's window depicting two men with candles—are the only remaining works of a Dutch-trained master in Gothic Bohemia.

Cost and Hours: 50 Kč, daily 9:00-18:00 in summer, shorter hours off-season.

Art Gallery of the Central Bohemian Region (GASK)

The former Baroque Jesuit college (on your left as you exit the cathedral) was converted into an art museum, which opened in 2010. It boasts the second-biggest exhibition space in the country (after the National Gallery in Prague), filled with ever-changing temporary exhibits of 20th- and 21st-century art.

The statues of saints on the artificial terrace in front of the gallery are a reminder of the building's Jesuit past. The Jesuits arrived here in 1626 with a mission: to make the Protestant population Catholic again. These chubby sandstone figures, just like those on the Charles Bridge in Prague, were initially commissioned as Counter-Reformation propaganda pieces.

Cost and Hours: Combo-ticket for all exhibits-220 Kč, single exhibit-80 Kč, Tue-Sun 10:00-18:00, closed Mon, Barborská 51-53, www.gask.cz.

Hrádek Castle and the Czech Museum of Silver (České Muzeum Stříbra)

This museum, located in Kutná Hora's 15th-century Hrádek castle, features an exhibit on mining and an intriguing horse-powered winch that once hoisted 2,000 pounds of rock at a time out of the mine. Don a miner's coat and helmet, and climb deep into the mine for a wet, dark, and claustrophobic 45-minute tour of the medieval shafts that honeycomb the rock beneath the town. Try to time your visit to join an English-language tour (ask for the charming Mr. Matuška, a retired miner). You can try calling ahead (the day before or the morning of your visit) to ask when English tours are scheduled—wait through the Czech recording, ask to speak with an English-speaker, and reserve a slot. Otherwise, drop by the museum soon after you arrive in Kutná Hora to find out the schedule and reserve.

Cost and Hours: 120 Kč, April-Oct Tue-Sun 10:00-18:00, closed Mon and Nov-March, tours generally every half-hour, tel. 327-512-159, www.cms-kh.cz.

Stone Fountain (Kamenná Kašna)

Because of intensive mining under the town, Kutná Hora has always struggled with obtaining clean drinking water. Water was brought to town by a sophisticated system of water pipes and then stored in large tanks. At the end of the 15th century, the architect Rejsek built a 12-sided, richly decorated Gothic structure over one of these tanks. Although no longer functioning, the fountain survives unchanged—the only structure like it in Bohemia (on the square called Rejskovo Náměstí).

Stone House (Kamenný Dům)

Notice the meticulous detail in the grape leaves, branches, and animals on this house's facade and up in its gable. Talented Polish craftsmen delicately carved the brittle stone into what was considered a marvel of its time. Skip the boring museum of local arts and crafts inside.

Cost and Hours: 50 Kč, Tue-Sun 10:00-17:00, closed Mon, Radnická 183, www.cms-kh.cz.

Alchemy Museum (Muzeum Alchymie)

The only one of its kind in the Czech Republic, situated in the surprisingly deep medieval cellars of this otherwise unassuming house, this museum features a laboratory dedicated to the pursuit of *prima materia* (primal matter). The English descriptions do a good job explaining the goals and methods of alchemy and the fate of its failed practitioners. The rare Gothic tower in the rear of the house is set up as an alchemist's study (complete with ancient books), looking much as it did when a prince used this vaulted space in his quest to purify matter and spirit.

Cost and Hours: 60 Kč, daily April-Sept 9:00-18:00, Oct-March 9:00-17:00, on the main square in the same building as the TI, tel. 327-512-378.

Nearby: Upstairs from the TI (in the same building) is another quirky museum, featuring a collection of baby strollers from the Victorian era to the present.

Italian Court (Vlašský Dvůr)

This palace, located on the site where Czech currency was once made, became Europe's most important mint and the main residence of Czech kings in the 1400s. Most of the present-day building, however, is a 19th-century reconstruction. Today, it hosts a moderately interesting museum on minting and local history. The entry fee gets you into the main Gothic hall (now a wedding chamber) and the Art Nouveau-decorated St. Wenceslas Chapel. The flower-filled square in front is also worth a look.

Cost and Hours: 70 Kč, April-Sept daily 9:00-18:00, shorter hours Oct-March, Havlíčkovo Náměstí.

Havlíček Square (Havlíčkovo Náměstí)

The monuments on this square are a Who's Who of important Czech patriots.

The statue in the middle of the square (and the square's namesake) is **Karel Havlíček** (1821-1856), the founder of Czech political journalism. From Kutná Hora, Havlíček ran an influential magazine highly critical of the Habsburg government. In 1851, he was forced into exile and detained for five years in the Tirolean Alps under police surveillance. His integrity is reflected by the quote inscribed on the statue: "You can try to bribe me with favors, you can threaten me, you can torture me, yet I will never turn a traitor." His motto became an inspiration for generations of Czech intellectuals, most of whom faced a similar combination of threats and temptations. Havlíček (whose name means "little Havel") was much revered in the 1970s and 1980s, when the *other* Havel (Václav) was similarly imprisoned for his dissent.

The bronze statue in front of the Italian Court honors the founder of Czechoslovakia, **Tomáš Garrigue Masaryk** (1850-1937; see sidebar on page 320). The brief inscription on the back of the pedestal recounts the statue's up-and-down history, which parallels the country's troubled 20th-century history: erected by Kutná Hora townspeople on October 27, 1938 (the eve of the 20th anniversary of Czech independence); torn down in 1942 (by occupying Nazis, who disliked Masaryk as a symbol of Czech independence);

erected again on October 27, 1948 (by freedom-loving locals, a few months after the communist coup); torn down again in 1957 (by the communists, who considered Masaryk an enemy of the working class); and erected once again on October 27, 1991. Notice that the Czechs, ever practical, have left a blank space below the last entry...

On the wall to the left of the gate, you'll find a small bronze tablet covered with barbed wire. This is an unassuming little **memorial** to the victims of the communist regime's misrule and torture.

Walk down the steps into a little park, and then turn right to reach a great viewpoint. It overlooks the tent-shaped roof of the cathedral and the scenic valley below. You might want to take a rest on nearby benches under some linden trees—and think about those whom the memorial commemorates.

Market (Tržiště)

This double row of stalls selling fake Nike shoes and cheap jeans is as much a part of Czech urban life today as farmers markets were in the past. The stalls are often run by Vietnamese immigrants, the Czech Republic's third-largest minority (after Slovaks and Poles). Many came here in the 1970s as part of a communist solidarity program that sent Vietnamese workers to Czech textile factories. They learned the language, adapted to the environment, and, after 1989, set off on a road to entrepreneurial success that allowed them to bring over friends and relatives (Mon-Fri 7:30-16:45, shorter hours Sat, closed Sun, near Stone House).

Near Kutná Hora

Sedlec Bone Church (Kostnice u Sedlci)

Located a mile away from the center of town, in Sedlec, this little church looks normal on the outside. But inside, the bones of 40,000 people decorate the walls and ceilings. The 14th-century plagues and 15th-century wars provided all the raw material necessary for the creepily creative monks who made these designs. Those who first placed these bones 400 years ago wanted viewers to remember that the earthly church is a community of both the living and the dead, a countless multitude that will one day stand before God. Later bone-stackers were more interested in design than theology...as evidenced by the chandelier that includes every bone in the human body.

Cost and Hours: 90 Kč, daily April-Sept 8:00-18:00, March

Sleep Code

(20 Kč = about $1, country code: 420)
S = Single, **D** = Double/Twin, **T** = Triple, **Q** = Quad, **b** = bathroom, **s** = shower only. Unless otherwise noted, prices include breakfast. To help you sort easily through these listings, I've divided the accommodations into three categories based on the price for a standard double room with bath:

$$$ Higher Priced—Most rooms 1,500 Kč or more.
 $$ Moderately Priced—Most rooms between 1,000-1,500 Kč.
  $ Lower Priced—Most rooms 1,000 Kč or less.

Prices can change without notice; verify the hotel's current rates online or by email. For the best prices, book direct.

---

and Oct 9:00-17:00, Nov-Feb 9:00-16:00, tel. 327-561-143, www.kostnice.cz.

Shuttle: The Bone Church runs a tourist minivan that can shuttle you from the church to sights in town (35 Kč/person, requires 3 passengers or pay the 105-Kč minimum fee, April-Sept 9:00-18:00, Oct-March 9:00-17:00, inquire at the desk, mobile 731-402-307).

Sleeping in Kutná Hora

Although one day is enough for Kutná Hora, staying overnight saves you money (hotels are much cheaper here than in Prague) and allows you to better savor the atmosphere of a small Czech town.

$$ Hotel u Vlašského Dvora and **Hotel Garni** are two renovated townhouses run by the same management. Furnished in a mix of 1930s and modern style, the hotels come with access to a fitness center and sauna. Hotel Garni is slightly nicer (Db-1,200 Kč, a few steps off main square at Havlíčkovo Náměstí 513, tel. 327-515-773, www.vlasskydvur.cz).

Eating in Kutná Hora

Pivnice Dačický has made a theme of its namesake, a popular 17th-century author who once lived in the house. Solid wooden tables rest under perky illustrations of medieval town life, and a once-local brew, also named after Dačický, flows from the tap. They serve standard Czech fare, as well as excellent game and fish. While its regulars still come here for the cheap lunch specials, during tourist season the crowd is mostly international. Service can be slow when a group arrives (daily 11:00-23:00, Rakova 8, tel. 327-512-248, mobile 603-434-367).

Dobrá Čajovna Teahouse also offers the chance to escape—not to medieval times, but to a Thai paradise. Filled with tea cases, water pipes, and character, this place is an ideal spot to dawdle away the time that this ageless town has reclaimed for you (daily 14:00-22:00, Jungmannovo Náměstí 16, mobile 777-028-481).

Restaurace Donna-U Žlutého Kola ("Yellow Wheels") serves the fastest, tastiest Czech dishes in town, attracting a local crowd. There's a long menu in English, but the lunch specials are only listed on a separate sheet in Czech. When the weather's nice, sit in the shady courtyard behind the restaurant (open daily, lunch specials until 15:00, on Havlíčkovo Náměstí, right above Hotel Garni).

Piazza Navona features irritating English-language advertising ("the only true Italian restaurant in town"), but it still draws loyal customers thanks to its decent food and superb location on the main square (open daily).

Terezín Memorial

Terezín (TEH-reh-zeen), an hour by bus from Prague, was originally a fortified town named after Habsburg Empress Maria Theresa (it's called "Theresienstadt" in German). It was built in the 1780s with state-of-the-art, star-shaped walls designed to keep out the Prussians. In 1941, the Nazis removed the town's 7,000 inhabitants and brought in 60,000 Jews, creating a concentration camp. Ironically, the town's medieval walls, originally meant to keep Germans out, were later used by Germans to keep the Jews in.

This was the Nazis' model "Jewish town," a concentration camp dolled up for propaganda purposes. Here, in this "self-governed Jewish resettlement area,"

Jewish culture seemed to thrive, as "citizens" put on plays and concerts, published a magazine, and raised their families. But it was all a carefully planned deception, intended to convince Red Cross inspectors that the Jews were being treated well. Virtually all of Terezín's Jews (155,000 over the course of the war) ultimately ended up dying either here (35,000) or in extermination camps farther east.

Petr Ginz, Young Artist and Writer

Born in 1928 to a Jewish father and non-Jewish mother, Prague teenager Petr Ginz excelled at art and was a talented writer who penned numerous articles, short stories, and even a science-fiction novel. Petr was sent to the concentration camp at Terezín in 1942, where he edited the secret boys' publication *Vedem (We Are Ahead)*, writing poetry and drawing illustrations, and paying contributors with food rations he received from home.

Some of Petr's artwork and writings were preserved by Terezín survivors and archived by the Jewish Museum in Prague. In 2003, Ilan Ramon, the first Israeli astronaut and the son of a Holocaust survivor, took one of Petr's drawings—titled *Moon Country*—into space aboard the final, doomed mission of the space shuttle Columbia.

The publicity over the Columbia's explosion and Petr's drawing spurred a Prague resident to come forward with a diary he'd found in his attic. It was Petr's diary from 1941 to 1942, hidden decades earlier by Petr's parents and chronicling the year before the teen's deportation to Terezín. *The Diary of Petr Ginz* has since been published in more than 10 languages.

In the diary, Petr matter-of-factly documented the increasing restrictions on Jewish life in occupied Prague, interspersing the terse account with dry humor. In the entry for September 19, 1941, Petr wrote, "They just introduced a special sign for Jews" alongside a drawing of the Star of David. He continued, "On the way to school I counted 69 'sheriffs,'" referring to people wearing the star.

Petr spent two years at Terezín before being sent to Auschwitz, where he died in a gas chamber. He was 16.

One of the notable individuals held at Terezín was Viennese artist Friedl Dicker-Brandeis. This daring woman, a leader in the Bauhaus art movement, found her life's calling in teaching children freedom of expression. She taught the kids in the camp to distinguish between the central things—trees, flowers, lines—and peripheral things, such as the conditions of the camp. In 1944, Dicker-Brandeis volunteered to be sent to Auschwitz after her husband was transported there; she was killed a month later.

Of the 15,000 children who passed through Terezín from 1942 to 1944, fewer than 100 survived. The artwork they created at Terezín is a striking testimony to the cruel horror of the Holocaust. In 1994, Hana Volavková, a Terezín survivor and the director of the Jewish Museum in Prague, collected the children's artwork and poems in the book *I Never Saw Another Butterfly*. Selections of the Terezín drawings are also displayed and well-described in English in Prague's Pinkas Synagogue (described on page 80).

Of the cultural activities that took place at Terezín, the best known was the children's opera *Brundibár*. Written just before the war, the antifascist opera premiered secretly in Prague at a time when Jewish activities were no longer permitted. From 1943 to 1944, the play, performed in Czech, ran 55 times in the camp. After the war it was staged internationally, and was rewritten and published in the US in 2003 as a children's book by Tony Kushner and Maurice Sendak (whose version later appeared on Broadway).

Today, Terezín is an unforgettable day trip from Prague for those interested in touring a concentration camp memorial and museum. Allow three to six hours to see the entire camp. With more time, stop in the nearby attractive town of Litoměřice (described later) for lunch before returning to Prague.

Getting to Terezín

The camp is about 40 miles northwest of Prague. It's most convenient to visit Terezín by **bus** (described next) or **tour bus** (see page 55).

Buses to Terezín leave hourly from Prague's Holešovice train station (Nádraží Holešovice, on Metro line C). When you get off the Metro (coming from the city center), head toward the front of the train, go upstairs, turn right, and walk to the end of the corridor. You'll see bus stands directly ahead, outside the station. The Terezín bus departs from platform 7 (direction: Litoměřice, buy ticket from driver). You'll arrive in Terezín 50 minutes later at the public bus stop on the main square, around the corner from the Museum of the Ghetto. Some buses also stop earlier, by the Small Fortress. The driver and fellow passengers may tell you to get off there, but my self-guided tour works best if you begin at the stop in town (after the bus passes a field of crosses on your right and travels across the river).

For bus schedules, see www.idos.cz—you want "Terezín LT" (be sure to check the return schedule, too; for details on getting back to Prague, see "Terezín Connections," later).

Orientation to Terezín

Cost and Hours: The 210-Kč combo-ticket includes all parts of the camp. Most sights, including the Museum of the Ghetto, Magdeburg Barracks, and Hidden Synagogue, are open daily April-Oct 9:00-18:00, Nov-March 9:00-17:30. The Columbarium and Crematorium are closed Sat. The Crematorium opens at 10:00 year-round and closes at 16:00 Nov-March, and the Small Fortress opens at 8:00 year-round and closes at 16:30 Nov-March.

Tours: Guided tours in English are offered if enough people re-

DAY TRIPS FROM PRAGUE

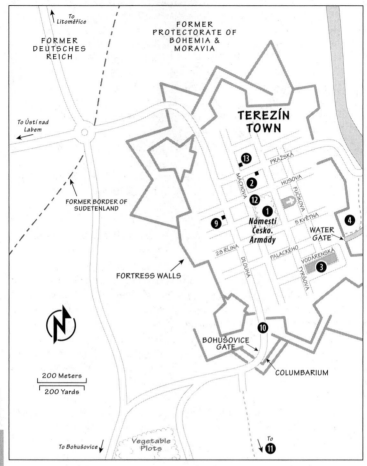

To Litoměřice

FORMER
DEUTSCHES
REICH

FORMER
PROTECTORATE OF
BOHEMIA &
MORAVIA

To Ústí nad
Labem

TEREZÍN
TOWN

13

PRAŽSKÁ

MÁCHOVA

2

HUSOVA

FUČÍKOVA

12

1

5 KVĚTNA

FORMER BORDER OF
SUDETENLAND

9

Náměsti
Česko.
Armády

WATER
GATE

4

28 ŘÍJNA

DLOUHÁ

PALACKÉHO

VODÁRENSKÁ

TYRŠOVA

3

FORTRESS WALLS

N

10

BOHUŠOVICE
GATE

COLUMBARIUM

200 Meters

200 Yards

To Bohušovice

Vegetable
Plots

To

11

DAY TRIPS FROM PRAGUE

quest them; call ahead to get the schedule and reserve a spot (included in entry).

Information: Tel. 416-782-225, mobile 606-632-914, www. pamatnik-terezin.cz.

Eating: In Terezín town, the **Parkhotel Restaurant** is the most elegant place for lunch (daily 10:00–22:00, around the block from Museum of the Ghetto at Máchova 163, tel. 416-782-260, cell 775-068-734).

The Small Fortress has a **cafeteria.** But avoid the stale sandwiches in the Museum of the Ghetto's dingy basement cafeteria, where most tour guides inexplicably bring their clients.

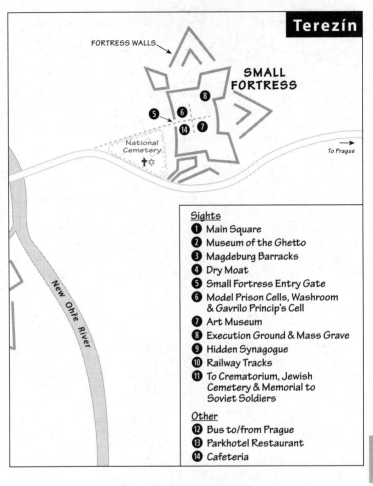

Terezín

FORTRESS WALLS

SMALL FORTRESS

❽

❺ ❻

❼
❶❹

National
Cemetery
✝ ✡

To Prague →

New Ohře River

Sights
❶ Main Square
❷ Museum of the Ghetto
❸ Magdeburg Barracks
❹ Dry Moat
❺ Small Fortress Entry Gate
❻ Model Prison Cells, Washroom
   & Gavrilo Princip's Cell
❼ Art Museum
❽ Execution Ground & Mass Grave
❾ Hidden Synagogue
❿ Railway Tracks
⓫ To Crematorium, Jewish
   Cemetery & Memorial to
   Soviet Soldiers

Other
⓬ Bus to/from Prague
⓭ Parkhotel Restaurant
⓮ Cafeteria

DAY TRIPS FROM PRAGUE

Self-Guided Tour

On this visit, you'll see Terezín town and the Small Fortress, which is a long half-mile walk to the east across the river.

• *The bus from Prague drops you off at Terezín town's spacious...*

Main Square (Náměstí Československé Armády): Picture the giant circus tent and barbed-wire fence that stood on this square for two years during the war. Inside, Jewish workers boxed special motors for German vehicles being used on the frigid Soviet front. As part of year-long preparations for the famous Red Cross visit (which lasted all of six hours on June 23, 1944), the tent and fence were replaced by flower beds (which you still see on the square today) and a pavilion for outdoor music performances.

• *Walk around the corner to the...*

Museum of the Ghetto: You can buy the Terezín combo-ticket here (note film showtimes posted near ticket desk). You'll find two floors of exhibits about the development of the Nazis' "Final Solution" and a theater showing four excellent films. One film documents the history of the ghetto, and two focus on children's art in the camp. The fourth is made up of clips from *Der Führer schenkt den Juden eine Stadt (The Führer Gives a City to the Jews)*, by Kurt Gerron. Gerron, a Berlin Jew, was a 1920s movie star who appeared with Marlene Dietrich in *Blue Angel*. Deported to Terezín, Gerron in 1944 was asked by the Nazis to produce a propaganda film. The resulting film depicts healthy (i.e., recently arrived) "Jewish settlers" in Terezín happily viewing concerts, playing soccer, and sewing in their rooms—yet an unmistakable, deadly desperation radiates from their pallid faces. The only moment of genuine emotion comes toward the end, when a packed room of children applauds the final lines of the popular anti-Nazi opera *Brundibár:* "We did not let ourselves down, we chased the nasty Brundibár away. With a happy song, we won it all." Even the Nazis were not fooled: Gerron and his wife were shipped to Auschwitz, and the film was never shown in public.

• *To learn more about living conditions in the camp, return to the main square and continue on Tyršova street to the...*

Magdeburg Barracks: Peek inside the large courtyard (you'll recognize it as the "soccer stadium" in Gerron's film), then continue upstairs. On the right are rooms reproducing the camp cabaret stage and exhibits documenting the prisoners' literary, musical, and theatrical activities. On the left is a meticulously restored camp dormitory, complete with three-tiered beds, eyeglasses, dolls, chessboards, and sewing kits.

• *As you exit the barracks (notice the high-water marks from the 2002 flood on the house opposite), turn right around the corner and walk 100 yards to a brick gate. You'll cross a bridge over a...*

Dry Moat: Imagine this moat filled with plots of vegetables, grown by starving Jews for well-fed SS officers.

Turn left and walk along the moat. The top of the fortification walls on the other side were once equipped with benches and pathways. When you reach the main road, turn right across the New Ohře River (the original course of the river was diverted here when Terezín was built).

• *Walk past the vast National Cemetery to the...*

Small Fortress: The fortress is marked by a black-and-white-striped gate. From 1940

to 1945, this fortress functioned as a Gestapo prison, through which 32,000 inmates passed (of whom nearly 10 percent died here)—chiefly members of the Czech resistance and communists. The 1,500 Jews interned here were treated with particular severity.

• *Inside the gate, turn left toward the notorious* Arbeit Macht Frei *sign (a postwar replica), painted above an arched gate. In the courtyard behind, you will first find...*

Model Prison Cells: The washroom in the left corner was built solely for the purpose of fooling Red Cross inspectors. Go ahead, turn the faucets: No pipes were ever installed to bring in water. The shower room farther to the left, on the other hand, was used to fool the Jews. Here they got used to the idea of communal bathing, so they wouldn't be suspicious when they were later taken to similar-

looking installations at Auschwitz. (There were no gas chambers at Terezín—most of the deaths here were caused by malnutrition, disease, and, to a lesser extent, execution.)

Before the Nazis, the Austrian monarchy used the Small Fortress as a prison. The little courtyard preserves the cell of the most famous prisoner from that time, Bosnian Serb **Gavrilo Princip,** whose assassination of Archduke Franz Ferdinand and his wife Žofie in 1914 sparked World War I (see sidebar on page 217). Princip died here in 1918 of tuberculosis.

• *Return through the* Arbeit Macht Frei *gate, then turn left into a large courtyard. On your right is an...*

Art Museum: This features two floors of paintings by prominent Czech artists, with themes of camp life and the Spanish Civil War.

• *Farther to the left is a path leading to the...*

Execution Ground and Mass Grave: Many of Terezín's victims were buried in mass graves along the fortress ramparts. The National Cemetery, outside the fortress, was created after World War II to hold remains exhumed from the mass graves (it now holds the last remains of 10,000 people).

• *At this point you could head to the handy cafeteria by the entry gate to the Small Fortress and take a break. The wood-and-metal chandeliers inside were produced by Jewish workers for the SS officers who once dined in these two rooms.*

With more time, consider continuing your tour in Terezín town *with the less-frequented sights that lie along or just off a main road called Dlouhá. At Dlouhá 17, look for the unique...*

Hidden Synagogue and Prisoner Housing: Although entry is included with your combo-ticket, you may need to ring the bell for the guard to open the door. Inside you'll find a courtyard; the bakery that used to be here hid the synagogue behind it. This is the only one of the camp's eight hidden synagogues that survived. The atmospheric space is still inscribed with two Hebrew captions, which are translated as "May my eyes behold, how You in compassion return to Sinai," and "If I forget Jerusalem, may my tongue rot and my right arm fall off." These words indicate that the prayer room belonged to a congregation of Zionists (advocates of a Jewish state), who, one would expect, were specifically targeted by the Nazis.

Upstairs, a few prisoners lived in a tight attic space. Even though the cramped rooms (reconstructed with period items) seem impossibly small, they were a far better accommodation than the mass housing in which most prisoners were interned. It's thought that a group of craftsmen who labored in a nearby workshop were "lucky" enough to live here.

• *Continue down Dlouhá toward the Bohušovice gate. On the ground, look for the remnants of...*

Railway Tracks: In the early years of the camp, Jews arrived at the train station in the nearby town of Bohušovice and then had

to walk the remaining two miles to Terezín. This was too public a display for the Nazis, who didn't want townspeople to observe the transports and become suspicious, so the Jewish prisoners at Terezín were forced to construct a railway line that led right to Terezín...and back out again to Auschwitz.

As you exit the walled-in area, on the right you will find Jewish and Christian ceremonial halls and the main morgue; on the left is a **Columbarium,** where the Nazis deposited cardboard boxes containing the ashes of dead prisoners. The Germans originally promised that the remains would be properly buried after the war, but in 1945, to erase evidence, the ashes of Terezín victims were dumped into the New Ohře River.

• *Continue along the road, then turn left past bucolic vegetable plots and fruit gardens to reach the...*

Crematorium, Jewish Cemetery, and a **Memorial to Soviet Soldiers:** Days before Terezín was liberated (on May 8, 1945), an epidemic of typhus spread through the camp. In the weeks after the war ended, scores of Soviet soldiers and medical workers who tried to contain the epidemic died, along with hundreds of former prisoners.

• *Our tour ends here. As you ponder Terezín, remember the message of all such memorials: Never again.*

Terezín Connections

The bus for **Prague** leaves from Terezín's main square (hourly, 50 minutes). If the return bus doesn't fit your schedule, consider taking a taxi from Terezín to the Bohušovice station (5 minutes from Terezín, trains to Prague depart nearly hourly, 1-1.5 hours). There is no taxi service from Bohušovice to Terezín, making the train a good option only for the return journey. If you're continuing from Terezín to **Dresden**, Germany, take the train from Bohušovice to Ústí, then switch to the international express train. For bus and train schedules, see www.idos.cz.

Near Terezín: Litoměřice

With a bustling, beautifully restored Renaissance square, Litoměřice (lee-TOH-myer-zheet-seh, pop. 26,000), located three miles north of Terezín, is a perfect lunch spot to lift your spirits after the bleakness of the camp. During the communist era, Litoměřice had the only seminary in the country. Today, there are still two huge Baroque churches here. Linger on the main square, Mírové Náměstí, and experience the pulse of this friendly, untouristy Czech town.

Getting to Litoměřice: Buses from Prague to Terezín continue on to Litoměřice (buses returning to Prague stop first in Litoměřice, then Terezín). If arriving by bus from Terezín, get off at the first stop after the bridge; from here it's a two-minute, slightly uphill walk to the main square.

Easier yet, it's a five-minute **taxi** trip between the Terezín Memorial and Litoměřice (about 150 Kč). The staff at Terezín's Museum of the Ghetto ticket office will be happy to call a taxi for you (such as Mr. Poláček's, based in Terezín, mobile 606-833-480).

Sights in Litoměřice: From the main square, several small streets filled with bakeries and convenience shops radiate outward. The onion-shaped tower is south, and the higher part of the square is due west. Stroll around and get lunch on the square. After lunch, climb up the onion-shaped tower of the **Town Hall** (the guide in the tower loves to talk), but skip the uninteresting museum on the square.

The short street next to the Town Hall leads onto the city walls, with good views. The statue at the viewpoint depicts the Romantic poet **Karel Hynek Mácha** (1810-1836), who wrote the most famous Czech poem, "Máj." He died in Litoměřice. In 1939, his body was ceremonially exhumed and transferred to the Slavín cemetery atop Prague's Vyšehrad hill. Mácha became a symbol of the irrepressible Czech spirit, stirring Czech nationalism during the occupations of first the Nazis, and later the communists. In November of 1989, demonstrating students were headed for the grave of Mácha when they suddenly decided that they were tired of the communists...and thus started the Velvet Revolution.

Eating in Litoměřice: The most convenient spot is the Czech fast-food joint **Joka,** which serves standard, ready-to-eat meals and good soups daily (at the top/northwest corner of the main square). You can get a sandwich, sit on the benches under trees by the fountain, and enjoy the view of the Renaissance-era townhouses. **Salva Guarda** is a bit stuffy and service is slow, but it's a decent sit-down option (daily 11:00-23:00, under the arches at the bottom/southeast corner of the square).

Litoměřice Connections: To reach Litoměřice's bus station for the trip back to Prague (hourly, 1 hour), walk east on the main street (Dlouhá) down from the square to an intersection, cross it, and continue in the same direction along Na Kocandě street (an easy 10-minute walk). The train station is nearby (though buses to Prague are preferable, as the train requires a transfer). For bus and train schedules, see www.idos.cz.

Konopiště Castle

Konopiště (KOH-noh-peesh-tyeh), the huge, Neo-Gothic residence of the Archduke Franz Ferdinand d'Este, is 30 miles south of Prague.

Construction of the castle began in the 14th century, but today's exterior and furnishings date from about 1900,

Archduke Franz Ferdinand (1863-1914)

Archduke Franz Ferdinand was the nephew of the Habsburg Emperor Franz Josef, who ruled from 1848 to 1916 (longer than Queen Victoria). Ferdinand was the impatient successor to the Austro-Hungarian throne. Local legends (whose veracity historians categorically deny) say that Franz Ferdinand even built a chapel at Konopiště for the sole purpose of praying that his old, hated uncle might soon die...but the emperor went on to outlive the young archduke.

Franz Ferdinand fell out of his uncle's favor when he married a beautiful but low-ranking Czech countess, Žofie Chotková (often known by her German name, Sophie). Žofie was "only" aristocratic, not royal. To get out of his relatives' sight, Franz Ferdinand bought Konopiště and moved here.

Obsessed with hunting, Franz Ferdinand traveled around the world twice, shooting at anything in sight: deer, bears, tigers, elephants, and crocodiles. He killed about 300,000 animals in all, many of whom stare morbidly at you as hunting trophies covering the walls at Konopiště.

In the Kaiser's Pavilion on the grounds of Konopiště, Franz Ferdinand met with German Kaiser Wilhelm and tried to talk him out of plotting a war against Russia. Wilhelm argued that a war would work to the mutual benefit of Germany and Austria: Germans wanted colonies, and Austria—crippled by the aspirations of its many nationalities—could use a war to divert attention from its domestic problems. But Franz Ferdinand foresaw that war would be suicidal for Austria's overstretched monarchy.

Soon after, Franz Ferdinand and Žofie went to Sarajevo, in the Habsburg-annexed territories of Bosnia and Herzegovina. On that trip, young Gavrilo Princip, a Bosnian Serb, shot the Habsburg archduke who so loved shooting. (Žofie was also killed.) Franz Ferdinand's assassination ironically gave the Germans (and their pro-war allies in the Austro-Hungarian administration) the pretext for starting the war against Serbia and its ally, Russia. World War I soon broke out. The event Franz Ferdinand had tried to prevent was, in fact, sparked by his death.

when the heir to the Habsburg throne, Archduke Franz Ferdinand, renovated his new home. As one of the first castles in Europe to have an elevator, a WC, and running water, Konopiště shows "modern" living at the turn of the 20th century. Touring the castle gives you a good sense of who this powerful Habsburg was, as well as a glimpse at one of the best medieval arms collections in the world (and lots of hunting trophies).

While the stretch between the parking lot and the castle entrance is overrun by tour groups, the **gardens** and the **park** are surprisingly empty. In the summer, the flowers and goldfish in the rose garden are a big hit with visitors. The peaceful 30-minute walk through the woods around the lake (wooden bridge at the far end) offers gorgeous castle views.

Tucked away in the bushes behind the pond is a pavilion coated with tree bark, a perfect picnic spot. This simple structure, nicknamed the **Kaiser's Pavilion,** was the site of a fateful meeting between the German Kaiser Wilhelm and the Archduke Franz Ferdinand (explained in the sidebar).

Cost and Tours: Entrance to the castle is by one-hour guided tour only. Choose from three different routes: Route I (220 Kč, includes public and guest rooms, hunting hall, and shooting range), Route II (220 Kč, includes the oldest part of the castle, armory, elevator, and chapel), and Route III (320 Kč, includes private top-floor rooms of Franz Ferdinand and his family). All tickets are 30 percent cheaper if you join a Czech-speaking tour (you'll be given an English audioguide).

While Route II gives you the most comprehensive look into the castle, its history, and celebrated collections, Route III—re-opened after the rooms were meticulously restored to match 1907 photographs—launches you right into a turn-of-the-20th-century time capsule. Space on Route III is limited to 8 people per hour: It's best to reserve a spot in advance by calling one day ahead or on the morning of your visit.

Hours: May-Aug Tue-Sun 9:00-12:30 & 13:00-17:00; April and Oct Tue-Fri 9:00-15:00, Sat-Sun 9:00-16:00; Sept Tue-Fri 9:00-16:00, Sat-Sun 9:00-17:00; closed Nov-March and Mon year-round.

Information: Tel. 317-721-366, www.zamek-konopiste.cz.

Getting to Konopiště Castle: Trains from Prague's Main Station drop you in Benešov (2/hour, 1 hour, www.idos.cz); a well-marked trail goes from the station to the castle (1.5 miles). To walk to the castle, as you exit the Benešov train station, turn left and walk along the street parallel to the railroad tracks. Turn left at the first bridge you see crossing over the tracks. Along the way you'll see trail markers on trees, walls, and lampposts—one yellow stripe between two white stripes. Follow these markers. As you leave town, watch for a marker with an arrow pointing to a path in the woods. Take this path to bypass the castle's enormous parking lot, which is clogged with souvenir shops and bus fumes.

Eating at Konopiště Castle: Three touristy restaurants sit under the castle, but I'd bring picnic supplies from Prague (or buy them at the grocery store by the Benešov train station). While the crowds wait to pay too much for lousy food in the restaurants, you'll enjoy the peace and thought-provoking ambience of a **picnic** in the shaded Kaiser's Pavilion. Or eat cheaply on Benešov's main square (try **U Zlaté Hvězdy**—"The Golden Star").

Karlštejn Castle

One of the Czech Republic's top attractions, Karlštejn Castle (KARL-shtayn) was built by Charles IV in about 1350 to house the crown jewels of the Holy Roman Empire. While it looks like a striking, fairy-tale castle from a distance, it's not much inside. The highlight of the castle's interior—the much-venerated and sumptuous Chapel of the Holy Cross (built to house the crown jewels)—  can be seen only with an advance reservation.

Cost and Tours: The Chapel of the Holy Cross—basically the only thing inside Karlštejn worth seeing—is part of tour Route II, which requires a reservation (300 Kč, hourly, 15 people maximum). To reserve a spot, send an email (rezervace@stc.npu.cz) with the date you'd like to visit. They'll reply with an available time slot and instructions for how to pay the 30-Kč/person reservation fee by credit card. Your reservation will be confirmed upon payment. Route I is nowhere near as interesting (270 Kč, no reservation required, bigger groups, shorter tour).

Hours: July-Aug daily 9:00-12:00 & 12:30-18:00; May-June and Sept Tue-Sun 9:00-12:00 & 12:30-18:00, closed Mon; March-April and Oct Tue-Sun 9:00-12:00 & 13:00-17:00, closed Mon; Nov-Feb Sat-Sun 10:00-12:00 & 13:00-15:00, closed Mon-Fri.

Information: Tel. 274-008-154 or 274-008-155, www.hrad-karlstejn.cz.

Getting to Karlštejn Castle: The castle, 20 miles southwest of Prague, is accessible by train (2/hour, 40 minutes, then a 20-minute walk; depart from Prague's Main Station in the direction of Beroun, www.idos.cz).

When you leave the Karlštejn station, turn right, walk to the next road, turn left, and cross the bridge over the river. From here, follow the pedestrian-only street up to the castle. Warning: This half-mile stretch has a concentration of crystal and souvenir shops as intense as Karlova street in Prague.

Hike to Srbsko: From Karlštejn Castle, an easy one-hour hike

along a well-marked trail (look for markers with one red stripe between two white stripes) leads you away from the tourists through a
quiet forest to Srbsko. There you'll find two good Czech restaurants
and a train station (the Karlštejn-Prague train stops in Srbsko).

Křivoklát Castle

Křivoklát (KREE-vohk-laht), an original 14th-century castle, is
beautiful for its simplicity and setting, amid the hills and deep
woods near the lovely Berounka River valley. Originally a hunting residence of Czech kings, it was later transformed into a royal
prison that "entertained" a number of distinguished guests, among
them the most notorious alchemist of the 1500s, Englishman Ed-
ward Kelly.

In summer, Křivoklát comes alive with craftspeople—wood-
carvers, blacksmiths, and basket-weavers—who work as if it were
the 15th century. The absence of tacky souvenir shops, the plain
Gothic appearance, and the background noise of hammers and
wood chisels give Křivoklát an engaging character.

The tour of the interior lasts a sensible half-hour. The highlight
is the king's audience hall, with its delicately arched ceiling.

Cost and Tours: 240 Kč with an English-speaking guide; 190
Kč if you go with a Czech group (pick up an explanation sheet in
English, and you'll be fine with the Czechs). It's 80 Kč to walk the
castle walls on your own.

Hours: Open May-Sept Tue-Sun 9:00-12:00 & 13:00-17:00,
closed Mon; April and Oct Tue-Sun 10:00-16:00, closed Mon;
Nov-Dec Sat-Sun 10:00-15:00, closed Mon-Fri; Jan-March Mon-
Sat 10:00-15:00, closed Sun.

Information: Tel. 313-558-440, www.krivoklat.cz.

Getting to Křivoklát Castle: Trains leave Prague's Main Station for Beroun (hourly, 40 minutes), running through the delightful valley of the dreamy Berounka River. In Beroun, transfer to
the cute little motor train to Křivoklát (dubbed by Czech hikers
the "Berounka Pacific"; every 2 hours, allow 1.5 hours total for trip
from Prague). From Křivoklát's train station, it's a 10-minute walk
uphill to the castle. At the train station, confirm the return schedule—one train leaves just before noon, and three others depart in
the afternoon. For train schedules, see www.idos.cz.

Sleeping and Eating at Křivoklát: $ **Hotel and Restaurant
Sýkora,** below the castle near the train station, has been a favorite
among Czech hikers since the 1930s. If you want to stay for an
evening concert in the castle courtyard or for a hike in the nearby
woods, sleep in one of the hotel's 11 renovated rooms (Db-600 Kč,

tel. 313-558-114, www.hotel-sykora.krivoklatsko.com, hotel.syko-ra@krivoklatsko.com, only Czech and German spoken). Insist on this promised price or cross the street to the nearby, much classier **$$ Hotel and Restaurant U Jelena** (Db-1,000 Kč, tel. 313-558-529, www.ujelena.eu, krivoklat@ujelena.eu).

Near Křivoklát: Nižbor and Lány

Nižbor

This village, which straddles the valley of the Berounka River, lies between Beroun and Křivoklát (it's the third stop on the little motor train after Beroun).

The main reason to stop in Nižbor is **Rückl Glassworks**, where you can witness the step-by-step production of traditional Czech crystal. As you get off the train, return to the first rail crossing—the entrance to the glassworks is just across the tracks (100 Kč; May-Sept Mon-Fri 9:30-14:30, closed Sat-Sun; Oct-April Mon-Sat 9:30-12:00, closed Sun; if an English-speaking guide isn't available, you'll be asked to tag along with a tour-bus group; factory shop and café open same hours, tel. 311-696-248, mobile 605-229-205, www.ruckl.cz). Tours last about 45 minutes and end in the gift shop, of course.

The small **castle** perched on the hill across the river houses a modest exhibit on Celtic archaeology. Nižbor was an important Celtic settlement just before the Christian era (50 Kč, May-Oct daily 10:00-17:00, closed Nov-April, tel. 311-693-100). The trail-head for a three-mile loop **trail** covering these Celtic sights (mainly in an open field) is immediately across the bridge in front of the Co-op supermarket.

Or, if you are in the mood for exploring the diversity of the forests, consider the following **woodland trail** (marked by signs—with a blue stripe between two white stripes—on trees, fences, and lampposts; 2-4 miles round-trip). Coming out of the glassworks gate, walk straight past the Keltovna restaurant and along the railroad tracks. After 100 yards, follow the blue-and-white marks and turn left up the hill, through a row of family houses. In another 100 yards you'll reach the edge of the forest. The trail then takes you over a small hill and down about a half-mile into a canyon with a creek, through a landscape that could soon be part of the Czech Republic's newest national park (see sidebar, next page). As you gaze at the surrounding slopes, notice the variety of trees: verdant ashes and alders growing along the moist creek-bed, leafy beeches on the lower slopes, and hardy oaks and pines clinging to the dry, rocky hilltops. It's about two miles to the end of the canyon; walk as far as you'd like or retrace your steps along the same route back to Nižbor.

DAY TRIPS FROM PRAGUE

Křivoklát National Park: Saving the Czech Republic's Diverse Forests

The Czech Republic's fifth national park may someday be created in the Křivoklát hills. While the country's four other parks lie in relatively remote locations along the border, the proposed 250-acre Křivoklát National Park is within a one-hour bike ride of the Zličín endpoint of the Prague subway system. The survival of such a diverse and extensive forest ecosystem in the immediate proximity of a metropolitan center—a miracle in heavily industrialized Central Europe—is due to its landscape and to human intervention.

A thousand years ago, the inaccessible canyons and rocky hills of the Křivoklát region made it the favorite hunting grounds of the Czech kings, who, for the next five centuries, preferred bears to humans, and discouraged local settlement. The royals eventually gave up Křivoklát, more people moved in, and logging increased with the demand for wood and charcoal. But the Fürstenberg family, who took ownership of Křivoklát in the 18th century, carefully replanted the cut-down areas with deciduous trees that matched the forests' original composition.

The communists stripped the visionary Fürstenbergs of their possessions and attempted to introduce large stands of fast-growing, imported spruce trees at Křivoklát, as they had in other parts of the Czech Republic (spruce can be harvested quickly for timber and paper-making). But local foresters and biologists defied the communists by continuing to protect Křivoklát's mix of native broadleaf trees.

In 1989, political changes opened the future of all of the Czech Republic's forestlands to public debate. The practice of reforesting with spruce trees came under increasing criticism, as the so-called "spruce monocultures" proved prone to windstorms

Eating in Nižbor: For lunch, consider either the modern **Keltovna restaurant** opposite the glassworks or the traditional **Restaurace U Lípy** across the bridge. The **Co-op supermarket** next to U Lípy has picnic supplies.

Continuing to Křivoklát: If you purchased a train ticket through to Křivoklát, you can get back on the Beroun motor train without purchasing a new ticket (check schedule carefully, trains go every two hours).

Lány

The village of **Lány,** about 15 miles north from Křivoklát Castle, is close to patriotic Czech hearts. The castle in Lány served as the Czech "Camp David" for both Tomáš Garrigue Masaryk (the first president of Czechoslovakia, between the World Wars) and Václav Havel (the contemporary "father of the Czech Republic" and first post-communist president of the nation).

and bark beetle infestations (whose frequency has only intensified with rising temperatures over the last two decades).

The state-run company that manages half of the country's forests says it aspires to long-term sustainability, but has been slow to discard the failed practices of the past. Cutting down groves of beech woods and planting battalions of spruce trees is a lot easier—and more profitable—than selectively protecting native plants. It's painfully obvious to any hiker that, rather than following scientific trends and preserving forests for future generations, unscrupulous forest managers are ransacking the country's wooded wealth.

Designating Křivoklát as a national park could save it. While "protected natural areas" (Křivoklát has been one since 1977) are managed by the increasingly out-of-control state-run company, national parks are administered directly by the ministry of environment and are subject to strict pan-European regulations. The purpose of the new national park is not simply to recognize the uniqueness of Křivoklát, but to wrest its control from those bent on erasing its distinctiveness—in an age when one would hope for better.

The battle over Křivoklát remains in the hands of the Czech Parliament, where the logging lobby and conservationists are both pressing their cases. But at least for the next couple of years, those who visit Křivoklát can experience Czech forests as they used to be—with a magnificent diversity of oak, beech, ash, alder, elm, maple, fir, pine, and even the infamous spruce—by hiking from Lány to Křivoklát (15 miles; see page 224 for details) or by strolling up the hill and into the woods from Nižbor's Rückl Glassworks (2-4 miles; see page 221 for details).

DAY TRIPS FROM PRAGUE

Masaryk and his family are buried in Lány's simple village cemetery. Masaryk's humble grave on a hill in the middle of the fields is a pilgrimage place for freedom-loving Czechs. The communists, wanting to erase Masaryk from the nation's memory, destroyed all statues of him (such as the one in Kutná Hora—described on page 204) and barely mentioned his name in history textbooks. During the communist era, Czechs risked their careers by coming here on the Czech Independence Day to put candles on Masaryk's grave. Imagine: Every year, on October 28, the police sealed off all roads to the village of Lány, and anyone who wanted access had to show an ID card. When you arrived at work the next morning, the boss would be waiting at the door, asking, "Where were you yesterday—and why?"

After 1989, Václav Havel—the symbol of the new Czech freedom—strove to restore dignity to the presidency. He went back to the tradition of the first Czech president, making Lány his home away from home. Havel's weekend sojourns here symbolized a return to Czech self-governance.

Getting to Lány: The bus leaves Prague's Hradčanská Metro station for the Lány/Kladno district (6/day, fewer on weekends, 1 hour, direction: Rakovník). Check the schedule at www.idos.cz. The bus first stops on the main square of the town, then at the cemetery. There is no public transportation from Lány to Křivoklát Castle, but it's a long but doable hike.

Hike to Křivoklát Castle: Consider making the 15-mile hike from Lány to Křivoklát Castle. From the cemetery, it's a five-minute walk to the trailhead on the main square, where you will also find two grocery stores for stocking up on supplies—there are no restaurants or stores until Křivoklát. With the help of a good map, follow the well-marked trail through woods and meadows (look for markers with one red stripe between two white stripes on trees, walls, and fences). This hike takes you through all the varieties of forests in Eastern Europe (beech, birch, poplar, oak, pine, spruce, fir), past a hidden 1950s dam, and to some stunning vistas. The *Praha-Západ* and *Křivoklátsko* hiking maps are excellent (sold in most Prague bookstores).

BEYOND PRAGUE

ČESKÝ KRUMLOV

Lassoed by its river and dominated by its castle, this enchanting town feels lost in a time warp. While Český Krumlov is the Czech Republic's answer to Germany's Rothenburg, it has yet to be turned into a medieval theme park. When you see its awe-inspiring castle, delightful Old Town of shops and cobbled lanes, characteristic little restaurants, and easy canoeing options, you'll understand why having fun is a slam-dunk here.

Český Krumlov (CHESS-key KROOM-loff) means, roughly, "Czech Bend in the River." Calling it "Český" for short sounds silly to Czech-speakers (since dozens of Czech town names begin with "Český"). However, "Krumlov" for short is OK.

The sharp bend in the Vltava provides a natural moat, so it's no wonder Český Krumlov has been a choice spot for eons. Celtic tribes first settled here a century before Christ. Then came German tribes. The Slavic tribes arrived in the ninth century. The Rožmberks—Bohemia's top noble family—ran the city from 1302 to 1602. You'll see their rose symbol all over town.

In many ways, the 16th century was the town's Golden Age, when Český Krumlov hosted artists, scientists, and alchemists from all over Europe. In 1588, the town became home to an important Jesuit college. The Habsburgs bought the region in 1602, ushering in a more Germanic period. After that, as many as 75 percent of the town's people were German—until 1945, when most Germans were expelled.

Český Krumlov's rich mix of Gothic, Renaissance, and Baroque buildings is easy to miss. As you wander, look up...notice the surviving details in the stonework. Step into shops. Snoop into back lanes and tiny squares. Gothic buildings curve with the winding streets. Many precious Gothic and Renaissance frescoes were whitewashed in Baroque times (when the colorful trimmings

of earlier periods were way out of style). Today, these frescoes are being rediscovered and restored.

With the town's rich German heritage, it was easy for Hitler to claim that this region—the Sudetenland—was rightfully part of Germany, and in 1938, the infamous Munich Agreement made it his. Americans liberated the town in 1945. Due to Potsdam Treaty-approved ethnic cleansing, three million Germans in Czech lands were sent west to Germany. Emptied of its German citizenry, Český Krumlov turned into a ghost town, partially inhabited by Roma (Gypsies—see sidebar on page 238).

In the post-WWII world drawn up by Stalin, Churchill, and FDR at Yalta, the border of the Soviet and American spheres of influence fell about here. Although the communist government established order, the period from 1945 to 1989 was a smelly interlude, as the town was infamously polluted. Its now-pristine river was foamy with effluent from the paper mill just upstream, while the hills around town were marred with prefab-concrete apartment blocks. The people who moved in never fully identified with the town—in Europe, a place without ancestors is a place without life. But the bleak years of communism paradoxically provided a cocoon to preserve the town. There was no money, so little changed, apart from a buildup of grime.

In the early 1990s, tourists discovered Český Krumlov, and the influx of money saved the buildings from ruin. Color returned to the facades, waiters again dressed in coarse linen shirts, and the main drag was flooded with souvenir shops.

With its new prosperity, the center of today's Český Krumlov looks like a fairy-tale town. In fact, movie producers consider it ideal for films. *The Adventures of Pinocchio* was filmed here in 1995, as was the opening sequence for the 2006 film *The Illusionist*.

After Prague, Český Krumlov is the Czech Republic's second-biggest tourist magnet (1.5 million visits annually), with enough tourism to make things colorful and easy—but not so much that it tramples the place's charm. This town of 15,000 attracts a young bohemian crowd, drawn here for its simple beauty, cheap living, and fanciful bars.

Planning Your Time

Because you can visit the castle and theater only with a guide (and English-language tours are offered just a few times a day), serious sightseers should reserve both tours first thing in the morning in person at the castle and theater (or call the castle), and then build your day around your tour times. Those who hate planning ahead on vacation can join a Czech tour anytime (English information sheets provided).

A paddle down the river to Zlatá Koruna Abbey is a high-

Parting of the Roses

A five-petal rose is not just the distinctive mark of Český Krumlov and the Rožmberk rulers (literally, "Lords from the Rose Mountain"). You'll find it, in five-color combinations, all over South Bohemia.

A medieval legend, depicted inside Český Krumlov's castle, explains the division of the roses in the following way: A respected nobleman named Vítek split the property he had accumulated during his lifetime among five sons. Each son was also assigned his own coat of arms, all of which shared the motif of a five-petal rose. The oldest son, Jindřich, received a golden rose in a blue field, along with the lands of Hradec and Telč. Vilém received a silver rose in a red field, with the lands of Landštejn and Třeboň. Smil was given a blue rose in a golden field and the lands of Stráž and Bystřice. Vok kept his father's coat of arms, a red rose in a white field, and became the lord in Rožmberk and Český Krumlov. Finally, the out-of-wedlock Sezima had to make do with a black rose and the tiny land of Ústí.

Over generations, the legend—which is corroborated by historical sources—served as a constant warning to the ambitious Rožmberks not to further split up their land. The Lords from the Rose Mountain were the rare Czech noble family that, for 300 years, strictly adhered to the principle of primogeniture (the oldest son gets all, and younger sons are subservient to him). Unlike Vítek, the patriarch, each successive ruler of the Rožmberk estates made sure to consolidate his possessions, handing more to his eldest son than he had received. As a result, the enterprising Rožmberks grew into the most powerful family in Bohemia. In 1501, their position as "first in the country after the king" became law.

light (three hours), and a 20-minute walk up to the Křížový Vrch (Hill of the Cross) rewards you with a fine view of the town and its unforgettable riverside setting. Other sights are quick visits and worthwhile only if you have a particular interest (Viennese artist Egon Schiele, puppets, torture, and so on).

The town itself is the major attraction. Evenings are for atmospheric dining and drinking. Sights are generally open 10:00-17:00 and closed on Monday.

Orientation to Český Krumlov

Český Krumlov is extremely easy to navigate. The twisty Vltava River, which makes a perfect S through the town, ropes the Old Town into a tight peninsula. Above the Old Town is the Castle Town. Český Krumlov's one main street starts at the isthmus and

heads through the peninsula. It winds through town and continues across a bridge before snaking through the Castle Town, the castle complex (a long series of courtyards), and the castle gardens high above. The main square, Náměstí Svornosti—with the TI, ATMs, and taxis—dominates the Old Town and marks the center of the peninsula. All recommended restaurants and hotels are within a few minutes' walk of this square. No sight in town is more than a five-minute stroll away.

Tourist Information

The helpful TI is on the **main square** (daily 9:00-19:00, July-Aug until 20:00, shorter hours in winter, tel. 380-704-622, www.ck-rumlov.info). Pick up the free city map. The 129-Kč *City Guide* book explains everything in Český Krumlov and includes a fine town and castle map in the back. The TI has a baggage-storage desk and can check train, bus, and flight schedules. Ask about concerts, city walking tours in English, and canoe trips on the river. A second, less-crowded TI—actually a private business—is just below the **castle** (daily 9:00-19:00, tel. 380-725-110).

Český Krumlov Card: This 200-Kč card, sold at the TI and participating sights, covers entry to the Round Tower, Castle Museum, Egon Schiele Art Center, and Museum of Regional History, and offers discounts at lesser sights. It does not cover the castle tours. Do the math to decide if it makes sense for you.

Arrival in Český Krumlov

By Train: The train station is a 20-minute walk from town (turn right out of the station, then walk downhill onto a steep cobbled path leading to an overpass into the town center). Taxis are standing by to zip you to your hotel (about 100 Kč), or call 602-113-113 to summon one.

By Bus: The bus station is just three blocks away from the Old Town. To walk from the bus-station lot to the town center, follow the "walking man" signs out of the lot to *Centrum*, veer right and downhill on the small road, and cross the main road past the Co-op grocery. Figure on 60 Kč for a taxi from the station to your hotel.

Helpful Hints

Festivals: Locals drink oceans of beer and celebrate their medieval roots at big events such as the Celebration of the Rose (Slavnosti Růže), where blacksmiths mint ancient coins, jugglers swallow fire, mead flows generously, and pigs are roasted on open fires (late June, www.ckrumlov.info). The summer also brings a top-notch international music festival to town, performed in pubs, cafés, and the castle gardens (mid-July-mid-Aug, www.festivalkrumlov.cz). During the St. Wenceslas celebrations, the square becomes a medieval market and the streets come alive with theater and music (Sept 28). Reserve a hotel well in advance if you'll be in town for these events.

Internet Access: Fine Internet cafés are all over town, and many of my recommended accommodations offer Wi-Fi or Internet access. The TI on the main square has several fast, cheap, stand-up stations. Perhaps the best cybercafé is behind the TI by the castle (tel. 380-725-117).

Bookstore: Shakespeare and Sons is a good little English-language bookstore (daily 11:00-19:00, a block below the main square at Soukenická 44, tel. 380-711-203, www.shakes.cz).

Laundry: Pension Lobo runs a self-service launderette near the castle. Since there are only a few machines, you may have to wait (200 Kč to wash and dry, includes soap, daily 9:00-20:00, Latrán 73).

Bike Rental: You can rent bikes at the **train station** (150 Kč/day with train ticket, prices slightly higher otherwise, tel. 380-715-000), **Vltava Sport Service** (see listing under "Canoeing and Rafting the Vltava" on page 241), and the recommended **Hostel 99.**

Tours in Český Krumlov

Walking Tours

Since the town itself, rather than its sights, is what it's all about here, taking a guided walk is the key to a meaningful visit. The TI sells tickets for two different guided walks. They are affordable, in English, and well worth your time. Both meet in front of the TI on the main square. No reservations are necessary—just drop in and pay the guide. The **Old Town Tour** offers the best general town introduction and is most likely to run (250 Kč, daily May-Oct at 10:30 and 15:00, Nov-April at 11:00, weekends only in Feb, 1.5 hours). The **Brewing History Tour,** which is the most intimate of the many brewery tours in this land that so loves its beer, takes you through the Eggenberg Brewery (200 Kč, daily May-Oct at 12:30, Nov-April at 13:00, weekends only in Feb, 1 hour). For a self-guided town walk, consider renting an **audioguide** from the TI (100 Kč/one hour).

Local Guides

Oldřiška Baloušková is a hardworking young guide who offers a wonderful tour around her hometown (400 Kč/hour, mobile 737-920-901, oldriskab@gmail.com). **Jiří (George) Václavíček,** a gentle and caring man who perfectly fits mellow Český Krumlov, is a joy to share this town with (450 Kč/hour, mobile 603-927-995, www.krumlovguide.cz, jiri.vaclavicek@gmail.com). **Karolína**

Kortušová is an enthusiastic woman with great organizational skills. Her company, Krumlov Tours, can set you up with a good local tour guide, palace and theater admissions, river trips, and more (guides-400 Kč/hour, mobile 723-069-561, www.krumlov-tours.com, info@krumlovtours.com).

Self-Guided Walk

▲▲▲Welcome to Český Krumlov

The town's best sight is its cobbled cityscape, surrounded by a babbling river and capped by a dramatic castle. All of Český Krumlov's

modest sights are laced together in this charming walk from the top of the Old Town, down its spine, across the river, and up to the castle.

• *Start at the bridge over the isthmus, which was once the fortified grand entry gate to the town.*

Horní Bridge: From this "Upper Bridge," note the natural fortification provided by the tight bend in the river. The last building in town (just over the river) is the Eggenberg Brewery (with daily tours—see "Tours in Český Krumlov," earlier). Behind that, on the horizon, is a pile of white apartment high-rises—built in the last decade of the communist era and considered the worst places in town to call home. Left of the brewery stands a huge monastery (not generally open to the public). Behind that, on Kleť Mountain, the highest hilltop, stands a TV tower that locals say was built to jam Voice of America broadcasts. Facing the town, on your left, rafters take you to the river for the sloppy half-hour float around town to the take-out spot just on your right.

• *A block downhill on Horní (Upper) street is the...*

Museum of Regional History: This small museum gives you a quick look at regional costumes, tools, and traditions. When you pay, pick up the English translation of the displays (it also includes a lengthy history of Krumlov). Start on the top floor, where you'll see a Bronze Age exhibit, old paintings, a glimpse of noble life, and a look at how the locals rafted lumber from Krumlov all the way to Vienna (partly by canal). Don't miss the fun-to-study ceramic model of Český Krumlov in 1800 (note the extravagant gardens high above the town). The lower floor comes with fine folk costumes and domestic art (50 Kč, daily 10:00-17:00, July-Aug until 18:00, Horní 152, tel. 380-711-674).

• *Below the museum, a little garden overlook affords a fine castle view. Immediately across the street, notice the Renaissance facade of...*

ČESKÝ KRUMLOV

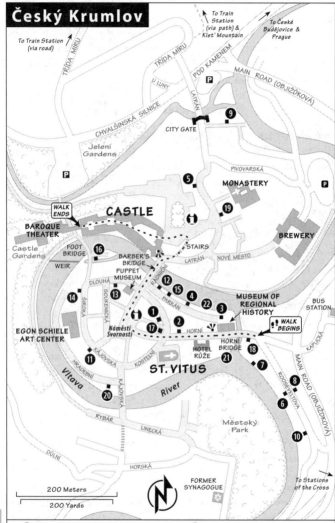

Český Krumlov

To Train Station (via road)

To Train Station (via path) & Klet' Mountain

To České Budějovice & Prague

TŘÍDA MÍRU

TŘÍDA MÍRU

U LUNY

POD KAMENEM

CHVALŠINSKÁ SILNICE

LATRÁN

MAIN ROAD (OBJÍŽĎKOVÁ)

CITY GATE

Jelení Gardens

PIVOVARSKÁ

MONASTERY

CASTLE

BAROQUE THEATER

WALK ENDS

Castle Gardens

FOOT BRIDGE

WEIR

BARBER'S BRIDGE

PUPPET MUSEUM

STAIRS

NOVÉ MĚSTO

LATRÁN

BREWERY

DLOUHÁ

SOUKENICKÁ

SIROKÁ

RADNIČNÍ

PARKÁN

MUSEUM OF REGIONAL HISTORY

BUS STATION

EGON SCHIELE ART CENTER

Náměstí Svornosti

HORNÍ

KÁJOVSKÁ

KOSTELNÍ

ST. VITUS

HOTEL RŮŽE

HORNÍ BRIDGE

WALK BEGINS

HRADEBNÍ

KÁJOVSKÁ

Vltava River

Městský Park

MAIN ROAD (OBJÍŽĎKOVÁ)

ROOSEVELTOVA

KAPLICKÁ

RYBÁŘ

LINECKÁ

DŮLNÍ

HORSKÁ

FORMER SYNAGOGUE

To Stations of the Cross

200 Meters

200 Yards

N

- ❶ Castle View Apartments
- ❷ Hotel Konvice
- ❸ Hotel Mlýn
- ❹ Pension Olšakovský
- ❺ Pension Danny & Launderette
- ❻ Pension Teddy
- ❼ Pension Myší Díra & Maleček Boat Rental
- ❽ Pension Anna
- ❾ Hostel 99 & Hospoda 99 Rest.
- ❿ Krumlov House Hostel
- ⓫ Na Louži Restaurant
- ⓬ Krčma u Dwau Maryí
- ⓭ Cikánská Jizba
- ⓮ Restaurace u Dobráka
- ⓯ Laibon Restaurant
- ⓰ Rybářská Restaurace
- ⓱ Krčma v Šatlavské
- ⓲ Restaurace Barbakán
- ⓳ Dobrá Čajovna Teahouse
- ⓴ Vltava Sport Service
- ㉑ Start Quickie River Float
- ㉒ End Quickie River Float & Start Zlatá Koruna Float

Hotel Růže: This former Jesuit college hides a beautiful courtyard. Pop inside to see a couple of bronze busts that stand like a shrine to the founders of Czechoslovakia. The one on the right, dedicated by Czech freedom fighters, commemorates the first Czechoslovak president, Tomáš Garrigue Masaryk (in office 1918-1934; see sidebar on page 320). The bust on the left recalls Masaryk's successor, Edvard Beneš (in office 1934-1948; see sidebar).

• *Walk another block down the main drag, until you reach steps on the left leading to the...*

Church of St. Vitus: Český Krumlov's main church was built as a bastion of Catholicism in the 15th century, when the Roman Catholic Church was fighting the Hussites. The 17th-century Baroque high altar shows a totem of religious figures: the Virgin Mary (crowned in heaven); St. Vitus (above Mary); and, way up on top, St. Wenceslas, the patron saint of the Czech people—long considered their ambassador in heaven. The canopy in the back, though empty today, once supported a grand statue of a Rožmberk atop a horse. The statue originally stood at the high altar. (Too egotistical for Jesuits, it was later moved to the rear of the nave, and then lost for good.) As you listen to the river, notice the empty organ case. While the main organ is out for restoration, the cute little circa-1716 Baroque beauty is getting plenty of use (see photos of the restoration work on the far wall; church open daily 10:00-19:00, Sunday Mass at 9:30, tel. 380-711-336).

• *Continuing on Horní street, you'll come to the...*

Main Square (Náměstí Svornosti): Lined with a mix of Renaissance and Baroque homes of burghers (all built on 12th-century Gothic foundations), the main square has a grand charm. There's continuity here. Lékárna, with the fine red Baroque facade on the lower corner of the square, is still a pharmacy, as it has been since 1620. McDonald's tried three times to get a spot here but was turned away each time. The Town Hall flies both the Czech flag and the town flag, which shows the rose symbol of the Rožmberk family, who ruled the town for 300 years.

Imagine the history that this square has seen: In the 1620s, the rising tide of Lutheran Protestantism threatened Catholic Europe. Krumlov was a seat of Jesuit power and learning, and the intellectuals of the Roman church allegedly burned books on this square. Later, when there was a bad harvest, locals blamed witches—and burned them, too. Every so often, terrible plagues rolled through the countryside. In a nearby village, all but two residents were killed by a plague.

But the plague stopped before devastating the people of Český Krumlov, and in 1715—as thanks to God—they built the plague monument that stands on the square today. Much later, in

234 Rick Steves' Prague & the Czech Republic

Edvard Beneš and the German Question

Czechoslovakia was created in 1918, when the vast, multiethnic Habsburg Empire broke into smaller nations after losing World War I. The principle that gave countries such as Poland, Czechoslovakia, and Romania independence was called "self-determination": Each nation had the right to its own state within the area in which its people formed the majority. But the peoples of Eastern Europe had mixed over the centuries, making it impossible to create functioning states based purely on ethnicity. In the case of Czechoslovakia, the borders were drawn along historical rather than ethnic boundaries. While the country was predominantly Slavic, there were also areas with overwhelmingly German and Hungarian majorities. One of these areas—a fringe around the western part of the country, mostly populated by Germans—was known as the Sudetenland.

At first, the coexistence of Slavs and Germans in the new republic worked fine. German parties were important power brokers and participated in almost every coalition government. Hitler's rise to power, however, led to the growth of German nationalism, even outside Germany. Soon 70 percent of Germans in Czechoslovakia voted for the Nazis. In September 1938, the Munich Agreement ceded the Sudetenland to Germany, and the Czech minority had to leave (for more on the Munich Agreement, see sidebar "The Never-Used Fortifications" on page 270).

Edvard Beneš was the first Czechoslovak secretary of state (1918-1934) and later became the country's second president (1934-1948), leading the Czechoslovak exile government in London during World War II. Like most Czechs and Slovaks, Beneš believed that after the hard feelings produced by the Munich Agreement, peaceful coexistence of Slavs and Germans in a single state was impossible. His postwar solution: move the Sudeten Germans to Germany, much as the Czechs had been forced out

1938, Hitler stood right here before a backdrop of long Nazi banners to celebrate the annexation of the Sudetenland. And in 1968, Russian tanks spun their angry treads on these same cobblestones to intimidate locals who were demanding freedom. Today, thankfully, this square is part of an unprecedented time of peace and prosperity for the Czech people.

• *The following three museums are grouped around the main square.*

Puppet Museum and Fairy Tale House: In three small rooms, you'll see fascinating displays of more than 200 movable creations

of the Sudetenland before. Through skillful diplomacy, Beneš got the Allies to sign on to this idea.

Shortly after the end of World War II, three million people of German ancestry were forced to leave their homes in Czechoslovakia. Millions of Germanic people in Poland, Romania, Ukraine, and elsewhere met with a similar fate. Many of these families had been living in these areas for centuries. The methods employed to expel them included murder, rape, and plunder. (Today, we'd call it "ethnic cleansing.")

In 1945, Český Krumlov lost 75 percent of its population, and Czechs moved into the vacated German homes. Having easily acquired the property, the new residents didn't take care of the houses. Within a few years, the once-prosperous Sudetenland was reduced to shabby towns and uncultivated fields—a decaying, godforsaken region. After 1989, displaced Sudeten Germans—the majority of whom now live in Bavaria—demanded that the Czechoslovak government apologize for the violent way in which the expulsion was carried out. Some challenged the legality of the decrees, and for a time the issue threatened otherwise good Czech-German relations.

Although no longer such a hot-button diplomatic issue, the so-called Beneš Decrees remain divisive in Czech politics. While liberals consider the laws unjust, many others—especially the older generations—see them as fair revenge for the behavior of the Sudeten Germans prior to and during the war. In the former Sudetenland, where Czech landowners worry that the Germans will try to reclaim their property, Beneš is a hugely popular figure. His bust in Český Krumlov's Hotel Růže is one of the first memorials to him in the country. The bridge behind the Old Town has been named for Beneš since the 1990s. The main square—the center of a thriving German community 70 years ago—is now, ironically, called "Square of Concord."

(overwhelmingly of Czech origin, but also some from Burma and Rajasthan). At the model stage, children of any age can try their hand at pulling the strings on their favorite fairy tale (80 Kč, daily 10:00-18:00, longer hours July-Aug, Dlouhá 29, tel. 380-713-422, www.krumlovskainspirace.cz). For more on Czech puppets, see the sidebar on page 178.

Torture Museum: This is just a lame haunted house: dark, with sound effects, cheap modern models, and prints showing off the cruel and unusual punishments of medieval times (100 Kč, daily 9:00-20:00, shorter hours off-season, English descriptions, Náměstí Svornosti 1, tel. 380-766-343).

Egon Schiele Art Center: This classy contemporary art gallery has temporary exhibits, generally featuring 20th-century

Czech artists. The top-floor permanent collection celebrates the Viennese artist Egon Schiele (pronounced "Sheila"), who once spent a few weeks here during a secret love affair. A friend of Gustav Klimt and an important figure in the Secession movement in Vienna, Schiele lived a short life, from 1890 to 1918. His cutting-edge lifestyle and harsh art of graphic nudes didn't always fit the conservative, small-town style of Český Krumlov, but townsfolk are happy today to charge you to see this relatively paltry collection of his work (120 Kč, daily 10:00-18:00 except closed Mon in Jan, café, Široká 71, tel. 380-704-011, www.schieleartcentrum.cz).

• *From the main square, walk up Radniční street and cross the...*

Barber's Bridge (Lazebnicky Most): This wooden bridge, decorated with two 19th-century statues, connects the Old Town and the Castle Town. In the center stands a statue of St. John of Nepomuk, who's also depicted by a prominent statue on Prague's Charles Bridge (see page 74). Among other responsibilities, he's the protector against floods. In the great floods in August of 2002, the angry river submerged the bridge (but removable banisters minimized the damage). Stains just above the windows of the adjacent building show how high the water rose.

• *After crossing the bridge, hike up the hill. Your next stop is Krumlov Castle.*

Sights in Český Krumlov

▲▲Krumlov Castle (Krumlovský Zámek)

No Czech town is complete without a castle—and now that the nobles are gone, their mansions are open to us common folk. The Krumlov Castle complex includes bear pits, a rare Baroque theater, groomed gardens—and the castle itself (www.castle.ckrumlov.cz).

Round Tower (Zámecká Věž)

The strikingly colorful round tower marks the location of the first castle, built here to guard the medieval river crossing. With its 16th-century Renaissance paint job colorfully restored, it looks exotic, featuring fancy astrological decor, terra-cotta symbols of the zodiac, and a fine arcade. Climb its 162 steps for a great view.

Cost and Hours: 50 Kč, daily 9:00-18:00, last entry 17:30.

Bear Pits (Medvědí Příkop)

At the site of the castle drawbridge, the bear pits hold a family of European brown bears, as they have since the Rožmberks added bears to their coat of arms in the 16th century to demonstrate their (fake) blood relation to the distinguished Italian family of Orsini (the name means "bear-like"). Featured on countless coats of arms, bears have long been totemic animals for Europeans. Pronouncing the animal's real name was taboo in many cultures, and Czechs still refer to bears only indirectly. For example, in most Germanic languages the word "bear" is derived from "brown," while the Slavic *medvěd* literally means "honey-eater."

Castle (Zámek)

The immense castle is a series of courtyards with shops, contemporary art galleries, and tourist services. The interior is accessible

only by tour, which gives you a glimpse of the places where the Rožmberks, Eggenbergs, and Schwarzenbergs dined, studied, worked, prayed, entertained, and slept. (By European standards, the castle's not much, and the tours move slowly.) Imagine being an aristocratic guest here, riding the dukes' assembly line of fine living: You'd promenade through a long series of elegant spaces and dine in the sumptuous dining hall before enjoying a concert in the Hall of Mirrors, which leads directly to the Baroque Theater (described next). After the play, you'd go out into the château garden for a fireworks finale.

Cost and Hours: To see the interior, you must take a one-hour escorted tour: Tour I (Gothic and Renaissance rooms, of the most general interest) or Tour II (19th-century castle life). Tours run June-Aug Tue-Sun 9:00-12:00 & 13:00-18:00, spring and fall until 17:00, closed Mon and Nov-March. Tours in Czech cost 150 Kč plus a 10-Kč reservation fee, leave regularly, and include an adequate flier in English that contains about half the information imparted by the guide (generally a student who's simply memorized the basic script). English tours are preferable, but cost more (250 Kč plus a 10-Kč reservation fee), run less frequently, and are often booked solid. Make your reservation when you arrive in town—just walk up to the castle office—or you can call 380-704-721, though the number is often busy. You'll be issued a ticket with your tour time printed on it. Be in the correct courtyard at that time, or you'll be locked out.

▲▲Baroque Theater (Zámecké Divadlo)

Europe once had several hundred Baroque theaters. Using candles for light and fireworks for special effects, most burned down. Today, only two survive in good shape and are open to tourists: one at Stockholm's Drottningholm Palace; and one here, at Krumlov Castle. During the 40-minute tour, you'll sit on benches in the theater and then go under the stage to see the wood-and-rope contrap-

Roma in Eastern Europe

Numbering 12 million, the Roma people constitute a bigger European nation than the Czechs, Hungarians, or the Dutch. The term "Gypsies," which used to be the common name for this group, is now considered both derogatory and inaccurate. It was derived from "Egypt"—the place from which medieval Roma were mistakenly thought to have originated. In the absence of written records, the solution to the puzzle of Roma ancestry had to wait for 19th-century advances in the science of linguistics.

The Roma are now thought to be descended from several low north-Indian castes (one of which may have given the Roma their name). A thousand years ago, the Roma began to migrate through Persia and Armenia into the Ottoman Empire, which later stretched across much of southeastern Europe. Known for their itinerant lifestyle, expertise in horse trading, skilled artisanship, and flexibility regarding private property, the Roma were both sought out and suspected in medieval Europe. In a similar way, gadjos (non-Roma) and their customs came to be distrusted by the Roma.

The Industrial Revolution removed the Roma's few traditional means of earning a livelihood, making their wandering lifestyle difficult to sustain. In the 1940s, Hitler sent hundreds of thousands of Roma to the gas chambers. After the war, communist governments in Eastern Europe implemented a policy of forced assimilation: Roma were required to speak the country's major language, settle in gadjo towns, and work in new industrial jobs. Today, few Roma can speak their own language well. Rather than producing well-adjusted citizens, the policy eroded time-honored Roma values and shattered the cohesiveness of their

tions that enabled scenes to be scooted in and out within seconds (while fireworks and smoke blinded the audience). Due to the theater's fragility, the number of visitors is strictly regulated. There are only five English tours a day, limited to 20 people per group, and generally sold out in advance. While it's a lovely little theater with an impressive 3-D effect that makes the stage look deeper than it really is, I wouldn't bother with the tour unless you can snare a spot on an English one. The theater is used only once a year for an actual performance, with attendance limited to Baroque theater enthusiasts. You can call 380-704-721 to get English-language tour times and reserve a space; but as with the castle tour, you will likely do best visiting the ticket office in person.

Cost and Hours: 300 Kč plus a 10-Kč reservation fee for English tour, 250 Kč plus a 10-Kč reservation fee for Czech tour, tours Tue-Sun May-Oct, no tours Mon and Nov-April; English departures at 10:00, 11:00, 13:00, 14:00, and 15:00; buy theater tour tickets at castle ticket office.

ČESKÝ KRUMLOV

traditional communities. It left the new Roma generation prone to sexual, alcohol, and drug abuse, and filled state-run orphanages with deprived Roma toddlers. When the obligation and right to work disappeared with the communist regimes in 1989, rampant unemployment and dependence on welfare joined the list of Roma afflictions.

As people all over Eastern Europe found it difficult to adjust to the new economic realities, they again turned on the Roma as scapegoats, fueling the latent racism that is so characteristic of European history. Many Roma now live in segregated ghettos, where even the most talented of their children are forced to attend schools for the mentally disabled. Those who make it against the odds and succeed in mainstream society typically do so by turning their backs on their Roma heritage.

In this context, the Roma in Český Krumlov are a surprising success story. The well-integrated, proud Roma community here (numbering 1,000 strong, or 5 percent of the town's population) is considered a curious anomaly even by experts. Their success could be due to a number of factors: It could be the legacy of the multicultural Rožmberks, or the fact that almost everyone in Český Krumlov is a relative newcomer. Or maybe it's that local youngsters, regardless of skin color, tend to resolve their differences over a beer in the local "Gypsy Pub" (Cikánská Jizba), with a trendy Roma band setting the tune.

While provincial politicians throughout the rest of Eastern Europe become national leaders by moving Roma into ghettos, Český Krumlov is living proof that Roma and *gadjos* can coexist happily.

Castle Museum (Hradní Muzeum)

An exhibit assembled from the castle's archives focuses on key moments in the lives of the town's various ruling families. While generally skippable, on summer Mondays it provides the only chance to peek inside the castle.

Cost and Hours: 100 Kč, April-Aug daily 9:00-17:00, Sept-March Tue-Sun 9:30-16:00, closed Mon.

Castle Gardens (Zámecká Zahrada)

This lovely, 2,300-foot-long garden crowns the castle complex. It was laid out in the 17th century, when the noble family would have it lit with 22,000 oil lamps, torches, and candles for special occasions. The lower part is geometrical and symmetrical—French garden-style. The upper part is wilder—English garden-style.

Cost and Hours: Free, May-Sept Tue-Sun 8:00-19:00, April and Oct Tue-Sun 8:00-17:00, closed Mon and Nov-March.

Near Český Krumlov

Zlatá Koruna Abbey (Klášter Zlatá Koruna)

Directly above the river at the end of a three-hour float by raft or canoe (see "Activities in Český Krumlov," later), this abbey was founded in the 13th century by the king to counter the growing influence of the Vítek family, the ancestors of the mighty Rožmberks. As you enter the grounds, notice the central linden tree, with its strange, cape-like leaves; it's said to have been used by the anti-Catholic Hussites when they hanged the monks. The short, guided abbey tour takes you through the rare two-storied Gothic Chapel of the Guardian Angel, the main church, and the cloister. After the order was dissolved in 1785, the abbey functioned briefly as a village school, before being turned into a factory during the Industrial Revolution. Damage from this period is visible on the cloister's crumbling arches. The abbey was restored in the 1990s and opened to the public only a few years ago.

Cost and Hours: 100 Kč for a tour in Czech—generally runs hourly, 180 Kč for an English tour, Tue-Sun 9:00-15:30, until 16:30 June-Aug, closed Mon and Oct-March, call 380-743-126 to pre-arrange an English tour, access via river float, www.klaster-zlatakoruna.eu.

Šumava Mountains

The well-rounded Šumava Mountains (SHOO-mah-vah) are, geologically, one of Europe's oldest ranges. Separating Bohemia from Bavaria, this long ridge, known in German on the Bohemian side as the Böhmerwald ("Bohemian Forest") and on the Bavarian side as the Bayerischer Wald ("Bavarian Forest"), also separates rivers that flow to the North Sea from those that empty into the Black Sea. This range was the physical embodiment of the Iron Curtain for 40 years: The first 10 miles or so within the Czech border were a forbidden no-man's-land, where hundreds of Czechs were shot as they tried to run across to Germany. In 1989 the barbed wire was taken down, and the entire area—more than 60 miles long—was declared the Šumava-Bayerischer Wald National Park. No development is permitted within the park, and visitors can't camp outside of designated areas. Since there's little industry nearby, these mountains preserve some of the most pristine woods, creeks, and meadows in Eastern Europe.

The gateway most easily accessible from Český Krumlov is the trailhead village of **Nová Pec,** a scenic 1.5-hour train ride away (5 direct trains/day). Nová Pec is located just beneath the slopes of the tallest mountain on the Czech side of the border, Plechý, a popular destination for hiking, biking, and cross-country skiing. Nová Pec's TI, which is 100 yards to the right of the train station, sells hiking and biking maps. You can rent bikes at the Pec train station (150 Kč/day with train ticket, slightly more without one, reserve a few

days ahead by calling 972-543-891 or emailing zstvlrdop@mail.
cd.cz) or three miles away toward Plechý next to the Plešný parking lot (mobile 723-380-138). Since bikes can be in high demand
in Nová Pec, it may be a better bet to rent a bicycle at the Český
Krumlov train station and bring it—for a 30 Kč surcharge—along
with you on the train. You can then return the bike at the station in
Nová Pec. Helmets are not included.

Sleeping near Nová Pec: Both of these recommended B&Bs
are about a mile outside of Nová Pec. Like almost everywhere else
in this border region, German and Czech are the only ways to communicate.

$$ Pension Za Pecí has five new, tastefully decorated rooms
(Sb-450 Kč, Db-900 Kč, optional dinner-100 Kč, tel. 388-336-
103, mobile 775-977-469, www.zapeci.com, mifudy@seznam.cz).

$$ Pension Hubertus sits on a sloping meadow and operates
its three rooms on solar power. Owner Eva will pick you up from
the train station if you ask (Sb-450 Kč, Db-900 Kč, mobile 602-
253-572, www.ubytovani.net/hubertus).

Activities in Český Krumlov

Český Krumlov lies in the middle of a valley popular for canoeing,
rafting, hiking, and horseback riding. Boat-rental places are convenient to the Old Town, and several hiking paths start right in town.

▲▲▲Canoeing and Rafting the Vltava

Splash a little river fun into your visit by renting a rubber raft or
fiberglass canoe for a quick 30-minute spin around Český Krumlov. Or go for a three-hour float and paddle through the Bohe-

mian forests and villages
of the nearby countryside.
You'll end up at Zlatá Koruna Abbey (described earlier), where the rafting company will shuttle you back to
town—or provide you with a
bicycle to pedal back on your
own along a bike path. This
is a great hot-weather activity. Though the river is far
from treacherous, be prepared to get wet.

You'll encounter plenty of inviting pubs and cafés for breaks
along the way. There's a little whitewater, but the river is so shallow
that if you tip, you can simply stand up and climb back in. (When
that happens, pull the canoe up onto the bank to empty it, since
you'll never manage to pour the water out while still in the river.)

Choose from a kayak, a canoe (faster, less work, more likely to tip), or an inflatable raft (harder rowing, slower, but very stable). Prices are per boat (2-6 people) and include a map, a waterproof container, and transportation to or from the start and end points. Here are your options:

Quickie Circle-the-Town Float: The easiest half-hour experience is to float around the city's peninsula, starting and ending on opposite sides of the tiny isthmus. Heck, you can do it twice (400 Kč for 1-2 people in a canoe or raft).

Three-Hour Float to Zlatá Koruna Abbey: This is your best basic trip, with pastoral scenery, a riverside pub about two hours down on the left, and a beautiful abbey as your destination (about 9 miles, 700 Kč for 1-2 people). From there you can bike back or catch a shuttle bus home—simply arrange a return plan with the rental company.

Longer and Faster Trips: If you start upriver from Krumlov (direction: Rožmberk), you'll go faster with more whitewater, but the river parallels a road, so it's a little less idyllic. Longer trips in either direction involve lots of paddling, even though you're going downstream. Rafting companies can review the many day-trip options with you.

Rental Companies: Several companies offer this lively activity. Perhaps the handiest are **Půjčovna Lodí Maleček Boat Rental** (open long hours daily April-Oct, closed Nov-March, at recommended Pension Myší Díra, Rooseveltova 28, tel. 380-712-508, www.malecek.cz, lode@malecek.cz) and **Vltava Sport Service** (April-Oct daily 9:00-18:00, closed Nov-March, Hradební 60, tel. 380-711-988, www.ckvltava.cz). Vltava also rents mountain bikes (320 Kč/day) and can bring a bike to the abbey for you to ride back.

Hiking

For an **easy 20-minute hike** to the Křížový Vrch (Hill of the Cross), walk to the end of Rooseveltova street, cross at the traffic light, then head straight for the first (empty) chapel-like Station of the Cross. Turning right, it's easy to navigate along successive Stations of the Cross until you reach the white church on the hill (closed), set in the middle of wild meadows. Looking down into the valley at the medieval city nestled within the S-shaped river, framed by the rising hills, it's hard to imagine any town with a more powerful *genius loci* (spirit of the place). The view is best at sunset.

For **longer hikes,** start at the trailhead by the bear pits below the castle. Red-and-white trail markers guide you on an easy six-mile hike around the neighboring slopes and villages. The green-and-yellow stripes mark a five-mile hiking trail up Kleť Mountain—with an altitude gain of 1,800 feet. At the top, you'll find the Kleť Observatory, the oldest observatory in the country (now a leading center for discovering new planets). On clear days, you can see the Alps (observatory tours-50 Kč, hourly July-Aug Tue-Sun 10:30-15:30, May-June Sat-Sun only, closed Sept-April and Mon year-round, www.hvezdarna.klet.cz).

Horseback Riding

Head about a mile and a half out of town, beyond the Křížový Vrch (Hill of the Cross), for horseback rides and lessons at Slupenec Horseback Riding Club.

Cost and Hours: 300 Kč-1 hour outdoors or in the ring, 2,200 Kč-all-day ride, helmets provided, Tue-Sun 10:00-18:00, closed Mon, Slupenec 1, worth a taxi trip, tel. 380-711-052, www.jk-slupenec.cz, René Srncová.

Sleeping in Český Krumlov

Krumlov is filled with small, good, family-run pensions offering doubles with baths from 1,000 to 1,500 Kč and hostel beds for 300 Kč. Summer weekends and festivals (see "Helpful Hints," earlier) are busiest and most expensive; reserve ahead when possible. Hotels (not a Krumlov forte) have staff that speak some English and accept credit cards; pensions rarely have or do either. While you can find a room upon arrival here, it's better to book at least a few days ahead if you want to stay in the heart of town. Cars are not very safe overnight—locals advise paying for a garage.

In the Old Town

$$$ Castle View Apartments, run by local guide Jiří Václavíček, rents seven apartments. These are the plushest and best-equipped rooms I found in town—the bathroom floors are heated, all come with kitchenettes, and everything's done just right. Their website describes each stylish apartment (1,900-4,800 Kč depending on size, view, and season; the big 4,800-Kč apartment sleeps up to 6, complex pricing scheme, reserve direct with this book for 10 percent off online prices, non-smoking, breakfast in a nearby hotel, Šatlavská 140, tel. 380-727-015, mobile 731-108-677, www.castleview.cz, info@castleview.cz).

$$$ Hotel Konvice is run by a German couple—and their two dogs—with a personal touch. Each room is uniquely decorated (Db-1,500-2,500 Kč, a block above the main square at Horní 144, tel. 380-711-611, www.boehmerwaldhotels.de, info@stadthotel-krummau.de).

Sleep Code

(20 Kč = about $1, country code: 420)
S = Single, **D** = Double/Twin, **T** = Triple, **Q** = Quad, **b** = bathroom, **s** = shower only. Unless otherwise noted, prices include breakfast. To help you sort easily through these listings, I've divided the accommodations into three categories based on the price for a standard double room with bath:

$$$ **Higher Priced**—Most rooms 1,500 Kč or more.
  $$ **Moderately Priced**—Most rooms between 1,000-1,500 Kč.
    $ **Lower Priced**—Most rooms 1,000 Kč or less.

Prices can change without notice; verify the hotel's current rates online or by email. For the best prices, book direct.

On Parkán Street, Below the Square

Secluded Parkán street, which runs along the river below the square, has a hotel and a row of small pensions. These places have a family feel and views of the looming castle above.

$$$ Hotel Mlýn, at the end of Parkán, is a recently opened and tastefully furnished hotel with more than 30 rooms and all the amenities (Sb-2,400 Kč, Db-3,000 Kč, elevator, free Wi-Fi, pay parking, Parkán 120, tel. 380-731-133, www.hotelmlyn.eu, info@hotelmlyn.eu).

$$ Pension Olšakovský, which has a delightful breakfast area on a terrace next to the river, treats visitors as family guests (Db-1,000-1,250 Kč, includes parking, Parkán 114, mobile 604-430-181, www.olsakovsky.cz, info@olsakovsky.cz).

On Latrán Street, at the Base of the Castle

A quiet, cobbled pedestrian street (Latrán) runs below the castle just over the bridge from the Old Town. It's a 10-minute walk downhill from the train station. Lined with cute shops, the street has a couple of fine little family-run, eight-room pensions.

$$ Pension Danny is a little funky place, with homey rooms and a tangled floor plan above a restaurant (Db-1,050 Kč, apartment Db-1,250 Kč, breakfast in room, Latrán 72, tel. 380-712-710, www.pensiondanny.cz, recepce@pensiondanny.cz).

On Rooseveltova Street, Between the Bus Station and the Old Town

Rooseveltova street, midway between the bus station and the Old Town (a four-minute walk from either), is lined with several fine little places, each with easy free parking. The key here is tranquility—the noisy bars of the town center are out of earshot.

ČESKÝ KRUMLOV

$$ Little **Pension Teddy** offers three deluxe rooms that share a balcony overlooking the river and have original 18th-century furniture. Or stay in one of four modern-style rooms, some of which also face the river (Db-1,250 Kč, deluxe Db-1,400 Kč, cash only, staff may be unhelpful, free Wi-Fi and Internet access, parking-200 Kč, Rooseveltova 38, tel. 380-711-595, mobile 724-003-981, www.pensionteddy.cz, info@pensionteddy.cz).

$$ Pension Myší Díra ("Mouse Hole") hides eight sleek, spacious, bright, and woody Bohemian contemporary rooms overlooking the Vltava River just outside the Old Town (Db-900-1,400 Kč, bigger deluxe riverview Db-1,900 Kč, prices include transfer to/from bus or train station, Internet access, Rooseveltova 28, tel. 380-712-853, www.malecek.cz). The no-nonsense reception, which closes at 20:00, runs the recommended boat rental company (Půjčovna Lodí Maleček, at the same address), along with three similar pensions with comparable prices: **Pension Wok** down by the river, **Pension Margarita** farther along Rooseveltova, and **Pension u Hada.**

$$ Pension Anna is well-run, with two doubles, five apartments, and a restful little garden. Its apartments are spacious suites, with a living room and stairs leading to the double-bedded loft. The upstairs rooms can get stuffy during the summer (Db-1,250 Kč, Db apartment-1,550 Kč, extra bed-350 Kč, Rooseveltova 41, tel. 380-711-692, www.pensionanna-ck.cz, pension.anna@quick.cz). If you book a standard Db and they bump you up to an apartment, don't pay more than the Db rate.

Hostels

There are several hostels in town. Hostel 99 (closest to the train station) is clearly the high-energy, youthful party hostel. Krumlov House (closer to the bus station) is more mellow. Both are well-managed, and each is a five-minute walk from the main square.

$ Hostel 99's picnic-table terrace looks out on the Old Town. While the gentle sound of the river gurgles outside your window late at night, you're more likely to hear a youthful international crowd having a great time. The hostel caters to its fun-loving young guests, offering a day-long river rafting and pub crawl, with rental bikes and a free keg of beer each Wednesday (65 beds in 4- to 10-bed coed rooms-300 Kč, D-700 Kč, T-990 Kč, Internet access-1 Kč/minute, laundry-200 Kč/load, use the lockers, no curfew or lockout, recommended Hospoda 99 restaurant, 10-minute downhill walk from train station or two bus stops to Spicak, Vezni 99, tel. 380-712-812, www.hostel99.cz, hostel99@hotmail.com).

$ Krumlov House Hostel is take-your-shoes-off-at-the-door, shiny, hardwood-with-throw-rugs mellow. Efficiently run by a Canadian, it has a hip and trusting vibe and feels welcoming to travelers of any age (24 beds, 6 beds in two dorms-300 Kč per bed, Db-800 Kč, 2-person apartment-900 Kč, family room, no breakfast but there is a guests' kitchen, DVD library, Wi-Fi, laundry facilities, Rooseveltova 68, tel. 380-711-935, www.krumlovhostel.com, info@krumlovhostel.com).

Eating in Český Krumlov

Krumlov, with a huge variety of creative little restaurants, is a fun place to eat. In peak times the good places fill fast, so make reservations or eat early.

Na Louži seems to be everyone's favorite little Czech bistro, with 40 seats in one 1930s-style room decorated with funky old advertisements. They serve inexpensive, tasty local cuisine and hometown Eggenberg beer on tap. If you've always wanted to play the piano for an appreciative Czech crowd in a colorful little tavern... do it here (daily 10:00-23:00, Kájovská 66, tel. 380-711-280).

Krčma u Dwau Maryí ("Tavern of the Two Marys") is a characteristic old place with idyllic riverside picnic tables, serving ye olde Czech cuisine and drinks. The fascinating menu explains the history of the house and makes a good case that the food of the poor medieval Bohemians was tasty and varied. Buck up for buckwheat, millet, greasy meat, or the poor-man's porridge (daily 11:00-23:00, Parkán 104, tel. 380-717-228).

Cikánská Jizba ("Gypsy Pub") is a Roma tavern filling one den-like, barrel-vaulted room. The Roma staff serves Slovak-style food (Slovakia is where most of the Czech Republic's Roma population came from). Krumlov has a long Roma history, and even today 1,000 Roma people live in the town (see "Roma in Eastern Europe" sidebar, earlier). While this rustic little restaurant—which packs its 10 tables under a mystic-feeling Gothic vault—won't win any culinary awards, you never know what festive and musical activities will erupt, particularly on Friday nights, when the owner's son's band, Cindži Renta (Wet Rag), performs here (Mon-Sat 15:00-24:00, closed Sun, 2 blocks toward castle from main square at Dlouhá 31, tel. 380-717-585).

Restaurace u Dobráka ("Good Man") is like eating in a medieval garage, with a giant poster of Karl Marx overseeing the action. Lojza, who's been tossing steaks on his open fire for years, makes sure you'll eat well. Locals know it as the best place for grilled steak and fish—expect to pay 350 Kč for a full meal. He charges too much for his beer in order to keep the noisy beer-drinkers away (open daily 17:30-24:00 from Easter until Lojza "has a shoebox full of money," Široká 74, tel. 380-717-776).

Laibon is the modern vegetarian answer to the carnivorous Middle Ages. Settle down inside or head out onto the idyllic river terrace, and lighten up your pork-loaded diet with soy goulash or Mútábúr soup (daily 11:00-23:00, Parkán 105).

Rybářská Restaurace ("Fisherman's Restaurant") doesn't look particularly inviting from the outside, but don't be discouraged. This is *the* place in town to taste freshwater fish you've never heard of (and never will again). Try eel, perch, shad, carp, trout, and more. Choose between indoor tables under fishnets or riverside picnic benches outside (daily 11:00-22:00, on the island by the millwheel, mobile 723-829-089).

Krčma v Šatlavské is an old prison gone cozy, with an open fire, big wooden tables under a rustic old medieval vault, and tables outdoors on the pedestrian lane. It's great for a late drink or roasted game (cooked on an open spit). *Medovina* is hot honey wine (daily 12:00-24:00, on Šatlavská, follow lane leading to the side from TI on main square, mobile 608-973-797).

Restaurace Barbakán is built into the town fortifications, with a terrace hanging high over the river. It's a good spot for old-fashioned Czech cooking and beer, at the top of town and near the recommended Rooseveltova street accommodations (open long hours daily, reasonable prices, Horní 26, tel. 380-712-679).

Hospoda 99 Restaurace serves good, cheap soups, salads, and meals. It's the choice of hostelers and locals alike for its hamburgers, vegetarian food, Czech dishes, and cheap booze (meals served 10:00-22:00, bar open until 24:00, at Hostel 99, Vezni 99, tel. 380-712-812). This place is booming until late, when everything else is hibernating.

Dobrá Čajovna is a typical example of the quiet, exotic-feeling teahouses that flooded Czech towns in the 1990s as alternatives to smoky, raucous pubs. Though directly across from the castle entrance, it's a world away from the touristic hubbub. As is so often the case, if you want to surround yourself with locals, don't go to a traditional place...go ethnic. With its meditative karma inside and a peaceful terrace facing the monastery out back, it provides a relaxing break (daily 13:00-22:00, Latrán 54, mobile 777-654-744).

ČESKÝ KRUMLOV

Český Krumlov Connections

All bus and train timetables are online at www.idos.cz.

Český Krumlov and České Budějovice

Almost all trains and some buses to and from Český Krumlov require a transfer in the city of České Budějovice, a transit hub just to the north.

In České Budějovice, the train and bus stations are next to each other: to transfer to a bus, exit the train station, turn left, and use the underpass to cross the street diagonally to the Mercury Centrum shopping center (the Autobusové Nádraží bus station is upstairs). Enter the shopping center and take the escalators to the third floor, following signs for *Bus*.

If you have time in České Budějovice between connections, consider a visit to the town's lovely main square, Náměstí Přemysla Otakara II (about a six-block walk from the stations). You can store your bags at the train station (lockers-60 Kc/day), then exit the station to the right, cross the street at the crosswalk, and head straight down Lannova třida (which becomes Kanovnická street) to the square.

By Train

From Český Krumlov by Train to: České Budějovice (6/day, 1 hour), **Prague** (8/day, 1/day direct, 4 hours; bus is faster, cheaper, and easier—see below), **Pec** (10/day, 1.25 hours), **Vienna** (6/day with at least one change, 5-6 hours), **Budapest** (6/day with at least one change, 10-15 hours).

By Bus

Buses go direct. The Český Krumlov bus station, a five-minute walk out of town, is just a big parking lot with numbered stalls for various buses (bus info tel. 380-711-190). The Student Agency bus company has an online reservation and ticket system, the newest buses, and a free drink for passengers (www.studentagency.cz).

From Český Krumlov by Bus to: Prague (7/day, 3.5 hours; 2 of the daily departures—12:00 and 16:45—can be reserved and paid for at TI, tickets can be bought from driver if seats are available, most buses leave and arrive from Na Knížecí stop in Prague, Metro: Anděl), **České Budějovice** (transit hub for other destinations; about 2/hour, 30-50 minutes, 30 Kč).

From České Budějovice by Bus to Třeboň, Telč, and Třebíč:
An express bus goes from České Budějovice to the Moravian city
of **Brno** (5/day Mon-Fri, 2/day Sat-Sun, 4.5 hours). Along the way,
it stops at **Třeboň** (30 minutes from České Budějovice), **Telč** (2
hours from České Budějovice), and **Třebíč** (3.25 hours from České
Budějovice).

By Shuttle Bus or Private Car

From Český Krumlov to Linz and Beyond: If you can get to Linz,
Austria, you'll have your choice of the fast trains running hourly
from Linz to Munich, Salzburg, and Vienna.

Two companies with similar pricing run shuttle buses to and
from Český Krumlov and **Linz** (3/day, 1.25 hours, 400 Kč), **Vienna** (1/day, 3 hours, 1,090 Kč), and **Salzburg** (1/day, 3 hours, 1,090
Kč). Be sure to book in advance, whether you're going with reliable
Sebastian Tours (mobile 607-100-234 or 608-357-581, www.sebas-
tianck-tours.com, sebastiantours@hotmail.com) or Pension Lobo
(tel. 380-713-153 or 777-637-374, www.shuttlelobo.cz, lobo@ck-
rumlov.cz; or reserve in person at Pension Lobo at Latrán 73 or at
the main square shuttle office; may cancel with short notice—reconfirm the day before).

TŘEBOŇ, TELČ, AND TŘEBÍČ

Many travelers to South Bohemia visit only Český Krumlov. While it's delightful, three nearby towns are less packaged, more authentic, and, for many, equally worthwhile.

If you draw a line between České Budějovice (the capital of South Bohemia) and Brno (the capital of Moravia), you'll go right through the "Three Ts": Třeboň is an inviting medieval town famous for its peat spas, network of manmade lakes, and fish specialties. Tiny Telč has the Czech Republic's most impressive main square. And busy Třebíč is home to the country's most intact historic Jewish quarter.

Getting Around the "Three Ts"

An express bus line between the big cities of České Budějovice and Brno stops in Třeboň, Telč, and Třebíč (5/day Mon-Fri, 2/day Sat-Sun; České Budějovice to Třeboň—30 minutes, to Telč—2 hours, to Třebíč—3.25 hours, to Brno—4.5 hours). You can reach České Budějovice easily by direct train from Prague (almost hourly, 2.5 hours) or from Český Krumlov (6/day, 1 hour). In České Budějovice, the bus and train stations are next to each other. Direct buses also connect these towns to Prague and other destinations; see "Connections" for each destination. For bus and train schedules, see www.idos.cz.

Planning Your Time

With good planning—letting bus departures dictate the amount of time you spend in each town—you could reasonably leave Český Krumlov early in the morning, visit Třeboň and Telč, and arrive in Třebíč by evening. With more time, consider an evening in Telč for village relaxation and hiking, or move on to Třebíč for a bigger, more city-like feel.

Třeboň

Třeboň (TREH-bohn, pop. 18,000), a well-preserved medieval town centered around an inviting Renaissance square, is a charming place to explore a unique biosphere of artificial lakes that date back to the 14th century.

Over the centuries, people have transformed what was a flooding marshland into a clever and delightful combination of lakes, oak-lined dikes, wild meadows, Baroque villages, peat bogs, and pine woods. Rather than unprofitable wet fields, the nobles wanted ponds that swarmed with fish—and today Třeboň remains the fish-raising capital of the Czech Republic. Landscape architects in the 16th century managed to strike an amazing balance between civilization and nature, which today is a protected ecosystem (about 15 percent covered by water) with

the biggest diversity of bird species in Eastern Europe. Nature enthusiasts come here to bird-watch, bike along dikes held together by the roots of centuries-old oaks, and devour the best fish specialties in the country.

While Třeboň enjoys plenty of tourism, its fish industry makes its relative affluence feel a little less touristy than other popular towns. Its peat spas have attracted patients from all over the world for decades, but since the facilities are small, Třeboň is never as overrun as some other, more famous spa towns.

Planning Your Time

With a full day in Třeboň, spend the morning enjoying the square, climbing up the Town Hall Tower, touring the Dean Church, and visiting the "Man and the Landscape" exhibition in the castle. (The castle itself and the brewery are less interesting.) After trying fish soup and trout for lunch, rent a bike and follow the educational trail along the ancient dikes. If it's hot, bring a bathing suit.

Soaking yourself in the peat of the spas is unforgettable; unfortunately, since the spa treatments are overbooked, it's difficult to get a spot (for booking details, see page 256). If you get in, build your day around it.

If you're here in October and November, lend a hand in the fascinating ritual of clearing the fish ponds, warming yourself with shots of potato rum as you wade through the mud.

Orientation to Třeboň

The old town—separated from newer construction by city walls, Renaissance gates, a water channel, and a castle garden—encircles the main square, Masaryk Square (Masarykovo Náměstí). Sights, hotels, restaurants, and ATMs are all within a couple blocks of Masaryk Square. From the train station, enter the square through the east gate. Standing in the middle of the square and facing west (with the station and gate at your back), the street to the left leads to the brewery and to Svět lake. The castle, which houses the "Man and the Landscape" exhibit, is at the far (west) end of the square.

Tourist Information

The TI, next to the Town Hall on Masaryk Square, hands out an exhaustive, glittering brochure called *The Region of Třeboň*, which includes a town map. With several days advance notice, they can reserve an English-speaking local guide (open daily 9:00-12:00 & 12:45-18:00, tel. 384-721-169, www.trebon-mesto.cz).

Arrival in Třeboň

The train station and the local bus stop are within easy walking distance from Masaryk Square.

By Train: Get off at the Třeboň-Lázně station—*not* the Třeboň-Město station. From Třeboň-Lázně, walk along the road directly in front of the station, and you'll reach Masaryk Square in five minutes.

By Bus: The bus from Prague leaves you at the main bus station, a 20-minute walk (or 100-Kč taxi ride, tel. 384-722-200) west of the old town. Most buses arriving from České Budějovice continue from the main station to the Sokolská stop, which is a short walk through the castle park to Masaryk Square.

Helpful Hints

Internet Access: The user-friendly **town library** (Mon-Fri 8:00-17:00, closed Sat-Sun) and **Café Bar-Computer Center Roháč** (daily 18:00-2:00 in the morning) are in the same building by the castle park, at Na Sadech 349. **Lázně Berta** is just outside the east gate (daily 6:00-22:00).

Bike Rental: Hotel Zlatá Hvězda (on Masaryk Square, tel. 384-757-111) and the **newsstand** directly across the square at #85 (tel. 384-722-867) both rent decent mountain and trekking bikes (30 Kč/hour, 100 Kč/half-day, 200 Kč/day, hotel requires driver's license as a deposit).

Sights in Třeboň

Masaryk Square (Masarykovo Náměstí)

Třeboň's fine main square is typical of squares in the region, lined with colorful facades artfully blending both Renaissance and Ba-

roque building styles. It was built by the town's 17th-century burghers, whose wealth came from the booming fish industry. The rectangular market plaza—with a humble plague column and fountain in the middle—feels just right. Grab a seat at one of the outdoor cafés, and watch local life circulate with the serenity of ducks on a lake.

While the tranquility comes naturally today, until 1989 it was a government requirement. At the square's lower end, above the bank door, a **propaganda relief** in the Social Realist style (but actually dating back to the 1930s) extols the virtue of working hard and stowing your money here for the common good. Higher up, a happy fisherman cradles a big fish, the reason for his wealth—and, since the 16th century, the wealth of Třeboň.

The **Town Hall Tower,** whose moderate height of 100 feet just fits with the size of the square, is worth the climb. Surveying the view from its top, you feel as if you can reach out and touch the circular old town. Beyond that, the lakes glimmer against the green backdrop of stately oaks (15 Kč, daily June-Sept 10:00-18:00, unpredictable hours Oct-May).

Across from the Town Hall, the impossible-to-miss, rampart-like white gable marks the famous 16th-century **Inn at the White Horse** (U Bílého Koníčka—look for the small horse on the facade).

At the other end of the square, notice the only modern building here, a **Spar supermarket.** Some 30 years ago, when the square was veiled in the shabby gray of communism, the regime decided to give it a facelift with a modern building that fit the medieval space like a UFO. After 1989, locals carefully added a facade and a new roof to the concrete box, effectively blending the former eyesore into the Old World townscape.

Castle (Zámek)

The castle is covered with rectangular sgraffiti, a characteristic decoration of the late 1500s (made by etching a design in plaster, revealing a different color underneath). As with other South Bohemian towns, all this sgraffiti is a reminder that the 16th century was Třeboň's heyday. Třeboň belonged to the Český Krumlov-based Rožmberk family. In 1600, Petr Vok—the last of the Rožmberks—moved here permanently after selling Český Krumlov to the emperor. He brought along his archive, still considered the most valuable collection of medieval documents in this part of Europe. The castle can only be visited with an escorted tour (likely in Czech, with an English flier). Your best basic castle visit is Route A, which includes Petr Vok's Renaissance rooms. Route B covers the 19th-century apartments, kitchens, and stables of the later, equally distinguished Schwarzenbergs.

Cost and Hours: 70-100 Kč for tours in Czech, English-language flier provided, buy at "cash box" ticket desk, tours go hourly or more, English tours cost more and must be reserved a week ahead by emailing zamek.trebon@seznam.cz, April-Oct Tue-Sun 9:00-11:45 & 12:45-17:00, closed Nov-March and Mon year-round, tel. 384-721-193, www.zamek-trebon.eu.

▲"Man and the Landscape" Exhibit

Located inside the castle, this is the best sight in town. Surprisingly modern, thoughtfully described in English, and further illuminated by excellent little video-on-demand terminals, the exhibit covers the things that make this town distinct: lake-making, the fish industry, the peat spa treatment, and the natural environment. A highlight is the theater (just after the stuffed animals), where you can watch a 13-minute video that takes you fishing early in the morning, and a 20-minute video that speeds you through a year with nature in Třeboň. An hour here is time well-invested.

Cost and Hours: 50 Kč, Tue-Sun 9:00-17:00, closed Mon, enter from garden just outside castle and city wall, tel. 384-724-912.

City Wall and Park

The greenbelt that circles the town just outside its 16th-century wall makes for a delightful 15-minute walk. Along the way, you'll pass the town's famous but underwhelming spas.

Dean Church and Augustine Monastery
(Děkanský Kostel a Augustiánský Klášter)

This Gothic church, with its unusual double nave (and obtrusive columns down the middle), is worth a look if open during your visit. A highlight is its delicately curved statue of the *Madonna and Child* (c. 1390, painted limestone). Its Ivory Soap sweetness and slinky S-shaped body are typical of late "beautiful style" Gothic. The artist, though anonymous, is known as the "Master of the Třeboň Madonna." The church once showcased more marvelous Gothic sculptures and altars, but these were deemed too valuable, so they were zipped off to the Museum of Medieval Art in Prague's St. Agnes Convent (see page 68). Frescoes in the adjoining cloister, badly neglected until after 1989, show scenes from the life of St. Augustine. While the monastery library is long gone, Augustinians were some of the most ardent medieval copyists in the time before Gutenberg's movable type revolutionized printing. Through the efforts of monks in this monastery, Třeboň became a center of medieval learning for Czechs and Austrians alike.

Cost and Hours: 30 Kč, July-Aug daily 9:00-11:30 & 13:30-17:00, or pop in just before the nearly nightly 18:30 Mass, if closed, ring the parish home next door, shorter hours off-season, Husova 142, rectory tel. 384-722-390.

Boating and Swimming

A motorboat sets out from the small wharf behind the brewery once an hour for a 30-minute (60 Kč) or 45-minute (90 Kč) cruise over the second-largest of Třeboň's lakes, Svět (daily 10:00-19:00). The nearest sandy beach is a 10-minute walk, to the right from the wharf along the dike.

Biking

The area is flat, so biking is a fun and convenient way to get around. A bike trip along the dirt trails on the ancient dikes is a great way to experience the land and water. Buy a cycling map from the TI, then follow the marked trails that snake along channels and through traditional villages.

Hiking

The best hiking is in the area of Nová Řeka (New River), directly east of town. Or catch a bus (or drive) to Chlum u Třeboně, and hike in the blueberry-filled pine woods along the Austrian border.

The Lakes of Třeboň

The medieval lake-builders of Třeboň created an ingenious landscape of regulated channels, marshes turned into lakes, and fields changed into marshes. Birds and animals new to the region began to dwell here. Peat provided a rich soil for pine trees and blueberry bushes.

The good lake-builders knew that small is beautiful... but, of course, not all of them were good. The most famous of Třeboň lake-builders was Jakub Krčín, the architect of the largest lakes, Svět and Rožmberk. Krčín was a man driven more by his ego than by practical considerations. Much of the water in his huge, deep lakes is a dead zone, lacking enough oxygen to support large fish colonies. Though less celebrated, his predecessor, Štěpánek Netolický, was more of a fishing expert. He built small lakes, and the fish in them thrived. His Golden Channel, which connects dozens of lakes, is the region's biggest marvel.

The Třeboň lakes were built for flood control as well as fishing. The marshy area around the town used to be regularly flooded by the Lužnice River, and the artificial lakes were designed to absorb the floods. In 2002, the largest floods in Czech history tested the work of those medieval lake-builders. While the 20th-century dams built on the Vltava River to protect Prague failed, Třeboň's 16th-century dams held, vindicating Krčín and keeping Třeboň's feet dry.

Peat Spa (Bertiny Lázně)

Třeboň is an important peat spa. Patients from all over the world come here for weeklong stays to get buried in the black, smelly sludge that's thought to cure aching joints and spines. Well...I guess it doesn't hurt to try. The complete peat bath *(slatinná koupel celková)* is combined with a full-body massage (don't try to sneak away before the nurse is finished with you). It's worth it to have the opportunity to fully judge the power of peat and experience the surreal *One Flew Over the Cuckoo's Nest* atmosphere of Czech medical institutions.

While it's smart to book a spa treatment several months ahead (you'll receive a prompt confirmation and a reminder one month before your appointment), you can often snare a last-minute spot if there's a cancellation. Call the spa or ask your hotelier to inquire for you (tel. 384-754-457, www.berta.cz, sestra@berta.cz). To get to the spa, go through the east gate of the city walls; the spa is just off to your left.

Sleep Code

(20 Kč = about $1, country code: 420)
S = Single, **D** = Double/Twin, **T** = Triple, **Q** = Quad, **b** = bath-room, **s** = shower only. Unless otherwise noted, credit cards are accepted and prices include breakfast. To help you sort easily through these listings, I've divided the accommodations into three categories based on the price for a standard double room with bath:

$$$ **Higher Priced**—Most rooms 1,500 Kč or more.
$$ **Moderately Priced**—Most rooms between 1,000-1,500 Kč.
$ **Lower Priced**—Most rooms 1,000 Kč or less.

Prices can change without notice; verify the hotel's current rates online or by email. For the best prices, book direct.

Sleeping in Třeboň

Although there are many pensions in Třeboň, most only take spa guests who stay for a couple of weeks. These two hotels welcome guests even for one- or two-night stays on short notice.

$$$ Hotel Galerie has 12 renovated rooms and an artistically decorated breakfast room. Notice the slightly buried storage room by the reception hall that now serves as a semi-open wine cellar—since Třeboň stands on floating sands, no house in town has a basement. The Galerie manager can usually set up a spa appointment even at the last minute—ask when you reserve (Sb-1,300 Kč, Db-1,850 Kč, Tb-2,400 Kč, Internet access and Wi-Fi, Rožmberská 35, tel. 384-385-293, mobile 724-093-876, www.hotel-trebon.cz, galerie@hoteltrebon.cz). The hotel also runs a decent restaurant on the ground floor with tasty, cheap lunch specials.

$ Hotel Bílý Koníček, on Masaryk Square, has managed to revamp all 23 of its rooms. Although still only a pale shadow of what was once a Renaissance inn—founded in 1544 and famous throughout the country—its rooms are a good value (standard Db-1,000 Kč, tel. 384-721-213, Masarykovo Náměstí 27, http://bilykonicekhotel.cz, hotel@hotelbilykonicek.cz).

Eating in Třeboň

Since the 1200s, Třeboň has lived on a steady diet of fish. The abundant variety of fish raised here is amazing...as are the chefs who cook that abundance. Austrians and Czechs alike drive for hours just to dine here. While you can find trout and carp throughout the country, the perch and pike from these lakes are unique. The pine woods south of the lakes are filled with blueberries—when it's the season, the blueberry dumplings are another must.

Šupina & Šupinka Restaurant ("Scale and Little Scale") is run by the local fishers' union, which makes sure the meals are top-notch. While the modern interior may not seem very atmospheric to visitors, it doesn't bother locals, who have good reason to consider this one of the best fish restaurants in the country. Dig into the rare and refined appetizers, which include fried carp sperm, cod liver, pickled herring, and local crab. If you have only one fish dinner in the Czech Republic, the native pike perch here would be your best choice (daily 10:30-24:00; from Masaryk Square, walk past the Spar supermarket along Petra Voka, then turn right into Novohradská Brána/Valy street; tel. 384-721-149).

Na Rožmberské Baště is a little eatery with warm wooden walls and nets and fishing rods hanging from the ceiling (you can borrow one and bring in your own catch to be cooked). They serve cheap, tasty meals made from everything that swims in the surrounding lakes (Mon-Sat 10:30-23:30, Sun 10:30-22:30, on Rožmberská, mobile 728-777-068).

Penzion a Restaurace U Míšků is a small, family-style place with fancy indoor seating and a pleasant garden courtyard, where they serve fish, steaks, and pasta (daily 11:00-23:00, near the Dean Church at Husova 11, tel. 384-721-698).

Schwarzenberská Pivnice is a large, colorful brewery/pub serving every variety of local Regent beer, including the fresh yeast kind you won't find in regular pubs. The only snacks available are Czech munchies, such as pickled sausage *(utopenec)* and pickled brie *(nakládaný hermelín)*—this place is for drinking (daily 10:30-23:00, in Regent Brewery at Trocnovské Náměstí 124, mobile 602-971-116).

Třeboň Connections

While buses between Třeboň and Prague are about as fast as the train (2.5 hours), bus departures are less frequent, and the bus station is far from the center of Třeboň. For bus and train schedules, see www.idos.cz.

From Třeboň by Train to: Prague (7/day, 2.5 hours, transfer at Veselí nad Lužnicí). If going from Prague to Třeboň, get off at Třeboň-Lázně, not Třeboň-Město.

From Třeboň by Bus to: Prague (2/day, 2.5 hours), **Český Krumlov** (10/day to České Budějovice, 30 minutes; then transfer to Český Krumlov—see page 248), **Telč** (5/day Mon-Fri, 2/day Sat-Sun, 1.5 hours), **Třebíč** (5/day Mon-Fri, 2/day Sat-Sun, 2.75 hours), **Brno** (5/day Mon-Fri, 2/day Sat-Sun, 4 hours).

Telč

Telč (pronounced "telch," pop. 6,000) is famous for its castle and its glorious square, considered by many to be the country's best. The old town—just a fat square with a thin layer of buildings—is surrounded by a sophisticated system of protective ponds and defensive walls. The  general lay of the land has changed little since the 1300s. After 1800, all new construction took place outside the core. Today, Telč remains an unspoiled, sleepy Czech town where neighbors chat in pastry shops, Vietnamese traders in medieval arcade stalls sell dirt-cheap textiles to country folks, and the smell of goat dung from a pasture across the lake permeates the town after nightfall.

There are basically no attractions aside from the square and the castle. Telč is made to order as a lunch stop on the way to or from Slavonice, Třeboň, and Třebíč, or on the longer haul between Prague, Brno, and Vienna. An overnight stay here can be a relaxing village experience.

Orientation to Telč

Everything you'll need—including ATMs, shops, hotels, and restaurants—is on the main square (Náměstí Zachariáše z Hradce), easily reachable on foot from the bus station. For a taxi, call 603-255-048 and expect basic English.

Tourist Information
The TI has information on area activities, train and bus schedules, and Internet access (Mon-Fri 8:00-18:00, Sat-Sun 10:00-18:00, shorter hours off-season, tel. 567-112-407, www.telc-etc.cz). Ask about their town audioguide or free downloadable audio tour. They can also help you find a room in one of the pensions on the square (see "Sleeping in Telč," later).

Helpful Hints
Festivals: Every year during the first two weeks of July, young musicians pour into Telč from all over Europe for the **French-Czech Music Academy,** which hosts workshops on classical music interpretation. The young virtuosos show off their skills

in a number of concerts and recitals (www.academie-telc.cz). The **Telč Vacations** (Prázdniny v Telči) festival, held during the first two weeks of August, makes the squares, gardens, and castle chambers come alive with folk music, open-air theater, and exhibitions (www.prazdninyvtelci.cz/eng).

Internet Access: The TI has one computer available to the public. The shop next to the TI also offers Internet access.

Bike Rental: You can rent bikes at the shop next to the TI (40 Kč/hour, 200 Kč/day, daily 9:00-18:00, tel. 567-243-562). Locals enjoy the half-day bike trip to the castle ruin of Roštejn and back (10 miles round-trip).

Boat Rental: During the summer, you can rent a boat for a lazy lake cruise. To get to the rental boats, walk through the gate between the castle and the square, then turn right on the path along the lake (40 Kč/hour; July-Aug daily 10:00-18:00; June Fri 13:00-18:00, Sat-Sun 10:00-18:00, closed Mon-Thu; no rentals Sept-May).

Sights in Telč

▲Main Square (Náměstí Zachariáše z Hradce)

Telč's spacious square, lined by fairy-tale gables resting on the characteristic vaulted arcades that still cover local shops and bakeries, is the most impressive in the Czech Republic. The uniqueness of the square lies in its enormous size, unexpected proportions in such a small town, and the purity of its style—of the 40 houses lining the square, there isn't a single one younger than 300 years. A fire devastated the town in 1553, and it was rebuilt of stone. A plague that ravaged the region in 1780 skipped Telč, so the plague column was built on the square to thank God.

Telč Castle

The castle is located at the end of the main square—you can't miss it. In its early years, this castle belonged to the clan of the Five Roses (symbolized by a golden rose on a blue field; see the "Parting of the Roses" sidebar on page 228). In the 1500s, the nobleman Zachariáš z Hradce (for whom the grand main square is named) imported a team of Italian artists, who turned the earlier Gothic palace into a lavish Renaissance residence. (Their work also influenced most of the burgher houses in the square.)

The castle can be toured only with an escort. You have two options: Tour A, the best basic castle tour, takes you through some

Gustav Mahler and Jihlava

Gustav Mahler (1860-1911) was the most important composer in Vienna at the turn of the 20th century. Mahler composed some of the last of the classical symphonies and was the first to venture into the musical never-never land of atonality (while his contemporary Arnold Schönberg, also Jewish, took up residence there). The age of harmony ended—by 1910 there was nothing to hold the world together, and shifts in art preceded the shots of World War I.

Mahler, born in the Czech village of Kaliště, spent the first 15 years of his life in Jihlava, at a house at Znojemská 4 that now functions as a vibrant cultural center and the composer's museum (tel. 567-167-132, www.jihlava.cz/gustavmahler). This is a worthwhile stop for music buffs en route from Prague to Telč.

stately Renaissance chambers. Tour B goes through the 19th-century apartments of the Lichtenstein family, who lived here until 1945. You'll most likely have a Czech-speaking guide and be given an English description to read as you go.

Cost and Hours: 90-110 Kč per tour, May-Aug Tue-Sun 9:00-12:00 & 13:00-17:00, April and Sept-Oct Tue-Sun 9:00-12:00 & 13:00-16:00, closed Nov-March and Mon year-round, last tour one hour before closing, www.zamek-telc.eu.

Regional Museum of Telč

While humble, this little five-room exhibit gives you an interesting insight into the town (check out the 1895 town model and the WWI and WWII photos). Everything is well-explained in the English pamphlet you can borrow as you enter.

Cost and Hours: 30 Kč, daily 9:00-16:30, in the castle complex.

Gallery of Jan Zrzavý (Galerie Jana Zrzavého)

Tucked away in the garden to the right of the castle entrance, this small gallery is worth a peek to learn about pointillism. Zrzavý, one of the most prolific Czech painters, had a style similar to earlier Impressionists, but used dots (or points) instead of lines to construct images. Paintings in the five-room gallery evolve from his teen years on through the troubled first half of the 20th century, but without the angst you might expect. Don't try to make much sense of it. Just enjoy looking at the artist's slices of local life, from steelworks to villages, represented in his unusual style.

Cost and Hours: 65 Kč, April-Oct Tue-Sun 9:00-12:00 & 13:00-17:00, Nov-March Tue-Sun 9:00-12:00 & 13:00-16:00, closed Mon year-round.

Sleeping in Telč

Many families living on or near the main square have turned parts of their homes into pleasant pensions that meld perfectly with the mellow feel of this town. At a pension, you get nicer rooms and more personal service for about half the price of the hotels, which bank on being the only places in town able to accommodate groups.

$$$ Penzion Galerie Telč, under the church tower across the square from the castle, has six spacious apartments above a café (Sb-1,100 Kč, Db-1,600-2,500 Kč, extra bed-350 Kč, tel. 222-532-547, www.hoteltelc.cz, info@pensiongalerie.cz).

$$$ Hotel Celerin, also on the main square, is slightly bigger than Penzion Galerie Telč. Some of its comfy rooms have traditional burgher furniture (Sb-980-1,200 Kč, Db-1,530-1,750 Kč, more expensive rooms face square, cheaper rooms face garden, Wi-Fi, closed off-season, tel. 567-243-477, www.hotelcelerin.cz, office@hotelcelerin.cz).

$ Penzion Patricia is run by a former high-school teacher (and her four-legged friends, Bibi and Borka) who, after 14 years in the US, returned to Telč with a mission: to turn her family's house into a showcase of Telč's hospitality. The eight rooms vary in size and style, but all come with queen-size beds imported from California. Breakfast is served on a terrace under the Romanesque church tower, and bonfires are lit in the garden along the former town walls, where you can grill meat or munch seasonal fruits (Sb-580 Kč, Db-980 Kč, Tb-1,350 Kč, two-night minimum in season, Internet access, next to Penzion Galerie Telč on the main square at #38, tel. 567-213-342, mobile 776-691-300, www.pensionpatricia-telc.eu, patricia_telc@volny.cz).

$ Penzion Steidler has the most tastefully furnished rooms in town and a narrow, blooming garden that stretches all the way to the lake (Sb-500 Kč, Db-800 Kč, suite-1,600 Kč, prices go up for one-night stays, breakfast-50 Kč, free Wi-Fi, parking-50 Kč, look for house #52 on the main square, tel. 567-243-424, mobile 721-316-390, www.telc-accommodation.eu, steidler@volny.cz).

$ Penzion Danuše is a well-managed, quiet place with four solid rooms (Db-1,000 Kč, Db suite-1,200 Kč, 30 yards off the main square at the corner of Palackého and Hradební 25, tel. 567-213-945, mobile 603-449-188, www.penziondanusetelc.cz, danuse.telc@seznam.cz).

Eating in Telč

All of these eateries are on the main square.

Šenk pod Věží ("Under the Tower") is ideal for a fancy Czech meal with extra touches. It has two small, atmospheric rooms with

100-year-old photographs and tranquil, outside seating in the back on the former town wall (daily 11:00-22:00, tel. 567-243-889).

Osvěžovna u Marušky, also directly beneath the tower, is popular with young locals who congregate here for coffee and cigarettes as much as for the food and beer. The walls are decorated by local artists and vacationing out-of-towners; jazz and classical concerts take place here twice a month (daily 11:00-24:00, mobile 603-398-128).

Pizzerie, on the corner by the plague column, has the best outside seating on the square and two modern, high-ceilinged rooms in the basement. Locals of all generations converge here for a surprisingly good and cheap Czech interpretation of the Italian theme. Sweet Czech ketchup rules the day, drowning every item on the long menu—be it pizza or pasta—in the same distinct flavor. Sicilian purists would not be amused (daily 11:00-22:00).

Telč Connections

From Telč to: Třeboň (5 buses/day Mon-Fri, 2/day Sat-Sun, 1.5 hours), **Třebíč** (5 buses/day Mon-Fri, 2/day Sat-Sun, 45 minutes), **Brno** (5 buses/day Mon-Fri, 2/day Sat-Sun, 2.5 hours), **Slavonice** (2 trains in morning, 3 in afternoon, 1 hour), **Prague** (3 trains/day, 4-5 hours, requires 2 changes—bus is better; 5 buses/day Mon-Fri, 3/day Sat-Sun, 2-3 hours; more with a transfer in Jihlava—3 hours total). Note that some buses to Prague may arrive at Prague's Roztyly station (on the red Metro line) rather than the main bus station, Florenc. For bus and train schedules, see www.idos.cz.

Třebíč

A few miles east of Telč is the big, busy town of Třebíč (TREH-beech, pop. 40,000), with another wonderful main square and, just over its river, the largest intact Jewish ghetto in the country. While Prague's Jewish Quarter is packed with tourists, in Třebíč you'll have an entire Jewish town to yourself. Třebíč's Jewish settlement was relatively small. Though lonely and neglected, its remains are amazingly authentic.

Orientation to Třebíč

Three hours in Třebíč is sufficient—everything's close by. The main square affords a fun slice-of-local-life look at a humble yet vibrant community, while the near-ghost town across the river was once the Jewish ghetto. The two main streets that run parallel to the river (which separates the ghetto from the Christian town) are connected by a maze of narrow passages, courtyards, and tunnels.

Tourist Information
The TI has two helpful branches: one on the main square and one in the ghetto's Rear Synagogue (both open daily 10:00-12:00 & 13:00-17:00, rental bikes at main square location, tel. 568-823-005, www.mkstrebic.cz).

Arrival in Třebíč
From the train station (with safe 24-hour luggage storage), cross the street behind the large waiting hall, and walk to the main square. To continue on to the ghetto, cross the river, following *Židovské Město* signs, marked with Stars of David. The cemetery is uphill.

Sights in Třebíč

▲Charles Square (Karlovo Náměstí)
Třebíč's main square is the third-biggest in the Czech Republic. A market square since the 13th century, it's still busy with a farmers market every morning. Třebíč was historically a mix of Christians and Jews, all living on the easy-to-defend bit of land between the river and the hill. As you'll see, that area is pretty tiny—and eventually the Christian community packed up and moved across the river for more space, establishing this square as the town's nucleus.

The statue of two Macedonian brothers—the saints Cyril and Methodius, who brought Christianity to Moravia and the Slavs in their own language, rather than Greek or Latin—was erected a thousand years after Methodius' death in 885. But forget all that history. Just circle the square, surveying today's Moravian scene. There are several fine pubs and cafés from which to people-watch. The small gallery in the four delightful vaulted rooms of the Painted House on the upper corner of the square is worth checking out to feel the artistic pulse of Moravia (next to the TI, displays temporary exhibits).

Opposite the bell tower, at #11, a lane leads across the river into the Jewish quarter, taking you directly to the Rear Synagogue (with a TI and small museum). Notice the grand views of the ghetto from the bridge.

▲Jewish Ghetto (Židovské Město)
The population of Třebíč's ghetto peaked in the 19th century at about 1,500. Only 10 Třebíč Jews survived the Holocaust. In the 1970s, the ghetto was slated for destruction, to be replaced by another ugly communist high-rise housing complex. But because the land proved unable to support a huge building project, the neighborhood survived. Today, it's protected by the government as the

largest preserved Jewish quarter in Europe. It comes back to life for one weekend a year during the Jewish festival (usually in late July).

Coming here, you enter a place where time has stopped: The houses are essentially as the Jews left them more than 60 years ago. Many of the houses were resettled by Roma (see sidebar, page 238), who have done little to change the look and feel of the place. In Třebíč today, only one woman has a Jewish father. (Because you must have a Jewish mother to be legally Jewish, the Jewish population is officially zero.) The government wants the ghetto to be a living neighborhood, not a museum. Lines of drying clothes and kids kicking around a soccer ball on the cobblestones make today's ghetto come alive. After dark, it's *the* place for edgy nightlife.

The **Rear Synagogue** (Zadní Synagoga) is the visitors center, with a branch of the TI, plus displays of artifacts and a model of the once-thriving local Jewish community (40 Kč, daily 10:00-12:00 & 13:00-17:00). You can also hire a guide here. At the TI, confirm the hours of the nearby cemetery (listed below).

The **Front Synagogue** (Přední Synagoga) has functioned since 1954 as a Hussite Christian church. Though the synagogue is generally locked, you can peek through its gate to see how it was retooled for the plain Hus-style worship.

Jewish Cemetery (Židovský Hřbitov)

A 20-minute walk above the ghetto, this evocative memorial park is covered with spreading ivy, bushes of wild strawberries, and a commotion of 9,000 gravestones (the oldest dating to 1631). Notice how the tombstones follow the assimilation of the Jews, from simple markers to fancy 19th-century headstones that look exactly like those of the rich burghers in Christian cemeteries.

Cost and Hours: Free, daily May-Sept 8:00-20:00, March-April and Oct 8:00-18:00, Nov-Feb 9:00-16:00, confirm hours at the Rear Synagogue TI before ascending the hill.

St. Procopius Basilica (Bazilika sv. Prokopa)

This enormous church looms over the town on a hill a five-minute walk above the main square and the ghetto. In a region of Baroque churches, this rich fusion of late Romanesque and early Gothic styles is a striking contrast. Unfortunately, it's viewable only with a tour.

Cost and Hours: 40 Kč, 45-minute tours start every 30 minutes, May-Sept Tue-Fri 9:00-12:00 & 13:00-17:00, Sat-Mon 13:00-17:00, shorter hours and less-frequent tours Oct-April, tel. 568-610-022.

Sleeping in Třebíč

$$ Hotel Solaster, near the bus station, is an attractive little place with 13 comfortable rooms, two suites, and flowers in the windows (Sb-990 Kč, Db-1,500 Kč, Wi-Fi, free covered parking, V. Nezvala 8, tel. 568-841-506, www.hotel-solaster.cz, recepce@hotel-solaster.cz).

$ Penzion u Synagogy, next to the Rear Synagogue, is as close as you can get to living in a Jewish ghetto, and includes free entry to the exhibits at the synagogue (Sb-470 Kč, Db-720 Kč, extra bed-120 Kč, Subakova 43, check in at Rear Synagogue TI, mobile 775-707-506).

$ Travellers' Hostel, near the Front Synagogue, has 55 dorm beds fitted into the meticulously restored home of a 16th-century baker. The oven still turns out warm bread, and a beer tap was installed even before the new roof, ensuring no guest leaves this party place without the two key elements of life (280 Kč per bunk in 8- to 10-bed dorm, 330 Kč in 4-bed dorm, Sb-600 Kč, Db-800 Kč, includes sheets and breakfast, Žerotínovo 19, tel. 568-422-594, mobile 777-637-417, www.travellers.cz, trebic@travellers.cz).

Eating and Drinking in Třebíč

Neptune Restaurant, facing the Front Synagogue, serves good soup, fish dishes, and cheap daily lunch specials. This is the best place in the Jewish quarter, with fine indoor or outdoor seating (daily 11:00-22:00, mobile 776-350-850).

Měsíční Čajovna ("Moon Teahouse"), on the upper street in the middle of the ghetto, is made for contemplating times gone by in the company of young English-speaking locals (Sun and Tue-Fri 15:00-21:00, Sat 16:00-23:00, closed Mon, Skalní 2).

Občerstvení Jordan, in the midst of the action at #23 on the main square, has outside seating perfect for a fast salad, sandwich, or ready-made daily special. Go inside and order by pointing at what you want (Mon-Fri 6:30-18:00, Sat 8:00-12:00, Sun 14:00-18:00).

Třebíč Connections

From Třebíč to: Telč (5 buses/day Mon-Fri, 2/day Sat-Sun, 45 minutes), **Třeboň** (5 buses/day Mon-Fri, 2/day Sat-Sun, 2.75 hours), **Brno** (5 buses/day Mon-Fri, 2/day Sat-Sun, 1.25 hours; also 10 trains/day, 1.25 hours), **Prague** (nearly hourly trains, 4-5 hours, transfer in Brno—bus is better; 7 buses/day, 2.5 hours). Note that some buses to Prague may arrive at Prague's Roztyly station (on the red Metro line), not the main bus station, Florenc. For bus and train schedules, see www.idos.cz.

SLAVONICE

Slavonice (SLAH-voh-neet-seh)—a charming little town of 2,700 people less than three miles from the Austrian border—is the perfect base for venturing into the most romantic of Czech landscapes. The town features two once-elegant Renaissance squares separated by a Gothic church and the Town Hall. In the surrounding countryside, hulking castle ruins top forested hills, deep woods surround lonely meadows, and WWII bunkers covered with sprawling blueberry bushes evoke the harsh realities of being a border town.

Centuries ago, this thinly populated borderland between Bohemia, Moravia, and Austria was filled with thieves and thugs—and was, therefore, nearly impossible to tax. Founded in the 1200s, the town was originally named Zlabings by the German settlers invited to colonize and civilize the region.

During the 14th century, when the main trade route between Prague and Vienna passed through here, Zlabings boomed. Most of the town's finest buildings date from this period. After the Thirty Years' War (1618-1648) the town declined, and, thanks to its sad fate, few new buildings broke the medieval architectural harmony.

Following World War II, Zlabings' German residents—90 percent of the population—were forced out by vengeful Czechs (see "Edvard Beneš and the German Question" sidebar on page 234). Czech people moved in and simply occupied the homes of the former residents—sitting on their sofas and even wearing their clothes.

The town became fully Czech (and was officially renamed Slavonice), and a curtain of barbed wire sealed it from the West on three sides. This region—always sparsely populated, even more so after its predominantly German population was removed—grew wilder and full of forests throughout the Cold War, when it earned the nickname "Czech Canada" (Česká Kanada).

After 1989, the deep woods of the military zone were opened up to hikers and cyclists, the border a mile south of Slavonice was reopened, and Austrians began flocking here for cheap lunches and shopping sprees, boosting business and bringing a new period of relative prosperity to Slavonice. The children you see playing in the streets today—the grandkids of those Czech settlers from 1945—are enjoying good times once again. But something about this town, at the end of the Czech world just 20 years ago, still feels like Česká Kanada.

Orientation to Slavonice

Everything of interest is on Slavonice's main square, Náměstí Míru. The train and bus stations are each within a few minutes' walking distance of the center (head for the church tower, which overlooks the square).

Tourist Information

The TI, on the main square, hands out useful tourist maps of the Slavonicko region and sells the detailed *Česká Kanada* hiking map. They also have good Internet access (daily 8:00-12:00 & 13:00-18:00, shorter hours off-season, free English audioguide, Náměstí Míru, tel. 384-493-320, www.slavonice-mesto.cz).

The roads in the area are rarely used and ideal for **biking**; you can borrow bikes from each of the listed hotels (see "Sleeping in Slavonice," later).

Sights in Slavonice

The city tower and the simple town museum are nothing special and probably not worth your time (both open daily June-Aug, weekends only May and Sept, closed Oct-April). Instead, consider the following attractions.

Underground Passages

The medieval cellars under the town, connected by an intricate network of underground passages, are a hit with children and thin, short people. Starting from the entrance (on the main square, next to the TI), you can slip on boots and an overcoat and follow your guide's flashlight, squeezing through a 30-minute subterranean tour of the town. While you'll see little more than dirty bricks, it's certainly a unique experience.

Cost and Hours: It costs 40 Kč to join an existing tour. If you're visiting when a tour isn't already scheduled, you'll pay 240

SLAVONICE

The Never-Used Fortifications

As soon as Adolf Hitler came to power in Germany in 1933, Czechoslovakia grew nervous about invasion. The area around Slavonice was part of the so-called Sudetenland: It belonged to Czechoslovakia, but was inhabited predominantly by ethnic Germans (see sidebar on page 234).

Czechoslovakia began constructing a ring of fortifications along its borders. Iron-enforced concrete bunkers were connected by underground tunnels.

By September 1938, when Hitler met with the French and British in Munich to claim the Sudetenland, these fortifications were filled with 1.5 million mobilized Czechs and Slovaks. Morale was high, and nobody doubted that the French and British would honor treaties with Czechoslovakia and help the young democracy. But instead, British Prime Minister Neville Chamberlain proclaimed to the British public, "Why should we care about the fate of a quarreling people about whom we know nothing?"—and signed off on the Munich Agreement, ceding the German areas of Czechoslovakia to Hitler without even inviting Czech representa-

Kč, the total cost of a tour for six people (July-Aug daily 9:00-18:00, call 775-906-330 to arrange a visit).

Sudetenland Defenses
Just outside Slavonice, hidden in a thick forest, is a network of armadillo-like concrete pillboxes and gun emplacements built by the Czechs in the 1930s, in anticipation of the Nazi takeover. The camouflaged mini-forts, barbed wire, and toy-like tank barriers evoke the futility of standing up to the Nazi war machine—you'll ponder the fine line between heroism and folly. A local duo is working to turn this area into the Museum of Fortifications. To get there, hike from Slavonice (1.25 miles) along the red-marked trail in the direction of Landštejn (see "Suggested Day Hike," later); or drive on the Slavonice-Stálkov road out of town and look for the *Muzeum Opevnění* sign on the left (park where you can and walk along the tiny road, then go through the lonely woods as if you were a 20th-century invader). You'll reach two bunkers fully equipped with 1930s periscopes and machine guns (daily July-Aug and on weekends May-June and Sept).

Landštejn Castle (Hrad Landštejn)
This region of thick forests and softly rolling hills is overseen by the stark ruins of the Gothic castle that once guarded the border. Though the castle itself is barren and looks like it was made of recently poured concrete, the commanding view from the top is worth the climb. On summer weekends, the castle serves as a venue for open-air folk and rock concerts.

tives to the negotiations. (Chamberlain won a Nobel Prize for this appeasement policy.) Alone, the Czechoslovak army—outnumbered by the Germans three to one—stood no chance. The frustrated soldiers were ordered home, and Czechs were forced out of the Sudetenland. Within six months, Hitler occupied the rest of the territory.

Today, the never-used bunkers along the hiking trails around Landštejn stand witness to the futility of appeasement policies and to the Czechs' bitter sense of betrayal. At the close of the war, this feeling led to the Czechs' siding with the Soviet Union, rather than with the unreliable French and British Allies. Ironically, the Munich Agreement probably saved Czechoslovakia from the fate of Poland, which was reduced to rubble during the war. Nevertheless, it took until 1989 for the Czechs to get over the frustration of the Munich Agreement in 1938, the communist takeover in 1948, and the failed "Prague Spring" uprising in 1968—moments when instead of being able to win their freedom, the Czechs had to give up without firing a single shot.

Cost and Hours: 70 Kč; June-Aug Tue-Sun 9:00-16:30, closed Mon; May and Sept Tue-Sun 9:00-15:30, closed Mon; April and Oct Sat-Sun 9:00-15:30, closed Mon-Fri; closed Nov-March; simple café inside castle gate, fancy Landštejnský Dvůr restaurant, two pubs by parking lot under castle; tel. 384-498-580, www.hradlandstejn.cz.

Getting There: Landštejn Castle is seven miles west of Slavonice, on the road to Nová Bystřice. Hardy travelers can reach the castle on foot (follow red-marked trail, see "Suggested Day Hike," next) or by bike (follow the road or get map at TI to go through the countryside). You can also reach it by bus (Slavonice-Nová Bystřice line, 3/day, weekdays only, 15 minutes, ask to be let off at Landštejn) or car (drive toward Nová Bystřice).

Suggested Day Hike: For a 14-mile hike, follow the red-marked trail from Slavonice to Landštejn via the work-in-progress Museum of Fortifications (described earlier), visit the castle (have lunch here), then descend along the yellow-marked trail in the direction of Dačice to Velký Troubný lake, a perfect swimming spot. From there, return to Slavonice along the red-and-white-marked nature trail.

SLAVONICE

Sleep Code

(20 Kč = about $1, country code: 420)
S = Single, **D** = Double/Twin, **T** = Triple, **Q** = Quad, **b** = bathroom, **s** = shower only. Unless otherwise noted, credit cards are accepted and prices include breakfast. To help you sort easily through these listings, I've divided the accommodations into two categories based on the price for a standard double room with bath:

$$ **Higher Priced**—Most rooms 1,100 Kč or more.
$ **Lower Priced**—Most rooms less than 1,100 Kč.

Prices can change without notice; verify the hotel's current rates online or by email. For the best prices, book direct.

Sleeping in Slavonice

All three recommended hotels are on the main square.

$$ Dům u Růže has 12 rooms in a restored late-19th-century house. Each room has its own bath and kitchen; the sauna and pool are 100 Kč/person extra (Sb-1,000 Kč, Db-1,300 Kč, Tb-1,950 Kč, breakfast-120 Kč, Wi-Fi, free parking, swimming pool, sauna, Náměstí Míru 452, tel. 384-493-004, mobile 603-493-879, www.dumuruze.cz, rezervace@hoteluruze.cz). They also rent bikes (30 Kč/hour, 200 Kč/day).

$$ Hotel Besídka, between the two parts of the square separated by the church, hides eight ultra-modern, bright rooms behind a magnificent Renaissance facade. The striking combination of ancient and postmodern styles was designed by (and named after) the architects-cum-actors of Prague's popular avant-garde theater, Sklep, who still converge here every New Year (Db-1,490 Kč, extra bed-490 Kč, free Wi-Fi, Horní Náměstí 522, mobile 606-212-070, www.besidka.cz). The hotel also runs the **Hostel Blue Star** (Modrá Hvězda) next door (from 200 Kč/bed) and a recommended restaurant downstairs.

$ Hotel Arkáda is more spartan (although all of the rooms were recently renovated) and seems designed for hikers (600 Kč/person for one-night stay, 400 Kč for two or more nights, extra bed-300 Kč, breakfast-100 Kč, Náměstí Míru 466, tel. 384-408-408, fax 384-408-401, www.hotelarkada.cz, info@hotelarkada.cz).

Eating in Slavonice

Restaurant Besídka is a welcoming place, with modern, artsy decor, a solid Czech menu, excellent pizzas, and divine blueberry dumplings. Their entertaining menu has choices ranging from the "Castro Breakfast" to "Cold and Chilly Tidbits" (daily 11:00-22:00, tel. 384-493-293, see Hotel Besídka listing, earlier).

Slavonice Connections

The only way in and out of Slavonice is by train via **Telč** (2 trains in morning, 3 in afternoon, 1 hour; see "Telč Connections" on page 263). For train schedules, see www.idos.cz.

OLOMOUC

Olomouc • Kroměříž

Olomouc (OH-loh-moats), the historical capital of Moravia, is a showcase of Baroque city planning. Today, it's the Czech Republic's fifth-largest city (pop. 100,700) and harbors Moravia's most prestigious university. Students rule the town. With its wealth of cafés, clubs, and restaurants, Olomouc is the place to taste vibrant local culture—without the hassles and scams of Prague.

Olomouc has pride. It's at a crossroads about 150 miles from each of the other great cities of the region (Prague, Wrocław, Kraków, Bratislava, and Vienna) and wants to play with the big boys. While it ruled Moravia from the 11th century until 1642, today it's clearly playing second fiddle to Prague in the modern Czech Republic. Locals brag that Olomouc has the country's second-most-important bishopric and its second-oldest university. Like Prague, it has its own fancy astronomical clock. Olomouc actually built its bell tower in the 19th century to be six feet taller than Prague's. Olomouc is unrivaled in one category: Its plague monument is the tallest and most grandiose anywhere.

Although Olomouc's suburbs sprawl with 1960s apartment complexes and factories, its historic core was spared Stalin's experiments in urban design. It's not lost in a time warp like the old-town areas of Český Krumlov, Telč, and Slavonice. It's simply workaday Moravia. Trams clatter through the streets, fancy boutiques sell stylish Versace fashions, and locals pack the busy pubs. Few tourists come here, so the town lives on its own booming economy.

In the mornings, proud farmers dig out their leeks and carrots and descend upon the colorful open-air market. Haná, the region that immediately surrounds Olomouc, is the most fertile in the Czech Republic. The big landowners here have never had trouble converting their meat, milk, and bread into gold and power. The

Olomouc's History

The fortune and misfortune of Olomouc has always come from its strategic location at the intersection of Eastern Europe's main east-west and south-north routes: Merchants, pilgrims, kings, and armies had to pass through the city.

Until the 1640s, Olomouc was the second-largest city in the Czech lands. The king's younger brother governed Moravian politics from here, while the archbishop kept the spirits (and the lands) of Moravians in God's hands—that is, his own.

Olomouc was trashed by passing armies during the Thirty Years' War (1618-1648) and occupied by Sweden for the last eight of those years. More than 70 percent of the town's population died in battles or from plagues, and the Moravian capital was moved to Brno. In 1709, Olomouc burned to the ground...only to emerge from the ashes with a Baroque flair during the Habsburg years. The new Olomouc—filled with churches, colleges, statues, and fountains—became the largest Baroque town in the country. But its prosperity again ended abruptly, as Prussia (occupying what is now western Poland and eastern Germany) threatened to invade Vienna—and Olomouc was right in the way. The Habsburgs had Olomouc's students and monks leave, and replaced them with soldiers who would defend the city. They surrounded Olomouc with tall, thick walls, and what once was a cultural center became an immense fortress. The Prussians laid siege to the city, but never managed to take it. The ring of walls and moats that protected the town also ended up preventing the encroachment of modern-day architecture into the historic center.

Olomouc eventually began to thrive again, but it remains overshadowed by Brno. Today, it still comes in second as the economic powerhouse of Moravia. But ever since Palacký University was founded here in 1946—on the grounds of the centuries-old theological university—Olomouc has been Moravia's intellectual center.

most distinguished landowner of all has always been the Church. Archbishops have ruled from here for a thousand years, filling the town with churches and monasteries. In 1946, these buildings were turned into departments of the new Palacký University.

Being a student town, Olomouc feels young and alive (though quiet during summer weekends and school vacations, when the students clear out). Olomouc has managed to blend the old and the new better than any other town in the country. The McDonald's on the Baroque main square is not an intruder, but simply a contented acknowledgment of modern times.

OLOMOUC

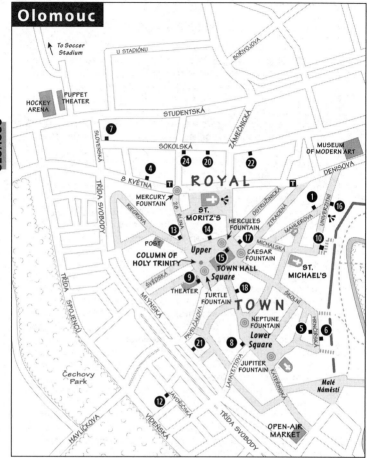

To generalize, the Moravians are seen as friendlier and more community-oriented than the more individualistic Bohemians. This shows in voting patterns. In Moravia, left-leaning parties tend to do better than the pro-business candidates who dominate the electorates in Prague and Plzeň (a city in western Bohemia). Traditions are also more prized in Moravia: Diverse regional dialects and folk customs have flourished here but have long since disappeared in Bohemia.

Anything labeled "Haná" is from this particular part of Moravia—you'll notice plenty of Haná pride here. Olomouc is a fine place to just kick back for a day or two in a beautiful Baroque town with its Haná-centric gaze fixed on the future. Nearby Kroměříž, an hour away by train, beckons day-trippers with its lavish castle and gardens.

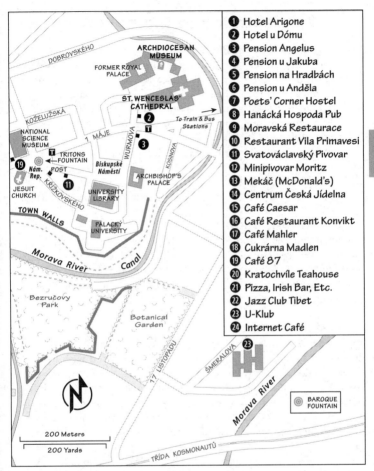

1 Hotel Arigone
2 Hotel u Dómu
3 Pension Angelus
4 Pension u Jakuba
5 Pension na Hradbách
6 Pension u Anděla
7 Poets' Corner Hostel
8 Hanácká Hospoda Pub
9 Moravská Restaurace
10 Restaurant Vila Primavesi
11 Svatováclavský Pivovar
12 Minipivovar Moritz
13 Mekáč (McDonald's)
14 Centrum Česká Jídelna
15 Café Caesar
16 Café Restaurant Konvikt
17 Café Mahler
18 Cukrárna Madlen
19 Café 87
20 Kratochvíle Teahouse
21 Pizza, Irish Bar, Etc.
22 Jazz Club Tibet
23 U-Klub
24 Internet Café

Planning Your Time

Olomouc is a delightful mix of Baroque space and 21st-century life. Don't approach the city as a sightseer; Olomouc is to be experienced and enjoyed. The only must-see "sights"—the two squares and the plague column—can be covered in an hour, but you can enjoy additional time in the city's restaurants, bars, and clubs.

If you're passing through, hop off the train for a three-hour lunch stop on the main square. Better yet, stay the night to relax and sample the rich nightlife. I enjoy the city enough to visit it as a long day trip from Prague. On a more leisurely visit, consider the worthwhile day trips to Kroměříž (with a sumptuous château, described later) and the Wallachia region (see next chapter).

Orientation to Olomouc

Olomouc's historic core is small, compact, and just five tram stops from the train station. The core has two parts: the original settlement around the former royal palace and cathedral, and the royal town (west of the cathedral). The royal town is concentrated around two connected squares: Upper Square (Horní Náměstí), with the Town Hall and plague column; and Lower Square (Dolní Náměstí), with many restaurants.

Part of Olomouc's charm is that it's a Baroque town on a medieval street plan. Everything of sightseeing interest is contained within its historic core, defined by the circular greenbelt that follows the town's old wall (much like the famous Planty in Kraków).

Tourist Information

Olomouc's main TI, in the Town Hall on the Upper Square, has plenty of well-written fliers describing the town's main sights (daily 9:00-19:00, tel. 585-513-385, www.olomouc-tourism.cz; there's also a TI at the train station). They sell tickets to concerts and can set you up with a local guide (500 Kč/hour, reserve ahead).

Arrival in Olomouc

By Train: Olomouc's circa-1950s train station (Hlavní Nádraží) is downright cute: Bright, happy peasants still greet you with their banners, rakes, and trays of *koláče* (pastries). As you exit through the main station hall, you'll see three information offices on the left. First is the railway center, with 24-hour help on train connections (tel. 972-741-620). Next is a simple TI that offers basic help—such as directions to hotels—and can sell you a good town map (daily 6:45-12:00 & 12:30-17:45, Internet access for 1 Kč/minute). Last is a city transit office, with information about trams and tickets (Mon-Fri 5:00-17:00, closed Sat-Sun).

Take the **tram** into the center. Trams #2, #4, and #6 stop in front of the train station and go past the cathedral (U Dómu, third stop), then continue to Koruna (fifth stop), right by the main square. Even if you're not arriving by train, consider riding the tram for an easy orientation to the city (see "Getting Around Olomouc," later).

Taxis are inexpensive (figure on 100 Kč to the center). Call Atlant-taxi (toll-free tel. 800-113-030) or Citytaxi (toll-free tel. 800-223-030).

Helpful Hints

Festivals: Olomouc's **Festival of Song** (early June, www.festamusicale.com) kicks off the event calendar. During the summer (July-Sept), the town organizes a cultural festival. Top Czech artists perform weekly under the open sky in the Town Hall courtyard or in one of the numerous churches and student clubs around town (www.olomouckekulturniprazdniny.cz). The Jesuit Konvikt (former monastery) simultaneously hosts a Baroque music festival. Outside of festival time, when school is in session (Sept-May), Olomouc is hopping, with good independent movie theaters and live music in bars. The town's main theater, **Moravské Divadlo,** regularly puts on opera performances (ticket office open Mon-Fri 9:00-18:00, closed Sat-Sun, located on the Upper Square next to the recommended Moravská Restaurace, tel. 585-223-533, www.moravskedivadlo.cz, pokladna@moravskedivadlo.cz).

Beer Spa: For an unforgettable memory, it's hard to beat soaking in a sudsy beer bath at the **Svatováclavský Pivovar** brewery (see page 290).

Pharmacy: A 24-hour pharmacy is on Aksamitova street.

Internet Access: U Dominika has mellow decor and comfy chairs (Mon-Fri 9:00-21:00, Sat-Sun 10:00-21:00, across the street from the Dominican monastery on the corner of Sokolská and Slovenská).

Bike Rental: Poets' Corner Hostel rents wheels by the day (for details, see hostel listing under "Sleeping in Olomouc," later).

Rickshaws: To cycle around on a rickshaw, look for the main stand in front of the TI on the square (50 Kč per ride, 100-Kč circuit goes around all fountains, 200 Kč also includes parks).

Local Guide: Štefan Blaho, who speaks English well, is a rare Olomouc guide ready to connect with curious visitors who figure out how much fun Olomouc is to visit—especially with a local (500 Kč/hour, tel. 581-208-242, mobile 602-729-613, www.olomouc-guide.cz, stefan@olomouc-guide.cz).

Getting Around Olomouc

Although Olomouc is walkable, I recommend taking a tram ride for a good orientation (see "Overview Tram Ride," below). Tickets are good for 40 minutes, so you can hop on and off (14 Kč, buy at *tabák* shops or yellow machines, or pay a little extra to buy on board from the driver).

Tours in Olomouc

Overview Tram Ride

The 10-minute tram ride from the train station (Hlavní Nádraží) to the Upper Square (stop: Koruna) is a handy way to get an overview of the city. It's easy. Trams #2, #4, and #6 make the route, going every few minutes.

In front of the train station stretches a modern town center with planned communist-era apartment blocks. While there are

OLOMOUC

The Baroque Fountains of Olomouc

Sprinkled around Olomouc's old town is a series of seven allegorical fountains with statues. Since pagan times, Olomouc—whose wealth has always been based on agriculture—has had a close relationship with water. Most of the fountains were inspired by classical mythology.

One features a statue of **Neptune,** the god of water. Another shows **Hercules** depicted as the guardian of Olomouc, holding the Moravian checkered eagle in his left hand and a mace in his right. **Jupiter,** the overlord of the gods, replaced an earlier sculpture of the only Christian saint who appeared on the fountains: St. Florian, protector from fires and floods.

The **Tritons** fountain—closely based on the one at Rome's Piazza Barberini—has the most developed composition: a pair of water spirits and a dolphin carrying a conch, with a fragile boy leading two dogs.

The culmination of the cycle is the equestrian statue of **Caesar,** who looks proudly toward Michael Hill (where legend says he founded Olomouc). The  water gods Morava and Danubius carry the coats of arms of Moravia and Lower Austria, and the dog represents Olomouc's fidelity to the Austrian emperor.

The **Mercury** statue is artistically the most successful. Mercury fulfilled the same role in classical mythology as the archangel Michael did in the Old Testament: He was the guide through the land of the dead and the messenger of the gods.

The modern **turtle fountain,** at the end of the Town Hall, is the most entertaining. The turtle, who lives a long life, symbolizes ancient Olomouc's ability to hang in there. The city's history in maps and documents is inscribed on the turtle's pillar. Contribute to a new tradition—though the statue is only a few years old, the tail (on the dolphin statue) already shows signs of being rubbed by visitors to assure their return to Olomouc. This fountain is a meeting place for young mothers and a fun place to watch toddlers enjoy the art.

The placement of the fountains and statues at the intersections of roads and squares—reminiscent of stage props in Baroque theater—imitates the spectacular cycle of Bernini's fountains in Rome. Since the second half of the 18th century, every view down any main street in Olomouc has ended with a sculpture. Look for these as you sightsee, and you'll better appreciate the town as theater.

plenty of drawbacks to the city's communist heritage, one good leftover from that era is Olomouc's fine, still-subsidized public transit. As you ride, notice that people often forgo owning a car because of dirt-cheap monthly passes. It's second nature here.

Going downtown from the station, you peel through the city's architectural layers of history. Crossing the three branches of the river, you pass through the university district before reaching the center. A red light at the front of the car indicates your next stop. Hop out at "Koruna," and head toward the big square (Upper Square) a block to your left.

Sights in Olomouc

Olomouc is divided between its royal town (surrounding the magnificent Upper Square, with its famous plague column) and its bishop's town, or cathedral district (the other end of town, with the bishop's palace and Archdiocesan Museum). The huge university sprawls between these two former centers of power. Visitors connect the two zones with an easy 10-minute walk. The sights here are listed in that order: Upper Square and its surroundings (market and churches), cross-town walk, and cathedral.

The Royal Town

Upper Square (Horní Náměstí)

Standing in front of the Town Hall, surrounded by the vast square and the many beautiful noble and bourgeois residences, you can imagine Olomouc's importance over the centuries. The fountain with an equestrian statue of Julius Caesar is dedicated to the legendary founder of the town (excavations reveal that it actually originated as a third-century Roman military camp—centuries after Caesar).

The Mahler Café is a reminder of the great composer Gustav Mahler (1860-1911). He lived and worked here until he moved to Vienna, claiming he needed better food.

Examine the town model. While designed for blind people, it gives anyone interested a feel—literally—for the medieval street plan, otherwise easily overlooked among all the Baroque grandeur.

On the square, take a look at the Town Hall, the fancy clock, the towering plague monument, and the seven mostly venerable fountains.

▲Town Hall

Olomouc's grand Town Hall is a testament to the city's 600 years of prominence in Moravia. The three wings around a rectangular courtyard once served as both council chambers and market halls. In the late 1400s, part of the building was converted into an armory, guards' house, and jail. On the outside, notice the beautiful

Mannerist loggia, used for the entry into the council chambers and for ceremonial purposes (such as the mayor's declarations to the public). The coats of arms of many nations show that Moravia was part of the vast and multiethnic Habsburg Empire.

The Town Hall is busy with local weddings—if you see a festively decorated car parked on the square, it's probably waiting to zip a bride and groom away. You can visit the Town Hall's interior and climb the tower only with an escort.

Cost and Hours: 15 Kč, 30-minute tour, daily at 11:00 and 15:00, book tickets and depart from the TI located within the Town Hall.

▲Astronomical Clock

The huge clock on the Town Hall was once far more complex than the one in Prague. Originally, it depicted the medieval universe divided into three spheres, but it was periodically rebuilt to correspond with new advances in knowledge. In 1898, purists worked to restore it to its original state. (A picture of this older version is in the window located a few steps to the left of the actual clock.)

Like Prague's clock, Olomouc's astronomical clock was intentionally destroyed by the Nazis in World War II. Today's version was rebuilt in 1953 by the communists, who had a flair for kitschy propaganda. In this one-of-a-kind clock made in the Socialist Realist style, you have earnest chemists and heroic mothers rather than saints and Virgin Marys. High noon is marked by a proletarian parade, when, for six minutes, a mechanical conga line of milkmaids, clerks, blacksmiths, medics, and teachers are celebrated as the champions of everyday society. Study the mosaic symbols of the 12 months (*leden* is January; circle down on the left—*červen* is June). The Haná region is agriculturally rich, so each month features a farm activity. As with any proper astronomical clock, there's a wheel with 365 saints, so you'll always know whose special day it is. But this clock comes with a Moscow-inspired bonus—red bands on the wheel splice in the birthdays of communist leaders (Lenin was born on the 112th day of the year in 1870; Stalin's saint was Toman—day 355). Note that the clock's designers were optimists—the year mechanism (on the bottom) is capable of spinning until A.D. 9999.

▲▲▲Column of the Holy Trinity
(Sousoší Nejsvětější Trojice)

The artistic pride of Olomouc is the tallest plague column in Europe. Squares throughout Eastern Europe are dotted with similar structures, erected by locals to give thanks for surviving the plague. This one was started in 1716 by a local man named Render, who

announced—with a confidence characteristic of the Haná region—
that he would create a work that in "its height and ornamentation would not have a peer in terms of excellence." He donated his
entire fortune, employing many great artists for decades to build
the monument. Sadly, he died before its consecration, which occurred in the presence of the Habsburg ruler Maria Theresa, the
Holy Roman Empress.

The Holy Trinity group on the highest point of the column
features God the Father making a blessing, Christ with a cross

sitting on a globe, and the dove in gold (representing the Holy Spirit) crowning everything.
Tumbling with the Trinity, the archangel Michael—holding his fiery sword and shield—
reminds us that the Church is in a constant
struggle with evil. A third of the way down
from the top of the column (past the golden
cannonball—embedded there as a reminder
of the 1758 Prussian siege), we see Mary—
the mediator between heavenly and earthly
spheres—carried off by angels during the Assumption.

The bottom third features three reliefs
with allegories of the Christian virtues (Faith, Hope, and Charity),
surrounded by six saints. Four of the saints are closely connected
with the life of Jesus (saints Joachim and Anne—the parents of St.
Mary—as well as St. Joseph and St. John the Baptist); the other
two are the patron saints of Olomouc (saints Jerome and Law-
rence). This particular arrangement of saints shows that universal
faith is often combined with a distinctly local myth and belief.

It all sits atop a tiny (and rarely open) chapel where Maria
Theresa knelt to pray—devout, yet green with envy. Olomouc had
a plague column grander than Vienna's.

Lower Square (Dolní Náměstí)

Below the Upper Square stretches the more workaday Lower
Square. Enjoy live music at the beer terrace or a bite at the fine
Hanácká Hospoda pub (described later, under "Eating in Olo-
mouc").

Find the communist-era **lamppost**
with its twin 1970s speakers. Locals remember growing up with these mouth-
pieces of government boasting of suc-
cesses ("This year, despite many efforts
of sabotage on the part of certain individuals in service of imperialist goals,
we have surpassed the planned output of
steel by 195 percent"); calling people to

"From Armories Make Libraries": John Amos Comenius (1592-1670)

This motto, which inspired the transformation of Olomouc's military fortress into a lively university campus, came from Comenius, a.k.a. Jan Amos Komenský, one of the Czech Republic's most influential teachers and writers (pull out a 200-Kč banknote to have a look at him). You'll find his dictum embedded in the pavement at the entrance to Olomouc's former central armory, which is the main university library today.

Comenius was born into the Moravian Brethren faith, which was founded on the pacifist ideals of the Czech religious reformer Petr Chelčický (c. 1390-1460). Having studied at universities in Germany, Comenius returned to Moravia as a young pastor to run the Protestant schools in Fulnek and Přerov. The beginning of the Thirty Years' War had a direct impact on him: His wife and two children died in a plague epidemic, and following the defeat of the Czech Protestants by the Catholic Habsburgs, Comenius had to choose exile over abandoning his faith. Personal misfortune went hand-in-hand with a professional one: During his escape through Poland, his entire library went up in flames, a fate that later befell many of his personal writings.

Surrounded by the chaos and destruction of war, Comenius believed that guns were no way to restore order—what the world really needed was a revolution in learning. He envisioned a liberal-arts education that would create citizens rather than specialists, and proposed a new teaching system based on the novel principle of "school through play." To promote this idea, he wrote extensively. His works included a textbook aimed at making learning Latin fun for children, one of the first scholarly treatments of preschool education, and *Orbis Pictus* ("World in Pictures"), the first children's encyclopedia. His most famous and acclaimed

action ("There will be no school tomorrow as all will join the farmers in the fields for an abundant harvest"); or quelling disturbances ("Some citizens may have heard about alien forces in our society taking advantage of this week's anniversary to spread unrest. This is to reassure you that the situation is firmly under control and nothing is happening in Olomouc or in Prague. Nevertheless, for their own safety, we suggest all citizens stay home").

Open-Air Market

As was the norm in medieval times, poor people traded tax- and duty-free items just outside the town walls. The city's market remains in the same spot, just outside the town wall a long block below the Lower Square. The town's circa-1900 brick market hall is of no interest today, but around it sprawls a colorful open-air market. While Moravian farmers sell their vegetables and herbs, Vietnamese traders hawk knockoff jeans and cheap sunglasses

work, *The Labyrinth of the World and the Paradise of the Heart* (written in Czech, not Latin), argued that all human knowledge and ambition is futile if unaccompanied by faith and charity. His fame spread across the Atlantic: In 1636, Comenius was asked to become the first president of Harvard University. Still hoping to return home (and afraid of sea journeys after he almost lost his life in a storm in the North Sea), Comenius declined the offer.

For the remainder of his wandering life, Comenius taught  and wrote in Poland, Hungary, the Netherlands, England, and Sweden, never able to return home. Alfons Mucha powerfully captured Comenius' tragic fate as a homeless exile—a fate later to be shared by thousands of free-spirited Czechs— in one of the canvases of his *Slav Epic* (see page 138).

During the communist era, Comenius' grave (in Naarden, near Amsterdam) became a shrine for Czech exiles; immediately after the fall of the Iron Curtain, the site was swamped with Czechs who came to pay their respects. Today, Comenius is considered one of the founders of modern education, and his legacy is alive far beyond Olomouc. In the Czech Republic and Slovakia, Comenius' birthday is celebrated as Teachers' Day, and the Comenius Medal is the highest UNESCO award for achievement in education.

(closed Sun, busiest on Wed and Sat, but fun any morning). The rough little snack bar sells *langoš* (a Hungarian cheese-and-grease doughnut, 13 Kč), cheap coffee, and good beer.

Churches

Since its origin, Olomouc has been the seat of bishops. The great number of churches—concentrated in such a small area—shows the strong presence of the Church here. Of the many churches in town, two are worth a peek (each one is a block off the Upper Square).

St. Michael's Church (Sv. Michal), located at the highest point in town, dominates Olomouc's skyline (free, open long hours daily). It's a fine, single-nave Baroque church full of illusory paintings, fake armor, and lovely Gothic frescoes hidden under Baroque whitewash. As it was rebuilt after looting by the Protestant Swedes during the Counter-Reformation, the Catholic propaganda is really cranked up. The three-domed ceiling—a reminder of the Trinity—is an unusual feature. From the cloister, stairs lead down to the 11th-century "rock chapel" and its tiny lake. The chair in the dark hole on the left is an invitation to pray or meditate. This humble grotto was the site of the first hermitage here on Olomouc's high rock. As Michael is the Christian antidote to paganism, archaeologists assume that this church sits upon a pagan holy spot.

St. Moritz's Church (Sv. Mořic) is a must-see for its pair of asymmetrical towers, which look more like fortresses. The church has an original Gothic vault, but its Gothic treasures are in a Prague museum. The altar and windows, while lovely, are Neo-Gothic, dating only from the 19th century. Climb the 200 steps to the tower to enjoy a commanding city view (15 Kč).

Strolling Between the Royal Town and the Cathedral

Connect the two sightseeing zones with a short walk along the city's main drag. Leaving the Upper Square on Ostružnická street, you'll pass real-estate offices (a home in a village or an apartment here goes for about 1.5 million Kč, or about $75,000) and lots of bookstores (supplying 17,000 local university students).

When you hit the main road, Denisova, notice the fine gas streetlamp that lit the street in 1899, when the tram first ran. Follow the tram line toward the lacy spire of the cathedral in the distance.

The mix of facades, from Gothic to Art Nouveau, masks narrow medieval buildings. At Univerzitní street, a quick detour to the right leads past the Vertigo Bar (where students believe a mind is a wonderful thing to waste) to the grand and renovated University building on the left (with its handy Café Restaurant Konvikt and a courtyard with a nice view over the town wall).

Continuing up the main drag, you pass the Museum of Modern Art (interesting) and the Natural Science Museum (boring). If you visit the **Museum of Modern Art** (50 Kč, free on Wed and Sun, open Tue-Sun 10:00-18:00, closed Mon, Denisova 47, www.olmuart.cz), save your ticket—it'll also get you into the Archdiocesan Museum (described later).

The big square called Náměstí Republiky is marked by a fountain inspired by Bernini's Triton Fountain in Rome (see "The Baroque Fountains of Olomouc" sidebar). The Jesuits, whose gorgeous church faces the square, founded the original university in the 16th century. This square marks the division between the royal town and the bishop's town. Ahead (past the square, veering a bit to the right), Mariánská street leads to the archbishop's stately 17th-century palace (closed to the public). On the slopes below the palace are Jesuit colleges (now university classrooms) and a Clarist convent (now a museum).

In the Bishop's Town, near the Cathedral

St. Wenceslas' Cathedral (Dóm Sv. Václava)

Supposedly, this has been the resident church of Olomouc's bishops ever since the Christian missionaries Cyril and Methodius visited in the ninth century. The present church has been rebuilt many times. While it maintains its Gothic lines, what you see is 19th-century pseudo-Gothic, with Neo-Renaissance paintings. The crypt houses a collection of liturgical ornaments—the second-largest in the country, after Loreta Church in Prague. Just inside the door, you can trace the lineage of local archbishops back 68 men, from today's archbishop to St. Methodius in 869.

Cost and Hours: Small fee possible, crypt generally open May-Oct 10:00-17:00, closed off-season.

▲Archdiocesan Museum

Opened in 2006, this is Olomouc's pride and joy. After his 1995 visit, Pope John Paul II asked the city to build this museum. The mission of this state-of-the-art museum is "In Glory and Praise—To Share a Thousand Years of Spiritual Culture in Moravia"...and it does just that.

Cost and Hours: 50 Kč, free on Wed and Sun, open Tue-Sun 10:00-18:00, closed Mon, Václavské Náměstí 3, same ticket also gets you into the Museum of Modern Art at Denisova 47, www.olmuart.cz.

Visiting the Museum: This former royal castle, once the king's principal Moravian residence, later became home to Olomouc's archbishop. The exterior is a mix of Romanesque and Gothic elements. Inside you'll wander among some of the finest medieval art in Eastern Europe (all well-described in English). The centerpiece of the treasury is a monstrance (Communion wafer holder) with 1,800 diamonds and seven pounds of pure gold (from 1750). The bishop's gilded coach understandably gave the Holy Roman Empress Maria Theresa more reason for envy.

Then, wearing slippers to protect the not-so-hardwood floor, you shuffle through the staterooms lined with well-lit paintings. Don't miss the painting depicting the ceremonial arrival of the new archbishop in Olomouc in the mid-1700s. Survey the town: Except for the McDonald's, it's all there. See how the artist, playing with perspective a bit, shows the gate on the left dividing the royal town from the bishop's town. This day was a good one for the bishop, as the secular royal town is filled with Christian pageantry.

OLOMOUC

Sleep Code

(20 Kč = about $1, country code: 420)
S = Single, **D** = Double/Twin, **T** = Triple, **Q** = Quad, **b** = bathroom, **s** = shower only. Unless otherwise noted, credit cards are accepted and prices include breakfast. To help you sort easily through these listings, I've divided the accommodations into three categories based on the price for a standard double room with bath:

$$$ Higher Priced—Most rooms 1,700 Kč or more.
  $$ Moderately Priced—Most rooms between 1,000-1,700 Kč.
    $ Lower Priced—Most rooms 1,000 Kč or less.

Prices can change without notice; verify the hotel's current rates online or by email. For the best prices, book direct.

Sleeping in Olomouc

$$$ Hotel Arigone, filling three tastefully renovated townhouses, is on the hill by St. Michael's Church. While some of the 53 rooms have 17th-century wooden ceilings and 19th-century-style furniture, most are furnished in a modern style and are accessible by elevator (Sb-2,000 Kč, Db-2,300 Kč, Internet access, rental bikes, parking, Univerzitní 20, tel. 585-232-351, www.arigone.cz, hotel@arigone.cz).

$$$ Hotel u Dómu, a six-room place on a quiet street next to the cathedral, is run with a personal touch that makes it popular with quirky visiting professors (Sb-1,400 Kč, Db-2,000 Kč, Tb-2,400 Kč, free Wi-Fi, free parking, Dómská 4, tel. 585-220-502, www.hoteludomu.cz, hoteludomu@email.cz).

$$$ Pension Angelus rents three rooms in a Baroque house with wooden beams and solid furniture (Db-1,850 Kč, Tb-2,450 Kč, free Wi-Fi, free parking, Wurmova 1, mobile 776-206-936, www.pensionangelus.cz, pensionangelus@email.cz).

$$ Pension u Jakuba rents six self-contained, Ikea-furnished apartments in a renovated 400-year-old house on a busy street. The pension also has seven quiet, modern rooms in a newly built annex in the courtyard (Sb-1,000 Kč, Db-1,200-1,500 Kč, Tb-1,950 Kč, Qb-2,500 Kč, breakfast-100 Kč, free Wi-Fi, parking available, 8 Května #9, to reach reception walk through passage into courtyard, tel. 585-209-995, mobile 777-747-688, www.pensionujakuba.com, ujakuba@iol.cz).

$ Pension na Hradbách rents four modern rooms, each with a personal touch (Sb-700 Kč, Db-1,000 Kč, Tb-1,500 Kč, no breakfast, Hrnčířská 3, tel. 585-233-243, mobile 602-755-848, www.pensionnahradbach.wz.cz, nahradbach@quick.cz).

$ **Pension u Anděla,** across the street, is well-suited to be on Hrnčířská ("Potter's street"), a quiet row of two-story village houses with brightly painted facades and window-boxes full of geraniums. Two of the four simply furnished rooms overlook the bastion and park (Sb-700 Kč, Db-850 Kč, no breakfast but in-room fridge, downstairs restaurant can make breakfast the night before on request, Hrnčířská 10, tel. 585-228-755, mobile 602-512-763, www.uandela.cz, info@uandela.cz).

$ *Hostel:* **Poets' Corner Hostel** fills two 1930s apartments near the town center. Tastefully furnished and immaculate, it's run as a family business by a friendly couple, Ian Martin (who's Australian) and Lucie Kyvalova (who's Czech). They have two young kids and a great enthusiasm for Olomouc. The hostel fits in perfectly with Olomouc's character as a student town and ultimate Back Door destination. The common room has sofas, armchairs, a decent library, Czech CDs (and no TV), and holds a wealth of information on Olomouc and the surrounding area (dorm beds-300-350 Kč, Sb-700 Kč, Db-900 Kč, Tb-1,200 Kč, free Wi-Fi, laundry service-150 Kč/load, ring doorbell at entryway to the right of the Charley Secondhand shop to get into Sokolská 1, mobile 777-570-730, www.hostelolomouc.com, reservation@hostelolomouc.com). The hostel also rents bicycles (100-200 Kč/day) and offers walking tours.

Eating in Olomouc

Try the sour, foul-smelling, yet beloved specialty of the Haná region, Olomouc cheese sticks *(olomoucké tvarůžky)*. The milk goes through a process of natural maturation under chunks of meat. Czechs figure there are two types of people in the world: *tvarůžky*-lovers and sane people. The *tvarůžky* are so much a part of the Haná and Czech identity that when the European Union tried to forbid the product, the Czech government negotiated for special permission to continue to rot their milk. Zip a few of these stinkers into a baggie, and you can count on getting a train compartment to yourself.

Restaurants

Hanácká Hospoda, on the Lower Square, is a simple, hearty village pub that serves regional specialties to visitors and locals alike. Choose between the woody, non-smoking Moravian beer-hall inside or the peerless square seating outside. Mozart came here to escape a smallpox epidemic in Vienna, and he lived above this restaurant. Enjoy the funky menu. Dish #007, Guttery Breath of the Knight of Loštice (a.k.a. *tvarůžky*—the stinky cheese sticks described above), comes with a lid, mints, and the offer of a toothbrush—they only have one, so please return it. Dishes #40 to #81 are good Olomouc favorites. Daily specials are available only in the basement room (Mon-Sat 10:00-24:00, Sun 10:00-20:00, kitchen closes two hours earlier, Dolní Náměstí, tel. 585-237-186).

Moravská Restaurace ("Moravian Restaurant"), on the Upper Square, is the one touristy place in town. If you're feeling homesick, step into this cozy, woody space, and you'll see happy tourists attracted by ads all over town, "authentic" Moravian folk costumes on the waiters, walls decorated with Moravian painted ceramics... and prices that will make you feel like you're back at home (essentially the same menu as Hanácká Hospoda for triple the price, daily 11:30-23:00, reservations recommended, Horní Náměstí, tel. 585-222-868, www.moravskarestaurace.cz).

Restaurant Vila Primavesi, to the left of St. Michael's Church, is located in a renovated, classy Art Nouveau villa—arguably one of Moravia's finest. The creative menu is rich in fish and game, and they have daily specials and a good wine selection. Seating is either inside, with ironed tablecloths, or on the terrace overlooking the city park (200-400-Kč entrées, daily 11:00-23:00, Univerzitní 7, tel. 585-204-852, mobile 777-749-288).

Svatováclavský Pivovar ("St. Wenceslas Brewery") is justifiably popular. It features seven kinds of unpasteurized beer brewed on the premises, an extensive menu, and the first "beer spa" in Olomouc. Reservations are strongly recommended for dinner (restaurant open Mon-Fri 8:00-24:00, Sat 11:00-24:00, Sun 11:00-21:00; spa open daily 14:00-20:00; beer bath-1,000 Kč, 2,000 Kč/2 people; free Wi-Fi for customers, Mariánská 4, tel. 585-207-517, www. svatovaclavsky-pivovar.cz).

Minipivovar Moritz, which brews fresh yeasty beer on-site, serves Bohemian cuisine and specialties from Galicia (the region of Poland just east of here). Dine in their atmospheric circa-1900 cellar or on the park-like square, in front of the dilapidated, picturesque Maria Theresa Gate. Taking its name from a German-Jewish industrialist (Moritz Fischer), it opened near a former synagogue in 2006 (precisely 100 years after the death of the man responsible for developing Olomouc into a modern manufacturing center). Today Moritz is one of the trendiest places in town. Head down to the basement to check out the kosher beer-making process, the unique *pivovod* (system of beer pipes that leads under the street to the outdoor bar on the square), and the portrait of Moritz's grandmother, who set the standard for hospitality that the owners hope to match (daily 11:00-23:00, on Palachovo Náměstí at Nešverova 2, tel. 585-205-560, reservations recommended in the evenings, www.hostinec-moritz.cz).

Mekáč (McDonald's), on the Upper Square, is filled with teenagers and moms with kids during the week. On a weekend, you can sit here and watch folks from the countryside, dressed in their Sunday best and coming to town for a "Bikmek" taste of the world.

Centrum Česká Jídelna ("Czech Eatery") is ideal if you're short on time and want some local-style fast food. They offer a world of traditional Czech dishes, ready and warmed, as well as an array of sandwiches and salads. Choose your meal by pointing at what you want (Mon-Fri 6:30-18:00, Sat 7:30-12:00, closed Sun, directly opposite the clock).

Café Caesar, filling the Gothic vaults in the Town Hall, is a popular pizza place with fine outside seating within a flea's hop of the plague monument (daily 9:00-1:00 in the morning, tel. 585-229-287). The little gallery next door, run by the café, promotes local artists.

Café Restaurant Konvikt is a modern-feeling place in the delightfully restored former Jesuit college. They cater primarily to businessmen, though some philosophy students also wander in here from the classrooms upstairs. In summer, they offer seating in a peaceful courtyard above the city walls and greenbelt (daily 11:00-24:00, Univerzitní 3, tel. 585-631-190).

Cafés and Teahouses

Olomouc is the Moravian university town, and every aspect of student life (except sleeping) happens right in the old center. Being a student town, Olomouc is lively and cheap during the school year but slower in July, August, and September (although foreign students coming here for summer programs in languages, music, and history are doing their best to make up for the annual vacation energy drain).

Café Mahler, on the Upper Square, is a stylish place for coffee and cake (Mon-Sat 8:00-22:00, Sun 10:00-21:00), while **Cukrárna Madlen,** between the Upper Square and the Lower Square, is the local ice-cream paradise (Mon-Sat 8:00-21:00, Sun 9:00-21:00).

Café 87 has the longest list of espresso drinks, iced coffees, frappés, pancakes, and desserts in town. The handful of Olomouc expats converge here daily just before lunch to have the chocolate cake, which is heavenly but highly addictive (daily 10:00-19:00, between the art and natural-history museums on Náměstí Republiky).

Kratochvíle Teahouse offers a wide array of freshly harvested tea leaves, as well as coffee, Moravian wines, and the increasingly popular hookahs (water pipes). This contemplative, bamboo-lined space also hosts exhibitions, concerts, and author readings (Mon-Fri 11:00-23:00, Sat-Sun 15:00-23:00, Sokolská 36, mobile 603-564-120).

Entertainment in Olomouc

Captain Morgan's Pizza, Bar Rasputin, The Crack Irish Bar, and **Club Belmondo** fill the massive red-brick 18th-century town wall with nightlife inspired by various corners of Europe. Fueled by the vibrant local crowd, these spots are open much of the day, but they don't really start to swing until around 21:00, when the disco and live music begin. All are free except Club Belmondo, which charges a 100-Kč cover. Head to the corner of Mlýnská and Pavelčákova, just across the Třída Svobody from Maria Theresa Gate.

Jazz Club Tibet has nothing to do with Tibet, but it does offer good food and live jazz twice a week in a modern, pub-like setting (Mon-Fri 11:00-24:00, Sat 12:00-24:00, closed Sun, Sokolská 48, tel. 585-230-399). Across the street, the **Metropol** movie theater screens a mixture of artsy and mainstream flicks.

Konvikt is a hip club right next to the restaurant of the same name (described earlier). In summer, it's a popular hangout for foreign students (Mon-Sat 14:00-24:00, closed Sun, tel. 585-631-191).

U-Klub, a 10-minute walk out of the center in the dorms, is the university's concert hall. Bands play folk, jazz, rock, punk…you name it (Šmeralova 12, tel. 585-638-117).

Olomouc Connections

Olomouc is on several major rail lines (including the one from Prague to Kraków). For bus and train schedules, see www.idos.cz.

From Olomouc by Train to: Kroměříž (hourly, 1-1.5 hours, transfer in Hulín; see "Getting to Kroměříž," next page), **Prague** (at least hourly, 2-3 hours), **Brno** (buses and trains at least hourly, 1.5 hours), **Rožnov pod Radhoštěm** (7/day, most connections require transfer in Valašské Meziříčí, allow 2 hours total; also consider bus), **Břeclav** (10/day, 2 hours, may transfer in Brno or Přerov), **Kraków** (5/day, 4.5-6 hours, transfer in Katowice, Poland, and possibly Přerov, Czech Republic; one 5-hour overnight train), **Vienna** (8/day, 3-4 hours, transfer in Brno, Břeclav, or Přerov), **Budapest** (6/day, 5-8 hours, transfer in Brno or Přerov).

From Olomouc by Bus to: Třeboň, Telč, and **Třebíč**—take the bus or train to **Brno** (see above), then take the bus in the direction of **České Budějovice** (5/day Mon-Fri, 2/day Sat-Sun—

see page 249 for connections out of České Budějovice), **Rožnov pod Radhoštěm** (hourly, 1.75-2.25 hours, most with change in Valašské Meziříčí).

Near Olomouc: Kroměříž

OLOMOUC

Whereas Olomouc was the official seat of the Moravian archbishops, Kroměříž (KROH-myehr-eezh) was the site of their lavish summer château. In 1948, this castle and its enormous gardens were nationalized and opened to the public. Kroměříž—showing off the richness of this corner of the Czech Republic—is the most lavish and best-renovated Rococo castle in the country. The 19th-century English-style park, with lakes, woods, and Chinese pavilions, is good for a walk or picnic.

While there are no other worthwhile sights in town, the pleasant square and streets filled with little bakeries offer a perfect complement to the grandeur of the archbishop's estate. The town and château of Kroměříž combine for a perfect half-day excursion from Olomouc, a wonderful opportunity to enjoy the genteel art and gentle life of small-town Moravia.

Getting to Kroměříž

From Olomouc, take one of the frequent trains in the direction of Přerov and Břeclav (hourly, 7:20 or 9:20 train is convenient). Get off at Hulín (the stop after Přerov on fast trains, 45 minutes), walk through the train station to the other side of the building, and hop on the small motor train to Kroměříž (departure scheduled to coincide with the arrival of Břeclav-bound trains, 8 minutes). Turn right out of the train station, then take the first left over the bridge. The main square (Velké Náměstí) and the entrance to the château are an easy 10-minute walk away.

On the way back, most trains from Kroměříž to Hulín connect with an Olomouc-bound train. For bus and train schedules, see www.idos.cz.

Tourist Information

The TI is on the main square, next to City Hall, and hands out a useful map with brief descriptions of all major sights, as well as a list of events (Mon-Fri 8:30-17:00, Sat-Sun 9:00-13:00, open weekdays until 16:00 May-Sept, closed Sun Oct-April, Velké Náměstí 115, tel. 573-321-408, www.kromeriz.eu).

Helpful Hints

Music: Throughout the summer, the city government joins forces with art schools and conservatories to enliven historical spaces with weekly concerts. The quality of the performers and the unique setting—in château halls and gardens—make a visit worthwhile (ticket booking and purchase at the TI on Velké Náměstí). The **Kroměříž Music Summer Festival** is in September (tel. 573-341-400).

Internet Access: The **TI** offers Internet access (first 15 minutes free). **DC Internet Café,** located on the main square, is right below the town museum (40 Kč/hour, Mon-Fri 10:00-19:00, Sat-Sun 13:00-19:00, Velké Náměstí 39).

OLOMOUC

Sights in Kroměříž

Archbishop's Château (Arcibiskupský Zámek)

Dominating the main square and the whole town, this château was rebuilt in Baroque style by archbishop Karel Lichtenstein (dubbed the "Moravian Richelieu") after  an earlier castle was severely damaged in the Swedish siege during the Thirty Years' War. The furniture and decorations are in the Rococo style (from the second half of the 18th century). The breathtaking chandeliers are made of Czech crystal.

The château is famous for one historic event: The Austrian parliament moved here from unstable Vienna during the tumultuous year of 1848, when a wave of revolutions spread across the Habsburg lands. The parliament drafted the first Austrian constitution in the château's main hall.

Hours: May-Sept Tue-Sun 9:00-17:00, closed Mon; April and Oct Sat-Sun 9:00-16:00, closed Mon-Fri; closed Nov-March; tel. 573-502-011, www.zamek-kromeriz.cz.

Tours: You can see the art gallery (described next) and climb the tower (50 Kč) on your own, but you can tour the château interior only with a guide (140 Kč with a Czech-speaking group). Try asking for an English-language tour—but be aware that you'll pay double, and you might be the only one on the tour. Tours run about every hour and last 70 minutes, with the time about evenly split between the first floor (eight rooms) and second floor (which has a beautifully painted ceiling depicting the history of the bishopric, and overlooks a stunning library interior with 80,000 books).

Art Gallery: Art-lovers should consider visiting the bishop's art gallery. Sure, it's not the Louvre, but it's the best Moravian collection of European paintings from 1400 to 1800, with works by Titian, Lucas Cranach, Albrecht Dürer, and Paolo Veronese (90 Kč, same hours as château).

Castle Garden (Podzámecká Zahrada)

This green space, filled with little ponds, exotic trees, and Chinese pavilions, offers a peaceful refuge. It's in the English style—wilder and more natural than the geometrically designed French gardens.

Cost and Hours: Free, July-Aug daily 5:30-20:30; May-June and Sept Tue-Sun 9:00-17:00, closed Mon; April and Oct Sat-Sun only, closed Mon-Fri; closed Nov-March.

Sleeping in Kroměříž

Kroměříž works best as a day trip from Olomouc, but if you want to attend a concert and stay the night, try **$$ Hotel Bouček.** This well-renovated, traditional townhouse on the main square rents 11 decent rooms (Sb-1,000 Kč, Db-1,500 Kč, extra bed-500 Kč, Velké Náměstí 108, tel. 573-342-777, www.hotelboucek.cz, hotel.boucek@seznam.cz).

Eating in Kroměříž

All of these eateries are on or just off the main square (Velké Náměstí).

Bistro u Zámku is a popular place to sip a frappé or iced coffee (daily, on the corner of main square next to the château).

Zámecká Myslivna ("Château Hunting Lodge") specializes in game. Your venison might have been shot by the archbishop, who still comes here during the summer (Sun-Thu 11:00-22:00, Fri-Sat 11:00-24:00, just off main square, Sněmovní Náměstí 41).

Radniční Kavárna is perfect if you want to eat on cushioned chairs outside, because it's a bit stuffy inside (daily 9:00-22:00, at top of main square across street from Town Hall).

Bistro Avion, a blue-collar self-service cafeteria on the main square, is good for a basic, filling meal (Mon-Fri 6:00-18:00, Sat 8:00-15:00, Sun 7:00-14:00). The place has no menu—just point to what looks good, and wash it down with Slovakia's best beer, Zlatý Bažant ("Golden Pheasant").

WALLACHIA

Rožnov pod Radhoštěm •
Pustevny

The mountainous region of Wallachia (vah-LAH-chee-ah)—where Slovakia and Poland meet the eastern edge of the Czech Republic—is ideal for an escape into nature, where you can enjoy both the ruggedness of the mountains and the easy tourist facilities of an accessible recreational area.

Wallachia (Valašsko) comprises three east-west ridges separating three long valleys. The Beskydy Mountains—the westernmost part of the Carpathian mountain range—make an impressive backdrop.

Wallachia has a sparse but proud population: the Wallachians (Valaši). They were originally Romanian shepherds who, following their sheep, drifted west along the pristine meadows and rugged canyons of the hauntingly beautiful Carpathians. In exchange for guarding the border, these shepherds received many privileges—most importantly, exemption from taxes.

Today, the Wallachians have their own tongue-in-cheek, tax-free "kingdom." In local restaurants and hotels, you can buy Wallachian "passports," which come with a brochure explaining in English why you should emigrate. The 90 Kč is a small price to pay for a passport when you consider that it frees you from the far-reaching clutches of the IRS.

Getting Around Wallachia

This region is best with a car. It's difficult, though doable, by public transportation. **Olomouc** is the nearest big city. To reach **Rožnov pod Radhoštěm** by train or bus from Olomouc, you'll need to transfer in Valašské Meziříčí (7 trains/day, allow 2 hours total; hourly bus, 1.75-2.5 hours). From **Rožnov,** a direct bus goes to **Prostřední Bečva/Pustevny** (4/day, 45 minutes). For bus and train schedules, see www.idos.cz.

Rožnov pod Radhoštěm

Rožnov pod Radhoštěm (ROHZH-novh pohd rahd-hosh-tyem), the largest town in the region and once a popular spa resort, may not be worth an overnight stay, but it certainly merits a visit for its Wallachian Open-Air Folk Museum.

▲Wallachian Open-Air Folk Museum (Valašské Muzeum v Přírodě)

The museum, which re-creates a traditional Wallachian village, is divided into three parts. Touring the "Little Wooden Town" is sufficient to give you a good sense of Eastern European mountain architecture, which blends here with elements of  Moravian house-building. The museum is also the resting place for the most distinguished Wallachians, among them the incredible runner Emil Zátopek, who won three gold medals at the Helsinki Olympics in 1952.

Cost and Hours: 180 Kč for all three parts; May-Sept daily 9:00-17:00; April Tue-Sun 9:00-17:00, closed Mon; Jan-March and Oct Tue-Sun 9:00-16:00, closed Mon; closed most of Nov and part of Dec (www.vmp.cz).

Tours: Although you can visit the complex on your own, you can more fully appreciate the site with an English-speaking guide—call a few days ahead to reserve (400 Kč for an hour-long tour, reserve at tel. 571-757-111 between 6:00 and 14:00, prohlidka@vmp.cz).

Getting There: On Rožnov's main square, you'll find direction markers for the museum (it's a 10-minute walk).

WALLACHIA

Pustevny

Pustevny (POO-stehv-nee, "Hermitage") is a small, pleasant resort atop the Beskydy (BEH-skih-dee) Mountains' most sacred ridge, in a spot where a legendary hermit once lived. The style of the mountain huts here is an imaginative combination of Art Nouveau and wooden village architecture. Peak season is June through August for hiking, and Christmas through Easter for skiing. During other months restaurants are open only on weekends.

The 30-minute **hike** from Pustevny along the red-marked trail on the ridge to-

ward the west will take you to a statue of Radegast, the old Slavic god of sun, friendship, and harvest. If you hike farther along the ridge for two miles, you'll reach the top of the sacred Radhošť mountain and statues of the Slavic ninth-century missionaries St. Cyril and St. Methodius. They hold a page of the beginning of the Gospel according to John, which they translated for the Slavic people more than 1,100 years ago. A wooden church dedicated to these two patrons of all Slavs stands behind the statue.

Hiking along the ridge from Pustevny in the opposite direction takes you through less-visited woods and into a virgin forest preserve at Kněhyně.

Getting to Pustevny

To get to Pustevny by **public transportation,** take a direct bus from Rožnov pod Radhoštěm (4/day, 45 minutes, stop is marked *Prostřední Bečva/Pustevny*).

If you're **driving,** you can reach the summit either from the south via Rožnov pod Radhoštěm and Prostřední Bečva, or from the north via Frenštát pod Radhoštěm and Trojanovice (which is linked to Pustevny by a scenic chairlift). From Frenštát, follow signs for Trojanovice, drive to the end of the road at the Ráztoka Hotel, then walk 500 yards to find the chairlift (50 Kč one-way, 80 Kč round-trip, in summer runs daily once an hour 9:00-18:00, off-season until 16:00, 15-minute ride). On arrival in Pustevny, be sure to check the schedule for the last chairlift back down to Troja-novice.

Sleeping and Eating in Pustevny

(20 Kč = about $1, country code: 420)
$$ Hotel Maměnka, a century-old, recently renovated historical landmark, fits sumptuously furnished rooms into a wooden structure that uniquely blends Art Nouveau with regional architecture (Db-1,300 Kč, suite Db-2,800 Kč, tel. 556-836-207, mobile 736-682-289, www.libusin-mamenka.cz, libusin@libusin-mamenka.cz). Its newly built **Koliba Valaška** annex, with similar rooms, is an opulent imitation of a shepherd's lodge. Hotel Maměnka is home to the classy-looking **Restaurant Libušín,** while the annex's **Restaurant Koliba** is geared more toward satisfying city Czechs' demand for rural fare in a traditional setting.

$$ Hotel Tanečnica, large and modern, is a solid, standard, circa-1980 Czech mountain lodge (Db-1,250 Kč, swimming pool, pay parking, tel. 556-835-341, www.hoteltanecnica.cz, hoteltanecnica@seznam.cz). The nearby **Koliba u Záryša** restaurant, with a more down-to-earth, scruffy shepherd's-hut setting than Restaurant Koliba, serves Wallachian food (such as cabbage soup and the pan-Carpathian specialty *halušky*—potato and flour gnocchi with sheep cheese and bacon) as well as the owner/cook's imaginative creations (such as oven-baked *živáňská pečeně*—a mixture of beef tenderloin, pork, or lamb in spices, wine, and vegetables).

WALLACHIA

MIKULOV WINE REGION

Mikulov • Pavlov and the Pálava Hills • Lednice and Valtice

The Mikulov region produces the Czech Republic's most famous wines. The locals here are known for their hospitality, which easily translates into the best customer service in the country. Historic Mikulov—the cultural center of South Moravia—has the look and feel of an Italian hill town. The village of Pavlov, set against the white stones and oak forests of the surrounding Pálava Hills, boasts beautiful rural architecture and hillside wine cellars. The large Lednice-Valtice complex of castles and 19th-century English-style parks is one of the largest manmade landscapes in Europe. Valtice, an ideal base for exploring the complex, is encircled by vineyards and has been dubbed "the wine capital of the Czech Republic." While popular with Czechs and Austrians, this region remains relatively undiscovered—adding to its many charms.

Getting Around the Mikulov Wine Region

The main railway junction of Břeclav is the gateway to the Mikulov wine region. For bus and train schedules, see www.idos.cz.

By Train from Břeclav to: **Mikulov** (10 trains/day, 30 minutes, goes through Valtice), **Valtice** (10 trains/day, 15 minutes), **Lednice** (8 buses/day Mon-Fri, 4/day Sat-Sun, 20 minutes; on summer weekends, a cute historical train runs between Břeclav and Lednice: 4/day, 20 minutes), **Prague** (9/day direct, 3 hours, most arrive at Prague's  Holešovice station), **Olomouc** (10/day, 2 hours, may transfer in Brno or Přerov).

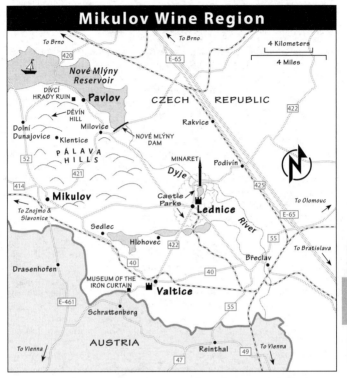

Mikulov Wine Region

By Bus from Břeclav to: Mikulov (10/day Mon-Fri, 5/day Sat-Sun, 1 hour), **Lednice** (10/day Mon-Fri, 5/day Sat-Sun, 15 minutes), **Pavlov** (10/day Mon-Fri, 5/day Sat-Sun, 45 minutes).

By Car: Although it's perfectly feasible to connect all these destinations by public transportation, you can rent a car in Břeclav (see "Helpful Hints," next). This is especially handy if you're arriving in the Czech Republic by train from Vienna or Budapest and want to rent a car.

By Bike: Most Czechs connect their wine-cellar visits by bicycle. Bikes can be rented either at Břeclav train station (ask at the ČD info desk) or at Rentbike in Mikulov (better quality, see "Helpful Hints," next). Bikes are allowed on trains.

Helpful Hints

Bike Rental: The best bikes in the region are at **Rentbike** in Mikulov (290 Kč/day, on the main square, Kostelní Náměstí 1, mobile 737-750-105, www.rentbike.cz).

Car Rental: The **Bors** rental office in Břeclav is convenient and rents Renaults (from 700 Kč/day, includes insurance, Mon-Fri 8:00-17:00, Sat 8:00-11:00, closed Sun, tel. 519-444-241,

Mikulov Wines

Czech wine is more than just a drink—it's a way of life. Although the Moravians might not have captured the sweetness of the Portuguese varieties, they did manage to ferment the taste of grapes into their own authentic culture. Without experiencing the wine tradition of southern Moravia, you will have missed a good part of the country's spirit.

Wine has been made in the Mikulov region since Roman times. Because no Roman soldier would fight without his daily two-liter ration of wine, and because it was difficult to transport unpasteurized wine over long distances, the 10th legion of Marcus Aurelius planted its own vines on this region's limestone hills (which reminded them of their homes in Tuscany). The Slavs and the Germans found the vines long after the Romans were gone and continued the tradition. In the 16th century, Anabaptist refugees from Switzerland brought new energy to the winemaking process. Today, the warm climate and the soil rich in calcium (from the limestone) make the Mikulov region one of the best wine-producing areas in Eastern Europe.

The most commonly used grapes are Ryzlink (Riesling), Veltlínské Zelené (Grüner Veltliner), Rulandské Bílé (Pinot Blanc), Chardonnay, and Sauvignon for whites. Svatovavřinecké (St. Laurent), Frankovka (Blaufränkish a.k.a. Lemberger), and Cabernet Sauvignon are used for reds. The locally bred grapes are Pálava and Aurelius.

The variety of grape is only one factor that contributes to each wine's distinct taste. Vintners discern wines by the type of soil in which they grow; the orientation of the slope (which de-

mobile 731-606-243, www.bors.cz, ondrej.holly.bors@dealer.renault.cz). To get to Bors from Břeclav's train station, it's a quick taxi ride (under 50 Kč) or a 10-minute walk (exit train station into park, turn left, walk along main street past the post office, go under a railway bridge, and find the Bors Renault dealership next door to the gas station).

Local Guides: Barbara and **Todd Hammond,** who are based in Valtice, guide individuals on bikes or by foot. With their insights on local customs, nature, and architecture, they make the wine region's dreamy landscapes come alive (400 Kč/hour, tel. 519-353-221, mobile 728-983-858, tb.km@worldonline.cz).

termines the amount of sun); and—most importantly—the sugar content. The best wines are from hand-picked late vintages, with sugar content reaching 27 percent.

The quirky local specialties are straw and ice wines. The grapes for straw wines mature in barns for months spread on dry straw. Ice wines—a Moravian and German specialty—are made from late-season grapes left to freeze while they are still on the vine. Since sugars and other solids do not freeze, pressing these grapes results in a small amount of concentrated, sweet wine. As these two wines are very difficult to make—the process is practically alchemy, and even the best vintners cannot predict which grapes will turn into a good straw or ice wine—they are also the most expensive. A tiny .3-liter bottle (about 10 oz.) costs more than 700 Kč.

The communists mismanaged wine production by planting bad shoots prone to diseases. Over the last 20 years, vintners have replaced most of these old vines with younger, better-quality ones. Moravian wines improve from year to year. Look for vintages from odd years—in the past decade these have been better than even years. Among older vintages, 2007 was outstanding.

The wine salon in the basement of Valtice Castle offers tastings and promotes 100 wines that have been chosen by experts as the best in the Czech Republic (see page 312).

One of the most prominent wine companies in the country is Reisten, the exclusive supplier to Prague's luxury restaurants and the president of the Czech Republic. Reisten produces its wines in Pavlov (see page 307).

MIKULOV WINE REGION

Mikulov

An important border town on the ancient "Amber Road" from the Baltic Sea to the Adriatic, Mikulov (MEE-kuh-lohv; think "Mikulov, not war") was briefly the unofficial capital of Moravia. When

the Austrian kings expelled the Jews from Austria in the early 1400s, they settled here on the border, gradually making up half the town's population and forming the largest Jewish community in what is now the Czech Republic outside of Prague. Jewish philosopher and scholar Judah Loew ben Bezalel—the famous Rabbi Loew—was the head Moravian rabbi here in the 16th century before moving to Prague. In the 19th century, the railway line to Vienna bypassed Mikulov, condemning it to a stagnation that mercifully protected it from Industrial Age construction.

Set between two hills that act as twin viewpoints—and with a beautifully restored main square dotted with cafés and wine bars—Mikulov today is the lively hub of South Moravia.

Tourist Information

The TI on the main square is a wealth of information about the entire region. They give out free maps and good biking information, and can help you arrange accommodations (Mon-Fri 8:00-18:00, Sat-Sun 9:00-18:00; shorter hours and closed Sat-Sun off-season; Náměstí 1, tel. 519-510-855 or 519-512-200, www.mikulov.cz).

Sights in Mikulov

The major sights in Mikulov are scattered between its hills and the town square. You can connect them with an easy up-and-down walk.

Strolling from the Main Square to Jewish Cemetery

Start your walk in the upper part of the main square. Look up at Holy Hill with the Church of St. Sebastian at the top. This is the destination of the annual pilgrimage to the **Black Madonna of Mikulov** (a statue of the Virgin Mary based on the famous Black Madonna of Loreto, Italy). The Madonna is usually housed in the large **Church of St. Wenceslas** on the main square, where you can also visit the ossuary in the church's crypt (free; church open July-Aug daily 10:00-12:00 & 13:00-18:00; Sept-June only during Mass held Sun at 8:00, Tue at 17:30, and Thu at 7:00; mobile 605-900-544).

At the foot of the square stands a prominent churchlike building, the **Tomb of the Dietrichstein Family.** These aristocrats ruled Mikulov from the 16th century to 1945 (60 Kč, April-May and Oct daily 10:00-17:00, June-Sept daily 9:00-18:00, closed Nov-March). The **Holy Trinity Column** in the middle of the square is a fine piece of late Baroque sculpture.

Above the square is the town's fortress: **Mikulov Castle.** The original castle burned down at the end of World War II and was rebuilt in 1950, so it lacks the period interiors of neighboring castles in Valtice and Lednice and isn't worth the 150-Kč admission.

From top of the square, step into the first castle courtyard (free to enter). Note the wrought-iron gate and coat-of-arms of the Dietrichstein family—there's two vintners' knives in the center. Walk through the castle's small park past a fountain and take the switchback trail toward the castle. As you gain altitude, the surrounding countryside comes into view.

From the park on the other side of the castle, take the staircase that descends down to Husova street, passing the only surviving **synagogue** in Mikulov. It's closed and will probably be under re-construction when you visit. To see other Jewish sights, turn right on Husova street, cross an intersection, and then turn right again, going up the hill to the **Jewish Cemetery** and **Ceremonial Hall.** This sight houses several small exhibits on the history and customs of the local Jewish community (30 Kč; June-Sept daily 10:00-18:00; April-May and Oct Tue-Sun 10:00-17:00, closed Mon; closed Nov-March; Hřbitovní Náměstí, tel. 519-510-388). Many Jewish visitors journey here from Vienna to pay their respects at the graves of famous rabbis. The oldest tombstone dates from 1603.

Hiking in the Mikulov Hills

For a panorama of the town, follow the blue-marked trail from the main square past the Stations of the Cross to Holy Hill and the Church of St. Sebastian.

For a perfect half-day hike from Mikulov to Pavlov, follow the red-marked trail from the main square up to the Kozí Hrádek castle ruins and then through the vineyards to Turold Hill. From here the trail continues along the road. After half a mile, turn left at the Sirotčí Hrádek hilltop ruin, returning to the road in the village of Klentnice (where you can get a bite to eat at the recommended Café Fara; check out its daily specials and traditional cakes). From here, the red-marked trail ascends up to Děvín Hill, the highest point of the Pálava Hills, and continues along the ridge to Maidens' Castle. From here, follow the green-marked trail down to the Baroque village of Pavlov. You can easily return to Mikulov by bus from Pavlov; see "Getting Around the Mikulov Wine Region," earlier.

Sleeping in Mikulov

All three recommended hotels lie along Husova street, in the heart of former Jewish district under the castle.

$$ Hotel Templ is situated in two delightfully restored houses, one Renaissance (with a former synagogue in the back), the other Art Nouveau (with a private garden). Each room is uniquely decorated, and all attic rooms have air-conditioning. An excellent restaurant is part of the business (Sb-1,400 Kč, Db-1,700 Kč, apartment with fireplace-2,500 Kč—firewood provided, Husova 50, tel. 519-323-095, www.templ.cz, info@templ.cz).

$$ Penzion Baltazar is a 19th-century house that preserves its historic spirit amid modern amenities (Sb-1,100-1,400 Kč, Db-1,500-1,800 Kč, Husova 44, tel. 519-324-327, mobile 720-611-712, www.pensionbaltazar.cz, info@pensionbaltazar.cz).

$$ Penzion Husa ("Goose") is the smallest of the historic hotels on Husova street, but has a garden and a terrace. The public

Sleep Code

(20 Kč = about $1, country code: 420)
S = Single, **D** = Double/Twin, **T** = Triple, **Q** = Quad, **b** = bathroom, **s** = shower only. Unless otherwise noted, credit cards are accepted, English is spoken, and breakfast is included. To help you sort easily through these listings, I've divided the accommodations into two categories based on the price for a standard double room with bath:

$$ **Higher Priced**—Most rooms 1,200 Kč or more.
$ **Lower Priced**—Most rooms less than 1,200 Kč.

Prices can change without notice; verify the hotel's current rates online or by email. For the best prices, always book direct.

spaces on the ground floor include a fully equipped kitchen (Sb-1,100-1,200 Kč, Db-1,200-1,600 Kč, no breakfast, Husova 30, mobile 731-103-283, www.penzionhusa.cz, info@penzionhusa.cz).

Eating in Mikulov

Restaurant Templ, in the recommended Hotel Templ, cooks the best food in town. **Restaurant Aquarium,** with a wall of fish tanks and great food, is a 10-minute walk from the center along Pavlovská street (Pavlovská 40, tel. 519-324-724). **Restaurace U Zajíce,** on the main square, is handy for its daily specials (Náměstí 3, mobile 728-541-511). **Café Dolce Vita, Café Petit,** and **Dobrý Ročník** ("Good Vintage Year") are three excellent places for coffee, pastries, or wine on the main square.

Mikulov Connections

From Mikulov by Train to: Valtice (10 trains/day, 15 minutes), **Břeclav** (10 trains/day, 30 minutes), **Vienna** (8 trains/day, 2 hours, transfer in Břeclav).

   From Mikulov by Bus to: Pavlov (10/day Mon-Fri, 5/day Sat-Sun, 20 minutes), **Lednice** (10/day Mon-Fri, 5/day Sat-Sun, 45 minutes), **Břeclav** (10/day Mon-Fri, 5/day Sat-Sun, 1 hour). For bus and train schedules, see www.idos.cz.

Pavlov and the Pálava Hills

The traditional, sleepy village of Pavlov stretches from the banks of a water reservoir toward the dramatic hilltop ruin of Dívčí Hrady ("Maidens' Castle"). In deep brick cellars, you can taste local wines and spicy Hungarian salami while listening to a local dulcimer band. Or take nature walks along the wooded slopes of the white Pálava Hills. Either way, you'll see Moravian village architecture at its best.

Sights in Pavlov

Wandering the Town

Česká street, stretching from under the hill to a parking lot above the church, is lined with traditional wine cellars. The owners sometimes rent out the small space on the first floor, wine is pressed on the ground floor, and extensive cellars run deep into the mountain. Look for farmsteads along the park by the church; they are some of the finest examples of rustic Baroque architecture in Moravia.

Wine Cellars

Ask your host whether a dulcimer band is playing in any of the wine cellars. Locals often bring their guitars along. September can be a wild month here as many arrive for harvest festivals and to drink the popular, slightly fermented wine juice (called *burčák*). One of the top wineries in the Czech Republic—**Reisten**—produces its wines in Pavlov on Vinařská street (April-Oct Mon-Sat 9:00-18:00, Sun 10:00-14:00; Nov-March Mon-Sat 9:00-17:00, closed Sun; coming from the recommended Pension Florián, turn left at the ramshackle Restaurace u Venuše and then look on your right for a small *Reisten* sign; mobile 724-793-429, www.reisten. net). **Paulus Winery,** in a newly renovated wine cellar, combines tradition with modern trends and is the most accessible of the many local wine cellars (Mon-Thu 10:00-20:00, Fri-Sat 10:00-24:00, Sun 10:00-19:00; weekends only in off-season; follow the green-marked trail uphill in the direction of the castle to Na Cimbuří 159, mobile 773-334-433, www.vinarstvipaulus.cz).

Nové Mlýny Reservoir

Three successive dams, planned for decades as part of an immense water regulation project, were built here shortly before the Velvet Revolution. They caused an ecological disaster: In the name of flood prevention, one of the last wetland forests in the Czech Republic was inundated—destroying precious flora and fauna. One of the intended benefits of the plan—to irrigate southern Moravia—also did not pan out. By the early 1990s, the collectivized fields and vineyards had been returned to individual owners. For these small producers, building channels or pumping water from the dams turned out to be too expensive. Still, the townspeople try to make the best of it. During the day, the yacht club at the bottom of the village rents paddleboats, canoes, and windsurfing boards. The shallow water is warm for most of the summer but, unfortunately, also too muddy to swim in.

Hiking in the Pálava Hills

For a good half-day hike, follow the green-marked trail from the church past the recommended Pension Florián, then up through the beech woods to the ruins of the Maidens' Castle (1.5 miles, 45 minutes). Continue on the red-marked trail to the highest point of the hills, called Děvín. Descend on the other side of the mountain to the village of Klentnice, where you can stop for lunch or home-made dessert at the recommended Café Fara. From here you can return to Pavlov by bus, or take your choice of trails: either along the blue-marked trail through the woods on the slopes of the Pála-va Hills, or along the educational winemaking route (marked by white signs with diagonal green stripes) through the vineyards east of the hills. If you have lots of energy, you can continue along the red-marked trail to Mikulov (see "Hiking in the Mikulov Hills," earlier) and take the bus back from there.

Sleeping and Eating in Pavlov

During the hot summer months and in September, getting a room on short notice can be difficult—book ahead.

$$ Hotel Pavlov is a suitable fallback if the pensions (listed next) are full (Sb-1,300 Kč, Db-1,600 Kč, Internet access, Klentnická 174, tel. 519-324-246, www.hotelpavlov.cz, info@hotelpavlov.cz).

Part of **$$ Café Fara** ("The Parish House"), in the nearby village of Klentnice, is a new, all-wood building, inspired by traditional Moravian architecture and winner of a historical renovation award. The historic parish house next door serves homemade meals and cakes (restaurant open daily until 20:00, Db-1,900 Kč, Tb/Qb-2,600 Kč, mobile 720-611-161, www.cafefara.cz, info@cafefara.cz).

$ Pension a Restaurace Florián, with six simple, clean rooms, is run by energetic Marie Jurigová—who doesn't speak English—and her three grown-up children who do—particularly Tonny, the youngest. Even if their place is booked up, ask for help arranging a room elsewhere. In the evenings, they run a wine cellar/restaurant behind the pension; on Saturdays a dulcimer band plays there. They also arrange visits to nearby wine cellars and can interpret if needed (D/Db-1,000 Kč, 5 percent discount with two-night stay and this book—mention when you reserve, Podhradní

195, tel. 519-515-323, mobile 736-760-463, www.pensionflorian.
cz, info@pensionflorian.cz).

$ Pension Pod Hradem ("Under the Castle"), recently built
above a 400-year-old wine cellar, is run by the Garčica vintner family. They pride themselves on having a garden with the best views
of the Pálava Hills and the Maidens' Castle. The young owners
studied winemaking in France and speak both French and English.
Tours of the wine cellar under the house, with samples of home-
made wines, are available on request (D/Db-1,000 Kč, two first-
floor doubles share a bathroom and large kitchen, two second-floor
doubles have their own bathrooms, Vinařská 237, tel. 519-513-375,
mobile 728-746-500, www.garcicovi.cz, penzion@garcicovi.cz).

Lednice and Valtice

MIKULOV WINE REGION

The twin towns of Lednice and Valtice—four miles apart and connected by a lush, walkable greenbelt—each boast a proud castle.
Located along the Austrian border southeast of Mikulov, they
make up one of the Czech Republic's most visit-worthy castle regions.

Since the 1200s, Lednice (LEHD-neet-seh, pop. 2,400)
and Valtice (VAHLT-eet-seh, pop. 3,600) have been part of the
Mikulov-based Lichtenstein family. The Lichtensteins were to
South Moravia what the Rožmberks were to South Bohemia: either caring benefactors who turned marshes and beech woods into
the promised land, or despotic aristocrats who mercilessly im-
poverished their serfs...depending on whom you ask. While the
Rožmberks died out in the early 1600s, the Lichtensteins thrived
during the Thirty Years' War (they wisely stayed loyal to the victorious Habsburgs) and continued to enrich the region until the
1940s. Valtice was their winter residence, but they summered at
Lednice (even though Lednice means "fridge," so named because
this stretch of the Dyje River is known for frequent frosts). Of the
two castles, Lednice is more interesting to tour.

An even more compelling
reason to make the short side-
trip from Mikulov or Břeclav
is the spectacular 19th-century
English-style park, which ex-
tends for miles between the
Lednice and Valtice castles.
Native oaks and exotic cedars
span their gnarled branches
over wild meadows and green

lakes, Romantic castles and Taj Mahal-style minarets rise in the middle of woods like apparitions, and rare birds silently glide through the sky.

Tourist Information

Lednice's TI, by the main parking lot in front of the entrance to the Lednice Castle, has free Wi-Fi and sells an inexpensive info brochure and maps of the garden complex (June-Sept Mon-Fri 8:00-17:00, Sat-Sun 9:00-17:00; shorter hours off-season and closed Sat-Sun Nov-March; Zámecké Náměstí 68, tel. 519-340-986, www.lednice.cz).

Valtice's TI is on the main square (April-Sept daily 9:00-17:00; Oct-March Mon-Fri 7:00-15:30, closed Sat-Sun; Svobody Náměstí 4, tel. 519-352-978, www.valtice.eu).

Sights in Lednice and Valtice

▲Lednice Castle (Zámek Lednice)

This castle is the Moravian answer to England's Windsor Castle, an immense structure built in the English Neo-Gothic style. Today, the castle houses the university for winemakers; anyone is welcome to sign up for a short summer course. To tour the palace, choose between three routes: Route I (ground-floor halls), Route II (prince's apartments), or Route III (picture gallery).

Cost and Hours: Route I or II-150 Kč each, Route III-50 Kč, English tour-50 Kč extra; May-Aug Tue-Sun 9:00-18:00, closed Mon; Sept Tue-Sun 9:00-17:00, closed Mon; April and Oct Sat-Sun 9:00-17:00, closed Mon-Fri except by reservation; closed Nov-March; tel. 519-340-128, www.zamek-lednice.info.

Castle Parks

From Lednice Castle, parks extend both north and south. The 19th-century nobles loved everything Romantic, peppering these woods with a quirky architectural hodgepodge: a Neo-Roman aqueduct, a Neo-Gothic castle ruin, a Neo-Greek temple, a victory column, a rendezvous pavilion, a minaret, and so on. Navigate between these perfect spots with the help of the map from the TI.

Cost: Depending on how many of the recommended park attractions you visit, plan on spending about 190-230 Kč per person.

Getting There: To reach the minaret from Lednice Castle, you can walk (one mile), hire a horse carriage (60 Kč/person, 30 minutes), or take a boat. Boats and carriages depart from the little dam just behind the castle; prices depend on the number of riders. Although most horse-carriage rides throughout Europe are tourist traps, here it feels appropriate to ride through the alleys like the nobles once did—even the school groups do it. A good plan is to ride to the minaret and walk back.

↪ Self-Guided Tour: Here are some highlights of the parks.

The **Palm Greenhouse,** located near the castle entrance, takes you from Moravia to the tropics (60 Kč, similar hours as castle but open even during winter). Notice the construction above you: one of the oldest examples of a cast-iron roof in Europe. Created in England in the 1830s, this innovation was one of the great technical marvels of the 19th century, enabling the construction of ever more spacious train stations and market halls as its use gradually spread through Europe.

From the greenhouse, it's a five-minute walk to the predator bird show; en route, you'll see a small **archery stand.** If you've ever dreamed of being William Tell, stop here and try your skill on the medieval and modern crossbows. No need to bring an apple or a son on which to set it—they provide the target discs and instruction (60 Kč for five shots, daily in summer, weekends only in spring and fall).

The 45-minute show of live **predator birds** features more than 20 kinds of birds from all over the world. The falcons, merlins, marsh harriers, buzzards, and goshawks demonstrate their hunting skills on simulated rabbits and quails. Some are breathtakingly fast, others comically slow. You can leave whenever you want (35 Kč for short visit, 70 Kč for whole show, pick up English brochure in ticket tent that describes every bird; July-Aug daily at 12:00, 14:00, and 16:30; April-June and Sept-Oct Sat-Sun at 12:00 and 14:00; call 608-100-440 for details).

My favorite part of the park stretches north, from the castle to the minaret. The **minaret** is an impressive bit of Romantic-era garden planning that copies the kind of Muslim-style minarets that flank the Taj Mahal in India. Those who climb its 302 winding steps (40 Kč) are rewarded with a grand view. Locals say that Count Alois Josef I intended to build a new church for the village of Lednice, but no plan seemed quite right to the villagers. Their pickiness finally irritated the count so much that he decided to build a mosque with a minaret instead of a church. The mosque never materialized, but the minaret did (completed in 1804). Since the ground around the Dyje River is made up of moving sands, the 200-foot-tall tower had to be anchored almost as deep underground, on beech and oak pilings. The minaret's architect, Josef Hardtmuth, was a versatile genius. The most successful of his patents was the idea of mixing graphite and mud and coating it with wood. The pencil factory he founded (which bears his name) is still one of the largest in Europe.

The four Arabic inscriptions on the sides of the minaret roughly translate: "There is no God except God, and Muhammad is his prophet. The world betrayed its people. Do not forsake your worldly possessions. There is no difference between wealth and renunciation. True happiness can be reached only in the world beyond. Only through industry and hard work can you reach well-being in this world. When fate stands against you, all plans lose meaning; indeed, without the help of fate, man does not reach redemption." Whoever utters the contents of the first inscription aloud is technically considered a Muslim.

Valtice Castle

While not as appealing as Lednice Castle, this winter residence of the Lichtenstein family is home to the Wine Salon of the Czech Republic, enormous castle cellars, and an extensive herb garden.

The **Wine Salon of the Czech Republic** (enter through the basement of the main castle entrance) exhibits and sells the best 100 Czech wines—selected annually in a vote by wine experts. The 1.5-hour wine tasting lets you make your own selections from featured wines (335 Kč; June-Sept Mon and Wed-Thu 9:30-17:00, Fri-Sun 10:30-17:00, closed Tue; Oct-Jan and March-May similar hours except closed Sun; closed Feb; tel. 519-352-072, www.salonvin.cz).

The 15th- and 17th-century **castle cellars** are rented by the leading local wine producer—Vino Chateau Valtice. Tours here include a look at the vats and tastes of three wines (60 Kč, July-Aug daily 10:00-18:00, May-June and Sept Sat-Sun only, closed Oct-April, enter to left of castle entrance, call ahead for tours in English, tel. 519-361-314, www.vsvaltice.cz).

The castle's **Tiree Chmelar Herb Garden** was founded by an American couple with Czech roots; it was designed by students at the Mendel University in Lednice (60 Kč; July-Aug daily 10:00-18:00; May-June and Sept Tue-Fri 16:00-18:00, Sat-Sun 10:00-18:00, closed Mon; closed Oct-April; enter to left of castle entrance, mobile 776-251-058, www.bylinkovazahrada-valtice.cz).

Valtice Underground (Valtické podzemí)

This complex is a unique labyrinth of interconnected cellars that has been restored and is now run by the Chateau Lednice winery. It's a great spot for dinner or wine-tasting. To get there, follow the red-marked trail from the main square along Růžová and then turn right onto Vinařská.

Cost and Hours: Cost varies with tour, May-Sept Tue-Fri 17:00-22:00, Sat 10:00-22:00, Sun 10:00-17:00, closed Mon; longer hours July-Aug; closed Mon-Thu and shorter weekend hours in April and Oct; closed Nov-March, mobile 724-331-563, www. valtickepodzemi.cz.

▲Museum of the Iron Curtain (Muzeum Železné Opony)

Near the border with Austria is a stark reminder of the Cold War. This museum exhibits uniforms, guns, and old photographs in the rooms of a former border-crossing station. You'll see the guards' quarters, a detention cell, and a piece of the barbed-wire fence that once divided Czechoslovakia and Austria. One room documents various imaginative attempts at illegal crossings, and a sober memorial lists the names and dates of those who were killed during their unsuccessful attempts. Your visit ends with a chilling 1980s propaganda film about the work of hunting down a "trespasser" *(narušitel)*. The museum's motto is "Freedom is the right to hit the road."

Cost and Hours: 70 Kč; July-Aug daily 10:00-17:00; April-June and Sept-Oct Fri-Sun 10:00-17:00, closed Mon-Thu; closed Nov-March; to arrange a visit outside normal hours or a guided tour call 519-340-130 or 608-968-388, Hraniční přechod 483, www.muzeumopony.cz.

Sleeping in Valtice

$$ Chateau La Veneria has six meticulous rooms, lavishly renovated with a woman's touch, in the former residence of the castle's chief groundskeeper. Breakfast is served in a gorgeous, secluded garden with a small waterfall; from here you have direct access to the castle parks. One could not find a better fit for visiting the opulent Lednice-Valtice complex (Db-1,550-1,950 Kč, in summer and on weekends reserve two months ahead, walk to the far end of the main square and then continue 200 yards along Růžová before turning left, K. Venerii 82, mobile 737-684-308, www.valtice-ubytovani-zamecek.cz, ivanabenadova@tiscali.cz).

$$ Penzion Prinz has nine spotless, air-conditioned rooms in the very center of town, run by two hospitable families who won the "Best Czech Pension" award in 2010 (Sb-920 Kč, Db-1,600 Kč, on the corner of the main square at Náměstí Svobody 1111, mobile 602-155-803, www.penzion-valtice.cz, prinz@penzion-valtice.cz).

MIKULOV WINE REGION

Lednice and Valtice Connections

Consider taking the bus to Lednice, walking through the gardens to Valtice (a level four-mile stroll), and then taking the train from there. For bus and train schedules, see www.idos.cz.

From Lednice to: Mikulov (10 buses/day Mon-Fri, 5 buses/day Sat-Sun, 45 minutes), **Vienna** (8 trains/day, 1.75 hours, transfer in Břeclav).

From Valtice to: Mikulov (10 trains/day, 15 minutes), **Prague** (hourly trains, 4 hours, 1 transfer), **Olomouc** (3 trains/day, 2.5-4 hours, several transfers).

CZECH HISTORY

The Czechs have always been at a crossroads of Europe—between the Slavic and Germanic worlds, between Catholicism and Protestantism, and between Cold War East and West. As if having foreseen all of this, the mythical founder of Prague—the beautiful princess Libuše—named her city "Praha" (meaning "threshold" in Czech). Despite these strong external influences, the Czechs have retained their distinct culture...and a dark, ironic sense of humor to keep them laughing through it all.

Charles IV and the Middle Ages

Prague's castle put Bohemia on the map in the ninth century. About a century later, the region was incorporated into the Ger-

man Holy Roman Empire. Within two hundred years, Prague was one of Europe's largest and most highly cultured cities.

The 14th century was Prague's Golden Age, when Holy Roman Emperor Charles IV (1316-1378) ruled. Born to a Luxemburger nobleman and a Czech princess, Charles IV was a dynamic man on the cusp of the Renaissance. He spoke five languages, counted Petrarch as a friend, imported French architects to make Prague a grand capital, founded the first university north of the Alps, and invigorated the Czech national spirit. (He popularized the legend of the good king Wenceslas to give his people a near-mythical, King Arthur-type cultural standard-bearer.) Much of Prague's history and architecture (including the famous Charles Bridge, Charles University, and St. Vitus Cathedral) can be traced

Typical Church Architecture

History comes to life when you visit a centuries-old church. Even if you wouldn't know your apse from a hole in the ground, learning a few simple terms will enrich your experience. Note that not every church has every feature, and a "cathedral" isn't a type of church architecture, but rather a designation for a church that's a governing center for a local bishop.

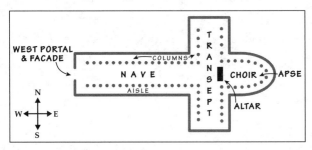

Aisles: The long, generally low-ceilinged arcades that flank the nave.

Altar: The raised area with a ceremonial table (often adorned with candles or a crucifix), where the priest prepares and serves the bread and wine for Communion.

Apse: The space beyond the altar, generally bordered with small chapels.

Barrel Vault: A continuous round-arched ceiling that resembles an extended upside-down U.

Choir: A cozy area, often screened off, located within the church nave and near the high altar, where services are sung in a more intimate setting.

Cloister: Covered hallways bordering a (usually square-shaped) open-air courtyard, traditionally where monks and nuns got fresh air.

Facade: The exterior surface of the church's main (west) entrance, viewable from outside and generally highly decorated.

Groin Vault: An arched ceiling formed where two equal barrel vaults meet at right angles. Less common usage: term for a medieval jock strap.

Narthex: The area (portico or foyer) between the main entry and the nave.

Nave: The long, central section of the church (running west to east, from the entrance to the altar) where the congregation sits or stands through the service.

Transept: In a traditional cross-shaped floor plan, the transept is one of the two parts forming the "arms" of the cross. The transepts run north-south, perpendicularly crossing the east-west nave.

West Portal: The main entry to the church (on the west end, opposite the main altar).

to this man's rule. Under Charles IV, the Czech people gained esteem among Europeans.

Jan Hus and Religious Wars

Jan Hus (c. 1370-1415) was a local preacher and professor who got in trouble with the Vatican a hundred years before Martin Luther. Like Luther, Hus preached in the people's language rather than in Latin. To add insult to injury, he complained about Church corruption. Tried for heresy and burned in 1415, Hus became both a religious and a national hero. While each age has defined Hus to its liking, the way he challenged authority while staying true to his beliefs has long inspired and rallied the Czech people. (For more on Hus, see page 62.)

Inspired by Hus' reformist ideas, the Czechs rebelled against both the Roman Catholic Church and German political control. This burst of independent thought led to a period of religious wars—and ultimately the loss of autonomy to Vienna. Ruled by the Habsburgs of Austria, Prague stagnated—except during the rule of King Rudolf II (1552-1612), a Holy Roman Emperor. With Rudolf living in Prague, the city again emerged as a cultural and intellectual center. Astronomers Johannes Kepler and Tycho Brahe flourished, as did other scientists, and much of the inspiration for Prague's great art can be attributed to the king's patronage.

Not long after this period, Prague entered one of its darker spells. The Thirty Years' War (1618-1648) began in Prague when Czech Protestant nobles, wanting religious and political autonomy, tossed two Catholic Habsburg officials out the window of the castle. (This was one of Prague's many defenestrations—a uniquely Czech solution to political discord, in which offending politicians were literally thrown out the window.) The Czech Estates Uprising lasted two years, ending in a crushing defeat of the Czech army in the Battle of White Mountain (1620), which marked the end of Czech freedom. Twenty-seven leaders of the uprising were executed (today commemorated by crosses on Prague's Old Town Square), most of the old Czech nobility was dispossessed, and Protestants had to convert to Catholicism or leave the country. Often called "the first world war" because it engulfed so many nations, the Thirty Years' War was particularly tough on Prague. During this period, its population dropped from 60,000 to 25,000. The result of this war was 300 years of Habsburg rule from afar, as Prague became a German-speaking backwater of Vienna.

Czech National Revival

The end of Prague as a "German" city came gradually. As the Industrial Revolution attracted Czech farmers and peasants to the cities, the demographics of the Czech population centers began

Typical Castle Architecture

Castles were fortified residences for medieval nobles. Castles come in all shapes and sizes, but knowing a few general terms will help you understand them.

The Keep (or Donjon): A high, strong stone tower in the center of the castle complex that was the lord's home and refuge of last resort.

Great Hall: The largest room in the castle, serving as throne room, conference center, and dining hall.

The Yard (or Bailey or Ward): An open courtyard inside the castle walls.

Loopholes: Narrow slits in the walls (also called embrasures, arrow slits, or arrow loops) through which soldiers could shoot arrows at the enemy.

Towers: Tall structures serving as lookouts, chapels, living quarters, or the dungeon. Towers could be square or round, with either crenellated tops or conical roofs.

Turret: A small lookout tower projecting up from the top of the wall.

Moat: A ditch encircling the wall, often filled with water.

Wall Walk (or Allure): A pathway atop the wall where guards could patrol and where soldiers stood to fire at the enemy.

Parapet: Outer railing of the wall walk.

Crenellation: A gap-toothed pattern of stones atop the parapet.

Hoardings (or Gallery or Brattice): Wooden huts built onto the upper parts of the stone walls. They served as watch towers, living quarters, and fighting platforms.

Machicolation: A stone ledge jutting out from the wall, fitted with

to shift. Between 1800 and 1900, though it remained part of the Habsburg Empire, Prague went from being an essentially German town to a predominantly Czech one. As in the rest of Europe, the 19th century was a time of great nationalism, when the age of divine kings and ruling families came to a fitful end. The Czech spirit was stirred by the completion of Prague's St. Vitus Cathedral, the symphonies of Antonín Dvořák, and the operas of Bedřich Smetana, which were performed in the new National Theater.

After the Habsburgs' Austro-Hungarian Empire suffered defeat in World War I, their vast holdings broke apart and became independent countries. Among these was a union of Bohemia, Moravia, and Slovakia, the brainchild of a clever politician named Tomáš Garrigue Masaryk (see sidebar). The new nation, Czechoslovakia, was proclaimed in 1918, with Prague as its capital.

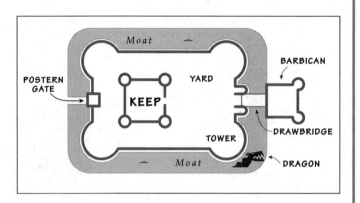

holes in the bottom. If the enemy was scaling the walls, soldiers could drop rocks or boiling oil down through the holes
and onto the enemy below.

Barbican: A fortified gatehouse, sometimes a stand-alone building located outside the main walls.

Drawbridge: A bridge that could be raised or lowered, using
counterweights or a chain-and-winch system.

Portcullis: A heavy iron grille that could be lowered across the
entrance.

Postern Gate: A small, unfortified side or rear entrance used during peacetime. In wartime, it could become a "sally-port"
used to launch surprise attacks, or as an escape route.

CZECH HISTORY

Troubled 20th Century

Independence lasted only 20 years. In the notorious Munich
Agreement of September 1938—much to the dismay of the Czechs
and Slovaks—Great Britain and France peacefully ceded to Hitler
the so-called Sudetenland (a fringe around the edge of Bohemia,
populated mainly by people of German descent; see sidebar on
page 270). It wasn't long before Hitler seized the rest of Czechoslovakia...and the Holocaust began.

For centuries, Prague's cultural makeup had consisted of a rich
mix of Czech, German, and Jewish people—historically, they were
almost evenly divided. But only 5 percent of the Jewish population
survived the Holocaust. And after World War II ended, the three
million people of Germanic descent who lived in Czechoslovakia
were pushed into Germany. Their forced resettlement—which led
to the deaths of untold numbers of Germans—was the idea, among
others, of Czechoslovak President Edvard Beneš, who had ruled
from exile in London throughout the war (see page 234). As a re-

Tomáš Garrigue Masaryk (1850-1937)

Tomáš Masaryk was the George Washington of Czechoslovakia. He founded the first democracy in Eastern Europe at the end of World War I, uniting the Czechs and the Slovaks to create Czechoslovakia. Like Václav Havel 70 years later, Masaryk was a politician whose vision extended far beyond the mountains enclosing the Bohemian basin.

Masaryk was born into a poor servant family in southern Moravia. After finishing high school, the village boy set off to attend university in Vienna. Masaryk earned his Ph.D. in sociology just in time for the opening of the Czech-language university in Prague. By then, he was married to an American music student named Charlotta Garrigue, who came from a prominent New York family. (The progressive Tomáš actually took her family name as part of his own.) Charlotta opened the doors of America's high society to Masaryk. Among the American friends he made was a young Princeton professor named Woodrow Wilson.

Masaryk was greatly impressed with America, and his admiration for its democratic system became the core of his gradually evolving political creed. He traveled the world and went to Vienna to serve in the parliament. By the time World War I broke out, in 1914, Masaryk was 64 years old and—his friends thought—ready

sult of both events (the Holocaust and the expulsion of Germans), today's Czech Republic is largely homogenous—about 95 percent Czechs.

Although Prague escaped the bombs of World War II, it went directly from the Nazi frying pan into the communist fire. A local uprising freed the city from the Nazis on May 8, 1945, but the Soviets "liberated" them on May 9.

The early communist era (1948-1968) was a mixture of misguided zeal, Stalinist repressions, and attempts to wed socialism with democracy. The "Prague Spring" period—initiated by a young generation of reform-minded communists in 1968—came to an abrupt halt under the treads of Soviet tanks.

The uprising's charismatic leader, Alexander Dubček, was exiled (and made a backwoods forest ranger), and the years following the unsuccessful revolt were particularly disheartening. In the late 1980s, the communists began constructing Prague's huge Žižkov TV tower (now the city's tallest structure)—not only to broadcast Czech TV transmissions, but also to jam Western signals. The

for retirement. But while most other Czech politicians stayed in Prague and supported the Habsburg Empire, Masaryk went abroad in protest and formed a highly original plan: to create an independent, democratic republic of Czechs and Slovaks. Masaryk and his supporters recruited an army of 100,000 Czech and Slovak soldiers who were willing to fight with the Allies against the Habsburgs, establishing a strong case to put on his friend Woodrow Wilson's Oval Office desk.

On the morning of October 28, 1918, news of the unofficial capitulation of the Habsburgs reached Prague. Local supporters of Masaryk's idea quickly took control of the city and proclaimed the free republic. As the people of Prague tore down double-headed eagles (a symbol of the Habsburgs), the country of Czechoslovakia was born.

On November 11, 1918, four years after he had left the country as a political unknown, Masaryk arrived in Prague as the greatest Czech hero since the revolutionary priest Jan Hus. The dignified old man rode through the masses of cheering Czechs on a white horse. He told the jubilant crowd, "Now go home—the work has only started." Throughout the 1920s and 1930s, Masaryk was Europe's most vocal defender of democratic ideals against the rising tide of totalitarian ideologies.

In 2001, the US government honored Masaryk's dedication to democracy by erecting a monument to him in Washington, DC. He is one of only three foreign leaders (along with Gandhi and Churchill) to have a statue in the American capital.

CZECH HISTORY

Metro, built at about the same time, was intended for mass transit, but was also designed to be a giant fallout shelter for protection against capitalist bombs.

But the Soviet empire crumbled. Czechoslovakia regained its freedom in the student- and artist-powered 1989 "Velvet Revolution" (so called because there were no casualties...or even broken windows); for more on the Velvet Revolution, see page 97. Václav Havel, a writer who had been imprisoned by the communist regime, became Czechoslovakia's first post-communist president.

"It's Not You, It's Me": The Velvet Divorce

In the autumn of 1989, hundreds of thousands of Czechs and Slovaks streamed into Prague to demonstrate on Wenceslas Square. Their "Velvet Revolution" succeeded, and Czechoslovakia's communist regime peacefully excused itself. But that was only the first step. In that age of new possibility, the two peoples of Czechoslovakia began to wonder if, in fact, they belonged together.

Notable Czechs

These prominent historical figures are listed in chronological order.

St. Wenceslas (907-935): Bohemian duke who allied the Czechs with the Holy Roman Empire. He went on to become the Czech Republic's patron saint, and it is he who is memorialized as a "good king" in the Christmas carol. For more on Wenceslas, see page 87.

Jan Hus (c. 1370-1415): Proto-Protestant Reformer who was burned at the stake (see page 317).

John Amos Comenius (Jan Amos Komenský in Czech, 1592-1670): "Teacher of Nations" and Protestant exile, whose ideas paved the way for modern education (see page 284).

Antonín Dvořák (1841-1904): Inspired by a trip to America, he composed his New World Symphony. For more on Czech composers, see page 184.

Tomáš Garrigue Masaryk (1850-1937): Sociology professor, writer, politician, and spiritual reformer. He was idolized during his lifetime as the "dearest father" of the Czechoslovak democracy (see sidebar in this chapter).

Jára Cimrman (c. 1853-1914): Illustrious but fictional inventor, explorer, philosopher, and all-around genius. Despite being overwhelmingly voted the "Greatest Czech of All Time" in a nationwide poll, he was not awarded the title (see page 108).

Alfons Mucha (1860-1939): You might recognize his turn-of-the-century Art Nouveau posters of pretty girls entwined in vines. Visit his museum in Prague, marvel at his stained-glass window in St. Vitus Cathedral, and view his magnum opus, the *Slav Epic* (see page 132).

Franz Kafka (1883-1924): While working for a Prague insurance firm, he wrote (in German) *The Metamorphosis* (man awakens as a cockroach), *The Trial*, *The Castle*, and other psychologically haunting stories and novels.

Milan Kundera (1929-): Wrote the novel *The Unbearable Lightness of Being* (which became a film), among others. For more on Czech authors and filmmakers, see page 351.

Václav Havel (1936-2011): The country's first post-Soviet president, also well-known as a playwright and philosopher (see page 352).

Madeleine Albright (1937-): Born in Prague as Marie Jana Korbelová, Albright was the first woman to serve as US Secretary of State, from 1997-2001, under Bill Clinton.

Martina Navrátilová (1956-): Tennis star of the 1980s. For more on Czech sports, see page 188.

Czech Borders 1914–Today

POLAND

BELARUS

NETH.

GERMANY

SLOVAKIA

Prague

UKRAINE

F
R
A
N
C
E

Vienna

SWITZ. AUSTRIA HUNGARY

SLOVENIA

CROATIA

SERBIA

ROMANIA

BOSNIA
HERZ.

ITALY

BULGARIA

GREECE

TURKEY

DCH

Habsburg Empire in 1914

Czechoslovakia (1918–1993)

Current Czech Republic Border

Current National Borders

Ever since they joined with the Czechs in 1918, the Slovaks felt they were ruled from Prague (unmistakably the political, economic, and cultural center of the country), rather than from their own capital. And the Czechs, for their part, resented the financial burden of carrying their poorer neighbors to the east. In the post-communist world, the Czechs found themselves with a 10 percent unemployment rate...compared with 20 or 30 percent unemployment in the Slovak lands. In this new world of flux and freedom, long-standing tensions came to a head.

The dissolution of Czechoslovakia began over a hyphen, as the Slovaks wanted to rename the country Czecho-Slovakia. Ideally, this symbolic move would come with a redistribution of powers: two capitals and two UN reps, but one national bank and a single

Czechs After Communism

Czech survivors of communist prisons (honored by the Monument to Victims of Communism; see page 110) feel a sense of injustice. Following World War II, many of the Czechs who collaborated with the Nazis were brought to justice. In contrast, after communism fell in 1989, few individuals responsible for the crimes committed by the communist regime faced retribution. In fact, when the country's industrial infrastructure was privatized in the early 1990s, former Communist Party big shots used their connections to take control of some of the country's new capitalist enterprises. Many of the old Party leaders morphed into the bosses of the new Czech economy.

The Czech Republic was the first post-communist country to ban informants of the secret police from public office (a policy called *lustrace,* or "lustration"). They were also the first to outlaw the propagation of communism (and other totalitarian ideologies). Even so, efforts to enforce this legislation have been less than successful. Many former agents have destroyed evidence, while others contend that they were not aware of their own cooperation.

In the early 1990s, stalwart members of the Communist Party fended off attempts at reform and preserved a fossil of an institution that still draws about 15 percent of votes in national elections. Today's "vanguards of progress" no longer preach class warfare, but instead they blend empty rhetoric ("We have a solution") with vague finger-pointing ("Who took away our hard-won securities?"). To become more palatable to a wider public and to

currency. The Slovaks were also less enthusiastic about abandoning the communist society altogether, since the Soviet regime had left them with a heavily industrialized economy that depended on a socialist element for survival.

Initially, many Czechs couldn't understand the Slovaks' demands. The first post-communist president of Czechoslovakia, Czech Václav Havel, made matters worse when he took a rare trip to the Slovak half of his country in 1990. In a fit of terrible judgment, Havel boldly promised he'd close the ugly, polluting Soviet factories in Slovakia, seemingly oblivious to the fact that many Slovaks still depended on these factories for survival. Havel left in disgrace and visited the Slovak lands only twice more in the next two and a half years.

In June of 1992, the Slovak nationalist candidate Vladimír Mečiar fared surprisingly well in the elections—suggesting that the Slovaks were serious about secession. The politicians plowed ahead, getting serious about the split in September of 1992. The transition took only three months from start to finish.

hide their Stalinist roots, they altered their symbol, exchanging the unsavory red star for a far more innocuous pair of cherries (allegedly to recall the Paris Commune of 1871).

Their nostalgic-about-the-good-old-times message registers mainly with Czechs who find it difficult to adapt to a more complex and risk-prone society. Many of them (including members of the younger generation) find communism's ordered worldview—familiar since childhood—to be the most easily comprehensible. Today, they read the newspapers for reassurance that capitalism is responsible for many social ills, that the European Union is German imperialism in disguise, and—in some extreme cases—that China is pairing up with Russia to defend humanity.

The idealistic Velvet Revolutionaries of 1989 thought that communism would naturally disappear over time—but they failed to realize how deeply the years of authoritarian rule had affected everyone, even its opponents. Today, Communist Party members are routinely re-elected into Parliament by older voters who find it difficult to keep up with changing times and look nostalgically to the past, and by young voters who didn't experience communism but vote Communist as a form of protest. Visitors surprised by the communist presence in a free Czech Republic can take it as a reminder that difficult experiences, individual as much as collective ones, take generations to process—especially if kept buried inside.

CZECH HISTORY

The people of Czechoslovakia never actually voted on the separation; in fact, public opinion polls in both regions were two-thirds *against* the split. This makes Slovakia quite possibly the only country in the history of the world to gain independence...even though its citizens didn't want it.

The Velvet Divorce became official on January 1, 1993, and each country ended up with its own capital, currency, and head of state. The Slovaks let loose a yelp of excitement, and the Czechs emitted a sigh of relief. For most the divorce dissolved tensions, and a decade and a half later, Czechs and Slovaks still feel closer to each other than to any other nationality.

Start of 21st Century to the Present

In recent times, the Czech Republic's most significant turning points occurred on May 1, 2004, when the country joined the European Union (see sidebar on page 130); and on January 1, 2008, when it entered the Schengen Agreement, effectively erasing its borders for the purposes of travel.

Václav Havel ended his second (and, constitutionally, last) five-year term in 2003, and died in 2011. While he's fondly remembered by Czechs as a great thinker, writer, and fearless leader of the opposition movement during the communist days, many consider him to have been less successful as a president. Some believe that the split of Czechoslovakia was partly caused by Havel's initial insensitivity to Slovak demands. For more on Havel, see page 352.

The next president, Václav Klaus, was the pragmatic author of the economic reforms in the 1990s. Klaus' surprising win in the 2003 election symbolized a change from revolutionary times, when philosophers became kings, to modern humdrum politics, when offices are gained by bargaining with the opposition (Communist votes in the Parliament were the decisive factor in Klaus' election).

In 2008, Klaus was narrowly re-elected by the Parliament for a second term, despite revelations of widespread corruption in the privatizing business sector. The scandal became the defining issue of the election, with Klaus and his Conservative Party denying responsibility for (and even the existence of) the abuses. The Greens and the Social Democrats had chosen as their candidate University of Michigan economic professor Jan Švejnar, the most outspoken critic of Klaus' reforms in the 1990s. And though public support was evenly divided between the two candidates, behind-the-scenes deals in the Parliament allowed the ruling conservatives to maintain their majority and keep Klaus in power. Public outrage at Klaus' controversial 2008 re-election eventually led to a change in the country's constitution, which allowed for the first election of a president directly by the people (rather than by the Parliament) in January of 2013.

The winner of this historic presidential election was Miloš Zeman, the other political heavyweight—apart from Klaus—of the 1990s. President Zeman, a populist intent on increasing his share of power, quickly began dismantling an unpopular administration whose main goal was to introduce fiscal austerity measures to reduce the country's growing debt—which set the stage for early parliamentary elections in late 2013.

In these elections the voters, disillusioned with the perceived corruption of the Social Democrats and the Conservatives, rejected the political status quo. Two newly emerged political entities, each formed around a successful businessman, gained almost a third of the votes. One of these new protest parties, ANO, eventually formed a ruling coalition with the Social and Christian Democrats, fueling hopes for more effective government and less corruption. But some say corruption will shrink

The Wisdom of Babička Míla ("Granny Míla")

Co-author Honza Vihan's grandmother, Bohumila Vihanová (February 17, 1907-August 18, 2008), was born in the Austro-Hungarian town of Prag (today's Praha), which was then ruled from Vienna. In the 101 years of her life, she lived under seven different governments: Habsburgs, interwar Czechoslovakia, Nazis, communists, post-communist Czechoslovakia, the Czech Republic, and the European Union. Wise beyond even her many years, she counseled family and visitors alike as follows:

- "I liked each change, because it always brought something new."
- "You must be able to take the best from whatever comes."
- "Nothing good that you do is ever lost; it always stays somewhere and surfaces when needed."
- "When the communists took over, that was bad—really bad. But then, my mother used to say, 'There's no point in crying over spilled milk. There's enough water in it already.' So I tried to get by, and somehow we managed to live through it all."
- "The main thing is to keep your inner balance."
- "You should never take yourself too seriously."
- "Let everyone believe whatever they want, as long as they behave accordingly."
- "Money will always be here. We won't."
- "Parents should never mix in their children's lives."
- "Good health and happy mind!"

only because business interests will now have direct access to the government.

While not without its problems, the Czech Republic is still enjoying a growing economy and a strong democracy, and Prague is one of the most popular tourist destinations in Europe.

APPENDIX

Contents

Tourist Information

The Czech national tourist office **in the US** is a wealth of information (tel. 212/288-0830, www.czechtourism.com, newyork@czechtourism.com). Their website includes a number of planning tools, descriptions of tourist regions and popular sights, and downloadable brochures and maps.

In the Czech Republic, your best first stop in every town is generally the tourist information office—abbreviated **TI** in this book. TIs are good places to get a city map and information on public transit (including bus and train schedules), walking tours, special events, and nightlife. Many TIs have information on the entire country or at least the region, so try to pick up maps for destinations you'll be visiting later in your trip. If you're arriving in town after the TI closes, call ahead with your questions or pick up a map in a neighboring town. Almost all the TIs in the Czech Republic are run by local governments, which means their information isn't colored by a drive for profit.

While TIs are eager to book you a room, use their room-finding service only as a last resort. They are unable to give hard opinions on the relative value of one place over another. The accommodations stakes are too high to go potluck through the TI. Even if there's no "fee," you'll save yourself and your host money by going direct with the listings in this book.

Communicating

Hurdling the Language Barrier

The language barrier in the Czech Republic is no bigger than in Western Europe. In fact, I find that it's even easier to communicate in Český Krumlov than it is in Madrid. Immediately after the Iron Curtain fell in 1989, English speakers were rare. But today, you'll find that most people in the tourist industry—and just about all young people—speak English well.

Of course, not everyone speaks English. You'll run into the most substantial language barriers in situations when you need to deal with a clerk or service person over age 40 (train station and post-office staff, maids, museum guards, bakers, and so on). Be reasonable in your expectations. Czech post-office clerks and museum ticket-sellers are every bit as friendly, cheery, and multilingual as ours are in the US. Luckily, it's relatively easy to get your point across. I've often bought a train ticket simply by writing out the name of my destination; the time I want to travel (using the 24-hour clock); and, if necessary, the date I want to leave (day first, then month, then year). Here's an example of what I'd show a ticket seller at a train station: "Olomouc - 17:30 - 15.7.2014."

Czech is a Slavic language closely related to its Polish and Slovak neighbors. Slavic pronunciation can be tricky. In fact, when the first Christian missionaries, Cyril and Methodius, came to Eastern Europe a millennium ago, they invented a whole new alphabet to represent these strange Slavic sounds. Their Cyrillic alphabet is still used today in the eastern Slavic countries (such as Serbia and Russia).

Fortunately, the Czechs long ago converted to the same Roman alphabet we use, but they've added lots of different diacritics—little markings below and above letters—to represent a wide range of sounds. An acute accent *(á, é, í, ó, ú, ý)* means you linger on that vowel;

it does not indicate stress, which invariably falls on the first syllable. The letter *c* always sounds like "ts" (as in "cats"). The little accent *(háček)* above the *č, š,* or *ž* makes it sound like "ch," "sh", or "zh" (as in "leisure"), respectively. A *háček* over *ě* makes it sound like "yeh."

Czech has one sound that occurs in no other language: *ř* (as in "Dvořák"), which sounds like a cross between a rolled "r" and "zh." Another unusual sound is *ň,* which is pronounced "ny" (as in "canyon"). These sounds are notoriously difficult for foreigners to duplicate; it's easiest just to replace them with simple "r" and "n" sounds.

Study the Czech survival phrases on page 359, and give it your best shot. The locals will appreciate your efforts. When navigating a town, these words can be helpful: *město* (MYEHS-toh, town), *náměstí* (NAH-myehs-tee, square), *ulice* (OO-leet-sah, street), *nábřeží* (NAH-bzheh-zhee, embankment road), and *most* (mohst, bridge).

If you speak German, it can come in handy—especially in the south of the country, where the economy depends in part on Austrian tourists from across the border.

Telephones

Smart travelers use the telephone to book or reconfirm rooms, get tourist information, reserve restaurants, confirm tour times, or phone home. This section covers dialing instructions, types of phones, and phone cards (for more in-depth information, see www.ricksteves.com/phoning).

How to Dial

Calling from the US to the Czech Republic, or vice versa, is simple—once you break the code. The European calling chart later in this chapter will walk you through it.

Dialing Domestically Within the Czech Republic

The following instructions apply whether you're dialing from a landline (such as a pay phone or your hotel-room phone) or a Czech mobile phone.

The Czech Republic has a direct-dial phone system (no area codes). To call anywhere within the Czech Republic, just dial the number. For example, the phone number of one of my recommended Prague hotels is 224-812-041. Whether you are calling from a Prague train station or from Český Krumlov, it's the same: just dial 224-812-041. All phone numbers in the Czech Republic are nine digits. If a number starting with 0800 doesn't work, replace the 0800 with 822.

If you're dialing within the Czech Republic using your US

mobile phone, you may need to dial as if it's a domestic call, or you may need to dial as if you're calling from the US (see "Dialing Internationally," next). Try it one way, and if it doesn't work, try it the other way.

Dialing Internationally to or from the Czech Republic
If you want to make an international call, follow these steps:

• Dial the international access code (00 if you're calling from Europe, 011 from the US or Canada). If you're dialing from a mobile phone, you can replace the international access code with +, which works regardless of where you're calling from. (On many mobile phones, you can insert a + by pressing and holding the 0 key.)

• Dial the country code of the country you're calling (420 for the Czech Republic, or 1 for the US or Canada).

• Dial the local number. (For specifics per country, see the European calling chart in this chapter.)

Calling from the US to the Czech Republic: To call the recommended Prague hotel from the US, dial 011 (the US international access code), 420 (the Czech Republic's country code), then 224-812-041.

Calling from any European country to the US: To call my office in Edmonds, Washington, from anywhere in Europe, I dial 00 (Europe's international access code), 1 (US country code), 425 (Edmonds' area code), and 771-8303.

Mobile Phones
Traveling with a mobile phone is handy and practical. There are two basic options: roaming with your own phone (expensive but easy) or buying and using SIM cards with an unlocked phone (a bit more hassle, but potentially much cheaper).

Roaming with Your US Mobile Phone: This pricier option can be worthwhile if you won't be making or receiving many calls, don't want to bother with SIM cards, or want to stay reachable at your US number. Start by calling your mobile-phone service provider to ask whether your phone works in Europe and what the rates are (likely $1.29-1.99 per minute to make or receive calls, and 20-50 cents to send or receive text messages). Tell them to enable international calling on your account, and if you know you'll be making multiple calls, ask your carrier about any global calling deals to lower the per-minute costs. When you land in Europe, turn on your phone and—bingo!—you have service. Because you'll pay for receiving calls and texts, be sure your family knows to call only in an emergency. Note that Verizon and Sprint use a different technology than European providers, so their phones are less likely to work abroad; if yours doesn't, your provider may be able to send you a loaner phone (arrange in advance).

Buying and Using SIM Cards in Europe: If you're comfortable with mobile-phone technology, will be making lots of calls, and want to save some serious money, consider this very affordable alternative: Carry an unlocked mobile phone, and use it with a European SIM card to get much cheaper rates.

Getting an **unlocked phone** may be easier than you think. You may already have an old, unused mobile phone in a drawer somewhere. When you got the phone, it was probably "locked" to work only with one company—but if your contract is now up, your provider may be willing to send you a code to unlock it. Just call and ask. Otherwise, you can simply buy an unlocked phone: Search your favorite online shopping site for an "unlocked quad-band phone" before you go, or wait until you get to Europe and buy one at a mobile-phone shop there. Either way, a basic model costs less than $50.

Once in Europe, buy a **SIM card**—the little chip that inserts into your phone (either under the battery, or in a slot on the side)—to equip the phone with a European number. (Note that smaller "micro-SIM" or "nano-SIM" cards—used in some iPhones—are less widely available.) SIM cards are sold at mobile-phone shops, department-store electronics counters, and some newsstand kiosks for $5-10, and usually include about that much prepaid calling credit (making the card itself virtually free). In most places, buying a SIM card is as easy as buying a pack of gum—and almost as cheap. (In some countries—including Italy, Germany, and Hungary—it can take a bit longer, because you have to show your passport and be registered.) Because SIM cards are prepaid, there's no contract and no commitment (in fact, they expire after just a few months of disuse); I buy one even if I'm in a country for only a few days.

When using a SIM card in its home country, it's free to receive calls and texts, and it's cheap to make calls—domestic calls average 20-30 cents per minute (though toll lines can be substantially more). Rates are higher if you're roaming in another country, but as long as you stay within the European Union, these fees are capped (about 30 cents per minute for making calls or 10 cents per minute for receiving calls). Texting is cheap even if roaming in another country. Particularly inexpensive SIM card brands let you call either within Europe or to the US for less than 10 cents per minute. In the Czech Republic, the major mobile phone companies are O2, T-Mobile, and Vodafone.

When purchasing a SIM card, always ask about fees for domestic and international calls, roaming charges, and how to check

European Calling Chart

Just smile and dial, using this key:
AC = Area Code, LN = Local Number.

European Country	Calling long distance within ...	Calling from the US or Canada to ...	Calling from a European country to ...
Austria	AC + LN	011 + 43 + AC (without initial zero) + LN	00 + 43 + AC (without initial zero) + LN
Belgium	LN	011 + 32 + LN (without initial zero)	00 + 32 + LN (without initial zero)
Bosnia-Herzegovina	AC + LN	011 + 387 + AC (without initial zero) + LN	00 + 387 + AC (without initial zero) + LN
Croatia	AC + LN	011 + 385 + AC (without initial zero) + LN	00 + 385 + AC (without initial zero) + LN
Czech Republic	LN	011 + 420 + LN	00 + 420 + LN
Denmark	LN	011 + 45 + LN	00 + 45 + LN
Estonia	LN	011 + 372 + LN	00 + 372 + LN
Finland	AC + LN	011 + 358 + AC (without initial zero) + LN	999 (or other 900 number) + 358 + AC (without initial zero) + LN
France	LN	011 + 33 + LN (without initial zero)	00 + 33 + LN (without initial zero)
Germany	AC + LN	011 + 49 + AC (without initial zero) + LN	00 + 49 + AC (without initial zero) + LN
Gibraltar	LN	011 + 350 + LN	00 + 350 + LN
Great Britain & N. Ireland	AC + LN	011 + 44 + AC (without initial zero) + LN	00 + 44 + AC (without initial zero) + LN
Greece	LN	011 + 30 + LN	00 + 30 + LN
Hungary	06 + AC + LN	011 + 36 + AC + LN	00 + 36 + AC + LN
Ireland	AC + LN	011 + 353 + AC (without initial zero) + LN	00 + 353 + AC (without initial zero) + LN
Italy	LN	011 + 39 + LN	00 + 39 + LN

APPENDIX

European Country	Calling long distance within ...	Calling from the US or Canada to ...	Calling from a European country to ...
Latvia	LN	011 + 371 + LN	00 + 371 + LN
Montenegro	AC + LN	011 + 382 + AC (without initial zero) + LN	00 + 382 + AC (without initial zero) + LN
Morocco	LN	011 + 212 + LN (without initial zero)	00 + 212 + LN (without initial zero)
Netherlands	AC + LN	011 + 31 + AC (without initial zero) + LN	00 + 31 + AC (without initial zero) + LN
Norway	LN	011 + 47 + LN	00 + 47 + LN
Poland	LN	011 + 48 + LN	00 + 48 + LN
Portugal	LN	011 + 351 + LN	00 + 351 + LN
Russia	8 + AC + LN	011 + 7 + AC + LN	00 + 7 + AC + LN
Slovakia	AC + LN	011 + 421 + AC (without initial zero) + LN	00 + 421 + AC (without initial zero) + LN
Slovenia	AC + LN	011 + 386 + AC (without initial zero) + LN	00 + 386 + AC (without initial zero) + LN
Spain	LN	011 + 34 + LN	00 + 34 + LN
Sweden	AC + LN	011 + 46 + AC (without initial zero) + LN	00 + 46 + AC (without initial zero) + LN
Switzerland	LN	011 + 41 + LN (without initial zero)	00 + 41 + LN (without initial zero)
Turkey	AC (if there's no initial zero, add one) + LN	011 + 90 + AC (without initial zero) + LN	00 + 90 + AC (without initial zero) + LN

APPENDIX

- The instructions above apply whether you're calling to or from a European landline or mobile phone.

- If calling from any mobile phone, you can replace the international access code with "+" (press and hold 0 to insert it).

- The international access code is 011 if you're calling from the US or Canada.

- To call the US or Canada from Europe, dial 00, then 1 (country code for US and Canada), then the area code and number. In short, 00 + 1 + AC + LN = Hi, Mom!

Smartphones and Data Roaming

You can take your smartphone to Europe, using it to make phone calls (sparingly) and send texts, but also to check email, listen to audio tours, and browse the Internet. You may have heard horror stories about people running up outrageous data roaming bills on their smartphones. But if you understand the options, it's easy to avoid these fees and still stay connected. Here's how.

For voice calls and text messaging, smartphones work like any mobile phone (as described under "Roaming with Your US Mobile Phone," earlier). To avoid roaming charges, connect to free Wi-Fi, and use Skype, FaceTime, or other apps to make cheap or free calls (see "Calling over the Internet," below).

To get online with your phone, you have two options: Wi-Fi and mobile data. Because free Wi-Fi hotspots are generally easy to find in Europe (at most hotels, many cafés, and even some public spaces), the cheap solution is to use Wi-Fi wherever possible.

But what if you just can't get to a hotspot? Fortunately, most providers offer an affordable, basic data-roaming package for Europe: $25 or $30 buys you about 100 megabytes—enough to view 100 websites or send/receive 1,000 text emails. If you don't buy a data-roaming plan in advance, but use data in Europe anyway, you'll pay staggeringly high rates—about $20 per megabyte, or about 80 times what you'd pay with a plan.

While a data-roaming package is handy, your allotted megabytes can go quickly—especially if you stream videos or music. To

your credit balance and buy more time. If text or voice prompts are in another language, ask the clerk whether they can be switched to English.

It's also possible to buy an **inexpensive mobile phone in Europe** that already comes with a SIM card. While these phones are generally locked to work with just one provider (and therefore can't be reused on future trips), they may be less hassle than buying an unlocked phone and a SIM card separately.

Mobile-Phone Calling Apps: If you have a smartphone, you can use it to make free or cheap calls in Europe by using a calling app such as Skype or FaceTime when you're on Wi-Fi; for details, see the next section.

Calling over the Internet

Some things that seem too good to be true...actually are true. If you're traveling with a smartphone, tablet, or laptop, you can make free calls over the Internet to another wireless device, anywhere in the world, for free. (Or you can pay a few cents to call from your computer or smartphone to a telephone.) The major providers are

keep a cap on usage and avoid incurring overage charges, you can manually turn off data roaming on your phone whenever you're not actively using it. (To turn off data and voice roaming, look in your phone's menu—try checking under "Cellular" or "Network," or ask your mobile-phone provider how to do it.) As you travel through Europe, you'll jump from hotspot to hotspot. But if you need to get online at a time when you can't easily access Wi-Fi—for example, to download driving directions when you're on the road to your next hotel—you can turn on data roaming just long enough for that task, then turn it off again. You can also limit how much data your phone uses by switching your email settings from "push" to "fetch" (you choose when to download messages rather than having them automatically "pushed" to your device). By carefully budgeting data this way, 100 megabytes can last a long time.

If you want to use your smartphone exclusively on Wi-Fi—and not worry about either voice or data charges—simply turn off both voice and data roaming (or put your phone in "Airplane Mode" and then turn your Wi-Fi back on). If you're on a long trip, are positive you won't be using your phone for voice or data roaming, and want to save some money, ask your provider about suspending those services altogether while you're gone.

By sticking with Wi-Fi wherever possible and budgeting your use of data, you can easily and affordably stay connected while you travel.

Skype, Google Talk, and (on Apple devices) FaceTime. You can get online at a Wi-Fi hotspot and use these apps to make calls without ringing up expensive roaming charges (though call quality can be spotty on slow connections). You can make Internet calls even if you're traveling without your own mobile device: Many European Internet cafés have Skype, as well as microphones and webcams, on their terminals—just log on and chat away.

Landline Telephones

Just like Americans, these days most Europeans make the majority of their calls on mobile phones. But you'll still encounter landlines in hotel rooms and at pay phones.

Hotel-Room Phones: Calling from your hotel room can be great for local calls and for international calls if you have an international phone card (described later). Otherwise, hotel-room phones can be an almost criminal rip-off for long-distance or international calls. Many hotels charge a fee for local and sometimes even "toll-free" numbers—always ask for the rates before you dial.

Public Pay Phones: While pay phones are common in the

Czech Republic, coin-operated phones are virtually extinct. To make calls from public phones, you'll need a prepaid phone card, described next.

Telephone Cards

There are two types of phone cards: insertable (for pay phones) and international (cheap for overseas calls and usable from any type of phone). A phone card works only in the country where you bought it, so if you have a live card at the end of your trip, give it to another traveler to use—most cards expire three to six months after the first use.

Insertable Phone Cards: This type of card can be used only at pay phones and can be purchased at any post office. It's handy and affordable for domestic calls, but more expensive for international calls. Simply take the phone off the hook, insert the prepaid card, wait for a dial tone, and dial away. The price of the call (local or international) is automatically deducted while you talk. Dialing 970 before the international access code (970-00-1 for calls to the US) saves you about half the price on international calls (20 cents per minute to the US or other EU countries), but is still more expensive than an international phone card.

International Phone Cards: With these cards, phone calls from the Czech Republic to the US can cost less than a nickel a minute. The cards can also be used to make local calls, and they work from any type of phone, including your hotel-room phone or a mobile phone with a European SIM card. To use the card, dial a local or toll-free access number, then enter your scratch-to-reveal PIN code. Some hotels block their phones from accepting these access numbers. (Ask your hotelier about access and rates before you call.)

A widely available brand in the Czech Republic is **Smartcall** (look for black-and-orange ads), sold at newsstands, exchange bureaus, Internet cafés, hostels, souvenir shops, and mini-marts in tourist towns such as Prague or Český Krumlov (they're not available in less touristy towns, such as Olomouc). The cards come in denominations of 150 Kč, 300 Kč, 500 Kč, and 1,000 Kč. Buy a lower denomination in case the card is a dud. Some shops also sell cardless codes, printed right on the receipt.

US calling cards, such as the ones offered by AT&T, Verizon, or Sprint, are a rotten value, and are being phased out. Try any of the options outlined earlier.

Useful Phone Numbers
Emergency Needs
Police: Tel. 158
Medical or Other Emergency: Tel. 112
Ambulance: Tel. 155

Embassies
US Embassy: Tel. 257-022-000 (24-hour line), emergency passport services Mon-Fri 8:00-11:30, in Prague's Little Quarter below the castle at Tržiště 15, http://prague.usembassy.gov, ACSPrg@state.gov
Canadian Embassy: Tel. 272-101-800, consular services Mon-Fri 8:30-12:30, north of the Castle Quarter at Ve Struhách 95/2, www.canadainternational.gc.ca/czech-tcheque, prgue-cs@international.gc.ca

Travel Advisories
US Department of State: Tel. 888-407-4747, from outside US tel. 1-202-501-4444, www.travel.state.gov
Canadian Department of Foreign Affairs: Canadian tel. 800-387-3124, from outside Canada tel. 1-613-996-8885, www.travel.gc.ca
US Centers for Disease Control and Prevention: Tel. 800-CDC-INFO (800-232-4636), www.cdc.gov/travel

Directory Assistance
Directory Assistance within the Czech Republic: Tel. 1188 (12-27 Kč/minute)
Internet "Yellow Pages" and "White Pages": www.zlatestranky.cz

Internet Access

It's useful to get online periodically as you travel—to confirm trip plans, check train or bus schedules, get weather forecasts, catch up on email, blog or post photos from your trip, or call folks back home (explained earlier, in "Calling over the Internet").

Your Mobile Device: The majority of accommodations in the Czech Republic offer Wi-Fi, as do many cafés, making it easy for you to get online with your laptop, tablet, or smartphone. Access is often free, but sometimes there's a fee. At hotels that charge for access, save money by logging in and out of your account on an as-needed basis. You should be able to stretch a two-hour Wi-Fi pass over a stay of a day or two.

Some hotel rooms and Internet cafés have high-speed Internet jacks that you can plug into with an Ethernet cable.

Public Internet Terminals: Many accommodations offer a guest computer in the lobby with Internet access for guests. If you ask politely, smaller places may sometimes let you sit at their desk for a few minutes just to check your email. If your hotelier doesn't have access, ask to be directed to the nearest place to get online. Internet cafés are easy to find in Prague; for specific listings, see page 44. Most other towns where I've listed accommodations also have Internet cafés. Many libraries offer free access, but they tend to have limited opening hours, restrict your online time to 30 minutes, and may require reservations.

Most computers are set to type using the Czech alphabet. To switch to English, click on the "CZ" at the bottom of the screen to toggle to "EN."

Security: Whether you're accessing the Internet with your own device or at a public terminal, using a shared network or computer comes with the potential for increased security risks. If you're not convinced a connection is secure, avoid accessing any sites (such as your bank's) that could be vulnerable to fraud.

Mail

You can mail one package per day to yourself worth up to $200 duty-free from Europe to the US (mark it "personal purchases"). If you're sending a gift to someone, mark it "unsolicited gift." For details, visit www.cbp.gov and search for "Know Before You Go."

The Czech postal service works fine, but for quick transatlantic delivery (in either direction), consider services such as DHL (www.dhl.com).

Transportation

By Car or Public Transportation?

Within Prague, a car is a worthless headache. If you're staying mostly in Prague and tackling a few convenient side-trips (such as Kutná Hora and Český Krumlov), public transportation works well. If you'll be venturing farther into the countryside, trains and buses will get you where you need to go—but renting a car gives you greater flexibility. For connecting Prague to international destinations (like Budapest or Kraków), stick with the train.

Public Transportation
Trains
Trains are fairly punctual (although you can expect the occasional late arrival) and cover cities well, but frustrating schedules make a few out-of-the-way destinations I recommend not worth the time and trouble for the less determined (try buses instead—described later).

Schedules: For Czech train and bus timetables, visit www.idos.cz (train info tel. 221-111-122, little English spoken). For trains, you can also check out Germany's excellent Europe-wide timetable at www.bahn.com. Consider buying the *Traťové Jízdní Řády*, a comprehensive, easy-to-use schedule of all trains in the country (includes English instructions, sold at major station ticket windows for 30 Kč). Although it's easy to look up a connection online, having the printed schedule and a map of railway lines gives you the freedom to easily change or make new plans as you travel.

Tickets and Tips: Tickets within the Czech Republic are valid for two days, and international tickets are good from three days to two months (the shorter-term ones are often cheaper). Your ticket is valid for travel along the entire stretch from Prague to your destination, not just for one trip on a specific train—so enjoy the flexibility it gives you, and hop on and hop off along the way. You'll rarely need a reservation, except for international night trains.

If you are traveling by train with one or more companions, ask for a group ticket. This gets you a 50 percent discount for every extra ticket (only the first person pays full price).

The Czech railway system has a rather complex system for discounts on international tickets. If you're heading to a city near the Czech border (such as Vienna, Bratislava, Dresden, or Nürnberg), it sometimes pays to buy two separate tickets: one to the Czech border, and another from the border to your destination. This also allows you to take advantage of particular discounts (such as the group discount) that apply only to domestic travel.

Railpasses: The Czech Republic is covered by a Czech Republic pass, a Germany-Czech or an Austria-Czech railpass, the five-country European East pass, the Global Pass, and the Select Pass. If your train travel will be limited to a handful of rides and/or short distances (for example, within the Czech Republic), you're probably better off without a pass—Czech tickets are cheap to buy as you go. But if you're combining Prague with international destinations, a railpass could save you money. For all the details, check out my free guide to Eurail passes at www.ricksteves.com/rail.

Buses
To reach many of the destinations in this book, buses are faster and

cheaper than trains, and may be more punctual. No reservations are necessary, but they're highly recommended if you're traveling on a popular route (such as from Prague to Český Krumlov). Bus timetables are online at www.idos.cz. To make online reservations, use www.studentagency.cz; if you're in Prague, visit the ticket office at the Florenc bus station (Metro: Florenc) or the Main Train Station (Metro: Hlavní Nádraží). For other routes, buy tickets online or directly from the driver as you board (exact change is appreciated; the driver might have difficulty breaking large bills). You'll be required to put big bags in the luggage compartment under the bus (12-24 Kč extra, depending on the distance), so have a small day bag ready to take on the bus with you. Most buses don't have bathrooms, nor do they stop for bathroom breaks.

Always let the bus driver know where you want to get off. Some stops may require a request (for example, the Small Fortress at Terezín Memorial), and most bus drivers are happy to let you know when your stop is coming up.

Czech Public Transportation

Legend:
----- Rail
- - - Bus

Renting a Car

If you're renting a car in the Czech Republic, bring your driver's license. You're also required to have an International Driving Permit—an official translation of your driver's license (sold at your local AAA office for $15 plus the cost of two passport-type photos; see www.aaa.com). While that's the letter of the law, I've often rented cars in the Czech Republic without having this permit. If all goes well, you'll likely never be asked to show the permit—but it's a must if you end up dealing with the police.

Rental companies require you to be at least 21 years old and to have held your license for one year. Drivers under the age of 25 may incur a young-driver surcharge, and some rental companies do not rent to anyone 75 or older. If you're considered too young or old, look into leasing (covered later), which has less-stringent age restrictions.

Research car rentals before you go. Especially during peak season, the best deals at Czech car-rental companies need to be arranged two to three weeks ahead. Renting from a local Czech company (see page 44) is as convenient as using a US agency; most

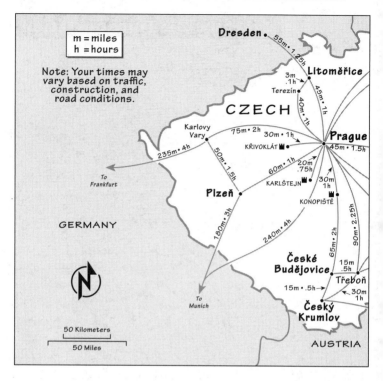

will bring the car to your hotel. There are about a hundred car-rental companies in Prague. Prima Rent is a good bet (see page 44). Or do a Google search from home, take your pick, and reserve by email.

Most of the major US rental agencies (including Avis, Budget, Enterprise, Hertz, and Thrifty) have offices throughout Europe. It can be cheaper to use a consolidator, such as Auto Europe (www.autoeurope.com) or Europe by Car (www.europebycar.com), which compares rates at several companies to get you the best deal. However, my readers have reported problems with consolidators, ranging from misinformation to unexpected fees; because you're going through a middleman, it can be challenging to resolve disputes that arise with the rental agency.

Regardless of the car-rental company you choose, always read the fine print carefully for add-on charges—such as one-way drop-off fees, airport surcharges, or mandatory insurance policies—that aren't included in the "total price." You may need to query rental agents pointedly to find out your actual cost.

For the best deal, rent by the week with unlimited mileage. To save money on fuel, ask for a diesel car. I normally rent the smallest, least-expensive model with a stick shift (generally much cheaper

Driving in the Czech Republic: Distance & Time

To Wrocław • 4h
170m

330m
6.5h
To Kraków

POLAND

REPUBLIC

225m • 5.5h
To Kraków

Kutná Hora

Olomouc
50m • 1.5h
Rožnov Pod Radhoštěm

60m • 1.25h

80m • 1.5h
Jihlava
40m
.5h
55m • 1h
30m • 1h
Kroměříž

95m • 2h
50m • 1h

Telč Třebíč
40m
1h
Brno
80m • 1.25h

40m • 1h
20m
.5h
25m
.75h
30m
.75h

15m • .5h
30m
1h
Moravský
Krumlov
35m • 1h
25m • .75h
Mikulov
SLOVAKIA

35m • 1h
Slavonice

45m • 1h

125m • 3h

Bratislava

Vienna

than an automatic). Almost all rentals are manual by default, so if you need an automatic, request one in advance; be aware that these cars are usually larger models (not as maneuverable on narrow, winding roads).

Czechs are once again proud of their locally built Škoda cars (since the 1920s, the Ford of Eastern Europe). Now owned by Volkswagen, Škoda is the biggest post-communist success story in the country. By renting one, you'll learn why most Eastern Europeans stay loyal to the brand, even as cheap Japanese cars inundate the market. (In an ironic twist, the word "Škoda"—which is the family name of an early owner of the company—also means "damage" in Czech.)

When renting, I usually get a Škoda Fabia; for more luggage space and more oomph, step up to the Škoda Octavia. On average, you should be able to get a Škoda with full insurance and unlimited mileage for $40-65 per day. Škodas usually have manual transmission and come with alarms; you might want to supplement the alarm with a lock for the steering wheel or stick shift.

You can sometimes get a GPS unit with your rental car or leased vehicle for an additional fee (around $15/day; be sure it's set to English and has all the maps you need before you drive off).

Or, if you have a portable GPS device at home, consider taking it with you to Europe (buy and upload European maps before your trip). GPS apps are also available for smartphones, but downloading maps on one of these apps in Europe could lead to an exorbitant data-roaming bill (for more details, see the sidebar on page 336).

Compare pickup costs (downtown can be less expensive than the airport) and explore drop-off options. Always check the hours of the location you choose: Many rental offices close from midday Saturday until Monday morning and, in smaller towns, at lunchtime.

When selecting a location, don't trust the agency's description of "downtown" or "city center." In some cases, a "downtown" branch can be on the outskirts of the city—a long, costly taxi ride from the center. Before choosing, plug the addresses into a mapping website. You may find that the "train station" location is handier. But returning a car at a big-city train station or downtown agency can be tricky; get precise details on the car drop-off location and hours, and allow ample time to find it.

When you pick up the rental car, check it thoroughly and make sure any damage is noted on your rental agreement. Find out how your car's lights, turn signals, wipers, and fuel cap function, and know what kind of gas the car takes. When you return the car, make sure the agent verifies its condition with you.

Car Insurance Options

When you rent a car, you are liable for a very high deductible, sometimes equal to the entire value of the car. Limit your financial risk with one of these three options: Buy Collision Damage Waiver (CDW) coverage from the car-rental company, get coverage through your credit card (if your card automatically includes zero-deductible coverage), or buy coverage through Travel Guard.

CDW includes a very high deductible (typically $1,000-1,500). Though each rental company has its own variation, basic **CDW** costs $15-35 a day (figure roughly 30 percent extra) and reduces your liability, but does not eliminate it. When you pick up the car, you'll be offered the chance to "buy down" the deductible to zero (for an additional $10-30/day; this is sometimes called "super CDW").

If you opt for **credit-card coverage,** there's a catch. You'll technically have to decline all coverage offered by the car-rental company, which means they can place a hold on your card (which can be up to the full value of the car). In case of damage, it can be time-consuming to resolve the charges with your credit-card company. Before you decide on this option, quiz your credit-card company about how it works.

Finally, you can buy collision insurance from a company such as **Travel Guard** ($9/day plus a one-time $3 service fee covers you for up to $35,000, $250 deductible, tel. 800-826-4919, www.travelguard.com). While Travel Guard is technically valid everywhere in Europe except the Republic of Ireland, some car-rental companies refuse to honor it, because they want to sell you their own insurance. Also note that various US states differ on which products and policies are available to their residents—check with Travel Guard and your car-rental company *before* you rent your car.

For more on car-rental insurance, see www.ricksteves.com/cdw.

Leasing

For trips of three weeks or more, consider leasing (which automatically includes zero-deductible collision and theft insurance). By technically buying and then selling back the car, you save lots of money on tax and insurance. Leasing provides you a brand-new car with unlimited mileage and a 24-hour emergency assistance program. You can lease for as little as 21 days to as long as six months. Car leases must be arranged from the US, and cars must be picked up and dropped off outside the Czech Republic (Munich is the closest city to Prague that has leasing services). One of many companies offering affordable lease packages is Europe by Car (US tel. 800-223-1516, www.europebycar.com).

Driving in the Czech Republic

Road Rules: Learn the universal road signs. Seat belts are required, and two beers under those belts are enough to land you in jail. Children under age 12 must ride in the back, and children under 80 pounds must have a child safety seat. Be aware of typical European road rules; for example, many countries require headlights to be turned on at all times, and it's generally illegal to drive while using your mobile phone without a hands-free headset. In Europe, you're not allowed to turn right on a red light, unless there is a sign or signal specifically authorizing it. Ask your car-rental company about

AND LEARN THESE ROAD SIGNS

Speed Limit (km/hr) — Yield — No Passing — End of No Passing Zone

One Way — Intersection — Main Road — Freeway

Danger — No Entry — No Entry for Cars — All Vehicles Prohibited

Parking — No Parking — Customs — Peace

APPENDIX

these rules, or check the US State Department website (www.trav-el.state.gov, click on "International Travel," then specify "Czech Republic" and click "Traffic Safety and Road Conditions").

Freeways: During the communist era, Eastern Europe's infrastructure lagged far behind the West's. With the Iron Curtain long gone, superhighways are popping up like crazy all over the Czech Republic. You'll sometimes discover that a much faster freeway option has been built between major destinations since your three-year-old map was published (a good reason to travel with the most up-to-date maps available). As soon as a long-enough section is completed, the roads are opened to the public. Only rarely are backcountry roads the only option (as with part of the trip between Prague and Český Krumlov). These can be bumpy and slow, but they're almost always paved (or, at least, they once were).

Fuel: Be sure you know which type of fuel your rental car takes. At about $2 per liter ($8 per gallon) for unleaded ("Natural 95"), gas in the Czech Republic is still somewhat cheaper than in Western Europe. If driving a diesel car, you're in luck—it's called "diesel" at the pump.

Tolls: If you're driving on highways in the Czech Republic, you're required to buy a toll sticker *(dálniční známka)* at the border, a post office, or a gas station (310 Kč/10 days, 440 Kč/1 month). Your rental car may already come with the necessary sticker—ask.

Parking: You'll pay about $10-15 a day to park safely in Prague. Formerly notorious for its Russian car-theft gangs, Prague is safer now—but it's still wise to be careful. Ask at your hotel for advice. In small towns, such as Třeboň or Slavonice, it's better to stay on the safe side when parking overnight. Again, ask your hotelier for advice. I keep a pile of coins in my ashtray for parking meters, launderettes, and wishing wells.

Cheap Flights

If you're considering a train ride that's more than five hours long, a flight may save you both time and money. When comparing your options, factor in the time it takes to get to the airport and how early you'll need to arrive to check in.

The best comparison search engine for both international and intra-European flights is www.kayak.com. For inexpensive flights within Europe, try www.skyscanner.com or www.hipmunk.com. If you're not sure who flies to your destination, check its airport's website for a list of carriers.

Well-known cheapo airlines include easyJet (www.easyjet.com) and Ryanair (www.ryanair.com). Smart Wings (www.smart-wings.com) is based in the Czech Republic.

Be aware of the potential drawbacks of flying on the cheap:

nonrefundable and nonchangeable tickets, minimal or nonexistent customer service, treks to airports far outside town, and stingy baggage allowances with steep overage fees. If you're traveling with lots of luggage, a cheap flight can quickly become a bad deal. To avoid unpleasant surprises, read the small print before you book.

Resources

Resources from Rick Steves

Rick Steves' Prague & the Czech Republic is one of many books in my series on European travel, which includes country guidebooks, city guidebooks (Rome, Florence, Paris, London, etc.), Snapshot

guides (excerpted chapters from my country guides), Pocket Guides (full-color little books on big cities), and my budget-travel skills handbook, *Rick Steves' Europe Through the Back Door*. Most of my titles are available as ebooks. My phrase books—for French, Italian, German, Spanish, and Portuguese— are practical and budget-oriented. My other books include *Europe 101* (a crash course on art and history designed for travelers); *Mediterranean Cruise Ports* and *Northern European Cruise Ports* (how to make the most of your time in port); and *Travel as a Political Act* (a travelogue sprinkled with tips for bringing home a global perspective). A more complete list of my titles appears near the end of this book.

Video: My public television series, *Rick Steves' Europe,* covers European destinations in 100 shows, with two episodes on Prague and the Czech Republic. To watch episodes online, visit www.hulu. com; for scripts and local airtimes, see www.ricksteves.com/tv.

Audio: My weekly public radio show, *Travel with Rick Steves,* features interviews with travel experts from around the world. All of this free audio content is available at Rick Steves Audio Europe, an extensive online library organized by destination. Choose whatever interests you, and download it via the Rick Steves Audio Europe smartphone app, www. ricksteves.com/audioeurope, iTunes, or Google Play.

Begin Your Trip at ricksteves.com

At our travel website, you'll discover a wealth of free informa-tion on European destinations, including fresh monthly news and helpful tips from thousands of fellow travelers. You'll find my latest guidebook updates (www.ricksteves.com/update), a monthly travel e-newsletter, my personal travel blog, and my free Rick Steves Audio Europe smartphone app (if you don't have a smartphone, you can access the same content via pod-casts). You can also follow me on Facebook and Twitter.

Our **online Travel Store** offers travel bags and accesso-ries that I've designed specifically to help you travel smarter and lighter. These include my popular bags (rolling carry-on and backpack versions), money belts, totes, toiletries kits, adapters, other accessories, and a wide selection of guide-books, planning maps, and DVDs.

Choosing the right **railpass** for your trip—amid hundreds of options—can drive you nutty. Our website will help you find the perfect fit for your itinerary and your budget.

Want to travel with greater efficiency and less stress? We organize **tours** with more than three dozen itineraries and more than 600 departures reaching the best destinations in this book...and beyond. We offer several tours that visit Prague and destinations in the Czech Republic, including our 8-day Prague and Budapest tour; our 12-day Berlin, Prague, and Vienna tour (which includes the charming village of Český Krumlov); and our 16-day Eastern Europe tour. You'll enjoy great guides, a fun bunch of travel partners (with small groups of generally 24 to 28 travelers), and plenty of room to spread out in a big, comfy bus when touring between towns. You'll find European adventures to fit every vacation length. For all the details, and to get our Tour Catalog and a free Rick Steves Tour Experience DVD (filmed on location during an actual tour), visit www.ricksteves.com or call us at 425/608-4217.

Maps

The black-and-white maps in this book are concise and simple, de-signed to help you locate recommended places and get to local TIs, where you can pick up a more in-depth map of the city or region (usually free).

A good city map is essential for your time in Prague. Bet-ter maps are sold at newsstands and bookstores. Before you buy a map, look at it to be sure it has the level of detail you want. Many of Prague's bookstores also have road, hiking, and cycling maps covering the entire country. One of the best is the Kiwi Map Store near Wenceslas Square (see page 179).

For drivers, I'd recommend a 1:100,000 atlas of the Czech Republic. If you have hiking plans (near Křivoklát, around Český

Krumlov, in the Šumava or Beskydy Mountains, around Třeboň, or near Slavonice), get the excellent 1:50,000 *Edice Klub Českých Turistů* maps, or the less detailed but sufficient 1:100,000 *Kartografie Praha* maps. Train travelers usually manage fine with the freebies they get at the local tourist offices.

Other Guidebooks

If you're like most travelers, this book is all you need. But if you're heading beyond my recommended destinations, $40 for extra maps and books can be money well spent.

The following books are worthwhile, though most are not updated annually; check the publication date before you buy.

Lonely Planet's guides to the Czech and Slovak Republics and Prague are thorough, well-researched, and packed with good maps and hotel recommendations. The Czech Republic and Prague Rough Guides are hip and insightful, written by British researchers.

Students and vagabonds will like the highly opinionated Let's Go series, which is updated by Harvard students. *Let's Go Eastern Europe* is best for backpackers who travel by train or bus, stay in hostels, and seek out the youth and nightlife scene.

Older travelers enjoy guides from Frommer's, even though, like the Fodor's guides, they ignore alternatives that enable travelers to save money by dirtying their fingers in the local culture.

The popular, skinny green Michelin Guides are excellent, especially if you're driving. Michelin Guides are known for their city and sightseeing maps, dry but concise and helpful information on all major sights, and good cultural and historical background. English editions are sold in Europe at gas stations and tourist shops. The encyclopedic Blue Guides are just right for scholarly types.

The Eyewitness series is popular for great, easy-to-grasp graphics and photos, 3-D cutaways of buildings, aerial-view maps of historic neighborhoods, and cultural background. But written content in Eyewitness is relatively skimpy, and the books weigh a ton. I simply borrow them for a minute from other travelers at certain sights to make sure that I'm aware of that place's highlights.

Recommended Books, Plays, and Movies

To learn more about the Czech Republic past and present, check out a few of these books, plays, and films.

Books and Plays

The most famous Czech literary classic is Jaroslav Hašek's *Good Soldier Švejk*, a darkly comic novel that follows the fortunes of its title character, a soldier in World War I's Austro-Hungarian army.

Novelist Bohumil Hrabal, writing in a stream-of-consciousness style, mixed tales he had heard in pubs from sailors, self-made

Václav Havel: An Authentic Life

Václav Havel (1936-2011) was a playwright first and a politician second. Author of more than 20 absurdist plays, Havel served as the first president of post-communist Czechoslovakia and was later elected to two terms as president of the Czech Republic.

At heart, Havel was an unassuming writer-critic—but circumstances propelled him into the roles of political dissident and humanitarian. Banned from Czech theater in the aftermath of the 1968 Prague Spring, Havel became an enemy of the communist state and was repeatedly jailed. Though public channels of expression were closed to him, his controversial essays and plays were circulated secretly, both to Warsaw Pact countries and to the West.

While staring down Czechoslovakia's communist regime during the 1989 Velvet Revolution, Havel and his fellow revolutionaries took to the streets with the chant, "Truth and love must prevail over lies and hatred." Havel acted as leader of the informal human-rights group Charter 77, which challenged the regime's suppression of Czech citizens. Their opposition began in defense of the right to freedom of expression—specifically, of a Czech counter-culture rock group, Plastic People of the Universe—that in 1976 was put on trial and convicted of disturbing the peace, essentially for performing without a permit. In Charter 77's manifesto, Havel persuasively argued that if one per-

philosophers, and kind-hearted prostitutes into enchanting fictions that deftly express the Czech spirit and sense of humor. His best works are *I Served the King of England*, *The Town Where Time Stood Still*, and *Too Loud a Solitude*. (Jiří Menzel turned some of Hrabal's writings into films—for more on Czech cinema, keep reading.)

Other well-known Czech writers include novelist and playwright Karel Čapek, who created the robot in the play *R.U.R.*; Milan Kundera, author of *The Unbearable Lightness of Being*, set during the 1968 Prague Spring uprising; and playwright—and Czechoslovakia's first post-communist president—Václav Havel, whose many essays and plays include *The Garden Party*, *Audience*, and *Temptation* (for more about Havel, see the sidebar).

The most famous Czech writer of all is the existentialist great, Franz Kafka, a Jewish Prague native who wrote in German. His surrealist stories include *The Metamorphosis*, about a man turning into a giant cockroach, and *The Trial*, about an urbanite being pursued and persecuted for crimes he knows nothing about.

Some lesser-known Czech writers are also worth discovering.

son's freedom is violated, everyone's freedom is violated. Through his writings, he articulated a message of hope and strength, stressing the importance of becoming a community "living in truth" and strong enough to stop conforming to Soviet ideologies.

The idea that so inspired the martyr Jan Hus and his 14th-century followers was the heretical realization that each human being has an intrinsic capacity to know what a just, free, and beautiful life is. Six centuries later, Václav Havel used his plays to explore what happens to a human being who rejects the guidance of this inner compass. His characters fixate on the abstractions of various mundane "truths" while forgetting their moral obligations to themselves and others. Havel saw love and truth not just as political slogans, but as everyday principles, and was himself catapulted by life into parts he had not scripted.

After serving two terms, Havel returned to his art, continuing to explore the ideas of freedom and morality. His death in 2011 at age 75 was marked by three days of national mourning and the renaming of Prague Airport as Václav Havel Airport Prague.

Havel will long be remembered for his clever use of art as a medium for political expression. Recently, the Human Rights Foundation established the "Václav Havel Prize for Creative Dissent" and bestowed it upon prominent activists including Ai Weiwei (China), Manal al-Sharif (Saudi Arabia), Aung San Suu Kyi (Burma), Ali Ferzat (Syria), Park Sang Hak (North Korea), and the Ladies in White (a Cuban opposition group).

Ota Pavel began his career as a sportswriter, translating athletic victories and defeats into compassionate epics. At the end of his life he produced two remarkable collections of simple, sadly humorous short stories whose main characters were fish and Pavel's witty Jewish father (collected in *How I Came to Know Fish*). In Arnošt Lustig's *Dita Saxová*, a young survivor of a concentration camp struggles to restart her life, while Josef Škvorecký's *The Cowards (Zbabělci)* describes the generation coming of age just after the World War II. Dominika Dery's *The Twelve Little Cakes* is a delightful memoir of her childhood (spent near Prague) at the end of communism in the late 1970s and early 1980s. So far, the definitive book of the 1989 generation is Jáchym Topol's *Sister*. Topol captures "the years after the Time exploded" in a rich mixture of colloquial Czech that's full of neologisms and borrowed German and English words. Alex Zucker's English translation does an excellent job of capturing these nuances.

Nobel Prize-winning poet Jaroslav Seifert experienced during his long life all the diverse movements of the 20th century—

Dadaism, Surrealism, communism, anti-communism—and created a medium of his own, in which everyone finds a poem to his or her own liking.

Films

The Czech film tradition has always been strong, and the 1960s were its heyday, giving birth to Jiří Menzel's *Closely Watched Trains* (an Oscar-winner based on Bohumil Hrabal's absurdist novel) and *Larks on the String*, Ivan Passer's *Intimate Lighting*, and Miloš Forman's *Firemen's Ball* and *Loves of a Blonde*. After his 1968 escape from communist Czechoslovakia, Forman made it big in the US with films such as *One Flew Over the Cuckoo's Nest* and *Amadeus*. Menzel went on to film five more of Hrabal's novels, including the acclaimed *I Served the King of England* (2006).

Two Czech filmmakers made a mark on the international stage after 1989: Jan Svěrák (*The Elementary School* and the Oscar-winning *Kolya*) and Jiří Hřebejk (*Divided We Fall*, nominated for an Oscar). More recently, Vít Klusák and Filip Remunda created a sensation with their hilarious, original, and disturbing documentary, *Czech Dream*, about the opening of a fake hypermarket invented and massively advertised by the directors themselves.

One of the most inspiring Czech artists is painter, animator, director, and surrealist Jan Švankmajer. His films *Alice, Faust, Conspirators of Pleasure,* and *Food* combine all of the author's artistic skills into a highly original style that is guaranteed to change the way you look at the world. His two most recent films—*Little Otík* and *Mad*—blend in more realism.

The Czechs have a wonderful animation tradition that successfully competes with Walt Disney in Eastern Europe and China. *Pat a Mat, Krteček (The Little Mole),* or *Maxipes Fík* are intelligent gifts to bring to your little ones at home.

Holidays and Festivals

This list includes selected festivals held in Prague and the Czech Republic, plus national holidays observed throughout the country. Many sights and banks close down on national holidays—keep this in mind when planning your itinerary. Before planning a trip around a festival, verify its dates by checking the festival's website or a local TI site. The Czech national TI (www.czechtourism.com) can provide specifics and a more comprehensive list of festivals. For sports events, see www.sportsevents365.com for schedules and ticket information.

Jan 1	New Year's Day
Jan 19	Anniversary of Jan Palach's death (flowers in Wenceslas Square)
Mid-March	One World International Human Rights Film Festival, Prague (www.oneworld.cz)
Easter Sunday and Monday	April 20-21 in 2014
April 30	Witches' Night (bonfires)
May 1	Labor Day and Day of Love
May 8	Liberation Day
Mid-May-early June	"Prague Spring" Music Festival, Prague (www.festival.cz)
Mid-May	Prague International Marathon, Prague (www.runczech.com)
Early June	Festival of Song, Olomouc (www.festamusicale.com)
Mid-June-late July	Prague Proms, Prague (music festival, www.pragueproms.cz)
Late June	Celebration of the Rose, Český Krumlov (medieval festival and knights' tournament, www.ckrumlov.info)
July 5	Sts. Cyril and Methodius Day
July 6	Jan Hus Day
July-Aug	Summer of Culture, Olomouc (www.olomouckekulturniprazdniny.cz)
Mid-July-mid-Aug	International Music Festival, Český Krumlov (www.festivalkrumlov.cz)
Early Aug	Telč Vacations Festival, Telč (folk music, open-air theater, exhibitions, www.prazdninyvtelci.cz/eng)
Sept	Dvořák Prague Music Festival, Prague (www.dvorakovapraha.cz)
Sept 28	St. Wenceslas Day (celebrates national patron saint and Czech statehood)
Autumn	International Jazz Festival, Prague (www.agharta.cz)
Oct 28	Independence Day
Nov 17	Velvet Revolution Anniversary
Dec	Christmas markets, Prague
Dec 5	St. Nicholas Eve, Prague (St. Nicholas, devils, and angels walk the streets in search of nice—and naughty—children)
Dec 24-25	Christmas Eve and Christmas Day
Dec 26	Feast of St. Stephen
Dec 31	St. Sylvester's Day, Prague (fireworks)

APPENDIX

Conversions and Climate

Numbers and Stumblers

- Europeans write a few of their numbers differently than we do. 1 = 1, 4 = 4, 7 = 7.
- In Europe, dates appear as day/month/year, so Christmas is 25/12/14.
- Commas are decimal points and decimals are commas. A dollar and a half is 1,50; one thousand is 1.000; and there are 5.280 feet in a mile.
- When counting with fingers, start with your thumb. If you hold up your first finger to request one item, you'll probably get two.
- What Americans call the second floor of a building is the first floor in Europe.
- On escalators and moving sidewalks, Europeans keep the left "lane" open for passing. Keep to the right.

Metric Conversions

A kilogram is 2.2 pounds and 1 liter is about a quart, or almost four to a gallon. A kilometer is six-tenths of a mile. I figure kilometers to miles by cutting them in half and adding back 10 percent of the original (120 km: 60 + 12 = 72 miles, 300 km: 150 + 30 = 180 miles).

1 foot = 0.3 meter	1 square yard = 0.8 square meter
1 yard = 0.9 meter	1 square mile = 2.6 square kilometers
1 mile = 1.6 kilometers	1 ounce = 28 grams
1 centimeter = 0.4 inch	1 quart = 0.95 liter
1 meter = 39.4 inches	1 kilogram = 2.2 pounds
1 kilometer = 0.62 mile	32°F = 0°C

Clothing Sizes

When shopping for clothing, use these US-to-European comparisons as general guidelines (but note that no conversion is perfect).

- Women's dresses and blouses: Add 30
  (US size 10 = European size 40)
- Men's suits and jackets: Add 10
  (US size 40 regular = European size 50)
- Men's shirts: Multiply by 2 and add about 8
  (US size 15 collar = European size 38)
- Women's shoes: Add about 30
  (US size 8 = European size 38-39)
- Men's shoes: Add 32-34
  (US size 9 = European size 41; US size 11 = European size 45)

The Czech Republic's Climate

First line, average daily high; second line, average daily low; third line, average number of days with some rain. For more detailed weather statistics for destinations throughout the Czech Republic (as well as the rest of the world), check www.wunderground.com.

J	F	M	A	M	J	J	A	S	O	N	D
31°	34°	44°	54°	64°	70°	73°	72°	65°	53°	42°	34°
23°	24°	30°	38°	46°	52°	55°	55°	49°	41°	33°	27°
13	11	10	11	13	12	13	12	10	13	12	13

Temperature Conversion: Fahrenheit and Celsius

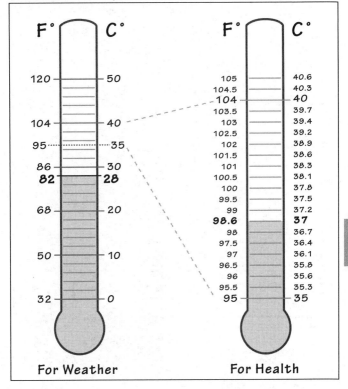

For Weather   For Health

APPENDIX

Europe takes its temperature using the Celsius scale, while we opt for Fahrenheit. For a rough conversion from Celsius to Fahrenheit, double the number and add 30. For weather, remember that 28°C is 82°F—perfect. For health, 37°C is just right.

Packing Checklist

Whether you're traveling for five days or five weeks, here's what you'll need to bring. Pack light to enjoy the sweet freedom of true mobility. Happy travels!

❑ 5 shirts: long- & short-sleeve
❑ 1 sweater or lightweight fleece
❑ 2 pairs of pants
❑ 1 pair of shorts
❑ 5 pairs of underwear & socks
❑ 1 pair of shoes
❑ 1 rainproof jacket with hood
❑ Tie or scarf
❑ Swimsuit
❑ Sleepwear
❑ Money belt
❑ Money—your mix of:
  ❑ Debit card
  ❑ Credit card(s)
  ❑ Hard cash ($20 bills)
❑ Documents plus photocopies:
  ❑ Passport
  ❑ Printout of airline eticket
  ❑ Driver's license
  ❑ Student ID, hostel card, etc.
  ❑ Railpass/train reservations/ car-rental voucher
  ❑ Insurance details
❑ Guidebooks & maps
❑ Address list (for sending emails & postcards)
❑ Notepad & pen
❑ Journal
❑ Daypack
❑ Toiletries kit:
  ❑ Toiletries
  ❑ Medicines & vitamins
  ❑ First-aid kit
  ❑ Glasses/contacts/ sunglasses (with prescriptions)
❑ Small towel/washcloth
❑ Laundry supplies:
  ❑ Laundry soap
  ❑ Clothesline
❑ Sewing kit

❑ Electronics—your choice of:
  ❑ Camera (& related gear)
  ❑ Mobile phone
  ❑ Portable media player (iPod or other)
  ❑ Laptop/netbook/ tablet
  ❑ Ebook reader
  ❑ Chargers for each of the above
  ❑ Headphones or earbuds
  ❑ Plug adapter(s)
❑ Alarm clock
❑ Earplugs
❑ Sealable plastic baggies
❑ Empty water bottle
❑ Postcards & photos from home

If you plan to carry on your luggage, note that all liquids must be in 3.4-ounce or smaller containers and fit within a single quart-size sealable baggie. For details, see www.tsa.gov/travelers.

Czech Survival Phrases

The emphasis in Czech words usually falls on the first syllable—though don't overdo it, as this stress is subtle and can vary slightly. A vowel with an accent (á, é, í, ú, ý) is held longer, but the emphasis is not necessarily on that syllable. The combination *ch* sounds like the guttural "kh" sound in the Scottish word "loch." The uniquely Czech letter *ř* (as in Dvořák) sounds like a cross between a rolled "r" and "zh"; in the phonetics, I've simplified it to "zh." Here are a few English words that all Czechs know: super, OK, pardon, stop, menu, problem, and no problem.

Hello. (formal)	Dobrý den.	DOH-bree dehn
Hi. / Bye. (informal)	Ahoj.	AH-hoy
Do you speak English?	Mluvíte anglicky?	MLOO-vee-teh ANG-lits-kee
Yes. / No.	Ano. / Ne.	AH-noh / neh
I (don't) understand.	Nerozumím.	NEH-roh-zoo-meem
Please. / You're welcome. / Can I help you?	Prosím.	PROH-seem
Thank you (very much).	Děkuji.	DYACK-khuyi
Excuse me. / I'm sorry.	Promiňte.	PROH-meen-teh
(No) problem.	(To není) problém.	(toh NEH-nee) proh-BLEHM
Good.	Dobře.	DOHB-zhay
Goodbye.	Nashledanou.	NAH-skleh-dah-noh
one / two	jeden / dva	YAY-dehn / dvah
three / four	tři / čtyři	tzhee / CHTEE-zhee
five / six	pět / šest	pyeht / shehst
seven / eight	sedm / osm	SEH-dum / OH-sum
nine / ten	devět / deset	DEHV-yeht / DEH-seht
hundred / thousand	sto / tisíc	stoh / TEE-seets
How much?	Kolik?	KOH-leek
local currency	koruna (Kč)	koh-ROO-nah
Write it.	Napište to.	NAH-pish-teh toh
Is it free?	Je to zadarmo?	yeh toh ZAH-dar-moh
Is it included?	Je to v ceně?	yeh tohf TSAY-nyeh
Where can I find / buy...?	Kde mohu najít / koupit...?	gday MOH-hoo NAH-yeet / KOH-pit
I'd like...(said by a man)	Rád bych...	rahd bikh
I'd like...(said by a woman)	Ráda bych...	RAH-dah bikh
We'd like...	Rádi bychom...	RAH-dyee BEE-khohm
...a room.	...pokoj.	POH-koy
...a ticket to _____. (destination)	...jízdenka do _____.	YEEZ-dehn-kah doh _____
Is it possible?	Je to možné?	yeh toh MOHZH-neh
Where is...?	Kde je...?	gday yeh
...the train station	...nádraží	NAH-drah-zhee
...the bus station	...autobusové nádraží	OW-toh-boo-soh-veh NAH-drah-zhee
...the tourist information office	...turistická informační kancelář	TOO-rih-stit-skah EEN-for-mahch-nee KAHN-tseh-lahzh
...the toilet	...véčé	VEHT-seh
men / women	muži / ženy	MOO-zhee / ZHAY-nee
left / right	vlevo / vpravo	VLEH-voh / FPRAH-voh
straight	rovně	ROHV-nyeh
At what time...	V kolik...	FKOH-leek
...does this open / close?	...otevírají / zavírají?	OH-teh-vee-rah-yee / ZAH-vee-rah-yee
Just a moment.	Moment prosím.	MOH-mehnt PROH-seem
now / soon / later	teď / brzy / později	tedge / BIR-zih / POHZ-dyeh-yee
today / tomorrow	dnes / zítra	duh-NEHS / ZEE-trah

In a Czech Restaurant

I'd like to reserve... (said by a man)	Rád bych zarezervoval....	rahd bikh ZAH-reh-zehr-voh-vahl
I'd like to reserve... (said by a woman)	Ráda bych zarezervovala....	RAH-dah bikh ZAH-reh-zehr-voh-vah-lah
...a table for one person / two people.	...stůl pro jednoho / dva.	stool proh YEHD-noh-hoh / dvah
Non-smoking.	Nekuřácký.	NEH-kuhzh-aht-skee
Is this table free?	Je tento stůl volný?	yeh TEHN-toh stool VOHL-nee
Can I help you?	Mohu Vám pomoci?	MOH-hoo vahm poh-MOHT-see
The menu (in English), please.	Jídelní lístek (v angličtině) prosím.	YEE-dehl-nee LEE-stehk (FAHN-gleech-tee-nyeh) PROH-seem
Service is / is not included.	Spropitné je / není zahrnuto.	SPROH-pit-neh yeh / NEH-nee ZAH-har-noo-toh
"to go"	s sebou	SEH-boh
with / without	s / bez	suh / behz
and / or	a / nebo	ah / NEH-boh
ready-to-eat meal (available now)	hotová jídla	HOH-toh-vah YEED-lah
meal on request (takes longer)	minutky	MIH-noot-kee
appetizers	předkrm	PZHEHD-krim
bread	chléb	khlehb
cheese	sýr	seer
sandwich	sendvič	SEHND-vich
soup	polévka	poh-LEHV-kah
salad	salát	SAH-laht
meat	maso	MAH-soh
poultry	drůbež	DROO-behzh
fish	ryby	RIH-bih
fruit	ovoce	OH-voht-seh
vegetables	zelenina	ZEH-leh-nyee-nah
dessert	dezert	DEH-zehrt
(tap) water	voda (z kohoutku)	VOH-dah (SKOH-hoht-koo)
mineral water	minerální voda	MIH-neh-rahl-nyee VOH-dah
carbonated / not carbonated (spoken)	s bublinkami / bez bublinek	SBOOB-leen-kah-mee / behz BOO-blee-nehk
carbonated / not carbonated (printed)	perlivá / neperlivá	PEHR-lee-vah / NEH-pehr-lee-vah
milk	mléko	MLEH-koh
(orange) juice	(pomerančový) džus	(POH-mehr-ahn-choh-vee) "juice"
coffee	káva	KAH-vah
tea	čaj	chai
wine	víno	VEE-noh
red / white	červené / bílé	CHEHR-veh-neh / BEE-leh
sweet / dry	sladké / suché	SLAHD-keh / SOO-kheh
glass / bottle	sklenka / lahev	SKLEHN-kah / LAH-hehv
beer	pivo	PEE-voh
light / dark	světlé / tmavé	SVYEHT-leh / TMAH-veh
Cheers!	Na zdraví!	nah zdrah-VEE
Enjoy your meal.	Dobrou chuť.	DOH-broh khoot
More. / Another.	Více. / Další.	VEET-seh / DAHL-shee
The same.	To samé.	toh SAH-meh
the bill	účet	OO-cheht
I'll pay.	Zaplatím.	ZAH-plah-teem
tip	spropitné	SPROH-pit-neh
Delicious!	Výborné!	VEE-bohr-neh

APPENDIX

INDEX

MAP INDEX

Audio Europe™